PAULINE THEOLOGY

Volume I:
Thessalonians,
Philippians,
Galatians,
Philemon

Edited by

Jouette M. Bassler

Fortress Press   Minneapolis

#23651812

PAULINE THEOLOGY, VOLUME I
Thessalonians, Philippians, Galatians, Philemon

Scripture quotations, unless otherwise noted, are from the Revised Standard Version of the Bible, copyright © 1946, 1952, and 1971 by the Division of Christian Education of the National Council of Churches.

Chapter 5, in revised form, is published in *The Thessalonian Correspondence* (BETL 87; Leuven: Leuven University Press, 1990), and is used here by permission.

Chapter 10, "The Theology of Galatians," adapted from *Jesus, Paul and the Law: Studies in Mark and Galatians,* by James D. G. Dunn. First published in Great Britain in 1990 by SPCK. Copyright © James D. G. Dunn 1990. Adapted and used by permission of Westminster/John Knox Press.

Interior design and typesetting: The HK Scriptorium, Inc.
Cover design: Ned Skubic

Library of Congress Cataloging-in-Publication Data

Pauline theology / edited by Jouette M. Bassler.
   p. cm.
   Includes bibliographical references.
   ISBN: 0-8006-2488-2: (v. 1 : alk. paper).
   1. Bible. N.T. Epistles of Paul—Theology. I. Bassler, Jouette M.
   BS2651.P284   1991
   227'.06—dc20   91-17665
                                   CIP

Manufactured in the U.S.A.   AF 1-2488
95   94   93   92   91   1   2   3   4   5   6   7   8   9   10

🝆 Contents

▣ Preface

"There are some things in Paul's letters hard to understand . . ."
2 Pet 3:16

FOR MANY YEARS the difficulties inherent in understanding Paul's theology were—ironically—obscured by the apparent success of various presentations of that theology. Whether interpreted, as in the magisterial works of Barth and Bultmann, from a consistent center or arranged under familiar doctrinal categories, Paul's thought seemed amenable to systematic organization. The question was usually not *whether* his thought could be understood as a coherent whole, but *how,* and several viable options seemed to be available. This comfortable state of affairs began to erode, however, in the 1970s and 1980s, when it became increasingly clear that the various presentations of Paul's theology tended to reflect the theological perspectives of Paul's interpreters more clearly than the theological emphases of the apostle himself. Moreover, as traditional models for understanding Paul's theology began to collapse, a counterreaction emerged in studies that denied the existence of any coherence to that theology. The very attempt to organize Paul's thought was viewed as misleading, for the apostle's thought was perceived to be filled with internal contradictions.

With the demise of old paradigms and suspicion in some quarters about the validity of *any* paradigms, the time was clearly ripe for a cooperative attempt by Pauline scholars systematically to reassess the way Pauline theology should be conceived. Methodological issues needed to be addressed, and the theology of the various letters needed to be heard afresh and apart from the dogmatic presuppositions of earlier ages. Thus in 1985 the Pauline Theology Consultation of the Society of Biblical Literature was formed. Several methodological decisions made by the Steering Committee of this consultation have informed the ongoing work of the consultation. The committee decided that the consultation should approach Paul's theology by studying first the way it came to expression in each letter, beginning with the shorter letters and proceeding to the longer ones. The purpose of following this sequence was to free the shorter letters from the theological dominance that the *Hauptbriefe* usually exercise on the Pauline corpus. To ensure further that the contours of the theology of each letter would be fairly delineated without premature assimilation to the *Hauptbriefe,* the committee also decided that the theology of each letter was to be defined without recourse to the other letters of the Pauline corpus. In addition, a gradual synthesis of Paul's theology was to be attempted by combining in stepwise increments the theologies of the various letters. This gradual and controlled combination of texts, beginning with the shorter letters and adding later the *Hauptbriefe,* was undertaken in hopes that some important but hitherto obscured theological patterns would emerge.

In the period from 1986 to 1988 the consultation (reconstructed in 1988 as the Pauline Theology Group of the SBL) addressed methodological issues; discussed the theologies of 1 and 2 Thessalonians, Philemon, Philippians, and Galatians; and attempted some partial syntheses of Paul's theology based on these letters. The chapters of this volume are drawn from the work of this period. Many of these papers were presented to the group under different titles and most have been rewritten in light of the group's discussion. A number of chapters are formulated as responses that challenge and integrate the conclusions of the primary papers. In content as well as structure, then, the volume preserves the dialogical quality of the work of the group.

Much has been accomplished. The distinctive theologies of the individual letters have begun to emerge with new clarity as a result of the approach embraced by this group. Methodological issues have been discussed in the abstract and tested in the concrete analyses of the letters. The various syntheses have highlighted recurring themes in the shorter letters of the corpus. Yet the work is far from over. Not only are there other letters to consider, but certain issues that have emerged from this work will require further clarification. How, for example, should the theology of a given letter be defined? Is it to be identified with the theological presuppositions of a letter, with the theological goals of the letter, or with the letter's argument? If theology is associated with the letter's argument, is it located in the surface structure of the argument or found in the deeper patterns that undergird it? The attempt to build a synthesis out of the theologies of the individual letters generates another set of questions. If all of Paul's words are addressed to and shaped for particular communities and their needs, how do we move from the concrete letters to a general statement about Pauline theology? Do we summarize and organize the words targeted for different communities, attempting, however, to retain Paul's categories of thought instead of imposing our own, or do we try to get behind Paul's specific words to the vision or convictions or beliefs that inform them? If so, how far behind Paul's words dare we or need we go and how shall we get there?

These and other questions are raised by the contributors to this volume. The reader is invited to enter into the energetic dialogue that marks the current state of research on the theology of the Pauline letters. We are in a period of rapid change. Neither the models of the past nor the deconstructive analyses of the present do justice to the creative flexibility of Paul's thought. New paradigms are needed for construing Paul's theology, paradigms that respect its flexibility and define the nature and locus of its coherence. The chapters that follow do not present the final word on this topic; they do, however, represent significant milestones along the way.

Abbreviations used in this volume can be found in the *Journal of Biblical Literature* 107 (1988) 579–96.

▣ Contributors

Paul J. Achtemeier
  Herbert Worth and Annie H. Jackson Professor of Biblical Interpretation
  Union Theological Seminary in Virginia

Jouette M. Bassler
  Associate Professor of New Testament
  Perkins School of Theology
  Southern Methodist University

J. Christiaan Beker
  Professor of New Testament Theology
  Princeton Theological Seminary

James D. G. Dunn
  Professor of Divinity
  University of Durham

Beverly Roberts Gaventa
  Professor of New Testament
  Columbia Theological Seminary

Richard B. Hays
  Associate Professor of New Testament
  Yale Divinity School
  Yale University

Robert Jewett
  Harry R. Kendall Professor of New Testament Interpretation
  Garrett-Evangelical Theological Seminary

Edgar Krentz
  Professor of New Testament
  Lutheran School of Theology at Chicago

David J. Lull
  Executive Director
  Society of Biblical Literature

J. Louis Martyn
  Edward Robinson Professor Emeritus of Biblical Theology
  Union Theological Seminary

Pheme Perkins
  Professor of Theology
  Boston College

Earl Richard
  Professor of Religious Studies
  Loyola University

J. Paul Sampley
  Professor of New Testament and Christian Origins
  Boston University

Robin Scroggs
  Edward Robinson Professor of Biblical Theology
  Union Theological Seminary

Stanley K. Stowers
  Professor of Religious Studies
  Brown University

N. T. Wright
  Chaplain and Tutor in Theology
  Worcester College
  University of Oxford

Bibliographies

Raymond F. Collins
  Professor of New Testament Studies
  Katholieke Universiteit Leuven
  Leuven

Edgar Krentz
  Professor of New Testament
  Lutheran School of Theology at Chicago

David J. Lull
  Executive Director
  Society of Biblical Literature

John Reumann
  Professor of New Testament
  Lutheran Theological Seminary at Philadelphia

Calvin J. Roetzel
  Arnold Lowe Professor of Religious Studies
  Macalester College

Part I

Methodology

1 FROM TEXT
TO THOUGHT WORLD

The Route to Paul's Ways[1]

J. Paul Sampley
Boston University

PAUL WAS A PREACHER of his gospel and a tutor of his churches, not a theologian. Of course, it is possible to argue that everyone has a theology and that a careful observer, given adequate information, could reconstruct it. In Paul's letters we have direct access to the communication of his thoughts as they intersect real life situations and only indirect access to the thought world from which his thoughts gain expression. Our reconstruction of what we might call a theology of Paul will always be a modern abstraction, a distillation that we gain from his thought world.

Given the nature of the sources with which we have to work, we may never be able to formulate even the core communication of Paul's teaching, but we should not be entirely without hope. In his letter to Corinth, Paul mentions that Timothy has presented to this church a brief summary of his "ways in Christ": "Therefore I sent to you Timothy, who is my beloved child, faithful in the Lord, to remind you of my ways in Christ, just as I teach them everywhere in every church" (1 Cor 4:17).[2] From this verse we know that there was a core representation of Paul's teaching, that it was possible for someone—like Timothy here—to grasp it and to communicate it on a visit, and that this same communication was at the center of what all of Paul's churches learned. Lacking Timothy, we must search the Pauline letters in an effort to reconstruct Paul's ways, but seeking them in highly situational letters will be a complex task.[3]

---

[1] The original title of this essay, given to me by the Steering Committee of the Pauline Theology Consultation of the Society of Biblical Literature when they asked me to contribute this essay, was "Overcoming Traditional Models by Synthesizing the Theology of Individual Letters."

[2] Unless noted otherwise, translations are mine.

[3] Surprisingly few essays in Pauline studies ask methodological questions. A refreshing

Before we proceed, we should state the governing assumption that underlies this paper and its suggestions: *Interpreters do not have direct, unhindered access
to Paul's thought world; that is, to the fundamental frame of reference within which
things made sense to Paul and out of which he operated.* They have direct access only
to his communication of his thoughts in his letters to various churches. Because of the
peculiar nature of Paul's letters, a modern quest after a theology of Paul must
proceed through a sequence that omits none of the following steps. (1) The
multiple effects of the epistolary situations and of Paul's rhetorical purposes
must be factored into a reading of Paul's communication of his thoughts.
(2) Thus we may establish the evidence for Paul's thought world. (3) From
that thought world we may venture a formulation of a theology of Paul.[4]
Any formulation of a theology of Paul from a surface reading of his letters
will be warped and sketchy.

I am also prepared to assume, until the preponderance of evidence indicates
otherwise, that Paul's thought world and the thoughts that it spawned are
relatively coherent.[5] As they are communicated in his letters, however, Paul's
thoughts are affected by so many considerations that they may often appear
if not contradictory at least in tension with one another. On the one hand,
this assumption leads one to expect a general coherence in Paul's thought
world. On the other hand, though, it stresses the fact that Paul's communication of his thoughts presents interpreters with the challenge of moving
beyond an unsophisticated surface reading of the texts to find the coherence
behind them.[6]

---

exception is Paul J. Achtemeier's call for "careful attention to . . . language . . . structure, and
context" ("'Some Things in Them Hard to Understand': Reflections on an Approach to Paul,"
Int 38 [1984] 267).

[4] It is also crucial that we carefully define just what is and is not meant by "theology," for
until we do so each of us will be looking for something different and our conversations with
one another will be all the more precariously grounded.

[5] I appreciate J. D. G. Dunn's comments on "contradiction" as a hermeneutic of "last resort."
He says: "Basic to good exegesis is respect for the integrity of the text and, in the case of
someone like Paul, respect for his intellectual calibre and theological competence. Such respect
includes a constant bearing in mind the possibility or indeed likelihood that the situations
confronting Paul were more complex than we can now be aware of, or include important aspects
which are now invisible to us" ("Works of the Law and the Curse of the Law [Galatians
3:10–14]," *NTS* 31 [1985] 523).

[6] When, on a surface reading, a passage does not make apparent sense or seem to fit what
is said elsewhere in the corpus, I prefer to acknowledge the difficulty and continue to seek an
understanding of how it might indeed fit Paul's thought. E. Käsemann rejects a tendency "to
take comfort in psychology" when what he terms "embarrassing moments" occur in the Pauline
text: "The temperament of the apostle is for ever breaking through the ordered pattern of
established rules. . . . Ought he [the interpreter] not rather to enquire whether the particularly
remarkable features of a given passage do not indicate the presence of an especially significant

I. MOVING FROM TEXT
TO THOUGHT WORLD:
GENERAL CONSIDERATIONS

The surface of the text in the Pauline letters does not grant the interpreter direct access to Paul's thought world, but only to Paul's communication of his thoughts to specific communities. Moving from the surface of the letters to a reconstruction of Paul's thought world thus requires particular care, for Paul's communication of his thoughts is fundamentally shaped by a number of factors—factors that sometimes even distort the thought world that inspires the communication.[7]

Paul's perception of the nature of the situation into which he writes. Paul's information is drawn from his own experiences in the churches, from letters exchanged with them, from emissaries sent from them, and from Paul's own agents. He treats in his letters topics that are relevant to the understanding of the situation he has gained from these sources.[8] What for the interpreter is only the slightest hint may for the original readers have been an allusion to material or an experience that they knew very well—the identity of the "famous brother" in 2 Cor 8:18, for example, or the "Anathema Jesus" of 1 Cor 12:3. Accordingly, interpreters sometimes encounter gaps in the text precisely at the point where their curiosity has been aroused. Because the agenda of Paul's letters is fundamentally set by his perception of the needs and struggles of a given community, we as outsiders to the situation may not be treated to a discussion that would disclose the link between apparently disparate features of Paul's thought world. Paul writes about the matters that he thinks he needs to treat, not about matters that would help us see how his thoughts cohere.

Moreover, Pauline studies, like early Synoptic Gospel investigations, have long been content to harmonize the various Pauline letters as if the different situations they address did not cause Paul to give distinctive slants to what seem to be related topics. Similar passages from different letters have been

---

statement and perhaps even the core of the whole chapter?" ("A Pauline Version of the 'Amor Fati,'" in *New Testament Questions of Today* [Philadelphia: Fortress, 1969] 218–19).

[7] My proposals in this essay are not intended to suggest that what I here outline is the only way to make advances in the study of the Pauline letters. I recognize and salute the gains of colleagues who, in ways other than those I offer here, are expanding the borders of Pauline studies: Wayne Meeks and Gerd Theissen in the application of sociological method, Richard Hays in his attention to narrative, Norman Petersen in his joining of sociological and narrative concerns, Abraham Malherbe and Hans Dieter Betz in their attention to rhetorical and parenetic conventions of the Greco-Roman world. The list could go on.

[8] See J. C. Beker's discussion of "contingency" in the following essay.

uncritically associated without inquiring after the possibility that they have different purposes. For example, although Romans 4 and Galatians 3 both treat Abraham as the father of all faithful, the arguments run in different directions. In Romans, Paul stresses Abraham's common parentage of Jews and Gentiles (the point, to oversimplify, is unity) whereas in Galatians he emphasizes how all became children of Abraham by faith (the point, again to oversimplify, is the primacy of faith).

Paul's casting of his thought in delicate balances and his eagerness to hold important matters in equilibrium. Paul holds fundamental matters in his thought world together in a delicate equilibrium: the faithfulness and freedom of God, for example, or what is already and what is not yet available to the believer. The balance between these items is delicate and can easily be upset, and then the richness and complexity of Paul's thought are diminished, for balances convey a larger picture than either item alone. It is not a case of either/or, but both/and—and not only both/and, but *both* and *and* in equilibrium.[9] So the Corinthians who claim that they already enjoy freedom in Christ are right, but they must not overlook the fact that they do not yet enjoy resurrection life. So God is free to do new things, but God is also faithful to the old promises. So Israel is still God's special people, but Israel is no different from the other nations. So love compels, but love is not served by compulsion.

When one member of a balanced pair is emphasized without respect for the other, something more than the neglected member is lost; even the emphasized point loses some of its power.[10] Of course, "all things are permissible." Paul nowhere denies that. But the full picture requires the balancing statements, "but not all things confer a benefit," or "not all things build up." Freedom is crippled when love is not firmly laced into it.

Conceiving Paul's thought in terms of balances has wide implications, because one's heuristic images or models shape and determine what one finds. For example, when scholars look for the center of Paul's thought, many find justification by faith there. Others have seen freedom at the center. But precisely because Paul's thought is cast in balances and not in isolated ideas, the nuclear model with its single "center" is not adequate. My model for construing Paul's thought is based on an analogy with electromagnetic fields. No

---

[9] See my essay "Romans and Galatians: Comparison and Contrast," in *Understanding the Word: Essays in Honor of Bernhard W. Anderson* (ed. J. T. Butler et al.; JSOTSup 37; Sheffield: JSOT Press, 1985) 315–39, where I employ the methodological care that I here advocate and where I discuss some delicate balances of Paul's gospel.

[10] The Pastoral Epistles can be seen as case studies in what happens to Paul's gospel when some of the delicate balances are allowed to lose their internal tension. In many particulars, Ephesians and Colossians can be viewed as halfway houses along that road.

single charge is sufficient to set up a field. The field comes into being when two poles, two different charges, exert an influence on each other. For something as complex as Paul's thought world, one must imagine a series of electromagnetic fields, each in tension within itself and each field of force arrayed in tension with all the others.

In particular, the rather widespread insistence that justification by faith is at the center of Paul's thought has led to an emphasis on Galatians for interpreting Paul, from Marcion to Luther and into our own time.[11] As a result, Paul is read heavily, and at times uncritically, under the influence of Luther, and certain topics like the law, rewards, and works are interpreted in predictable ways. Under the model I am proposing, justification by faith would have a prominence in Paul's thought world, but neither it *nor any other concept* would be said to be at the center.

A related but often-overlooked problem emerges: when Paul sees one of these delicate balances twisted askew by his churches or by his opponents, he usually responds not by reaffirming the balance but by stressing the neglected pole. Thus, any adequate interpretation of Paul depends on a reconstruction of the argument of the opponents and a careful estimation of Paul's rhetorical strategy. Because Paul focuses so frequently on the position of his opponents, our capacity to understand Paul is directly proportionate to our ability to understand Paul's opponents. We thus need a more credible, sensitive, and sympathetic reckoning of these opponents and their positions. Yet the matter is even more complex: Paul, in his concern to restore lost balance, sometimes *over*emphasizes the neglected pole. Thus, for example, he responds to the Corinthians' individualistic enthusiasm by stressing their communal claims and responsibilities. So the *nature* and the *degree* of Paul's polemical or apologetic intent and his rhetorical strategy must be discerned if our interpretation is to recover what Paul would have seen as the proper balance. Otherwise we will confuse a statement shaped by Paul's polemic or by his rhetorical purposes with what he might have said in a moment less governed by passion.[12]

How are Paul's polemical and apologetic sections to be interpreted? How can we learn to determine just how much Paul may overstate his case in order

[11] When last we had a Society of Biblical Literature seminar on Paul, we began our study with Galatians—over my objections. Daniel Patte makes Galatians his point of entry for the study of Paul! (*Paul's Faith and the Power of the Gospel: A Structural Introduction to the Pauline Letters* [Philadelphia: Fortress, 1983]).

[12] E. A. Judge notes that "such is the subtlety of the lost rhetorical art, that until we have it back under control we can hardly think we know how to read passages which both by style and content belong to Paul's struggle with rhetorically trained opponents for the support of his rhetorically fastidious converts" ("Paul's Boasting in Relation to Contemporary Professional Practice," *AusBR* 16 [1968] 48).

to restore a particular balance? Our answer must be informed by the customary rhetorical and polemical practices of his own time, and the only way to achieve this will be more work in the rhetorical handbooks. We need ultimately to be able to distinguish the various polemical strategies that Paul employs.[13]

Paul's evangelistic flexibility. Working out of his own relatively coherent thought world, Paul behaves—and probably writes—quite differently in different circumstances. Paul was sometimes viewed as an authoritative, even dictatorial, figure, and awareness of this image could have occasioned his opening *correctio* in Rom 1:11–12: "For I long to see you in order that I may impart some spiritual gift to you, to strengthen you, that is, that we may receive encouragement with you through each other's faith, both yours and mine." But the authoritative Paul is not the only Paul to be found in the letters. There is also the flexible Paul who describes his missionary policy as one of great adaptability: to the Jews he becomes as one under the law whereas to the Gentiles he becomes as one outside the law (1 Cor 9:19–23). It is this Paul who can forgo the use of his charisma of glossolalia for the well-being of the community (1 Cor 14:18–19), who can personally be ready to depart this life but accept the need to stay on (Phil 1:23–26), who can consider not going to deliver the collection to Jerusalem (1 Cor 16:3–4) but later change his mind and go even though it is dangerous for him to do so (Rom 15:25–32), whose other travel plans change so much that some Corinthians find him untrustworthy (2 Cor 1:15–18), who can accept support from the Philippians or manage well without it (Phil 4:10–13), who doggedly refuses any support from the Corinthians (2 Cor 11:9–10) and presents his practice of self-support as a model in Thessalonica (1 Thess 2:9–12) and yet accepts frequent support from the faithful at Philippi (Phil 4:16; 2 Cor 11:9), and who relates to some believing communities as one among equals (Phil 4:15; Phlm 17; note also Phil 1:1, where he does not designate himself as apostle but as a slave along with Timothy) but with others energetically defends his apostolic status (1 Cor 1:1; 2 Cor 1:1; Gal 1:1).

Further study will show that this pervasive flexibility is not merely pragmatic; it offers a fundamental insight into Paul's thought world. The gospel and love *require* flexibility: "in order that I might by all means save some" (1 Cor 9:22); "only that in every way, whether with false motives or in truth, Christ is proclaimed" (Phil 1:18); "on account of love I prefer to appeal to

[13] I would venture the hypothesis, for example, that Paul feels he is on safer personal ground in his debate with the Galatians than when he writes 2 Corinthians 10–13 to the Corinthians. One can take the liberties of Galatians (Gal 1:6; 3:1, 3; 4:11, 20; 5:12) only when one is confident of the readers' deep personal loyalty and a storehouse of goodwill.

you" (Phlm 9). Rigid patterns and set programs do not always fit the demands of the gospel.

More clarity about Paul's flexibility and an identification of when and why it is employed will heighten our awareness of those times and places where Paul is inflexible. Then we may be better able to assess whether an individual point of inflexibility reveals a fundamental principle that Paul is committed to defend.

Paul's use of pre-Pauline traditions. The difficulty of penetrating behind Paul's communication of his thoughts to a recognition of the thought world that spawned them is compounded by Paul's frequent use of pre-Pauline traditions. These include Christian hymnic, creedal, and liturgical formulations as well as scripture quotations and allusions. When, for example, Paul writes to the Romans, most of whom he does not know, he very freely draws on earlier church traditions and signals absolutely no awkwardness in expressing his own thoughts through those traditions. There was, of course, a reason for employing this strategy in this letter: it had the important impact of identifying Paul and his gospel with traditions that the Romans might have known as their own. Yet whenever there is confusion in his churches, Paul reminds them of the traditions that he received and passed along to them. On occasion his argument is shaped by those traditions (1 Cor 15:3–50).

For Paul, of course, there was only one gospel. That conviction lay behind his struggle with the Galatians and behind the earlier debate at the Jerusalem conference mentioned in that letter (Gal 2:1–10). Thus Paul welcomed other church traditions as avenues through which he could advance his concerns. It is clear, though, that we need to reexamine the way traditions — and scripture — function in Paul's letters.

The nature of Paul's letters thus requires special care of the interpreter. The influence of the various situations on Paul's rhetorical strategies must be considered and due regard must be given to his flexibility. Only then can we hope to move from Paul's communication of his thoughts to the thought world in which the desire to communicate was grounded. Moreover, we cannot even begin a reconstruction of Paul's thought world until we have analyzed each letter.

II. MOVING FROM TEXT
TO THOUGHT WORLD:
SPECIFIC PROCEDURES

We need to establish some questions that, when applied systematically to the letters, will turn up clues to the coherencies of Paul's thought world.

These questions must first be applied rigorously to each letter and then to the collection as a whole. When the individual letters are compared with one another, a feature of a given letter that had initially gone unnoticed might gain in significance when seen alongside a similar feature in another letter. Indeed, when viewed together, these features could provide clues to a basic aspect of Paul's thought. Thus the effort to reconstruct Paul's thought world by looking at the letters *together* will yield more data than the original investigations of the individual letters. Consider, for example, Paul's comment in Phil 2:4: "Let each of you look not to the things pertaining to oneself, but to matters pertaining to others." An interpreter could reasonably wonder whether this was a bit of counsel particular to the Philippian situation and be tempted to pass it by. But when these words are reinforced by 1 Cor 10:24 ("Let no one seek the thing pertaining to oneself, but the thing pertaining to the other") and by the similar comment in 1 Cor 10:33 (". . . not seeking my own advantage, but that of the many"), the interpreter could confidently treat Phil 2:4 as an established principle of Paul's thought world.

This brings us to the point where we can begin to establish procedures for gathering data as we move from letter to letter. I have decided to present these procedures in the form of questions which, if pursued, might promise some yield toward a reconstruction of Paul's thought world. With each, a short illustrative example is offered. The order is not intended to suggest any ranking or sequencing, nor is the list intended to be exhaustive. Others surely will propose different questions and may even amend some of mine.

1. Where does Paul self-correct? That device was recommended by rhetoricians as a way to have the reader understand exactly what was being said.[14] "I am astonished that you are so quickly turning away . . . to another gospel—there is not another!" (Gal 1:6–7). "But now, knowing God, or rather having been known by God, . . ." (Gal 4:9).

2. Where does Paul say something is evident, clear, or plain (δῆλος)? "It is clear that by the law no one is justified before God" (Gal 3:11). "But when it says, 'All things are put in subjection under him,' it is plain that he is excepted who put all things under him" (1 Cor 15:27 RSV). Does 2 Cor 5:5 function in this same way?

3. When is something authoritatively written off? "But when they measure themselves by one another, and compare themselves with one another, they are without understanding" (2 Cor 10:12 RSV).

4. What matters are treated as indifferent? Is there a pattern? Likewise, what counts? "Therefore we aspire, whether we are at home or away, to please [the Lord]" (2 Cor 5:9). "For neither circumcision is something nor

---

[14] The treatment of Rom 1:11–12 above can serve as an example here also.

uncircumcision . . ." (Gal 6:15; see also 1 Cor 7:19; Gal 5:6). Rom 14:5–9 illustrates that such a pattern of identifying indifferent matters (no doubt a Stoic echo) is widespread in Paul's letters.

5. What does Paul expect from all churches? "As in all the churches of the saints . . ." (1 Cor 14:33b RSV). "If any one is disposed to be contentious, we recognize no other practice, nor do the churches of God" (1 Cor 11:16 RSV; see also 1 Cor 4:17).

6. In a related way, what is always expected of the believers? They are to "rejoice in the Lord always" (Phil 4:4 RSV) and "hold fast to prayer" (Rom 12:12; see also 1 Thess 5:17). The counterpart to this question is also worth pursuing: What is one *never* to do? "Do not be indolent in earnestness" (Rom 12:11). "Do not set the mind on things too high" (Rom 12:16; see also 11:20). "Never avenge yourselves" (Rom 12:19 RSV). Care must be taken here, for Paul's especially warm and positive relationship with the Philippians enables him to write, "Therefore, my beloved, as you have always obeyed, so now, not only as in my presence but much more in my absence, . . ." (Phil 2:12 RSV).

7. Are there not patterns within Paul's arguments which, if studied, could yield insights into coherencies in his thought world? We can identify at least three types of significant patterns.

(a) Does Paul present a basic point from which, or in light of which, he reasons? If so, he understood this point as already established with the community and as basic to his view. An example would be his reference to "the present distress" in 1 Cor 7:26.

(b) Within an argument, what can be made of Paul's references to what the readers already know? We can conclude that Paul—and probably his readers— accepted as true or normative the matter that was already known to them. An example is found in Gal 3:2, where Paul asks the Galatians to draw upon the truth of their experience: "This only do I want to learn from you: from works of the law did you receive the Spirit or from hearing with faith?" Note also the way the references to what "we know" (1 Cor 8:1, 4) function in the larger context of that chapter.

(c) Have we properly noted the various ways that Paul grounds his arguments? He frequently moves with careful deliberation toward the telling point of his argument. Thus, for example, in 1 Cor 7:31 he grounds his previous advice in the eschatological conviction that "the form of this world is passing away" (RSV). This pattern abounds in Paul's writings and thus provides a rich resource that needs to be examined (see also 1 Cor 7:35; 8:6; 11:1; 12:26; 15:34, 50; 2 Cor 4:15; 9:8; 10:18; Gal 3:18, 20).

Closely related to this is another feature of Pauline argumentation. Often Paul's arguments contain what we might call an indirect witness to his thought world. When Paul brings to a disputed matter something that he

believes to be beyond dispute and then argues from the imported consideration, these considerations function very much like the grounding statements
just noted. An example is found in Paul's response to the Corinthian charge
that he vacillates and makes his plans κατὰ σάρκα. In the space of a few verses
he twice argues from the faithfulness of God: "as surely as God is faithful . . . ," and "all the promises of God find their Yes in [Jesus Christ]" (2 Cor
1:18, 20 RSV). Likewise, in a hardship list Paul provides an indirect witness
to his view of possessions: ". . . as having nothing, and yet possessing everything" (2 Cor 6:10 RSV; see also 1 Cor 3:21-23; 7:29-31).

8. What can the *structure* of some of Paul's arguments tell us about primary
assumptions within his thought world? Several structures can be noted.

(a) Some "if . . . then" constructions suggest integral connections that exist
within Paul's thought world. "But if a son also an heir" (Gal 4:7).

(b) Questions that assume a known answer will tell us what Paul thinks
is already established. "Therefore, is the law against the promises?" (Gal
3:21).[15] "Shall we make the Lord jealous? Are we stronger than he?"
(1 Cor 10:22).

(c) The "not only" part of a "not only . . . but also" statement is also understood as an established point from which to argue; therefore, we can use such
information as a building block in our reconstruction of Paul's thought
world. "We have regard for what is good not only before the Lord but also
before people" (2 Cor 8:21).

(d) Relative clauses modifying "God," "Christ," or the "Holy Spirit" are
rich sources of information about Paul's thought world. Examples include
". . . Jesus who rescues us from the coming wrath" (1 Thess 1:10) and
". . . God, who calls you into God's own reign and glory" (1 Thess 2:12).

9. What about statements that are repeated from letter to letter? "God is
faithful" (1 Cor 1:9 RSV; 2 Cor 1:18). Or consider the following statements:
"For it is necessary that all of us appear before the tribunal of Christ, so that
each one may receive a recompense for the things done in the body" (2 Cor
5:10); and "[God] will recompense each according to the works of that one"
(Rom 2:6). Care must be taken, however, to detect when similar statements
were generated by similar situations.

10. In prayers, what does Paul give thanks for? What does he cite for com-
mendation? Paul's words in Philemon 4-5 bear directly on the situation of
that letter, but they also portray the kind of life that he elsewhere encourages:
"I give thanks to my God always, remembering you in my prayers, because
I hear of your love and the faith which you have toward the Lord Jesus and
all the saints."

---

[15] See S. K. Stowers, *The Diatribe and Paul's Letter to the Romans* (SBLDS 57; Chico, CA:
Scholars Press, 1981).

11. In a related matter, should we note when Paul urges a person or an entire congregation to "do so more and more" (1 Thess 4:1, 10 RSV)? Equally significant are his frequent assertions to continue "just as you are doing" (1 Thess 5:11).

12. Should we not note ideal portraits that Paul sketches, whether of a proper worship service (1 Cor 14:24–25, 26–33) or of an ideal fellow worker (2 Cor 8:16–17)? In an analogous fashion, Paul's praise of the faith or love or steadfastness of an individual, a church, or even believers across an entire Roman province provides an insight into what Paul considers to be proper living in accord with the gospel.[16]

13. What shall we make of the frequency with which Paul mentions goals in his letters? At the very least we can surmise that such matters were of importance to Paul in dealing with his different churches and they were probably a prominent feature of his thought world. The goals are defined by a few oft-repeated phrases: to please God (Rom 8:8; 1 Cor 7:32; 1 Thess 2:4; 4:1; cf. 1 Thess 2:15), to glorify God (Rom 15:6, 9; 1 Cor 6:20; 2 Cor 9:13; Gal 1:24; cf. Rom 1:21), to walk worthily of God (1 Thess 2:12) and to the glory of God (1 Cor 10:31; Phil 2:11). The investigation should be expanded, however, to include such expressions as "pursue love" (1 Cor 14:1).

14. What do Paul's frequent admonitions to imitate his behavior reveal? Paul does what he thinks all believers should do: he lives according to the gospel. Thus his life is a reflection of his gospel, and attacks upon him are sometimes countered with a defense of his gospel while questions about his gospel are often answered by reference to his own life. Accordingly, if we wish to reconstruct Paul's thought world we must not ignore his oft-sounded call to his churches to model their behavior after his. The most sweeping such admonition is found in Philippians: "What you have learned and received and heard and seen in me, do; and the God of peace will be with you" (4:9 RSV; see also 1 Cor 4:16; 11:1; Gal 4:12; Phil 3:17; 1 Thess 1:6). Most often Paul presents himself as the model, but sometimes his coworkers are pictured as his imitable doubles (1 Cor 3:5–9). In a variant of this theme, Paul sometimes applies the problems of others to himself (1 Cor 4:6–7; 9:1–27).

15. What information can we glean from the postscripts of Paul's letters? These sections of the letters (1 Cor 16:13–18, 21–22; 2 Cor 13:11–13; Gal 6:11–17; 1 Thess 3:11; 5:12–22), often personally penned, offer possibilities for our inquiry because they often focus on issues that initially prompted the letter. Because of the summary nature of these postscripts, however, particular care must be taken to identify any polemical material peculiar to that situation.

---

[16] Paul encourages the Corinthians by describing the zeal of the Macedonians (2 Cor 8:1–5) and vice versa (2 Cor 9:2; see also 1 Thess 1:7–8).

16. How shall we evaluate the *sententiae* or gnomic sayings that Paul cites in his letters? Maxims show up in the Pauline letters in a variety of ways. Frequently, Paul strings them together, usually toward the end of a letter (Rom 12:9–21; 2 Cor 13:11–12; Phil 4:4–9; 1 Thess 5:12-22). In these circumstances, they stand alongside each other like photographs in a gallery, each a vignette of the faithful life in practice.[17] Sometimes, however, a maxim stands by itself at the heart of an argument. In such instances, the statement often functions as the foundation upon which the argument is structured: "Let all things be done decently and in order" (1 Cor 14:40). "For God is not a God of confusion but of peace" (1 Cor 14:33 RSV). These gnomic statements are valuable for a reconstruction of Paul's thought world because they are offered as premises of the argument, material that is beyond dispute. (See section 7c above.)

The slogans that show up in Paul's letters, even when they are championed by his opponents, may have originated with Paul and his penchant for *sententiae,* and insofar as they did, they shed light on Paul's preaching. Some examples of this are widely recognized: "an idol is nothing in the world," and "there is no God except one" (1 Cor 8:4). The statement "all things are permissible" (1 Cor 6:12; 10:23; see also Rom 14:2–3) may also belong in this category. To be sure, some of these maxims may amount to little more than conventional wisdom, but even that should tell us something fundamental about Paul's thought world.

In closing, I would suggest an analogy between Pauline studies and Synoptic studies. One of the first things we learn as we encounter the Synoptic Gospels is this dictum: "The gospels are primary sources for the life and faith of the early church; they are secondary sources for the life and faith of Jesus." In Pauline studies, we are not in quite the same position, but perhaps we are closer to it than we think. I restate the adage this way: Paul's letters are primary sources not only for the apostle's apprehension of the situation into which he writes but also for his efforts to instruct, correct, encourage, and lead his churches; they are, however, sometimes oblique, and always limited, avenues to his thought world. Yet the more skilled we become in interpreting the way Paul communicates his thoughts, the more we will have laid the base for a careful reconstruction of the thought world from which those thoughts arose.

---

[17] Studies that set Paul in the broader culture are important in this as in other regards; see, e.g., W. A. Beardslee, "Plutarch's Use of Proverbial Forms of Speech," *Semeia* 17 (1980) 110–12.

2 RECASTING PAULINE THEOLOGY

The Coherence-Contingency Scheme
as Interpretive Model

J. Christiaan Beker
Princeton Theological Seminary

THE FIRST SECTION EXPLICATES the coherence-contingency scheme and eluci-
dates some of its features; the second section addresses some critical
problems associated with the scheme.

I. EXPLICATION

The coherence-contingency scheme assumes that Paul is primarily not a
systematic theologian or a pastoral counselor but an *interpreter* who both in
his exegesis of the Old Testament and in his appropriation of Christian tradition adapts and reformulates previous interpretation in a distinctive and
innovative manner. It is not Paul the theologian (as Marcion celebrates him)
or Paul the successful missionary (as Acts celebrates him) which marks the
primary distinctiveness of the apostle in early Christian thought, but rather
Paul the interpreter of the gospel. Therefore, an adequate interpretation of
Paul must focus on that element of his thought which constitutes "the heart
of the matter" and without which all other Pauline issues remain peripheral,
namely, the precise character and function of Paul's interpretive activity.

Paul's hermeneutic is shaped by a complex interaction of coherence and
contingency. By "coherence" I mean the stable, constant element which
expresses the convictional basis of Paul's proclamation of the gospel: he
refers to it as "the truth of the gospel" (Gal 2:5, 14), apostasy from which
elicits an apocalyptic curse (Gal 1:8, 9; see also Phil 1:27; 2 Thess 1:8; 2:12).
By "contingency" I mean the variable element, that is, the variety and particularity of sociological, economic, and psychological situations which Paul
faces in his churches and on the mission field. Thus through the interaction
between coherence and contingency, the abiding Word of the gospel
becomes a word on target, thereby fulfilling its function as gospel.

Paul's hermeneutic not only distills a specific core out of the variety of gospel traditions in the early church but also "incarnates" that core into the particularity of historical occasions and contexts. . . . It is Paul's interpretive achievement that he combines particularity and universality, or diversity and unity, in such a way that the gospel is neither simply *imposed* on historical occasions as a ready-made "orthodox system" nor simply *fragmented* into fortuitous and accidental intentions of thought. . . . Unless Paul's "core" is viewed in its "contingent" eventfulness, it sinks away into the abstraction of a system. Yet, unless the "contingent" character of the gospel interacts with its coherent core, Paul's hermeneutic becomes opportunistic and incidental, if not chaotic.[1]

This description of the coherence-contingency scheme in my book on Paul needs correction and explication in several ways: (a) What precisely is the *content* of the coherent structure of the Pauline gospel? (b) What precisely constitutes the *interaction* between coherence and contingency? Is it possible or even desirable to draw *clear distinctions* between the bipolar concepts, coherence and contingency, as if they can be compartmentalized into distinct conceptual units? (c) To what extent is the coherence-contingency scheme too severely *abstract* and rationalistic to do justice to Paul's hermeneutic?

The Content of the Coherent Structure of Paul's Gospel

The use of the term "coherence" rather than "core" is crucially significant for my project, and therefore the occasional use of the latter term in my book *Paul the Apostle* is misleading. The term "core" is not only reminiscent of Rudolf Bultmann's distinction between *core* and *husk* (separating a central conviction from its linguistic expression) but suggests as well the presence of a center or *Mitte* in Paul's thought which controls all the other Pauline expressions and elaborations. Thus, the term "core" suggests a fixed, non-pliable substance; it has been the main interpretive device to designate the center of Paul's thought since the Reformation. Even when Albert Schweitzer located the center of Paul's thought in his eschatological mysticism, rejecting the doctrine of justification as its central core and advocating instead a two-crater theme (eschatological mysticism and rabbinic-juridical thought),[2] the quest for an explicit doctrinal core or center continued, whether located in the mysticism of "being in Christ," in righteousness, or in sacramental participation.

The term "coherence," however, suggests a fluid and flexible structure. In

---

[1] J. C. Beker, *Paul the Apostle: The Triumph of God in Life and Thought* (Philadelphia: Fortress, 1980) 351 (emphasis added).

[2] A. Schweitzer, *The Mysticism of Paul the Apostle* (New York: Macmillan, 1955) esp. 223–26.

contrast to a fixed core and a specific center or particular symbol, it points to a field of meaning, a network of symbolic relations that nourishes Paul's thought and constitutes his "linguistic world." At this point it may be helpful to refer to the remarks of Hendrikus Boers, who identifies the search for coherence as a primary task of New Testament scholarship. After referring to attempts at a solution by W. Wrede, K. Barth, R. Bultmann, E. Käsemann, D. Patte, and myself, he writes:

> The cumulative value of these contributions is that they help clarify one of, if not *the* most fundamental problem in Pauline interpretation. However, none of them succeed in identifying a center which makes it possible to integrate the diversity of the Apostle's thinking into a coherent whole. Such a center cannot be found in *any particular Pauline idea,* such as Beker's eschatological triumph of God, or Patte's patterns of convictions. The center of Paul's thought transcends every instance of its expression.[3]

Boers demonstrates the necessity of clarifying my definition of "coherence." A symbolic universe is not an "idea," nor is "coherence" to be classified as a "center," core, or *Mitte,* that is, as something so specific that Boers can charge me with making "of a single apple [in the sense of Plato's *Laches*] the center of Paul's thinking."[4]

I suggest that Jewish apocalyptic is the substratum and master symbolism of Paul's thought because it constituted the linguistic world of Paul the Pharisee and therefore formed the indispensable filter, context, and grammar by which he appropriated and interpreted the Christ-event, the ἀποκάλυψις Ἰησοῦ Χριστοῦ (Gal 1:12; see also 1:16; 2:2). The interaction between coherence and contingency as the conjunction of the apocalyptic substratum with contingent contexts is evident not only in the private experience of Paul's call but also in the communal activity of Paul's missionary mandate. The coincidence of "conversion" and apostolic call in the Damascus experience (Gal 1:15) demonstrates that "the truth of the gospel," that is, the apocalyptic interpretation of the cross and resurrection of Christ, is not only the abiding solution to Paul's private contingency (in answering the crisis of his personal life) but also the abiding solution to the various problems of his churches (in answering their several crises).

In positing Jewish apocalyptic as the master symbolism of Paul's thought, I do not suggest that Paul adopts Jewish apocalyptic as a literary genre or uses Jewish apocalypses as literary *Vorlagen.* Moreover, I am not interested in semantic explorations of the meaning of the concept "apocalyptic" in

---

[3] H. Boers, "The Foundations of Paul's Thought: A Methodological Investigation—The Problem of the Coherent Center of Paul's Thought," *ST* 42 (1988) 61 (emphasis added).

[4] Ibid., 58.

relation to Paul.[5] Rather, I maintain that apocalyptic *motifs* dominate Paul's thought, that Paul's modifications of the Christian tradition are *not* due to Hellenistic-Jewish or Philonic influences but are modifications of an *apocalyptic* substratum.

Coherence cannot be restricted to one particular "contingent" symbol—for instance, to the eschatological triumph of God, as I proposed in my book[6]—because it implies a network of symbolic relations and does not refer to one specific idea or *Mitte*. Therefore I agree with J. Louis Martyn's objection to my proposition that "the situational demands (in Galatians) suppress the apocalyptic theme of the gospel."[7] The coherence of the gospel, then, is constituted by the apocalyptic interpretation of the death and resurrection of Christ. W. Wrede said long ago that in Paul "all references to the redemption as a completed transaction swing around at once into utterances about the future."[8] In other words, the coherence of the gospel involves a series of affirmations which are stamped by apocalyptic thought and which in turn cannot be divorced from their ultimate point of reference, namely, the imminent apocalyptic triumph of God.

The Interaction between Coherence and Contingency

The nature of this interaction is probably the most crucial issue in the analysis of Paul's hermeneutic. The *fluidity* of this interaction in Paul seems to make a proper delineation of the boundaries of the coherent and the contingent very difficult, if not impossible. Two points need to be emphasized here.

(1) The relation between coherence and contingency assumes quite different forms in Jewish casuistry and in later Christian orthodoxy. There the coherence-contingency scheme revolves around the relation of universal principles or precepts to specific cases. In Judaism, for instance, the status of the Law of Moses is an eternally given and fixed literary document which Mishna and Midrash must make applicable to new historical circumstances. In Christian orthodoxy fixed creedal or dogmatic formulations (see, for instance, "the deposit of truth" in 1 Tim 6:20) become as it were sacred texts which in a clearly *separate* hermeneutical move must subsequently be explicated and applied to contingent situations.

The hermeneutical situation in Paul, however, is quite different. Fixed or

---

[5] L. E. Keck, "Paul and Apocalyptic Theology," *Int* 38 (1984) 229–41.

[6] Beker, *Paul the Apostle,* ix; see the comments of H. Boers, quoted above, and R. P. Martin's review of this book in *JBL* 101 (1982) 463–66.

[7] See Martyn's review of *Paul the Apostle* in *WW* 2 (1982) 194–98; see *Paul the Apostle,* x, 58.

[8] W. Wrede, *Paul* (London: Philip Green, 1907) 111.

written creedal formulations simply did not yet exist in the early churches. All they had were floating oral traditions. Hymnic, baptismal, and eucharistic fragments circulated along with succinct confessions and traditional benedictions (see, for instance, 1 Cor 8:6; 12:3; 15:3–5; and 2 Cor 13:13). This circumstance helps to explain the hermeneutical fluidity in Paul and early Christianity as simply a necessity.

> The church then was held together less by dogmatic uniformity than by hermeneutical multiformity. The unity of the church was the focus, and theological diversity served that purpose. In this context of multiformity, Paul may indeed have been the first "dogmatic" theologian in the sense that he could not sacrifice the specificity of "the truth of the gospel" to the unity of the church. Indeed, the unity of the church and the truth of the gospel constitute the permanent uneasy dialectical components of Paul's apostolate and thought.[9]

These earlier remarks make me now see more clearly that Paul's struggle in maintaining both the truth of the gospel and the unity of the church is directly related to the coherence-contingency issue of his hermeneutic. Hermeneutical fluidity between coherence and contingency in Paul is in this case all the more surprising because he formulated more clearly than other early Christian theologians the coherent structure of the gospel, that is, the abiding truth of the gospel, and so bequeathed to Christianity the beginnings of a doctrinal "orthodox" structure.

The reciprocal relation between coherence and contingency effects a fluid relation of the coherent truth of the gospel to the various contingent situations of the moment so that the coherence of the gospel does not become a static, unalterable structure of thought. Martyn refers to this hermeneutical process as a "circular" movement between coherence and contingency,[10] which aptly describes the "contextual" nature of the coherent "text" in Paul. The contingent nature of Paul's hermeneutic involves the inevitable risk that its inherently occasional and opportune character might become opportunistic and self-serving. However, the crux of the matter must be kept in mind: all interpretation—if it is to be interpretation rather than transliteration—involves risk. Thus Paul must risk in his own interpretation the proper relation of coherence and contingency—a risk that involves compromise, if not accommodation, and possibly opportunistic omissions and additions. After all, charismatic authority and apostolic insight are not synonymous with inerrancy and infallibility!

(2) For Paul the locus of the interaction between coherence and contingency is the Holy Spirit, which has the function of the διαχρίσεις

---

[9] Beker, *Paul the Apostle,* 130.
[10] Martyn in *WW* 2 (1982) 197.

πνευμάτων (1 Cor 12:10). In other words, the Holy Spirit—like the Paraclete in John—is both *detective* and *judge:* it detects the proper bond between coherence and contingency and subsequently evaluates the adequacy of the hermeneutical translation. In this context we must recall the awareness in the Pauline churches of the living presence of the risen Lord as the Spirit and its activity in prophetic utterances.[11] Therefore the interrelation between νοῦς and πνεῦμα (1 Corinthians 14; 2 Corinthians 4) characterizes the hermeneutical strategy of coherence and contingency by the members of the body of Christ in the Pauline church.

The Coherence-Contingency Scheme

To what extent is the coherence-contingency scheme too abstract? The conception of a coherence-contingency scheme suggests a thought process preoccupied with a coherence theory of truth and thus tends to forget that Paul was a pragmatic missionary and propagandist. Paul seems more interested in persuasion, emotional appeal, and moral exhortation in his letters than in the academic pursuit of coherence and consistency of thought. His primary interest is to advance the missionary outreach of the gospel, to convert people to the God of Jesus Christ, and to keep his churches together and maintain their unity. Thus, the interpreter of Paul may discover that a disclosure theory of truth may provide a more profitable means of access to Paul's hermeneutic than a coherence theory of truth.

The coherence-contingency scheme is not, however, an abstract, intellectual hermeneutical activity in the Pauline church. It would, for instance, be a mistake to concentrate exclusively on the nature of coherence, on the implications of a coherence theory of truth in comparison with a correspondence theory of truth, or on the logical consistency of argumentation and its inductive or deductive sequences. Although it is necessary to defend Paul's thought against detractors like E. P. Sanders and H. Räisänen,[12] who posit that there are basic contradictions between Paul's convictions or intuitions and their rational explications, we must remember that Paul was a *pragmatic* hermeneutician—a missionary and a propagandist who interwove thought with praxis and a convictional base of *logos* with the rhetoric of *ethos* and *pathos.*[13]

---

[11] See below, p. 23.

[12] E. P. Sanders, *Paul, the Law, and the Jewish People* (Philadelphia: Fortress, 1983); H. Räisänen, *Paul and the Law* (Philadelphia: Fortress, 1986); see the earlier criticisms of F. Nietzsche, E. Renan, and P. A. de Lagarde.

[13] See S. J. Kraftchick, "Ethos and Pathos Appeals in Galatians Five and Six: A Rhetorical Analysis" (Ph.D. diss., Emory University, 1985).

The coherence of the gospel "incarnates" itself into the contingencies of the mission field in such a way that—to use modern language—a coherence theory of truth serves the objective of a disclosure theory of truth. In other words, the ὑπακοή of the Gentiles, the δύναμις and transforming power of the gospel to turn the hearts of people from idolatry to authentic worship, constitutes the essence of Paul's apostolic hermeneutic. In fact, because the locus of the interaction between coherence and contingency is the Holy Spirit, and because the body of Christ in turn is the locus of the Spirit, the body of Christ constitutes the place where the hermeneutical activity takes place. Within the unity of the Spirit, the members of the body in their diversity, multiformity, and mutuality plot the necessary strategies for their contingent situation in accordance with the coherent truth of the gospel. Indeed, the body of Christ constitutes a pneumatic democracy where—under the guidance of the apostle and his coworkers—the members of the body "find out," "test," and "approve" (δοκιμάζειν) "what is the will of God, what is good and acceptable and perfect" (Rom 12:2).[14] Thus, the hermeneutic of coherence-contingency is not an abstract or individualistic activity of the apostle, nor an activity of learned rabbis in a rabbinic school, but a pragmatic consensus-building activity in the body of Christ, where relevant and authentic "gospel" strategies are devised for particular problems.

II. CRITICAL PROBLEMS

The Dialogical Dialectic of the Scheme

The dialogical dialectic of the coherence-contingency scheme may be applicable to a particular letter, but is it a sufficient method for the corpus of the Pauline letters as a whole? Does the scheme involve a rigidity that fails to do justice both to the lively, contingent flow of Paul's thought (i.e., to its developmental or progressive character) and to its intuitive, incidental, and *ad hoc* features?

Notwithstanding the increasing interest in a developmental theory, which posits a progressive theological journey of Paul from 1 Thessalonians to Romans and/or Ephesians,[15] the objections to it raised by J. Lowe and V. P.

---

[14] See below, p. 23.

[15] See, e.g., C. H. Dodd, *The Apostolic Preaching and Its Developments* (London: Hodder & Stoughton, 1936); L. Cerfaux, *The Church in the Theology of St. Paul* (New York: Herder & Herder, 1959); C. H. Buck and G. Taylor, *Saint Paul: A Study of the Development of His Thought* (New York: Scribner's, 1969); F. F. Bruce, *Paul, Apostle of the Heart Set Free* (Exeter, Devon: Paternoster, 1977); G. Lüdemann, *Paul, Apostle to the Gentiles: Studies in Chronology* (Philadelphia: Fortress, 1984); W. Wiefel, "The Jewish Community in Ancient Rome and the Origins of

Furnish in their articles of 1941 and 1970 still stand.[16] The developmental theory often allows hypothetical preunderstandings to enter the debate, when, for instance, a new chronology of Paul's career and letters serves to expand the time limit of the letters' composition and thus to accommodate a possible theological development, or when Colossians and Ephesians are accepted as genuine letters of Paul so as to make room for the "mature" theology of an "older" Paul. Moreover, the concept "development" needs much more careful analysis. For instance, does it refer to an extrapolation of existing thought or to innovative thought structures? Furthermore, does it refer to peripheral or central thought structures? A possible shift in Paul's thought with respect to the interim state of the dead is clearly of quite different significance than would be, for instance, a shift with respect to the law or christology. In the light of these issues, the coherence-contingency scheme protects us from assuming all too easily the shifting character of the coherence of Paul's gospel, as if Paul's coherence were nothing but a culturally conditioned, contingent structure.

The Interaction between Coherence and Contingency

The reciprocal and circular interaction between coherence and contingency evokes some critical problems.

Is it possible to construe Paul's coherence with linguistic precision? When H. Boers states that "the center of Paul's thought transcends every instance of its expression," or when D. Patte defines it as "a system of convictions," or when E. P. Sanders separates Paul's "basic convictions" from his "divergent statements" and arguments, there is real gain in these observations, because they represent a movement away from a rigid dogmatic center or *Mitte* of Paul's hermeneutic.[17] Nevertheless, the gain does not match the loss, because once we divorce an experiential reality—a conviction or an intuition—from its linguistic expression, we attempt to go "behind the text" to its "pre-textual" location in Paul's "mental bank." This means that we reduce Paul's apostolic intent of proclaiming an intelligible and clear gospel (note

---

Roman Christianity," in *The Romans Debate* (ed. K. P. Donfried; Minneapolis: Augsburg, 1977) 100–119; and U. Schnelle, *Wandlungen im paulinischen Denken* (Stuttgart: Katholisches Bibelwerk, 1989).

[16] J. Lowe, "An Examination of Attempts to Detect Development in St. Paul's Theology," *JTS* 42 (1941) 129–42; V. P. Furnish, "Development in Paul's Thought," *JAAR* 38 (1970) 289–303.

[17] Boers, "Foundations of Paul's Thought," 2; D. Patte, *Paul's Faith and the Power of the Gospel: A Structural Introduction to the Pauline Letters* (Philadelphia: Fortress, 1983) 20–21; Sanders, *Paul, the Law, and the Jewish People,* 147–48.

his emphasis on νοῦς in 1 Cor 14:14–19 and on the φανέρωσις τῆς ἀληθείας in 2 Cor 4:2) to some sort of "psychological *Mitte*."

Does the coherence find adequate expression in the contingency, or does the contingency regularly compromise—if not drown and overwhelm—the coherence? Do contingent situations compel Paul to make statements that are inconsistent with his coherent thought?[18] For instance, if—as I propose—Paul's manner of conjoining coherence and contingency constitutes the *proprium* of his hermeneutic, it should constitute a major criterion for determining the Pauline or pseudo-Pauline character of a letter like Colossians. It would seem that the realized eschatology of Colossians, with its spatial rather than temporal thought pattern, qualifies as such a criterion. One could argue, however, that Paul's coherence is always qualified by contingency, so that the exclusively christological focus of Colossians—which seems to deviate from Paul's theocentric eschatology—is necessitated by the pressures of the contingent situation in Colossae, that is, by the Colossian heresy. Does not this mean that Colossians' realized eschatology cannot be appealed to as a criterion of its pseudo-Pauline character?[19]

An Inherent Conflict in the Coherence-Contingency Hermeneutic

If the body of Christ—as "the temple of the Holy Spirit" (1 Cor 3:16)—is the place where the hermeneutical activity of coherence-contingency takes place, that is, if the body of Christ is engaged in consensus building and in strategies to meet its various contingencies, who will decide the adequacy and relevance of the coherence-contingency debate? Who decides what constitutes "the new coherence," that is, the new product of thought which is the result of the interaction of the gospel's coherence and the contingency of the moment and which motivates the strategic praxis of the church?

On this issue Paul seems involved in a conflict between two convictions: (a) the conviction of the presence of the Spirit within the communal body of Christ, which establishes a pneumatic democracy in the body of Christ and in turn explains the lack of normative "offices" in the Pauline church; and (b) the conviction of his own unique apostolic call and authority, which establishes Paul as the normative interpreter of the gospel who requires the

---

[18] Sanders, *Paul, the Law, and the Jewish People;* and Räisänen, *Paul and the Law.*

[19] I offer this observation as a carrot to my critics, because I myself am persuaded that Colossians transgresses Paul's coherent conviction on this issue (note the omission in Colossians of the resurrection of the dead, its peculiar understanding of "hope," its almost Johannine conception of the eschatological future as φανέρωσις [3:4]).

church to be obedient to his own construal of coherence-contingency relations.

This conflict raises the question whether the outcome of the coherence-contingency hermeneutic is a product of Paul's private idiosyncratic musings or truly a gift of the communal Spirit within the unity of the body of Christ (Rom 12:1–2; 1 Cor 14:26–33a). The hermeneutical activity of the Pauline church seems caught in the conflict between Paul's insistence on his *personal* "charismatic authority," on the one hand, and the *communal* authority of the church, on the other.

Indeed, Paul often appeals not to the assent of the local church in which he functions as *primus inter pares* but to the external warrant of the authority of his unique apostolic office as the guarantee for the truth of his coherence-continuity scheme. Therefore it comes as no surprise that the post-Pauline church was compelled to develop a hierarchy of offices in order to guarantee its hermeneutical "orthodoxy," that is, to maintain the proper interpretation of the gospel for the church's various circumstances.

III. A FINAL WORD

It seems to me that the coherence-contingency method—notwithstanding its problems—provides a welcome *via media* between the extremes of a purely sociological analysis and a dogmatic imposition of a specific center on Paul's thought. The danger of the "sociological captivity" of Paul's thought, which threatens to evaporate the abiding theological truth-claim of the gospel, parallels in many ways the danger of a dogmatic imposition, either in terms of the dogmatic loci of a catechism or in the guise of a purely dogmatic dialectic of cross and resurrection with its *sub contrario* character of life and death.[20]

The reciprocal and circular interaction of coherence and contingency maintains the truth-claim of both the "dogmatic" (coherence) and the "sociological" (contingency), because it does not explore the dialectic of interacting theological concepts—such as Käsemann's *sub contrario* thesis or K. Barth's "infinite qualitative difference between time and eternity"—but rather focuses on a different kind of dialectic: that between the truth of the gospel and its "incarnational" relevance for people's concrete lives and circumstances.

---

[20] See E. Käsemann, "The Saving Significance of the Death of Jesus in Paul," in *Perspectives on Paul* (Philadelphia: Fortress, 1971) 32–59.

3 FINDING THE WAY
TO PAUL'S THEOLOGY

A Response to J. Christiaan Beker and J. Paul Sampley

Paul J. Achtemeier
Union Theological Seminary in Virginia

THE BASIC PROBLEM faced by anyone who seeks to find and define Paul's "theology," a problem reflected in the work of both J. Christiaan Beker and J. Paul Sampley as well as in all of the material in this volume, centers on the fact that we confront in the Pauline letters not so much a theology as a theologian engaged in theological reflection. That reflection, furthermore, is directed not to systematic statements but to the solution of problems that have arisen in different churches facing the varying complexities of attempting to live out the implications of the Christian faith preached to them by Paul and others. Thus, what one confronts in Paul's letters are reflections on how the gospel intersects with the world in which his readers live and how they are to think and act in that world under the rubric of that gospel. That in its turn reflects the fact that what Paul preached, by his own admission, was not a theology but "the gospel" (see, e.g., Rom 1:16; 1 Cor 4:15; 15:1; 2 Cor 11:4; Gal 2:2; 1 Thess 2:4). What he wanted to say and what he wanted his readers to accept fall under that rubric.

If we seek the underlying coherence of Paul's "theology," we must recognize that finding it will be a complex procedure. We must take into account the fact that Paul's theology exists under the rubric of "gospel," which itself contains not only materials unique to Paul but also materials he received and accepted from a Christian tradition that existed prior to his becoming an apostle (e.g., 1 Cor 11:23). It is to the daunting quest for a reflective model that will allow us to recover the theological coherence of that gospel that the proposals of Beker and Sampley are directed. Although the papers of Beker and Sampley address the same problem — namely, how to isolate from the welter of situation-conditioned material present in Paul's letter that material which represents positions or expressions which themselves do not depend

25

on a given contingent situation for their validity — they do so in somewhat different ways. Beker reflects on some refinements in the "coherence-contingency" model with which he has been working for some time, and Sampley suggests some generative questions on the basis of which we may be led to discover the coherent center of Pauline theology.

I.

In order to clarify the issues that emerge from Beker's proposals, let me use those proposals as an example of the way the coherence-contingency model may be applied and illustrate through them what I see as both the strengths and the shortcomings of Beker's reflections. The task I shall undertake, therefore, is to use the insights of Beker's model to aid in the process of clarifying the relationship between the coherence of Beker's understanding of his interpretive model and the contingent expressions and discussions of it he has presented here and elsewhere.

In undertaking this task, I do not wish to posit an internal contradiction in the coherence of Beker's model, even though some of his contingent expressions may suggest that as a possible assumption. Nor do I want to propose some sort of chronological development in his thought, nor the possible influences of some key events on that supposed development (important as they may or may not be), simply because I do not possess enough detailed data to allow me to do that. Furthermore, the fact that Beker says some things in this paper that are different from what he has said elsewhere — for example, in his magisterial *Paul the Apostle* — could lead one to conclude that he has changed his mind about the coherent center of his thought, or that discussions into which he has entered have led him to alter in a decisive way his earlier thinking. I do not, however, take that to be the case. Rather, I suspect that those discussions have shown him certain problems in the contingent expressions of his thought and have led him to find other and better contingent expressions that are more apposite to the coherent center of his thought. One assumes that the relationship between what has just been said about the problem of the contingent expression of the coherent center of Beker's thought and the substance of our discussion about Paul is clear.

There is another point in our discussion of Beker's paper that bears equally on its substance, and that is the question of the relationship of an experiential reality — for example, a conviction or an intuition — to its linguistic expression. Beker professes concern that the explication of that relationship is an "attempt to go 'behind the text' to its 'pre-textual' location in Paul's 'mental bank'" (p. 22). Yet in a sense that is exactly what his paper represents. That it is possible to sense a coherent whole as yet unavailable to precise linguistic expression is the experience of anyone who, involved, say, in a discussion such as this, realizes that a given linguistic expression of what one had in mind has not achieved its desired clarity. To be able to realize concerning one's own linguistic expression that one's thought has not been clearly expressed is an indication of the existence of a coherent center existing apart from its linguistic expression. Beker's paper is clearly enough his attempt to give linguistic expression to the coherent center of his own thought about the coherence-contingency model of interpreting Paul; the fact that he quotes from his book (p. 351; p. 16 of his paper) and then clarifies that quotation shows that that is exactly what is going on here.

With that introduction, several aspects of the critique I want to pursue have been laid down. Let me say at this point, however, that I am in wholehearted agreement with what Beker is seeking to do. I agree, for example, that one cannot find a development in Paul's thinking, since one is simply incapable of determining the order of composition of the letters we have. Even the placing of 1 Thessalonians as the earliest of Paul's letters rests, one suspects, on the often-unspoken assumption that early Christian thought developed from greater to lesser expectation of an immediate parousia. When applied to Paul, this seems to suggest an early date for 1 Thessalonians, since in that letter such an expectation apparently has caused a problem. That the nature of the problem—enough people have died since the congregation was founded so that now questions are starting to arise about Christ's return— points to a later rather than an earlier date is a problem honored more by ignoring than by discussing it.

I agree also that Paul was a coherent thinker—and often far more skilled in rhetoric than his critics want to believe. Careful attention to language, rhetorical structure, and context will often show supposed contradictions to rest more with careless exegesis than with Paul. One must wonder, for example, when one confronts the debate about the origin and significance of the thought expressed by δικαιωθέντες in Rom 5:1, whether the debaters have bothered to look at the immediately preceding verse, where being set right with God is clearly tied to the event of Christ's resurrection (4:25), giving plenty of reason for its appearance as accomplished in 5:1. Efforts to prove Paul a confused thinker on the basis of that kind of "debate" and "exegesis" say more about the debaters than about Paul.

This critique is therefore one performed by an *amicus curiae,* sympathetic to the attempt by Beker to demonstrate to the court of scholarly opinion the validity of his interpretive insight into the problem of understanding the theological thought of the apostle Paul.

Basic to my problem in understanding Beker's paper remains the relationship between coherence and contingency. Beker presents numerous attempts to clarify "coherence" in the paper. He begins with the definition on p. 15: coherence is the "constant element [*sic*] which expresses the convictional [*sic*] basis of Paul's proclamation of the gospel." It can also be equated with the "truth of the gospel" (Gal 2:5, 14; see also pp. 17, 24). Many other terms are used to define "coherence": it is the "coherent structure" of the Pauline gospel (p. 16); it represents a "field of meaning," a "network of symbolic relations," Paul's "linguistic world" (p. 17); it involves a "series of affirmations . . . stamped by apocalyptic thought"; it is "constituted by the apocalyptic interpretation of the death and resurrection of Christ" (p. 18); it can be termed the "coherent truth of the gospel" (p. 21) or Paul's "coherent thought" (p. 23). All of these are attempts to locate the coherence of Paul's theology apart from its contingent expression in his letters—but, equally important, apart from any dogmatic core or *Mitte* which could be expressed in the absence of its contingent application. Indeed, given Beker's thought on this matter, one wonders whether he could imagine that Paul himself ever thought of that coherence apart from its contingent expression. I suspect he could not, and I would agree with him.

It is precisely when Beker uses terminology suggesting mutual interaction between coherent center and contingent expression that I find that interrelationship puzzling. There is, he writes, a "reciprocal and circular interaction of coherence and contingency" (p. 22). This is a thought, it seems to me, that may need to be protected from itself, since it is open to many unpleasant ramifications. Of some Beker is aware: one such ramification is the suggestion that at some point a "new coherence" could emerge as the result of some dispute or another, such as the one reflected in Galatians. How different is finding such a "new coherence" from finding that Paul "chang(ed) his mind" or "develop(ed) his thought"? Given the possibility of a "new coherence," I find it hard to see how Beker can distinguish between interpretations that take into account legitimate interaction and those that do not, and hence which he would consider illegitimate (e.g., an interpretation of such interaction that would lead one to be able to justify Colossians as authentic). Beker needs to be careful in offering that "carrot to his critics" (p. 23 n. 19) lest those critical rabbits take a hand or an arm along with the carrot!

That ability to differentiate between legitimate and illegitimate "circular and reciprocal" relationships must further presume an ability to locate at least some of the content of the coherence of Paul's thought. For example, in discussing the possible "development" of Paul's thought, Beker, I think rightly, suggests that there is a difference between a possible shift in Paul's thinking with respect to "the interim state of the dead" and a shift with respect to the "law or christology" (p. 22). Yet on what basis is this decision made? If it is not simply to be personal preference or theological prejudice, one must have some way of knowing what Paul himself regarded as "peripheral" to his coherent "thought structures" and what is "central" (the terms are used on p. 22). That brings us back to the knotty problem of "core" or *Mitte* — concepts not easily jettisoned for the sake of convenience in meeting the objections of one's critics. To throw out the whole notion of a consistent core at the center of Paul's coherence is to throw the baby out with the bathwater. As Beker's statement on peripheral and central thought structures shows, however, the baby is still in the tub, and Beker needs to deal with his need for that core in the clear expression of his own thought.

There are other questions: What does it mean to say that "coherence . . . suggests a fluid and flexible structure" (p. 16)? Is the emphasis on "structure," in which case the interrelationships of the various elements of the thought structure can be rearranged without affecting the "truth of the gospel"? Or is the emphasis on "fluid and flexible," with the implication that the thought structures themselves belong to the contingent expression of that "truth of the gospel," in which case all later distinctions between peripheral and central (e.g., interim state of the dead and law, authenticity of Colossians) simply reflect the shape of the central thought structures *at that particular moment*. At that point, not only is the baby out with the bathwater, but the tub and the mother are as well!

There are questions of meaning: What does it mean to say that "the interrelation between νοῦς and πνεῦμα . . . characterizes the *hermeneutical strategy of coherence and contingency* by the members of the body of Christ in the Pauline church" (p. 20; my emphasis)? Does the πνεῦμα energize νοῦς as coherence energizes contingency? Is the interrelationship between coherence and contingency simply a "strategy" without in any way being central to a gospel which itself was incarnated in a contingent human being? Can one even know about such an interrelationship without knowing *something* of the content of the coherent center?

What does it mean to say that the Holy Spirit is the "locus of the interaction between coherence and contingency" (p. 19), when it is also stated that the "place" (= locus?) where this interaction, this hermeneutical activity, takes place is the body of Christ, that is, the church (p. 21)? Is the implication that the life of the body of Christ is sustained and directed by the Holy Spirit? Is that what is meant by the statement that "the Holy Spirit is both detective and judge" in this hermeneutical translation, evaluating its adequacy? That is, are (Spirit-led) members of the (Spirit-filled) body of Christ responsible for both the expression and the critique of the adequacy of any given contingent expression of the coherent center of the faith? We need further reflection on these contingent expressions of the coherent center of Beker's thought about the Holy Spirit in the relationship of contingency and coherence in Paul's thought.

Another question: What is the relationship in Beker's paper between "the substratum and master symbolism of Paul's thought," which consists in Jewish apocalyptic (p. 17), and the coherent center of the truth of the gospel? If Jewish apocalyptic forms "the indispensable filter, context, and grammar" of Paul's appropriation and interpretation of the Christ-event—a point with which I completely agree—does it not in fact give us a clue about the content of the coherent center of Paul's thought and of his thought structure, of his grasp of "the truth of the gospel" (p. 17)? Although I am not clear on what the "crisis of his [Paul's] personal life" was, I do agree that the apocalyptic framework did constitute a noncontingent element in Paul's grasp and proclamation of the gospel and hence was part of Paul's "abiding solution" to the problems of his churches (p. 17). Yet having said that, must one not also say that we have here a clear indication of the nature of that core of Pauline thought which manifests itself in all its contingency as Paul sought to address varied problems in varied locations and situations?

A penultimate word: I am not so pessimistic as Beker appears to be about expressing some of the content of the coherent center of Paul's thought, even running the risk of finding there a core or *Mitte,* always with the reservation that it receives no totally noncontingent expression in the letters we have. Yet much can be learned about this matter, I would argue, from the nature of Paul's call/conversion as Christian apostle as that is referred to, obliquely to be sure (I resist the temptation to say "contingently"), in such a passage as Phil 3:4-14. In this passage Paul is discussing the contrast between his former set of values as a Pharisee (v. 6) and his present set of values as one who "knows Christ," a set of values that has caused him to regard those former values as worthless (v. 8). Here if anywhere we should expect some reference(s) to that central set of values he now holds which have led to such a transvaluation of his life story. The subjects mentioned—law, righteousness, faith, suffering, resurrection—must surely belong to that central core, that *Mitte* of the gospel for which he willingly discarded all that he had formerly held in highest regard.

Again, in the more polemical correspondence with the Christians in Corinth, the crucified and risen Christ once more plays a key role in those places where Paul points to what he regards as central to his life and activity as an apostle of Christ (1 Cor 2:2) or to the validity of the faith of his readers (15:14, 17). In these letters, both in the irenic Philippians and in the highly polemical 1 Corinthians, the crucified and risen Christ plays a key role.

Indeed, given the fact that Paul himself identifies as absolutely and non-contingently central to the faith the resurrection of Christ (1 Cor 15:14, 17: without it faith is null and void) and the belief that God brought it about (Rom 10:9b), one suspects that Christ risen from the dead by God's power in fact belongs to the noncontingent, central aspects of Paul's Christian theology.

A final word: None of this is to indicate displeasure with what Beker has written or what he intends with what he has written. What I have said is, I repeat, the critique of a friend who shares fully in the task to which Beker has set himself and who senses major dangers precisely where he does in some current trends of Pauline scholarship. These reflections are therefore offered to enrich our ongoing discussion of the problem of understanding the theology of the Apostle to the Gentiles, among whose number we also find ourselves.

II.

In his paper on a proper approach to Pauline theology, J. Paul Sampley operates from a perspective that is not so chary of finding a core or *Mitte* in terms of theological assertions which, though given contingent expression in the letters, yet belong to the noncontingent bedrock of Pauline theological convictions.

Sampley points helpfully to the fact that Paul himself describes a situation with Timothy and the Corinthian Christians where we may validly conclude that "there was a core representation of Paul's teaching" (p. 3) which it was possible for someone like Timothy to understand and communicate (1 Cor 4:17). That same "core representation" is of course implied in such passages as Gal 1:6–9, where Paul identifies it as the "gospel" he preached and to which he expected allegiance (see also Gal 2:2, 5; 1 Thess 2:4). I take such an observation to be a step forward in the theoretical justification for the existence of such a "center" for Pauline theology. Sampley combines that with two presuppositions which I think are also of central theoretical importance for the task of finding that center: (1) that "Paul's thought world and the thoughts that it spawned are relatively coherent" and (2) that there is therefore the possibility that we may move "beyond an unsophisticated surface reading of the texts to find the coherence behind them" (p. 4).

Possessed of such theoretical justification for the attempt to find the theological center—Paul's "gospel," if you will—Sampley then outlines some ways one may move beneath the surface to a "reconstruction of Paul's thought world." As a first step, he considers some factors that shape the way Paul communicates his thought, which one must hence consider in any attempt at reconstruction. Those factors are not novel but are nonetheless essential, and anyone undertaking more than a surface reading of the Pauline letters must constantly bear them in mind.

The first one that Sampley notes is the fact that Paul expresses himself in accordance with his own perception of the situation. Although this point is not in itself complex, one must understand it as saying no less, but also no more, than it actually does. It means no less than this: given the nature of the Pauline letters, which respond to actual situations in the actual life of real Christian communities (and in one instance to an individual Christian in a concrete situation, namely, Philemon), we are entirely dependent on Paul's perception of the situation to which he is responding. We do not have a non-contingent expression of what Paul felt represented the coherent center of the faith. All we have are contingent expressions controlled and shaped by what Paul thought would be appropriate and effective in response to the situation he was addressing. It will therefore be up to us to infer which elements in his response belong to the central core of his gospel and what the connection may be between the various theological points Paul scores. We depend on what Paul felt it important to say, given his perception of the situation.

But that statement also means no more than it says. That is, it does not say that if we could determine that Paul had misunderstood the situation or that his perception of it had been faulty, then somehow his response would similarly have been faulty and in need of correction. From the point of view of eliciting Paul's theology, it is irrelevant whether or not his perception of the problem was accurate. Paul will draw in his arguments from the same gospel and will apply what he draws in the same way whether his perception of the situation corresponds to the perception of others or not. But whether his perceptions of the situation were correct or not, his responses are all we have, and it is from them, not from the hypothetical accuracy or inaccuracy of his perception of the positions and problems of others, that we must determine his theology, his gospel.

Although Sampley does not employ his first point in an attempt to determine the relative degree of accuracy of Paul's perception of a given situation and hence the appropriateness or inappropriateness of his response to that situation, it is nevertheless necessary, it seems to me, to avoid the kind of implications that can be, and have been, derived from such a proposition. What Sampley intends with the observation is clear enough: he simply wants to clarify the point that Paul does not expound his entire theology or even say all that might be related to a given issue; he discusses only those aspects of his thought (or, perhaps better, his "gospel") which he feels are immediately relevant to the point(s) at issue. This drives home the disturbing likelihood that much that was central to Paul's gospel, that which was clear and convincing and hence not misunderstood (or whose misunderstanding could have been cleared up in person), will not be discussed. That in itself is enough to ensure humility on the part of those seeking the reconstruction of Paul's gospel! Fortunately (!), much that appears to have been central was misunderstood, especially by the (for this purpose invaluable) Corinthian Christians, but the caveat remains nonetheless.

I would quarrel, however, with Sampley's interpretation of Paul's use of Abraham in Galatians 3 and Romans 4 in making this point. I think it wrong to say that whereas the use of Abraham in Galatians 3 is to stress the primacy of faith, the point of discussing Abraham in Romans 4 is unity. Since Romans 4 is Paul's justification of the correctness of the affirmation contained in 3:31 (law and gospel are not fundamentally opposed, since the law itself is grounded in faith), I would urge that the point in Romans is equally the primacy of faith, although I would grant that it is made from another perspective and within a different context from that of Galatians. I mean such an observation to confirm rather than dispute Sampley's basic point (we depend on Paul's perception of the situation), since that basic point stands even when exegetical results may differ.

Sampley's second point—that Paul casts his thought in delicate balances, both poles of which must be kept in equilibrium—is important for its emphasis on the dynamic quality of Paul's thought. Paul does not have copybook maxims that he trots out as the occasion may (or may not) make appropriate. Paul has an understanding of the gospel of God's act for humanity in Christ which is incapable of flat and unchanging formulations regardless of differing circumstances. The complexity of the divine–human relationship demands complexity of the explication of that relationship. Sampley is correct to point to an overdependence of Pauline interpreters on Luther and the doctrine of justification by faith as the central core of Paul's gospel, an overdependence that leads interpreters to play down or even ignore some other important elements of that gospel, such as the final judgment, in which the Christian's performance will play a part. Sampley is also correct to point out that the understanding of such bipolar balances must be based not on what would seem good to the modern reader in that particular polemical situation, but rather in terms of the structures of rhetoric and polemic prevalent in Paul's own culture. We do indeed need to know enough about ancient rhetoric to recognize at what points Paul is making use of it and thus what points he wants to make.

The third point—that Paul's reaction to various situations is no less dynamic than the gospel he holds—adds further complexity to the process of recovering that gospel, but again it is a necessary complexity. Because Paul is fundamentally a missionary and expresses his theology in the service of that mission, the flexibility required of a successful mission imposes itself on the way Paul expresses himself. This is most useful, as Sampley points out, in determining the importance of those times when Paul finds himself unable to be flexible, as when he confronts the denial at Corinth of the importance of Christ's resurrection.

Sampley's fourth point – that Paul uses pre-Pauline traditions – needs little further comment. It must be used with care, however, since unless we possess the original form (as in the case of some Old Testament quotations), the reconstruction of the shape of that pre-Pauline tradition can lead to laby-rinths of speculation whose unprofitability has not always been recognized. Whether, for example, Paul depends on earlier tradition in Rom 1:2–4 or 3:24–26 has finally little bearing on what Paul meant to say with that tradi-tion in its present form and context, or whether the thought contained there could have been part of the central core of Paul's gospel. Its present meaning must be determined by its present wording in the present context, and there is no reason why pre-Pauline tradition, adapted or not, could not have been integral to Paul's own gospel, however idiosyncratic one may think it was.

In his final section, Sampley proposes some specific procedures to aid us in recovering the "coherencies of Paul's thought world" (or of his gospel, as I prefer to call it, since "thought world" can also apply to the Hellenistic culture within which all of Paul's thoughts necessarily took place, whether related to his gospel or not; it is therefore a needlessly ambiguous phrase). Sampley formulates these procedures in terms of questions that must be "applied rigorously to each letter and then to the collection as a whole," and he supplies us with sixteen of them, two of which have, respectively, three and four subheads.

There is no need to rehearse them; they are catalogued with commendable clarity and forthrightness in the paper. One can also appreciate the fact that Sampley presents his list as neither exhaustive nor hierarchical. The questions are intended to indicate a manner of approach for locating Paul's coherent center rather than to give a blueprint for the reconstruction of that center. For that reason he anticipates that others may differ with individual formula-tions of the questions and may want to propose others – an anticipation that will surely prove correct.

III.

Let my closing comment be in that vein, by pointing to a kind of question I think needs also to be in any list of this kind. Sampley touches on it in ques-tion 7, subpoint (a), when he asks if there are basic points "from which, or in light of which, he [Paul] reasons." I think this leads in a direction far too important to be relegated to a subhead. Rephrased, the question would ask about those generative statements or beliefs that seem to underlie larger developments in Paul's letters. Are there positions to be found in Paul's letters, whether articulated or implied, that appear to generate, and hence account for, larger superstructures of argument and assertion?

One such generative position would surely be the resurrection of Christ from the dead, already mentioned at the conclusion of the discussion of Beker's paper. There, as we saw, it is given as a noncontingent component of valid Christian faith: without that component, faith has no point; it is futile and empty. An added qualification is given in Rom 10:9b, namely, that such a resurrection is an act of God. Such an affirmation is therefore of central importance for Paul, but can we show that it is also generative of other beliefs and to that extent foundational for Paul's gospel? I think we can.

If God is the one who is at work in Christ's resurrection, for example, then Christ's resurrection would be understood as God's vindication of Christ's wrongful death, since God did not want him dead, but alive. That in its turn would mean that those Jewish religious authorities who had determined that Jesus was an opponent of God, and hence deserved death, were wrong. Thus Jesus' death must have some meaning other than that he received the fate justly meted out to those cursed of God. That in its turn would have some significant implications in regard to the law. If it was in reliance on the law that the Jewish authorities had reached that determination, finding in their interpretation of that law that it was God's will that Jesus be killed, then their interpretation of the law was wrong. That in its turn meant that the law had no defense against such misinterpretation and misuse and that it could be made to serve some purpose other than God's will. Indeed, it could justify a (sinful) opposition to that will, allowing Christ to be understood as opposed and cursed by God. If the law was thus revealed as an unreliable, even sin-infested revelation of God's will, then until something happened that healed the law of its infestation of sin, following the law could lead only to opposition to God (Rom 7:13–23!).

A further consequence can be drawn. Contained in that law, now revealed to be infested by the power of sin, were the commands of sacrifice for the expiation of sin. Such commands also then are infected by the perverse power of sin, which can lead astray those who follow the law, and hence the sacrifices therein commanded no longer are valid for sin's expiation. That in its turn would offer an explanation for the necessity of Christ's death: he now breaks the power of sin by providing a valid sacrifice for sin's expiation.

That Jesus rose from the dead by God's power would generate other consequences as well. For example, since the only framework within which resurrection had any real religious validity was within the apocalyptic framework of understanding—it was there one of the signs of the end-time, as was, in some strands at least, the appearance of the messiah—the resurrection of Jesus would be a powerful indication that that way of understanding reality and the course of God's dealing with humanity was valid. This would lead one to interpret the events surrounding the career, death, and resurrection of Jesus from such an apocalyptic perspective. One could continue such examples of the way a generative conviction begets a further network of coherent beliefs (e.g., how one enters and maintains a relationship to God, the nature of the new religious community, the relationship of the Christian to secular culture), but this is perhaps sufficient to show how the identification of such generative convictions allows one to reconstruct certain coherences within the contingent expressions of Paul's gospel.

The final word must be one of appreciation for the seminal work of both Beker and Sampley on the problem of recovering Paul's gospel. Beker has set the parameters of the discussion with his formulation of the contingency-coherence model. Sampley has provided a fruitful analysis of the way one moves from (contingent) text to (coherent) thought world (or gospel) and has provided examples of a specific way that move may be undertaken. The ensuing discussion of Pauline theology will continually betray the debt owed to both of them.

Part II

The Theology of the Thessalonian Correspondence

4 EARLY PAULINE THOUGHT

An Analysis of
1 Thessalonians

Earl Richard
Loyola University, New Orleans

THIS STUDY BEGINS by considering briefly several issues that bear on the interpretation of 1 Thessalonians: chronology, the relevance of Acts 17, and the document's composite as well as epistolary character. There follow two major parts of the analysis. In the first of these, I approach the document's thought by examining what Paul presumes in it about God, Christ, and Christian reality, whether from his Hellenistic Jewish, Greco-Roman, or Jewish Christian background.[1] In the second main section, I treat concepts Paul explicitly discusses or emphasizes as the result of the Thessalonian situation: (1) Paul's great concern (and relief) that the new converts have survived the challenge of being Christians in an inimical environment and (2) Paul's responses to the queries from Thessalonica.[2] A brief final section examines the results of the study to underscore what is theological background in 1 Thessalonians, what is theological focus, and what is foretaste of the thought of the later Pauline letters.[3]

---

[1] A descriptive approach, similar to that employed by J. Reumann ("The Theologies of 1 Thessalonians and Philippians: Contents, Comparison and Composite," in *Society of Biblical Literature 1987 Seminar Papers* [ed. K. H. Richards; Atlanta: Scholars Press, 1987] 521–36), seems best suited to an examination of the accepted concepts that author and audience share in their epistolary exchange.

[2] This part focuses on the epistolary situation as providing the surest access to the document's thought; see J. P. Sampley's essay, "From Text to Thought World: The Route to Paul's Ways" (pp. 3–14 above).

[3] On the problem of examining a particular letter's thought as opposed to providing an overview of Pauline theology, see J. M. Bassler, "Paul's Theology: Whence and Whither? A Synthesis (of sorts) of the Theology of Philemon, 1 Thessalonians, Philippians, Galatians, and 1 Corinthians," in *Society of Biblical Literature 1989 Seminar Papers* (ed. David J. Lull; Atlanta: Scholars

I. INTRODUCTORY CONSIDERATIONS

Pauline Chronology

The letters of Paul, not Acts, should determine Pauline chronology.[4] If one gives Paul priority in this matter, important chronological possibilities follow: earlier dating of the Corinthian ministry and correspondence (especially in relation to the Gallio episode), priority of the Thessalonian and Philippian correspondence, an earlier date for these than allowed by standard chronology, and reexamination of the authentic letters' temporal and local references.[5] Thus I am led to date the Thessalonian correspondence, Paul's earliest extant letters, in the early to mid-forties.[6]

The Relevance of Acts 17

Though there are basic disagreements (beyond chronology) between the Lucan and Pauline accounts, many commentators continue to rely on the narrative of Acts for the historical and theological framework of the Thessalonian correspondence.[7] Often the theme of persecution by Jews is imported from Acts 17 to interpret Paul's use of θλῖψις terminology and both to confirm the authenticity and to explain the anti-Judaic character of 2:14–16.[8] Since Luke provides a Jewish context to the mission, some presume that the community is Jewish — a conclusion contradicted by Paul in 1:9: "you turned

---

Press, 1989) 413–17; see also the surveys and syntheses of Pauline thought presented in this volume for a better sense of later Pauline development.

[4] See R. Jewett, *A Chronology of Paul's Life* (Philadelphia: Fortress, 1979). G. Lüdemann (*Paul, Apostle to the Gentiles: Studies in Chronology* [Philadelphia: Fortress, 1984]) revives the important insights of J. Knox (*Chapters in a Life of Paul* [Nashville: Abingdon, 1950]). See also J. Murphy-O'Connor, "Pauline Missions before the Jerusalem Conference," *RB* 89 (1982) 71–91; and E. Richard, "Contemporary Research on 1 (& 2) Thessalonians," *BTB* 20 (1990) 107–15.

[5] These issues receive further attention in my *Jesus, One and Many: Christological Concepts of New Testament Authors* (Wilmington: Glazier, 1988) 239–62, where I discuss the critical need to revise Pauline chronology.

[6] In partial agreement with Lüdemann, *Apostle to the Gentiles*, 262.

[7] Recently, however, T. Holtz (*Der erste Brief an die Thessalonicher* [EKKNT 13; Zurich: Benziger, 1986] 15–18), E. Best (*A Commentary on the First and Second Epistles to the Thessalonians* [HNTC; New York: Harper & Row, 1972] 2–7), and W. Marxsen (*Der erste Brief an die Thessalonicher* [Zurich: Theologischer Verlag, 1979] 13–22) have expressed skepticism in this regard.

[8] For a defense of the theme of persecution and of the authenticity of 2:14–16, see K. P. Donfried, "Paul and Judaism: 1 Thessalonians 2:13–16 as a Test Case," *Int* 38 (1984) 242–53; idem, "The Theology of 1 Thessalonians as a Reflection of Its Purpose," in *To Touch the Text: Biblical and Related Studies in Honor of Joseph A. Fitzmyer, S.J.* (ed. M. P. Horgan and P. J. Kobelski; New York: Crossroad, 1989) 243–60; and R. Jewett, *The Thessalonian Correspondence: Pauline Rhetoric and Millenarian Piety* (FFNT; Philadelphia: Fortress, 1986).

to God from idols." The synagogue scenario of Acts is also contradicted by recent discussion which suggests instead a Hellenistic manner of missionizing for Paul and his associates.[9] Furthermore, the three sabbaths of Acts 17:2 do not provide sufficient time for the Pauline mission or for repeated contacts with Philippi, and the Pauline data do not mesh with those of Acts regarding either the occasion of composition or the presence and movement of *dramatis personae*.[10] All of this suggests methodological caution in the use of Luke to read Paul.

The Composite Character of 1 Thessalonians

The claim that 1 Thessalonians is not a unified composition is an old one, but defense of the letter's integrity is vehement.[11] A major problem in discussions is the focus on W. Schmithals's complex dissection of the correspondence (involving both 1 and 2 Thessalonians)[12] rather than an examination of the text's inherent difficulties. These involve the probable interpolation of the un-Pauline 2:14–16[13] and the document's unique double thanksgiving. In addition, 3:11–4:2 sounds like a conclusion, and there is temporal tension and content difference between chaps. 1, 4–5, on one hand, and 2:17–3:13, on the other. Thus, I defend the composite character of 1 Thessalonians, whereby a short earlier missive (2:13–4:2) has been inserted into a later Thessalonian letter,[14] and I envision distinct situations for these two documents. I note, finally, that the presumption of integrity rests on the assumption that accepting the document as it is presents fewer problems than

[9] See, e.g., studies of Paul the artisan (R. F. Hock, *The Social Context of Paul's Ministry: Tentmaking and Apostleship* [Philadelphia: Fortress, 1980]), Paul and house-churches (W. A. Meeks, *The First Urban Christians: The Social World of the Apostle Paul* [New Haven: Yale University Press, 1983]), and Paul as itinerant, philosopherlike preacher (A. J. Malherbe, *Paul and the Thessalonians: The Philosophic Tradition of Pastoral Care* [Philadelphia: Fortress, 1987]).

[10] For further discussion of the themes of persecution, Pauline missionary work, and the relation of Acts 17 to 1 Thessalonians, see Richard, "Contemporary Research."

[11] See, most recently, R. F. Collins, "Apropos the Integrity of 1 Thess," in *Studies on the First Letter to the Thessalonians* (BETL 66; Leuven: University Press, 1984) 96–135; and Jewett, *Thessalonian Correspondence*, 31–46.

[12] W. Schmithals, "The Historical Situation of the Thessalonian Epistles," in *Paul and the Gnostics* (Nashville: Abingdon, 1972) 123–218.

[13] See B. A. Pearson, "1 Thessalonians 2:13–16: A Deutero-Pauline Interpolation," *HTR* 64 (1971) 79–94; D. Schmidt, "1 Thess. 2:13–16: Linguistic Evidence for an Interpolation," *JBL* 102 (1983) 269–79; and G. Lyons, *Pauline Autobiography: Toward a New Understanding* (SBLDS 73; Atlanta: Scholars Press, 1985) 202–7.

[14] My arguments for adopting this position are more fully developed in *Jesus, One and Many*, 248–52; see also Murphy-O'Connor, "Pauline Missions," 82.

theories defending its composite nature.[15] Either position operates with a certain degree of conjecture, so the results of the analysis must speak for themselves.

The Epistolary Character of 1 Thessalonians

Study of 1 Thessalonians must respect the nature of epistolary literature; it must recognize that a letter presumes more than it states, is by definition "occasional," and gives a limited perspective on its author's thought. Thus, because of its focus on limited topics (worthy ministry in chap. 2, concern and relief about survival in chap. 3, and ethical and eschatological issues in chaps. 4–5), the document does not present a summation of early Pauline thought. 1 Thessalonians also seems to presuppose two different "occasions" for its composition, both in temporal and in logical terms. Epistolary study is thus necessary, but recently it has been a mixed blessing. Instead of examining Hellenistic letters for typological parallels,[16] some scholars prefer to have the Pauline letters conform to an imagined Pauline letter type, particularly the "rhetorical genre" whose constituent parts consist of *exordium, narratio, probatio, peroratio,* or some variation thereof.[17] Paul, even early Paul, becomes a sophisticated rhetorician rather than a letter writer. Such an approach overlooks the document's inherent problems, does not do justice to examining the types of letters Paul could and did write, and ignores the activity involved in the preservation and publication of the letters.

II. PAUL'S THEOLOGICAL PRESUPPOSITIONS

What do Paul and his Thessalonian audience share in terms of language and concepts as the background and context of their exchange? Whether the terminology and concepts reached him as tradition or were initiated by the

---

[15] B. J. Johanson, for example, posits the integrity of the letter as a presupposition for a holistic reading, which is then said to confirm that assumption (*To All the Brethren: A Text-Linguistic and Rhetorical Approach to 1 Thessalonians* [Stockholm: Almqvist & Wiksell, 1987]).

[16] S. K. Stowers, *Letter Writing in Greco-Roman Antiquity* (Library of Early Christianity 5; Philadelphia: Westminster, 1986); J. L. White, *Light from Ancient Letters* (Philadelphia: Fortress, 1986).

[17] See, e.g., H. D. Betz's proposed outline of Galatians (*Galatians: A Commentary on Paul's Letter to the Churches in Galatia* [Hermeneia; Philadelphia: Fortress, 1979]), Jewett's proposals for 1 and 2 Thessalonians (*Thessalonian Correspondence*), and recent studies of 2 Thessalonians by these two scholars' respective students: G. S. Holland, *The Tradition That You Received from Us: 2 Thessalonians in the Pauline Tradition* (HUT 24; Tübingen: Mohr [Siebeck], 1988); and F. W. Hughes, *Early Christian Rhetoric and 2 Thessalonians* (JSNTSup 30; Sheffield: JSOT Press, 1989).

Pauline missionary group is not without interest.[18] What concerns me, however, are not the general presuppositions that Paul derives from his Judeo-Christian background, but what he presumes *in this letter* about God, Christ, and Christian reality. In all his letters he speaks often about God, even in this, his earliest, where the noun θεός appears thirty-four times (excluding two occurrences in 2:14–16, which I view as a later interpolation). Clearly, Paul has inherited both the monotheistic faith of Hellenistic Judaism and its early appropriation by Jewish Christians.[19]

Paul's notion of God was that held by his fellow Jews: faith simply is "faith in God," to whom one turns as the one, living, and true God (1:9). Even the heathen is defined as one "who does not know God" (4:5). These concepts derive from traditional formulas which express Israel's unrelenting monotheistic faith. This is a God of peace (5:23), to whom one renders thanks, who chooses human beings out of love that they might render service in view of the kingdom and glory (1:4, 9; 2:12; 4:1), whose will is to sanctify all who believe (4:3; 5:18), who has destined humanity for holiness, that is, for a pleasing and unblamable life (2:4, 12; 3:13; 4:1, 7). So God is at work in believers, grants them the Spirit, and sends them envoys, who are approved and given courage to preach (2:4, 13; 4:8). God's apocalyptic role is stressed throughout the document and defined through concepts Paul and his audience have inherited from Jewish and Christian apocalyptic discourse and now presuppose in their dialogue.[20]

---

[18] See G. Friedrich, "Ein Tauflied hellenistischer Judenchristen, 1. Thess. 1,9f," *TZ* 21 (1965) 502–16; T. Holtz, "'Euer Glaube an Gott': Zu Form und Inhalt von 1 Thess 1,9f," in *Die Kirche des Anfangs: Festschrift für Heinz Schürmann zum 65. Geburtstag* (ed. R. Schnackenburg et al.; Leipzig: St. Benno, 1977) 459–88; idem, "Traditionen im 1. Thessalonicherbrief," in *Die Mitte des Neuen Testaments: Einheit und Vielfalt neutestamentlicher Theologie: Festschrift für Eduard Schweizer zum siebsigsten Geburtstag* (ed. U. Luz and H. Weder; Göttingen: Vandenhoeck & Ruprecht, 1983) 55–78; R. F. Collins, "Tradition, Redaction, and Exhortation in 1 Thess 4,13–5,11," in *Studies,* 154–72; and I. Havener, "The Pre-Pauline Christological Credal Formulae of 1 Thessalonians," in *Society of Biblical Literature 1981 Seminar Papers* (ed. K. H. Richards; Chico, CA: Scholars Press, 1981) 105–28.

[19] See R. F. Collins, "The Theology of Paul's First Letter to the Thessalonians," in *Studies,* 230–52.

[20] For a survey of the literature on the eschatology of 1 Thessalonians, see Jewett, *Thessalonian Correspondence;* Richard, "Contemporary Research"; see also J. H. Neyrey, "Eschatology in 1 Thessalonians: The Theological Factor in 1,9–10; 2,4–5; 3,11–13; 4,6 and 4,13–18," in *Society of Biblical Literature 1980 Seminar Papers* (ed. P. J. Achtemeier; Chico, CA: Scholars Press, 1980) 219–31.

The "narrative" concerning God's dealings with humanity or the overarching summary of these traditional themes seems best understood as part of Paul's theological presuppositions; see R. B. Hays, "Crucified with Christ: A Synthesis of the Theology of 1 and 2 Thessalonians, Philemon, Philippians, and Galatians," pp. 231–34 below. On occasion the story, or at least part

Paul's notion of God was also deeply affected by the Christ-event. The name and title "Jesus Christ" appear seventeen times in 1 Thessalonians (excluding two occurrences in 2:14–16), often in conjunction with the title χύριος. This is only half as often as the thirty-four occurrences of θεός, but these figures are less stark if one recognizes the theological character of 2:1–12 (θεός nine times, "Christ" once), if one notes the reference to Jesus as Son in 1:10, and if one accepts most absolute uses of χύριος (the title used alone) as referring to Jesus.[21] Moreover, there is a fundamental correlation between theology and christology even at the level of background. For example, four times God is called "Father," twice in formulaic statements (1:1; 3:11) and twice where God and the Lord Jesus are associated in an eschatological context (1:3; 3:13). Thus, attributing the title "Father" to God leads invariably to an associated statement about Jesus, the Son (1:10). The three occurrences of the expression "our Father" suggest further that, in the tradition assumed by Paul and his readers, the theme of God's fatherhood encompassed not only Jesus' special sonship but also that of Christian believers.[22] We might also note the close association of theological and christological motifs in the creedal statements of 1:9–10; 4:14; and 5:9–10.

Also of interest is Paul's appeal both to theology and christology in discussing the new Christian reality. If believers are beloved and chosen by God (1:4), they are nonetheless made to "increase and abound in love" by the Lord (Jesus, 3:12).[23] One is exhorted in the Lord Jesus to live a life pleasing to God (4:1). Sanctification is God's work, which is established in Christ Jesus (4:2; 5:18, 23). The gospel is both from God (2:2, 8, 9) and about Christ (3:2). The missionaries are both "apostles of Christ" and coworkers of God in the service of the gospel of Christ (2:6; 3:2). Additionally, several stark features of 1 Thessalonians—its decided focus on the future, heightened eschatological tone, and extensive use of apocalyptic imagery—relate to Paul's view of the Christian reality.[24] One is called to live a "life worthy of God" in view

---

of it, moves to the foreground; see my comments below on 1:2–10 as a recounting of the Thessalonian community's story.

[21] In general agreement with R. F. Collins, "Paul's Early Christology," in *Studies*, 269–74.

[22] Collins, "Theology of Paul's First Letter," 232–34.

[23] Bassler's insistence that election is a fundamental conviction of Paul's thought is correct ("Paul's Theology," 420), but it would seem that such a theme forms part of the background rather than the theological focus.

[24] E. Krentz is right in seeing the thought of 2 Thessalonians as being focused "entirely" on the "apocalyptic future" ("Through a Lens: Theology and Fidelity in 2 Thessalonians," p. 54 below). That of 1 Thessalonians, while stressing the future, is influenced by the audience's eschatological concerns and the writer's developing notion of the new Christian reality and presupposes the interrelation between the past, present, and future components of the Christ-event.

of the future kingdom and glory, "to be kept sound and blameless" or to "have hearts established in holiness before God," again in view of a future event, the Lord's coming (2:12; 3:13; 5:23). Apocalyptic imagery is found not only in the explicit discussion in chaps. 4–5 but also in the language and tone of the other chapters. For example, the difficulties of the missionaries and those of the community are given an apocalyptic nuance when Paul speaks of "Satan hindering" the mission or of "the Tempter enticing" the community (2:18; 3:5). In addition, the four verses that mention the Spirit receive a heightened apocalyptic tone from contextual description (1:5, 6; 4:8; 5:19), and the two prayer texts, by invoking God's presence, enhance the apocalyptic sense of the closeness of heaven and earth (1:3; 3:9).

Writer and audience presume shared concepts and ideology; they assume many things about God, Christ, and Christian reality, concepts which do not yet form the center of the document's message but which nonetheless indicate the range and background of Pauline thought. These are the accepted or known concepts and images which both allow communication between letter writer and audience and provide the context or rationale for the writer's discussion and advice. We turn now to what Paul discusses or emphasizes as a result of the twofold Thessalonian context.

III. PAUL'S THEOLOGICAL FOCUS

The Early Letter

The first situation, that is, the reason for the composition and sending of the first, short missive (2:13–4:2), is precisely the missionaries' great concern whether, and relief that, the new converts have survived the challenge of being Christians in a less-than-hospitable environment. The letter begins with a short, well-developed thanksgiving (2:13) which announces the major themes of the missive. After speaking of the pain of separation, the repeated attempts to return to Thessalonica, and the circumstances of Timothy's mission, the letter focuses on Timothy's message and its consequences. In 3:6 one finds the clearest statement of the letter's two main themes, for Timothy's splendid news is about the community's genuine faith ("your faith and love") and about the mutual relation between community and missionaries.[25]

From beginning to end the letter underscores the relationship between the community and the missionaries, a relationship that extends from the initial preaching, to the intense personal (and mutual) sense of separation, to the

---

[25] Best, *Thessalonians*, 140; I. H. Marshall, *1 and 2 Thessalonians* (NCB; Grand Rapids: Eerdmans, 1983) 94–95.

equally intense desire to pay the community a visit (2:17–18; 3:6, 9, 11).[26] The
letter's emotional language adds to the sense of the missionaries' attachment
to and concern for the converts: "We were made childless by separation from
you for just a short time, in person but not in heart" (2:17). The intense desire,
the frustrated chances to return, and the absence of news made the wait
unbearable. Timothy's message, however, confirms that the relationship is
mutual and convinces the missionaries that they can look forward, with less
anxiety but no less anticipation, to a future visit (3:10–11).

1 Thess 3:2 and 5 are crucial for their focus on the community's faith. In
3:2 it is said that Timothy is sent "to strengthen and encourage (them) regarding (their) faith." The Thessalonians' faith is the central issue, for v. 3 adds:
"so that no one be dissuaded (σαίνεσθαι) by the present difficulties." There is
fear that the community might fall away from its commitment.[27] Verse 5
further stresses that the crucial issue in Paul's mind is the community's
survival: *I* "sent to inquire about your faith for fear the Tempter had successfully tempted you and that our work would be without effect." Timothy's
"splendid news" then is a counterstatement to the missionaries' fears.

The missive therefore is written in response to Timothy's newly arrived
report and rhetorically addresses past, present, and future considerations.
Statements about the missionaries' attachment to the newly founded community, about their desire and attempts to visit, and about "gladly agreeing
to remain alone in Athens" add pathos to the letter. These statements about
past concerns emphasize the present, joyful reaction to Timothy's report
(3:7). Despite difficulties, the missionaries "are encouraged" precisely because
of the *Thessalonians'* faith.[28] The anxiety is gone since it is clear that they
"stand firm in the Lord" (3:8), and the attitude is now one of prayer and joy
(3:9). The entire letter, in fact, reflects the missionaries' joy on hearing
Timothy's report. But there is unfinished business, and so the writer
addresses future concerns. If the anxiety is gone, the desire to visit has not
been satisfied, except in Timothy's case. Thus Paul prays that God and the
Lord Jesus (3:10–11) may allow them this visit, its purpose being stated in
the enigmatic phrase "to supply what is still lacking in (their) faith" (3:10).
The issue cannot be defective faith, for Timothy's report is about the Thessalonians' "faith and love" (3:6). Granted that their love for one another and for

---

[26] It is in this sense that 2:13 must be understood; the stress is on human agency.

[27] The evidence for the interpretation of σαίνεσθαι is notoriously weak, whether one opts for
the standard, but conjectural, translation "be moved" or "agitated" (BAGD 740; RSV) or the more
etymological meaning "be dissuaded." The context of the first missive, I believe, favors the
second option.

[28] The emphasis is indicated by the position of ὑμῶν, which here precedes the noun.

all can increase, it is nonetheless a *lived* faith. The missionaries wish to return to impart further teaching to the young community. In the meantime, the community is told, "you know what instructions we gave you through the Lord Jesus" (4:2).[29]

The Later Missive

The second situation, that presumed by the second, longer letter (1:1–2:12 + 4:3–5:28), is a study in contrast. This letter presupposes a new time frame and offers different content and structure. Time has elapsed since the founding, for the reputation of the converts is well known and they have contributed to the missionary effort (1:7–8). One also encounters a maturing community in need of advice; in effect, the second part of the letter reads like a series of responses to questions, a fact that brings us to the issue of structure. The letter's dominant structural feature is the recurring περὶ τῆς/τῶν in 4:9, 13 and 5:1, which introduces topics of discussion. In the light of the excellent parallel with 1 Corinthians, one should thus see 2:1–12 as addressing an oral report and the remainder as responding to questions from Thessalonica.[30]

1 Thess 1:2–10, which is described as "one long untidily constructed sentence,"[31] is the letter's extended thanksgiving. This thanksgiving period achieves one of its traditional functions: namely, it prepares for subsequent discussion. The preaching of the gospel, the missionaries' conduct, and their reception and imitation (1:5–6, 9) announce the theme of the ministry in 2:1–12. Mention of the community's faith, life, and perseverance, as well as references to the Spirit, prepare for the ethical injunctions of 4:3–12. Various hints in the thanksgiving period ("hope in our Lord Jesus Christ," "waiting for the Son's return," 1:3, 10) point to the later treatment of eschatological issues in chaps. 4 and 5.

Yet, interestingly, the thanksgiving period also recounts the story of the community. Paul tells the beginning of the story as one of God's love and choice (1:4) and then describes the mission or coming of the gospel, the missionaries' conduct (1:5, 6), the community's acceptance of the gospel message (1:9–10), and the repercussions of the Thessalonian mission throughout Greece.[32] The function of this story is to underscore the statement in v. 3, which provides the thanksgiving's theological focus: we remember "before

---

[29] Marshall, *1 and 2 Thessalonians*, 99.
[30] See Richard, *Jesus, One and Many*, 251, 282–84.
[31] Best, *Thessalonians*, 65.
[32] The story in this instance acquires a rhetorical function, because it serves both as *captatio benevolentiae* and *mimesis* for the writer's discussion and advice.

our God and Father your work of faith, labor of love, and steadfastness of hope in the Lord Jesus Christ." The community is firm in its convictions, active in its commitment, and at work for the good of others. It is against this background that one must read the letter.

1 Thess 2:1–12 marks a shift in focus from the response of the converts described in chap. 1 to the missionaries' behavior in Thessalonica. The passage has traditionally been read as a defense against accusations,[33] but A. J. Malherbe has recently shown that most of the terms used by Paul here in describing his work and that of his coworkers are in fact those used by Dio Chrysostom in rebuking Cynic philosophers. But what false philosophers are *accused* of doing (error, uncleanness, deception, flattery, greed, etc.) Paul *denies* he and his coworkers have done. In fact, Paul says, their motivation was theological ("pleasing God") and their method gentle (like a nurse or a father) and self-giving. Malherbe concludes that "one is not obliged to suppose that Dio [also Paul] was responding to specific statements that had been made about him personally."[34] Thus the passage is hortatory in purpose, for, in the words of I. H. Marshall, it "presents the missionaries as a pattern for the converts to follow."[35] Yet Marshall is right in insisting that something in the situation at Thessalonica must have motivated such a description and defense of the apostolic mission.[36]

Since there is really no evidence of opponents in this letter, the passage must relate to the community's situation. The first missive indicates that there were accute difficulties in establishing and maintaining the community. The second letter recalls these; the community began in the midst of difficulty (1:6) and the missionaries preached ἐν πολλῷ ἀγῶνι (2:2). This expression is usually translated "in the face of great opposition" but probably refers to the fierce rhetorical struggle encountered by public speakers as they attempted to persuade their audiences.[37] The apostles initially competed with other preachers for the converts' loyalty, fostered their survival and growth within an enticing pagan environment, and now return to the subject through an autobiographical, heartwarming treatment of the initial mission. Apparently the problems encountered earlier by the converts have not disappeared and the missionaries have been warned of this. The parenetic discussion

---

[33] The opponents are variously described as judaizers, Jewish authorities, Gnostics, or members of the Thessalonian community.

[34] A. J. Malherbe, "'Gentle as a Nurse': The Cynic Background to I Thess ii," *NovT* 12 (1970) 217; see also idem, "Exhortation in First Thessalonians," *NovT* 25 (1983) 238–56; and idem, *Paul and the Thessalonians.*

[35] Marshall, *1 and 2 Thessalonians,* 61.

[36] Ibid.

[37] Malherbe, *Paul and the Thessalonians,* 46–52.

throughout chaps. 4 and 5 invariably contrasts the beliefs and behavior of the non-Christian neighbor (4:5, 13; 5:3) to those of the believer who already knows these things; in 4:10–12 the apostles return more directly to the issue by addressing extra- and intra-community problems.[38]

What then is the focus of chap. 2? The text functions as exhortation, that is, as reassurance that the mission was indeed God's work. Malherbe states:

> While the moral philosopher was impelled by an awareness of his own moral freedom, acquired by reason and the application of his own will, to speak boldly to the human condition and demand its reformation, Paul regards his entire ministry, as to its origin, motivation, content and method, as being directed by God. God grants him the boldness to speak, and what he says is not philosophical or rational analysis of the human condition, but the gospel of God.[39]

The origin, motivation, and goal of the Thessalonian mission then are theological; missionaries are entrusted by God (not themselves) to preach the gospel of God (not rational analysis) that the audience might lead a life worthy of God now and gain future entry into the kingdom.

1 Thess 4:3–5:28 comprises two major sections of the letter: 4:3–5:11, which consists of responses to questions, and 5:12–28, which represents the letter's final parenesis and closing. Much attention has been devoted to these verses: 4:3–8 on sexual ethics and holiness; 4:9–12 on brotherly love and Christian conduct; two eschatological passages, one about believers who die before the Lord's return (4:13–18) and another concerning the time of the end (5:1–11); and 5:12–22 consisting of admonitions. Of interest are two overall considerations.

First, it is agreed that Paul's parenesis relies on traditional Hellenistic moral tradition, whether it be sexual ethics, relation to neighbors, or attitudes toward the death of loved ones. Yet it is clear that Paul is more interested in the theological motivation for action and behavior than in particular acts. 1 Thess 4:3–8 focuses on holiness (ἁγιασμός [vv. 3, 7]), not on the rational life,[40] and concludes with a reference to God's gift of the Holy Spirit (v. 8). In 4:9–12 Christian love is said to be divine in origin (God-taught) and leads to a quiet life of work, respect, and independence among Roman neighbors. The eschatological texts emphasize theological and christological motivation and conclude by stressing the discussion's parenetic function. As Malherbe notes about 4:13–18: "Paul is not providing eschatological instruction to inform his readers, but to console those who are grieving";[41] and (about

---

[38] 5:12–22 should also be read in this manner.
[39] Malherbe, "Exhortation," 249.
[40] Ibid., 251.
[41] Ibid., 254.

5:1–11, I would add) to encourage them to give one another strength in view of the ominous Day of the Lord.

Second, it should be noted that rhetorically each passage has a teleological thrust: that is, each discussion ends with a statement of its purpose. The section on sexual morality ends by insisting that God calls to holiness (with the gift of the Holy Spirit [vv. 7–8]). That on brotherly love focuses on Christian behavior, while the eschatological texts speak of "being always with or living with the Lord" (4:17; 5:10). Thus, the teaching of the second missive relates directly to the community's queries. Paul borrows traditional concepts, both Hellenistic and Judeo-Christian, and either operates within their purview or builds on their foundation.

IV. BACKGROUND, FOCUS, OR FORETASTE

It would seem from the foregoing that the distinction between theological background and theological focus is crucial, in methodological terms, when examining the thought of a particular letter. The former concerns those things which writer and audience accept and which provide the fabric of discourse; it thus serves a communicative function. The latter involves the author's principal concerns, whether providing information, consolation, or exhortation; it conveys the author's explicit intention. Both of these form part of Pauline theology or thought; their relative importance depends on the role they play in Pauline thought generally or the extent to which they are developed or rhetorically engaged.[42]

What, then, in 1 Thessalonians is background? Paul presumes a given understanding of God, Christ, and Christian reality which not only permeates his correspondence but is also taken for granted by his audience in these two missives. The facts — that God chooses and is petitioned in prayer; that Jesus is God's Son and is the means of salvation; and that believers are called to lead a life worthy of God and to love one another and all — are accepted by writer and audience and allow for meaningful communication. Their function is subsidiary to the document's principal concerns.

In the first missive, the author's focus is on the community's faith and love and its reciprocal concern for its parents in the faith, the missionaries. In the

---

[42] Rhetoric or argument has an important function to play in this process, but it is doubtful that an author's thought is to be found in or limited to a letter's mode of argumentation. Instead, I agree with Sampley that argument has to do with "proper balance" and is therefore closely linked to an author's and audience's situation ("From Text to Thought World," pp. 6–8 above). Appreciating or understanding Paul's argument in any given context is essential for perceiving his thought; see, e.g., K. A. Plank, *Paul and the Irony of Affliction* (Atlanta: Scholars Press, 1987).

second missive, the purpose is both to reassure the community and to respond to its deep concerns. Thus Paul offers thankful reassurance concerning their genuine faith, love, and hope, and narrational reassurance that the work of the Thessalonian mission was God's work. He also presents responses which illustrate the sanctified or love-inspired life, give grounds for consolation to those who grieve, and offer strength to those who are apprehensive.

What, finally, is foretaste of later Pauline development? In this regard, it should be noted that certain terms and concepts appear little or not at all in 1 Thessalonians: δίκαιος, νόμος, wisdom, truth, the flesh/body dichotomy, sin, and apostolic terminology. Other features, however, are particularly prominent: the parousia, the use of us/you discourse and other forms of direct address, and the emphasis on apostolic presence (first missive), on conversion, and on parenesis. Many themes appear as constant factors in the Pauline letters and are destined for later development: christological data, the role of the Spirit, the use of the ἐν Χριστῷ formula, and the stress on faith, love, hope, community, and Christian behavior.[43]

Although 1 Thessalonians does not offer a summation of Pauline thought, even of early Pauline thought, this composite document does provide a fixed point for such a study and a vantage from which to accomplish such a review.

---

[43] See I. H. Marshall, "Pauline Theology in the Thessalonian Correspondence," in *Paul and Paulinism: Essays in Honour of C. K. Barrett* (ed. M. D. Hooker and S. G. Wilson; London: SPCK, 1982) 173–83.

5 THROUGH A LENS

Theology and Fidelity
in 2 Thessalonians[1]

Edgar Krentz
Lutheran School of Theology at Chicago

2 THESSALONIANS DOES NOT present abstract or theoretical theology; it is rather a response to human need, hope, and aspiration in a time of persecution. The fundamental conviction that God is a God of justice who will vindicate his suffering church underlies this theology and gives it unity.[2] All theologoumena in the letter are related to this central apocalyptic conviction, which functions as a lens to focus the letter's theology on the traumatic situation of the church. I propose in this paper to describe this theology on the presupposition that Paul is not the author of 2 Thessalonians.[3]

I. APOCALYPTIC AS THEOLOGICAL LENS

The theology of 2 Thessalonians arises out of the interplay between the negative situation of the community and the writer's response in terms of

---

[1] Revision of a paper first read to the Consultation on Pauline Theology at the meeting of the Society of Biblical Literature in Atlanta, GA, 24 November 1986; the original title was "Through a Prism: The Theology of 2 Thessalonians." A revised version of this paper was read to the Colloquium Biblicum Lovaniense on the Thessalonian Correspondence on 17 August 1988, under the title "Traditions Held Fast: Theology and Fidelity in 2 Thessalonians"; it is to be published in *The Thessalonian Correspondence* (BETL 87; Leuven: University Press).

[2] The term "theology" is used in many different senses; see E. Farley, *Theologia: The Fragmentation and Unity of Theological Education* (Philadelphia: Fortress, 1983) 31–44, with nn. 4, 6; G. A. Lindbeck, *The Nature of Doctrine* (Philadelphia: Westminster, 1984) 112–23.

[3] I argued the case for the non-Pauline origin of 2 Thessalonians in "A Stone that Will Not Fit," a paper circulated to the members of the Society of Biblical Literature Seminar on the Thessalonian Letters (1985). Two recent dissertations also present the case: G. S. Holland, *The Tradition That You Received from Us: 2 Thessalonians in the Pauline Tradition* (HUT 24; Tübingen: Mohr [Siebeck], 1988); F. W. Hughes, *Early Christian Rhetoric and 2 Thessalonians* (JSNTSup 30; Sheffield: JSOT Press, 1989).

apocalyptic eschatology.[4] God's vindication of his faithful people is the lens through which the writer surveys his theological terrain. What does not serve his message is either treated in perfunctory fashion or omitted entirely, for persecution is the grim reality out of which the letter arises. The Thessalonians are suffering persecution (ἐν πᾶσιν τοῖς διωγμοῖς ὑμῶν καὶ ταῖς θλίψεσιν αἷς ἀνέχεσθε, 1:4) from non-Christians (τοῖς μὴ εἰδόσιν θεὸν καὶ τοῖς μὴ ὑπακούουσιν τῷ εὐαγγελίῳ τοῦ κυρίου ἡμῶν 'Ιησοῦ, 1:8; see also 2:12) because of the "royal rule of God" (βασιλεία τοῦ θεοῦ, 1:5).[5] The writer is himself experiencing such opposition. He asks for prayers that he might be delivered from "evil and pernicious people" (τῶν ἀτόπων καὶ πονηρῶν ἀνθρώπων, 3:2), faithless outsiders who clearly oppose "the word of the Lord" (3:1; see also 1:8). The situation is thus one of external opposition to the community and the good news that called it into being.

Persecution, however, is only the first stage in the growing opposition to the community and its God. The opposition will develop in intensity, for at present a force (τὸ κατέχον, 2:6) or a person (ὁ κατέχων, 2:7) holds the persecution in check. The removal of that restraining person will be the καιρός (2:6) for the ultimate revelation of ὁ ἄνθρωπος τῆς ἀνομίας (2:3),[6] the nadir of apocalyptic misfortune. The "Man of Lawlessness," however, is destined for destruction.

The reference to this Man of Lawlessness introduces the cosmic dimension of the opposition to the church addressed in 2 Thessalonians. He is ultimately the "Evil One" from whom the Thessalonians need to be protected (3:3), the great enemy of God (2:4), the parody of the Lord Jesus. The παρουσία of the Man of Lawlessness κατ' ἐνέργειαν τοῦ σατανᾶ (2:9) is accompanied by a show of power in signs and miracles that are a lie and by the deceit of injustice

---

[4] This paper will not engage in extensive dialogue with the modern literature but will concentrate on reconstructing the theology from the text itself.

[5] I use the convenient term "Thessalonians" from the letter itself without thereby affirming that the community actually lived in this Macedonian city. 2 Thessalonians itself gives not one clue to the geographical location or the character of the church addressed, unless one accepts the prescript in 2 Thess 1:1 as evidence.

J. M. Bassler argues that suffering punishment preserves the future reward of the elect ("The Enigmatic Sign: 2 Thessalonians 1:5," *CBQ* 46 [1984] 496–510). Such an interpretation gives a positive value to suffering persecution itself as a proleptic certainty of ultimate vindication. (Unless otherwise noted, the translations of biblical texts are my own.)

[6] This language is taken over from apocalyptic tradition; 2 Thessalonians never uses the term νόμος and shows no interest in the Torah. W. Gutbrod argues that ἀνομία in 2:3 "does not derive from OT Law, but simply means sin or unrighteousness," as in 2 Cor 6:14 ("ἀνομία," *TDNT* 4. 1086). See also E. von Dobschütz, *Die Thessalonicher-Briefe* (MeyerK 10; 7th ed.; 1909; reprint, Göttingen: Vandenhoeck & Ruprecht, 1974) 272; W. Trilling, *Der zweite Brief an die Thessalonicher* (EKKNT 14; Neukirchen-Vluyn: Neukirchener Verlag, 1980) 83 n. 309.

(2:9–10).[7] This description clearly puts the persecutors into an apocalyptic context, for the persecutors in the present and the archenemy of God in the future are of a piece, enemies of God who set themselves against the gospel and who are characterized by ἀνομία (2:3, 7), ἀδικία (2:12), and the ἀπάτη ἀδικίας (2:10).[8] They are the purveyors of the "great lie" (2:9), who are themselves ultimately deceived into believing their own falsehood (2:11). The irony of these words is difficult to overestimate.

II. JUDGMENT ON THE OPPRESSORS

The writer's use of apocalyptic language and an apocalyptic schema assures the readers that their suffering and persecution must be understood from the ultimate outcome already determined by God and God's agent, Jesus.[9] The writer evaluates the present entirely in the light of the apocalyptic future. At that time God will even out the past by "repaying those causing tribulation with tribulation, but the persecuted with refreshment" (1:6–7),[10] a kind of balancing of accounts based on the old "law of retribution."[11] The process by which this will be accomplished is already under way. God is sending (πέμπει, a present tense, 2:11) a deceiving force (ἐνέργεια πλάνης)[12]

---

[7] Rev 13:5–8 speaks in similar fashion of the beast from the sea as a parody of God who is addressed blasphemously with the words of Exod 15:11: "Who is like the beast and who is able to make war with him?" See also Rev 13:13.

[8] The phrase is ambiguous. The genitive ἀδικίας is either a genitive of quality or description ("every wicked deceit"; so E. Best, *A Commentary on the First and Second Epistles to the Thessalonians* [HNTC; New York: Harper & Row, 1972] 307; see also von Dobschütz, *Thessalonicher-Briefe,* 288) or source ("all deceit that originates in unrighteousness"; so J. E. Frame, *A Critical and Exegetical Commentary on the Epistles of St. Paul to the Thessalonians* [ICC 38; New York: Scribner's, 1912] 270). I. H. Marshall says that ἀδικία is used of the opposition to God in the end-time in *Pss. Sol.* 17:23–29 and *Diogn.* 9:1 (*1 and 2 Thessalonians* [NCB; Grand Rapids: Eerdmans, 1983] 202).

[9] See Bassler, "Enigmatic Sign," 506–9.

[10] The term ἄνεσις is rare in Paul, occurring elsewhere only in 2 Cor 2:13; 7:5; 8:13.

[11] This balancing of accounts may suggest the content of the "mystery" referred to in 2:7. Though von Dobschütz applies the term to "die allegemeine Sittenverderbnis der Endzeit" (*Thessalonicher-Briefe,* 281) and Frame regards it as a reference to the "secretly developing lawlessness" that will culminate in apostasy on earth (*Thessalonians,* 264), Best more correctly describes the force that works against God as "an open secret" and argues that the power active in ἐνεργεῖται (2:7) is God's (*Thessalonians,* 293). G. Bornkamm points out that the allusion to the mystery must be understood "in relation to the imminent revelation of the ἄνομος (2:6–8). . . . He is disclosed as a power which hastens not only towards its full manifestation but also towards its destruction by the κύριος" ("μυστήριον," *TDNT* 4. 823). Bornkamm's insight should be combined with 2 Thess 2:11–12. The mystery is the ironic fact that the deception practiced by the persecutors and the Man of Lawlessness will ultimately ensure their destruction and the vindication of the persecuted.

[12] The use of ἐνέργεια supports Best's interpretation of ἐνεργεῖται in 2:7; see n. 11 above.

that brings error on the opponents. They believe their own lie (2:11) and consent to iniquity (2:12); God's apocalyptic act confirms them in their opposition. Thus their ultimate punishment is assured.

Jesus, the κύριος, is the agent of God's ultimate vengeance (ἐκδίκησις, 1:8). 2 Thess 1:5–10 is dominated by apocalyptic and judicial language. Jesus the Lord will be revealed from heaven in company with the angels of his power (1:7) as a punishing and purifying fire (ἐν πυρὶ φλογός, 1:8). The angels are the heavenly entourage that demonstrates the Lord's power (Zech 14:5), and the flaming fire stresses both his divine character (Exod 3:2) and his punishing role (Dan 7:9–12). Jesus is the executor of God's "righteous judgment" (δικαία κρίσις, 1:5)[13] on the persecutors; he takes vengeance on those who do not know God (διδόντος ἐκδίκησιν τοῖς μὴ εἰδόσιν θεόν, 1:8), that is, on those who do not obey the gospel of our Lord Jesus.[14] Disobedience to the gospel is equivalent to not knowing God. The punishment (δίκη, 1:9) for this is eternal destruction. Only those who have come to believe the writer's testimony,[15] as the Thessalonians have, will be among the "holy ones" who acclaim and marvel at the Lord Jesus when he comes (1:10).

Chapter 2 presents a similar picture of Jesus as the avenging judge. Whereas 2 Thess 1:5–10 is written in terms of the future fate of the persecutors, 2:3–12 broadens the picture to include the cosmic dimensions of the Evil One who will be destroyed by Jesus. The culmination of the anti-God activity will be the ἀποστασία, the rebellion (a political term), signaled by the revelation of ὁ ἄνθρωπος τῆς ἀνομίας, ὁ υἱὸς τῆς ἀπωλείας, the "Man of Lawlessness, the Son of Destruction" (2:3). (The two phrases are similar in formation to two well-known christological titles in the gospels: ὁ υἱὸς τοῦ ἀνθρώπου, ὁ υἱὸς τοῦ θεοῦ.) This revelation will show the "Man of Lawlessness" to be what he in fact is, one destined for destruction (2:8) as the enemy of God (2:3–4). The ἐπιφανεία τῆς παρουσίας of the Lord Jesus will follow when the power restraining the Man of Lawlessness is removed, and then the Lord [Jesus] will destroy the Lawless One by the breath of his mouth and make him ineffectual (καταργήσει) by the epiphany of his parousia (2:8).

---

[13] The term κρίσις is not in Paul's theological vocabulary outside of this passage. It is found in the deutero-Pauline 1 Tim 5:24. Of the words formed from the stem *κριν-, only κρίμα, κατάκριμα, and κρίνω occur with some frequency in Paul—and often without a primarily apocalyptic sense.

[14] The stress falls on the word "gospel." Paul uses the language of obedience in relation to faith or Christian conviction (ὑπακοὴ πίστεως, Rom 1:5; see also Rom 6:16; 15:18; 16:19; [16:26]; 2 Cor 10:5; οὐ πάντες ὑπήκουσαν τῷ εὐαγγελίῳ, Rom 10:16), but does so to stress that believing is the *only obedience that the gospel calls for.*

[15] μαρτύριον (1:10) is also a legal term, correlating with the extensive use of legal terminology in 1:5–10: δικαία κρίσις (1:5), δίκαιος, ἀνταποδίδωμι (1:6), ἐκδίκησις (1:8), δίκην τίνω (1:9), ἐπιστεύθη τὸ μαρτύριον (1:10).

"All who do not believe the truth, but consent to injustice" (εὐδοκήσαντες τῇ ἀδικίᾳ, 2:12), who "did not receive the love of the truth in order to be saved" (2:10), will be condemned by the Lord Jesus. In this context, salvation (εἰς τὸ σωθῆναι, 2:10) is equivalent to escaping the condemnation of Jesus at the appearance of his coming. Salvation for the Thessalonians then is vindication at the parousia of the Lord Jesus.

III. JESUS IN 2 THESSALONIANS

This concentration on the future vindication of the church determines the christology of 2 Thessalonians. It is not Jesus, the Crucified and Risen One (as in Rom 4:24–25; 8:34; 10:9), but Jesus, the future judge *par excellence* who will destroy the persecutors of the suffering community, who is presented as the κύριος (1:8–10; 2:8).[16] The title never refers to Jesus' past. His major characteristic is power, exercised in the destruction of the Man of Lawlessness by the breath of his mouth (2:8)[17] and in the punishment of the persecutors (1:9). Because of this exercise of power, he will be acclaimed gloriously by the community at his coming with the panoply of power (messengers of his power and flaming fire, 1:7–8).

Consonant with that use of the title Lord, Jesus' significance for the readers lies entirely in the future (a consistent apocalyptic view), but the future casts light on the present life and activity of the Thessalonians. They must be clear about his παρουσία and their (future) "gathering before him" (ἐπισυναγωγὴ ἐπ' αὐτόν, 2:1), since their present activity is grounded in Jesus' parousia, not in his resurrection made effective in Christians by their baptism (cf. Rom 6:4–11). They can be certain that the Lord "will establish them and protect them from the Evil One" (3:3), and thus the Lord's future role is the basis for the appeal of the letter about life in the present: παραγγέλλομεν . . . ἐν ὀνόματι τοῦ κυρίου ἡμῶν (3:6).[18] The Thessalonians are praised because their faith and love are active (1:3), an activity immediately identified as ὑπομονὴ

---

[16] κύριος is the primary designation for Jesus in 2 Thessalonians: 1:1, 2, 7, 8, 9, 12 [*bis*]; 2:1, 8, 14, 16; 3:1, 3, 4, 5 (?), 6, 12, 18. It occurs in reference to him either absolutely, with the name Jesus, or with Jesus Christ. 2 Thess 3:16 describes Jesus as the Lord of peace (ὁ κύριος τῆς εἰρήνης), a phrase modeled on 1 Thess 5:23. Only once is ὁ Χριστός used absolutely of Jesus (3:5). See R. F. Collins's paper, "The Language of 2 Thessalonians," part IV of "The Gospel of Our Lord Jesus," to be published in *The Thessalonian Correspondence.*

[17] See *Pss. Sol.* 17:33–35. The Davidic king there does not trust in horses, chariots, or war chest. Rather he exercises power by the word of his mouth.

[18] The ἡμῶν is textually uncertain. Note the frequency of παραγγέλλω in 2 Thessalonians: 3:4, 6, 10, 12; 1 Thessalonians more frequently uses παρακαλέω: 2:11; 3:2, 7; 4:1, 10, 18; 5:11, 14. It is consistent with this that there is little appeal to past knowledge in 2 Thessalonians. Οἴδατε occurs only in 2 Thess 1:8; 2:6; and 3:7, whereas in 1 Thessalonians it appears in 1:5; 2:1, 2, 5, 11, 17; 3:3, 4, 6; 4:2, 4, 5; 5:2, 12.

. . . ἐν πᾶσιν τοῖς διωγμοῖς ὑμῶν καὶ ταῖς θλίψεσιν αἷς ἀνέχεσθε (1:4). Endurance in persecution is action in anticipation of apocalyptic vindication. There is no explicit reference back to the great salvific events in the life of Jesus. No earlier creedal formulas are cited; Jesus is nowhere named or described as one whose life, death, or resurrection forms the basis of the present life or the future hope of the suffering Thessalonians. Nothing corresponds to the λόγος τοῦ σταυροῦ of 1 Cor 1:18. There is no reference to Jesus' death as sacrifice for sin or as defeat of sin, no reference to proclamation. The verb κηρύσσειν is not used. There is no allusion to baptism as the locus where life is shaped by dying with Jesus and where one is freed from sin to live a new kind of life that is enslaved to righteousness. The only event in Jesus' career that is significant for the Thessalonians is his future revelation in power and glory on the "Day of the Lord" (2:2; see also 1:10). His parousia will also be his revelation as Lord, their benefactor and vindicator.[19]

IV. GOD IN 2 THESSALONIANS

Whereas Jesus' role is restricted to the future, God's activity in the past is the basis of hope. God is, *proprie dicta,* the theological center of 2 Thessalonians. He is, for example, the chief apocalyptic actor; Jesus is his agent.[20] The key passage is 2 Thess 2:13–14: God chose (εἵλατο) the Thessalonians as the "firstfruits toward salvation because of the sanctification of the spirit and faith in the truth."[21] This election is not only the basis for the conviction that they are presently loved by the Lord (ἀδελφοὶ ἠγαπημένοι ὑπὸ κυρίου, 2:13)

---

[19] Paul uses the title "Lord" frequently. However, he consistently relates the lordship of Jesus to his resurrection from the dead. The community in Corinth, for example, addresses the resurrected Jesus with the acclamation κύριος Ἰησοῦς, but 2 Thessalonians makes no use of that acclamation (1 Cor 12:3; see also Phil 2:11; Rom 10:9). 1 Thessalonians twice refers to Jesus' resurrection (1:10; 4:14). See R. F. Collins, "Recent Scholarship on Paul's First Letter to the Thessalonians," in *Studies on the First Letter to the Thessalonians* (BETL 66; Leuven: University Press, 1984) 20–23.

[20] D. E. H. Whiteley says the letter is permeated with "the sense of God and His providence" (*Thessalonians in the Revised Standard Version* [New Clarendon Bible; London: Oxford University Press, 1969] 19). Whiteley's phraseology is apt, but "justice" is a more important characteristic of God in the letter, as the use of δίκαιος (1:6) and ἐκδίκησις (1:8) shows. Therefore God must punish the ἀδικία (2:10) of the persecutors (2:11–12).

[21] Reading ἀπαρχήν with B F G P 33 81 etc., not ἀπ' ἀρχῆς with ℵ, D Ψ it Ambrosiaster, etc. (the text translated by the rsv). M. Dibelius argues convincingly for the priority of "firstfruits" (*An die Thessalonicher I, II; An die Philipper* [HNT 11; 3d ed.; Tübingen: Mohr (Siebeck), 1937] 51). Citing Philo, he points out that this term is a title of honor for Israel; it does not imply any priority in standing: διότι τοῦ σύμπαντος ἀνθρώπων γένους ἀπενεμήθη οἷά τις ἀπαρχὴ τῷ ποιητῇ καὶ πατρί (*Spec. Leg.* 4.180).

but also the foundation for their future hope: God has called them[22] by the writer's gospel "so that you may obtain the glory of our Lord Jesus Christ" (εἰς περιποίησιν δόξης τοῦ κυρίου, 2:14). This language is apocalyptic (see 1:7–10). Because God has called them, they also are the ἐκκλησία τοῦ θεοῦ (1:4) that suffers for the "royal rule of God." That suffering is described as a demonstration of the "just judgment of God" (ἔνδειγμα τῆς δικαίας κρίσεως τοῦ θεοῦ, 1:5), because it ultimately leads to the public demonstration of God's just actions.

God's fundamental character, according to 2 Thessalonians, is justice. Justice is shown when God repays the persecutors of his assembly with persecution[23] and gives rest to the persecuted. God is the ultimate vindicator of his assembly. Twice God is called "our father" (1:1; 2:16), but it is striking that he is never addressed as "the [God and] Father of our Lord Jesus Christ" (cf. 2 Cor 1:3) or as the one "who raised him [Jesus] from the dead" (cf. Rom 4:24; 8:11; 10:9; etc.). God is not primarily the creator or giver of life in this letter, but the executor of justice for the people whom he called. He is their father, as he was Israel's father.[24] He does not respond directly to evil but works through an agent (another apocalyptic facet) to vindicate in the future. That correlates strikingly with the language about Jesus in the letter.

God's justice also determines the content of the gospel in 2 Thessalonians. The gospel is the announcement that God, "who called the Thessalonians to possess the glory of our Lord Jesus," will faithfully carry out his plan for them. God's justice demands an agent of power. The εὐαγγέλιον τοῦ κυρίου ἡμῶν ᾽Ιησοῦ (1:8) describes how Jesus' parousia will execute punishment on the oppressors and call forth admiration among the faithful (1:10). In the present, God makes his called people worthy of their calling by the "sanctification of the spirit" (2:13). In this connection 2 Thess 2:13–16 is of prime importance. God called the Thessalonians as firstfruits of salvation through the good news. God's own self is tied to the promise of future salvation, and that is good news.[25] Indeed, his righteous judgment is already evident in the life of the Thessalonians (1:4–5). He chose the Thessalonians as the firstfruits of salvation (here clearly a future, anticipated event, 2:13) and called them through the good news of that future destiny (2:14). He is thanked for their growing faith and love (1:3) and has loved and comforted them in the past

---

[22] The terms εἵλατο and ἐκάλεσεν reflect election theology.

[23] Note the wordplay on the stem *θλιβ- in 1:6–7.

[24] Deut 14:1; 32:6; Isa 64:8; see G. Quell, "πατήρ," *TDNT* 5. 959–74, esp. pp. 970–74; for Israel as God's son, see Exod 4:22; Hos 11:1.

[25] Holland points out that there is no appeal to the past reception of the gospel as the basis for the readers' faith and love (as in 1 Thess 1:5b; 2:1–2); rather, their future salvation is the basis of their conviction of "God's righteous judgments" (1:5–10) (*Tradition*, 63–64).

(2:16). These verbs used of God are highly instructive.[26] These actions of God all have future components: God will send a spirit of delusion on the wicked to guarantee their ultimate condemnation (2:11). He will vindicate the Thessalonians by punishing their persecutors (1:6–10) and will, it is hoped, make the Thessalonians worthy of their call (1:5). God's justice will thus be a demonstration of his love for them, shown in their election and ultimate vindication. All that is included in the gospel.[27]

Grace (χάρις) is not of major significance in this letter. The term occurs twice in stock formulas (1:2; 3:18). Elsewhere grace is set into a future eschatological context (1:7–12). The Thessalonians will glorify the name of our Lord Jesus when he comes as end-time judge. This will demonstrate that God has made them worthy of their calling and filled them with all approbation of goodness and every work of faith. Jesus' parousia is thus subsumed under the reality of God's grace, and God's grace is the standard according to which Jesus' name is glorified (κατὰ τὴν χάριν τοῦ θεοῦ ἡμῶν καὶ κυρίου Ἰησοῦ Χριστοῦ, 1:12). This pattern of events (God's past and present actions for the community and their future consequences) accords with God's grace. The writer repeats this idea later when he describes God as "our Father who loves us and gives eternal exhortation and good hope in grace" (ὁ πατὴρ ἡμῶν ὁ ἀγαπήσας ἡμᾶς καὶ δοὺς παράκλησιν αἰωνίαν καὶ ἐλπίδα ἀγαθὴν ἐν χάριτι, 2:16). Grace is thus founded in the character of God in 2 Thessalonians, not in the cross and resurrection of Jesus in the past.

V. THE LIFE OF THE COMMUNITY

The church is called to actions that reflect these convictions about the justice of God. Faith is the reaction to the writer's testimony that God will vindicate his church (ἐπιστεύθη τὸ μαρτύριον ἡμῶν ἐφ' ὑμᾶς, 1:10). Faith is also equivalent to "knowing God" (θεὸν εἰδέναι, 1:8).[28] Just as God is πιστός (3:3), so the reaction to God is πίστις. To deny God's eschatological plan is lack of faith (3:2).[29] Faith implies correlative action. When the writer appropriates

---

[26] J. M. Bassler called attention to these verbs in her response to this paper at the Society of Biblical Literature meeting in 1986.

[27] In "Pauline Presuppositions," a paper read to the Colloquium on the Thessalonian Letters (to appear in *The Thessalonian Correspondence*), J. Plevnik argues that 1 Thessalonians presupposes "a broad antecedent catechesis" that included the soteriological significance of the death and resurrection of Jesus and the present lordship of Jesus in history. None of that is present in 2 Thessalonians.

[28] Faith is directed to God who is faithful, not to the "God who raised Jesus from the dead." The persecutors do not know God; that is, they do not see that their ultimate fate is determined by God (see 1:8–9; 2:10).

[29] Hughes's translation of 3:2, "for not all are trustworthy," obscures the significance of πίστις (*Christian Rhetoric*, 14). The rsv's "for not all have faith" is better.

the phrase ἔργον πίστεως (1:11) from 1 Thess 1:3, he conceives of the work of faith as fidelity under pressure.[30] Thus he speaks of boasting "on behalf of your endurance and faith (ὑπὲρ τῆς ὑπομονῆς ὑμῶν καὶ πίστεως) in all your persecutions and afflictions" (1:4).

This action of faith takes a number of forms. (1) Because Christians know and trust God's fidelity to his electing choice, they "ought to thank God" (ἡμεῖς δὲ ὀφείλομεν εὐχαριστεῖν τῷ θεῷ, 2:13; see also 1:3). These two references to thanksgiving as obligatory response "owed" to God form an *inclusio* about the extensive discussion of God's eschatological actions for his community on behalf of his royal rule. The stress in "we ought" is less on moral obligation than on thanksgiving as the truly commensurate response to God's action. Because the writer is opposed by evil men, the Thessalonians are also asked to pray on behalf of the "word of the Lord" (ὁ λόγος τοῦ κυρίου, 3:1), that is, the "account of the Lord" and his eschatological act of salvation. Prayer is a work of faith in the face of the reality that "faith does not belong to everyone" (3:2).

(2) The Thessalonian Christians are called to action that befits a community experiencing persecution as it waits for apocalyptic deliverance; that is, they are called to obedience (3:14). That means standing fast by holding on to the traditions firmly (στήκετε καὶ κρατεῖτε [2:15] is a hendiadys), whether taught them by discourse or letter (ἃς ἐδιδάχθητε εἴτε διὰ λόγου εἴτε δι᾽ ἐπιστολῆς ἡμῶν). 2 Thessalonians is itself one presentation of that tradition, a tradition that stressed the role of God in apocalyptic vindication and called on Christians to be faithful.[31] They are to wait for the appearance of the Lord and thereby show their obedience to the gospel and their faith in the truth. They anticipate that the Lord will direct them into the love of God and the endurance of Christ (3:5). The writer assures them that the faithful Lord will preserve them from the Evil One (3:3), the demonic opponent of 2:3–10. Love of God is expressed in endurance under persecution, that is, in being established in every good word and deed (2:17).

(3) The community is also to remain pure. They are to avoid every member who does not live according to the "tradition" (περιπατοῦντος . . .

---

[30] The juridical character of the language suggests the translation "evidence" or "proof" for the term πίστις here. See my comments in E. Krentz, J. Koenig, D. H. Juel, *Galatians, Philippians, Philemon, 1 Thessalonians* (Augsburg Commentary on the New Testament; Minneapolis: Augsburg, 1985) 55, 107, and now, with full citation of the evidence in Philo and Josephus, D. Hay, "Pistis as 'Ground for Faith' in Hellenized Judaism and Paul," *JBL* 108 (1989) 461–76.

[31] W. Trilling argues that the gospel "liegt im Zeugnis des Apostels vor" (*Untersuchungen zum zweiten Thessalonicherbrief* [ETS 27; Leipzig: St. Benno, 1972] 112). It is identified with the truth that people either reject in favor of the lie or adhere to faithfully. The gospel thus has a clearly apocalyptic orientation in 2 Thessalonians. There is no basis in 2 Thessalonians for including in these traditions any reference to christological or soteriological formulas.

μὴ κατὰ τὴν παράδοσιν ἣν παρελάβοσαν παρ' ἡμῶν, 3:6). The tradition is the apocalyptic interpretation of the community's life as one that expects vindication for fidelity. 2 Thess 3:14 makes the need for community purity clear: the recipients of the letter are to identify[32] Christians who do not obey its teaching and avoid all social contact with them—though the writer tempers his severity in 3:15.[33] Paul's example shows how faith works (3:7–9), while the description of the disorderly (3:11–12) functions as a reinforcement of the demand for proper life in the waiting community.

Jesus, the powerful end-time judge, is given a proleptic status of power in this book. He is paralleled with God as an effective actor for the community as it waits for the revelation of his glory (2:16; 3:16). He is described in ways applied elsewhere in the Pauline corpus to God himself. The authority of Jesus Christ is invoked by the writer to reinforce his parenesis (παραγγέλλο-μεν . . . ἐν ὀνόματι τοῦ κυρίου ἡμῶν Ἰησοῦ Χριστοῦ, 3:6). Jesus' future role is the measure of what "doing good" (3:13), "standing fast" (2:15), and "approving the good and doing the work of faith" (1:11) are.

VI. CONCLUSION

2 Thessalonians surprises one with the narrow focus of its thought. All the resources the author uses (past election, christology, tradition, gospel) stress future salvation and are directed to the life of waiting under pressure. There is not a hint of the life of the community in worship, its structure, or its local leadership. The role of the spirit in this letter is at best minimally described (2:2, 8, 13); it is not present in the community as the effective presence of the risen Lord. The great past events are the call and election of the community by God, not the death and resurrection of Jesus. There is no reference to the creedal confession of Christ, no cultic enactment or memorial of Jesus' death and resurrection. Baptism is nowhere alluded to, unless one reads it into the word "call." In short, the community is shapeless, without specific charismata. 2 Thessalonians is essentially a letter with one theme: faithful endurance under persecution. Fidelity is holding on to the tradition(s) presented in the letter itself. The writer ransacks the resources of apocalyptic thought

[32] According to BAGD, σημιόω means to "mark, take special notice of" someone. MM point to Polybius 5.78.2 (σημειωσάμενοι τὸ γεγονός) as a parallel to the disapproval implied in this passage (s.v. σημειόω). The use in Greek medical texts in the sense of "diagnose" is similar (LSJ, s.v. 2).

[33] Hughes uses these data to develop the theory that 2 Thessalonians is written to combat opponents "within the Pauline circles" (see 2:1–2). He suggests that Colossians and Ephesians represent the type of eschatology that disturbs the author of 2 Thessalonians (*Christian Rhetoric*, 80–86). The theory is attractive.

to underscore his theme. His goal is to rouse his readers to steadfast waiting as the apocalyptic calendar unrolls.

Measured by Greek rhetorical standards, 2 Thessalonians is a form of deliberative oratory. It has a clearly philosophical ἦθος, concerned with the moral character of the readers. One can scarcely make any judgment about its rhetorical ἦθος (i.e., about the appropriateness of content to speaker, audience, and subject), since both writer and readers are without sharp contours. In γνώμη (the consistency, adequacy, and economy of the ideas presented) 2 Thessalonians gets high marks. The letter makes almost no use of rhetorical τέχνη, the art of embellishment practiced by Greek rhetoricians since the time of Gorgias. Its λέξις or Ἑλληνισμός (i.e., its purity, clarity, and elegant variety of diction) is correct but unvaried. The emotional tenor remains the same throughout.[34]

These comments about rhetoric have little directly to do with our analysis of the theology of the letter, but they support the suggestion that the epistle deals with one theme consistently spun out—fidelity to the apocalyptic tradition. The lens through which all of the language of 2 Thessalonians is refracted is the expectation of apocalyptic vindication through the agent of a just God. The readers are to respect that tradition by demonstrating its effect on their present actions. To change to a musical metaphor, 2 Thessalonians has only one theme, but plays it well.

---

[34] These four categories of rhetorical analysis (ἦθος, γνώμη, τέχνη, λέξις) are taken from Pseudo-Dionysios, *On the Examination of Speeches* (Bibliotheca Teubneriana [Usener-Radermacher, 1904] 2.374–387) and *On Mistakes in Speeches* (2.359–374); see D. A. Russell, *Criticism in Antiquity* (Berkeley and Los Angeles: University of California Press, 1981) 7–12.

6 A MATRIX OF GRACE

The Theology of 2 Thessalonians
as a Pauline Letter

Robert Jewett
Garrett-Evangelical Theological Seminary

THE APOCALYPTIC THEOLOGY of 2 Thessalonians has frequently been seen as so different from the other Pauline letters that it is often argued that the letter must be pseudonymous. The absence of the law-gospel dialectic and of technical anthropological terms such as flesh in antithesis to spirit also seems to require either a forgery hypothesis of some kind or an audience-and-situation theory. After weighing the alternatives in a study published several years ago, I opted for Pauline authorship and a unique audience situation to account for the peculiar details in this letter.[1] My assumption in this study is that 2 Thessalonians was written in response to a deepening congregational crisis in the period several months after the reception of 1 Thessalonians in AD 50. The first Thessalonian letter had failed to rectify the sudden crisis of millenarian faith that had occurred after unexpected persecution and the death of congregational members. A group of radicals who had abandoned their occupations in the belief that the millennium had already dawned, the ἄτακτοι, continued their socially offensive activities, even citing Paul's first letter as proof that the Day of the Lord had already arrived (2 Thess 2:2). 2 Thessalonians was dictated by Paul as a mixed letter of denial and reproof, a deliberative discourse designed to show the absurdity of this radically realized eschatology and to bring the ἄτακτοι under control. The *partitio* (2 Thess 2:1–2) announces the two topics for discussion in rebuttal of millenarian radicalism: the true status of the parousia and the eschatological involvement of believers.[2] Each of these topics is developed later in the letter

---

[1] Robert Jewett, *The Thessalonian Correspondence: Pauline Rhetoric and Millenarian Piety* (Philadelphia: Fortress, 1986).

[2] Ibid., 83, 86; for a more detailed discussion of the rhetorical function of the *partitio*, see F. W.

as a formal proof (2:3–12 and 2:13–3:5). The central theme in this apocalyptic theology, reflecting the earliest stage of theological development visible in Paul's letters, is thus the tension between the "already" and the "not yet." This theme, however, rests on assumptions Paul shares with a congregation whose faith had been evoked in response to good news not only about a future apocalyptic triumph but also about salvation already achieved by Christ.

I. SHARED THEOLOGICAL ASSUMPTIONS

In Pauline letters, the material in the epistolary introduction establishes common ground with the congregation. In contrast to the main body of the letter, where Paul often develops new concepts in contrast to those held by the congregation, the introductory material tends to be traditional and formulaic, certain to be shared by Paul's conversation partners. In the thanksgiving (2 Thess 1:3–10) and the intercessory prayer (2 Thess 1:11–12) we encounter the apocalyptic tension that Paul apparently shares with his churches and now rehearses as the basis for his subsequent argument. The "kingdom of God" that is currently visible in the embattled suffering of believers (1:5) will soon be fully manifest with the return of Christ, when vengeance is enacted against evildoers (1:8–10).[3] The πίστις and ὑπομονή of believers in the present moment of adversity, apparently consisting of adherence to the new age being ushered in through the gospel, are evidence of divine intervention for which Paul gives thanks (1:4).[4] Both faith and love are growing in the congregation, indicating the presence of divine power (1:3). So the transformation already visible in the congregation is a direct result of "the grace of our God and the Lord Jesus Christ" (1:12; see also 1:2), giving hope of future participation in the glory of the kingdom of God (1:10–12).[5]

Hughes, *Early Christian Rhetoric and 2 Thessalonians* (JSNTSup 30; Sheffield: JSOT Press, 1989) 56–57.

[3] J. M. Bassler argues for a *Leidenstheologie* in 1:5, in which the punishment of the elect is thought to preserve their reward in the age to come ("The Enigmatic Sign: 2 Thessalonians 1:5," *CBQ* 46 [1984] 496–510, esp. pp. 502, 509).

[4] See Roger D. Aus, "The Liturgical Background of the Necessity and Propriety of Giving Thanks According to 2 Thes 1:3," *JBL* 92 (1973) 438: "It is precisely in this situation of suffering that the author of 2 Thessalonians tells the addressees that he and his fellow Christians ought to give thanks to God, as is proper, because the Thessalonians' faith is growing abundantly and their love for one another is increasing; they are steadfast and are demonstrating their faith (vss. 3–4)."

[5] See C. H. Giblin, *The Threat to Faith: An Exegetical and Theological Re-Examination of 2 Thessalonians 2* (AnBib 31; Rome: Pontifical Biblical Institute, 1967) 112: "If glory among the faithful stands at the very end of the eschaton, it is, he adds, because faith in Paul's testimony has stood at its beginning."

The imminence of this future fulfillment is evident in the reference to those afflicted in Thessalonica, who will shortly experience along with Paul the "rest" when Christ returns (1:7).

Salvation by grace in 2 Thessalonians provides the basis both of the current experience of faith, love, and patient endurance and of the anticipation of future participation in the kingdom of God. The grace of God revealed in Christ is received by those who respond in faith to Paul's gospel, which evidently proclaimed wrath against the evil age, from which believers would be preserved (1:9–12). The underlying theological matrix of the letter is thus an apocalyptic theology of grace and wrath in which Christ is the primary actor.

The details in the opening of 2 Thessalonians appear to correlate closely with formulaic references later in the letter to salvation through Christ. For instance, 2:13 refers to the divine election to salvation that the Thessalonians had experienced, involving them in a process of spiritual sanctification and "faith in the truth." In 2:16–17; 3:3–5; and 3:16 the Lord is described as being involved in the congregation's present and future well-being. Since 2 Thessalonians lacks an explicit discussion of christology, it is necessary to steer between the unacceptable alternatives of reading the later theology of the cross back into this early letter or denying any role for Christ's death and resurrection in this apocalyptic theology. The aorist participles ἀγαπήσας and δούς in 2:16 point back to a single act of benefaction in which God and Christ were both involved, "probably that of the death and resurrection of Christ."[6] The formulaic clues throughout the letter point toward Jesus as the "apocalyptic benefactor," whose grace has already been received and whose triumph bringing additional benefactions is anticipated.[7] Given the prevalence of benefactor metaphors in the Greco-Roman world,[8] it is unnecessary to assume the presence of the elaborate construct of Paul's later theology to interpret this basic language of grace. What remains clear is that Paul's gospel had been the means by which this apocalyptic message was announced and a new "calling" given to believers, assuring their participation in this future triumph (2:14).

It was the future dimension of the apocalyptic salvation, an anticipated participation in the "glory of our Lord Jesus Christ" (2:14), that had been misunderstood in Thessalonica. In contrast to millenarian radicals, who eliminated apocalyptic tension by the announcement of the unqualified

---

[6] E. Best, *A Commentary on the First and Second Epistles to the Thessalonians* (HNTC; New York: Harper & Row, 1972) 320.

[7] See F. Danker and R. Jewett, "Jesus as the Apocalyptic Benefactor in Second Thessalonians," forthcoming in *The Thessalonian Correspondence* (BETL 87; Leuven: University Press).

[8] See F. W. Danker, *Benefactor: Epigraphic Study of a Graeco-Roman and New Testament Semantic Field* (St. Louis: Clayton, 1982).

arrival of the kingdom of God, Paul insisted on the dialectic between current ambiguity and future fulfillment. The theology of 2 Thessalonians therefore appears to be a classic example of what J. C. Beker contends was character-istic of Paul's apocalyptic theology as a whole: "With the Christ-event, history has become an ellipse with two foci: the Christ-event and the Parousia, or the day of God's final victory."[9]

II. THE PROOF THAT THE PAROUSIA
HAS NOT YET COME

The first proof in 2 Thessalonians, as announced in the *partitio* (2:1–2), is that the Day of the Lord has not arrived as the radicals had claimed (2:3–12). The "not yet" scheme is developed as a refutation of a contrary view cited in the *partitio* that "the Day of the Lord has already come." Five signs must precede such an event, according to Paul's apocalyptic scenario, and their absence proves the falsity of a radically realized eschatology. The appearance of the "rebellion" (2:3) and the "Man of Lawlessness" (2:3), the removal of the "restrainer" (2:6–7), the destruction of the lawless one (2:8), and finally the rise of "delusion" (2:11–12) are all required before anyone can think that the end of history has arrived. Since the rhetorical interaction between Paul and his audience is so rarely taken into account by interpreters, this scenario is frequently understood as implying a long-term postponement of the parousia and thus as evidence of a non-Pauline theology. I agree that it is a postponement, but of an end already fallaciously announced as present. In the context of millenarian radicalism, the false sense of "already" needed to be countered by the "not yet," stated in thoroughly apocalyptic terms.

In addition to the theological insistence on the futurity of apocalyptic fulfillment, this proof contains language that indicates a conservative adher-ence to the value of the law. The Antichrist figure is identified as an opponent of the law (2:3, 8), and the "mystery of lawlessness" (2:7) is depicted as already at work as a sign of the imminence of the end.[10] The context indicates that lawlessness was thought to involve "rebellion against God,"[11] and it may well include the kind of libertinistic behavior in which the ἄτακτοι were

---

[9] J. C. Beker, *Paul the Apostle: The Triumph of God in Life and Thought* (Philadelphia: Fortress, 1980) 160.

[10] J. E. Frame, *A Critical and Exegetical Commentary on the Epistles of St. Paul to the Thessalonians* (ICC 38; New York: Scribner's, 1912) 264.

[11] I. H. Marshall, *1 and 2 Thessalonians* (NCB; Grand Rapids: Eerdmans, 1983) 195; see also G. Friedrich, *Der zweite Brief an die Thessalonicher* (Göttingen: Vandenhoeck & Ruprecht, 1976) 266.

involved.[12] This language assumes that there is a demonic force operating in those who oppose the law, so that the "lawless" stand flatly in opposition to Christ.[13] At this stage in Paul's theology, there is no possibility of a polemical attitude toward the law that became characteristic of the later letters.[14] As far as I can tell from 2 Thessalonians, the obligation to obey the Torah still remains intact, and it appears perfectly consistent that no hint of an antithesis between law and gospel is given.

The first proof contains language implying an ambivalence between free will and predestination in connection with the phenomenon of apocalyptic delusion (2:9–12). Those who fall prey to the deception of the "lawless one" are described as having "refused to love the truth and so be saved." But this element of willful rejection of God is combined with the apocalyptic motif of the "delusion" sent by God to confirm the belief in falsehood.[15] J. B. Lightfoot described the three phases of damnation implicit in this passage: (1) the human rejection of the truth, (2) a divinely ordained delusion, and (3) the ultimate punishment.[16] As I. Howard Marshall remarks, "Whatever one may say about divine predestination, the lost carry the responsibility for their own perdition."[17] The phrases "having faith in" or "loving the truth" (2:12, 10) evoke the horizon of accepting or rejecting the gospel[18] as the key to the judgment scheme in this apocalyptic theology.

III. THE PREVAILING OF BELIEVERS UNTIL THE PAROUSIA

The second proof in the letter (2 Thess 2:13–3:5) provides assurance for believers in the present moment of testing: when the parousia arrives they will surely "obtain the glory of our Lord Jesus Christ" (2:14). It is clear that, in contrast to the inclinations of the ἄτακτοι, such glory is not presently available to the church. It is reserved to the apocalyptic future. This portion of Paul's "already/not yet" scheme opens with a thanksgiving concerning the election of the Thessalonian Christians to salvation but moves to the necessity of standing firm in faith. The close proximity of "gospel" (2:14)

---

[12] See Jewett, *Thessalonian Correspondence,* 102–7, 172–75.

[13] See J. Ernst, *Die eschatologischen Gegenspieler in den Schriften des Neuen Testaments* (Regensburg: Pustet, 1967) 27–32.

[14] See R. Jewett, *Paul's Anthropological Terms: A Study of Their Use in Conflict Settings* (AGJU 10; Leiden: Brill, 1971) 109–11.

[15] See Roger D. Aus, "God's Plan and God's Power: Isaiah 66 and the Restraining Factors of 2 Thess 2:6-7," *JBL* 96 (1977) 550.

[16] J. B. Lightfoot, *Notes on Epistles of St. Paul* (New York: Macmillan, 1904) 117.

[17] Marshall, *1 and 2 Thessalonians,* 203.

[18] See Best, *Thessalonians,* 309.

and "traditions" (2:15) suggests that despite the use of a term often employed elsewhere for the transmission of moral teaching, Paul wishes to include the traditions about Christ as the crucified and returning savior that had been central in his proclamation and reiterated in his earlier letter.[19] The parallel between "our gospel" in 2:14 and "the gospel of our Lord Jesus" in 1:8 indicates the substantive content of Paul's earlier christological preaching. In the immediately following verses (2:16–17) Christ is the one who provides "comfort" and ethical firmness during the interim before the parousia. The benediction in these two verses reiterates the previous actions of Christ in providing love, comfort, and hope "through grace," thus confirming our assessment in section I that 2 Thessalonians provides a potent fusion of grace within an apocalyptic scheme of salvation. Grace provides the basis for the acceptance of apocalyptic ambiguity in this letter.

The request for prayerful intercession in behalf of Paul's missionary activities in 3:1–2 presupposes that Christian leaders as well as followers face continued threats from the old age. In contrast to the millenarian radicals who declared the presence of the parousia and hence the final elimination of evil, Paul takes realistic account of these threats. What he argues in 3:3 is that Christ is capable of strengthening the faithful to resist evil and of guarding them "from the evil one."[20] Although they may suffer or die, they have assurance that they are not finally under the power of the demonic forces. The assurance formula that Paul uses in the next sentence pertains not to their escaping the impact of malevolence but rather to their remaining faithful during testing. Hence, the benediction that concludes this proof deals with the action of Christ to provide firm directedness on the part of Christians toward God who loves them and Christ who steadfastly stands by them through all adversity.

IV. THE EXHORTATION TO DEAL WITH THE ΆΤΑΚΤΟΙ

In 2 Thess 3:6–15 Paul turns to the source of the millenarian confusion. In 3:6 he urges withdrawal from the ἄτακτοι. In view of the extensive discussion of work in these verses, several commentators prefer the option

---

[19] Ibid., 317: "In our passage *traditions* relates to doctrine rather than to worship or behaviour." James M. Reese (*1 and 2 Thessalonians* [New Testament Message 16; Wilmington: Glazier, 1979] 99) and Albrecht Oepke (*Die Briefe an die Thessalonicher* [NTD 8; Göttingen: Vandenhoeck & Ruprecht, 1979] 185) insist that behavioral instructions are implied in the choice of this term.

[20] On the likelihood that ἀπὸ τοῦ πονηροῦ refers to the demonic "evil one," see F. F. Bruce, *1 and 2 Thessalonians* (WBC; Waco: Word, 1982) 200.

"loafers" to translate this term.[21] Recent commentators such as E. Best and F. F. Bruce and translations such as J. Moffatt's and the Revised Standard Version favor this option.[22] But the definitive study of this term by Ceslas Spicq has shown that the basic meaning of the term is standing against the order of nature or of God. The word was typically used in military contexts to depict someone who would not keep step or follow commands. Spicq terms this group the "refractaires,"[23] which should be rendered the "obstinate" or "insubordinate" in English.[24] Resistance against authority is therefore implied by this term, a conclusion that is strongly supported by the reference to refusing to accept the Pauline tradition in 3:6. C. H. Giblin concurs in the judgment that "the ἄτακτοι are troublemakers, not just economic parasites," and moreover that they were "responsible for the deception on the topic of the parousia. . . ."[25] In view of the likelihood that the congregation had been providing sustenance for this group of radicals, the command in 3:6 implies the withdrawal of support. The theological basis for this command is laid out in the apostolic imitation scheme of 3:7–10. Paul had the right to financial support but refrained from using it in order to provide a model for economic responsibility. He goes on to provide a multileveled rationale for work: acceptance of the apostolic command, independent self-support (3:12), and having the means to do good for others (3:13). Therefore, adherence to the "traditions" Paul had brought to Thessalonica entailed repudiating the abandonment of daily occupations that characteristically accompanies millenarian excitement.

V. CONCLUSION

The letter ends on the theme of the ethical stance required for living in the world while expecting its imminent transformation with the parousia of

---

[21] George Milligan, *St. Paul's Epistles to the Thessalonians: The Greek Text with Introduction and Notes* (London: Macmillan, 1908) 152–54; Frame, *Thessalonians*, 197; for a more ample development of this approach, see J. E. Frame, "οἱ ἄτακτοι (I Thess. 5.14)," in *Essays in Modern Theology and Related Subjects Gathered and Published as a Testimonial to Charles A. Briggs* (New York: Scribner's, 1911) 194: ". . . οἱ ἄτακτοι in I 5.14 is to be translated straightway 'the loafers.'"

[22] Best, *Thessalonians*, 230; Bruce, *Thessalonians*, 122.

[23] Ceslas Spicq, "Les Thessaloniciens 'inquiets' etaient ils des paresseux?" *ST* 10 (1956) 1–13, esp. p. 12. This view was reaffirmed in *Notes de Lexicographie Neo-Testamentaire* (Göttingen: Vandenhoeck & Ruprecht, 1978) 1. 159.

[24] See Marshall, *1 and 2 Thessalonians*, 150; Béda Rigaux, *Saint Paul: Les épîtres aux Thessaloniciens* (Ebib; Paris: Gabalda, 1956) 582–83; for an earlier statement of this conclusion, see Wilhelm Bornemann, *Die Thessalonicherbriefe, völlig neu bearbeitet* (MeyerK 10; Göttingen: Vandenhoeck & Ruprecht, 1894) 236–37.

[25] Giblin, *Threat to Faith*, 144, 147.

Christ. The "already/not yet" scheme appears to operate on the ethical as well as on the theological level. The "peace" that is the subject of the final benediction (3:16), in contrast to the premise of millenarian radicalism, is not the absence of adversity. It cannot be a once-and-for-all benefit, such as millenarians might expect, but rather comes "at all times in all ways" (3:16). The peace of Christ is the constant gift of divine grace that provides sustenance for a beleaguered congregation continuing to face political as well as economic woes.[26] The underlying matrix of the theology of 2 Thessalonians is thus logically reasserted in the final words: the grace of the apocalyptic Christ will see them through (3:18).

---

[26] See Jewett, "The Form and Function of the Homiletic Benediction," *ATR* 51 (1969) 25.

7 PEACE IN ALL WAYS

*Theology in the Thessalonian
Letters: A Response to R. Jewett,
E. Krentz, and E. Richard*

*Jouette M. Bassler
Perkins School of Theology*

THE THESSALONIAN CORRESPONDENCE seems an unlikely place to begin a quest for Paul's theology. The authorship of one of the letters is hotly contested and the other is rarely cited for its theological content. Yet because these letters have been so overshadowed by the longer, weightier letters of the Pauline corpus, they offer a unique opportunity for testing the efficacy of the methodology embraced by the contributors to this volume. If other Pauline letters are excluded from consideration, will the distinctive contours of the theology of *these* letters emerge more clearly? The three papers by Professors Krentz, Jewett, and Richard demonstrate that this is indeed the case, but they also demonstrate that temporarily eliminating the rest of the Pauline corpus from one's purview does not eliminate all the factors that can influence one's reading of the theology of a letter. Indeed, the three papers present case studies in how other presuppositions can influence this reading. Robert Jewett, for example, has presupposed Pauline authorship of 2 Thessalonians, whereas Edgar Krentz has analyzed the same text under the presupposition of non-Pauline authorship. In what follows I will show how their different presuppositions regarding authorship have inevitably led Jewett and Krentz to radically different assessments of the theology of 2 Thessalonians. I will also propose a complementary approach to the theology of the letter, one that attempts to proceed without any overt presuppositions about its authorship.

Authorship is not an issue in Earl Richard's analysis of 1 Thessalonians, but the integrity of the letter is, for he assumes that the canonical epistle comprises two originally independent letters. Even more significant, however, is his methodological assumption that a distinction can be made

71

between Paul's theological presuppositions in the letters and his contextualized arguments. The result is a complex analysis that distinguishes not only between the theological presuppositions behind the argument and the argument itself but also between the quite different arguments of the two letters. Yet the theology of this letter, insofar as theology is defined as Paul's appropriation and application of scripture and Christian traditions to the specific situation of the Thessalonian community,[1] seems more properly located at the interface between theological presuppositions and contextual argument, rather than defined through their distinction. I propose, then, that once the main features of the theological background and focus have been identified, an analysis of how they are integrated in the argument of 1 Thessalonians is necessary to define the theological contours of that letter.

I. 2 THESSALONIANS:
AN *INCLUSIO* OF PEACE

Jewett and Krentz not only start with different presuppositions about the authorship of 2 Thessalonians, but they also work with somewhat different understandings of what constitutes the theology of the letter. Krentz's analysis, for example, reflects the standard doctrinal headings of systematic theology. To understand the theology of the letter according to this format, then, is to understand what the (unknown) author said about eschatology ("Judgment on the Oppressors"), christology ("Jesus in 2 Thessalonians"), theology ("God in 2 Thessalonians"), and ethics ("The Life of the Community"), and Krentz organizes comments scattered throughout the letter under these four headings. Jewett, however, approaches the question from a rhetorical perspective. For him, to understand the theology of the letter is to understand the theological assumptions shared by Paul and the Thessalonians and the dialogical quality of the arguments that Paul presents in refutation of the millenarian radicalism extant in the community.

Whether approaching the question doctrinally or rhetorically, however, both agree that the letter presents a one-sided emphasis on apocalyptic eschatology. For Krentz this apocalyptic eschatology defines the theology of the letter. It is the "lens through which the writer surveys his theological terrain" (p. 53) or, to change the optical metaphor slightly, the "lens through

---

[1] See, e.g., N. T. Wright, "Putting Paul Together Again: Toward a Synthesis of Pauline Theology," pp. 195–97 below; R. B. Hays, "Crucified with Christ: A Synthesis of the Theology of 1 and 2 Thessalonians, Philemon, Philippians, and Galatians," pp. 227–29 below; and J. M. Bassler, "Paul's Theology: Whence and Whither? A Synthesis (of sorts) of the Theology of Philemon, 1 Thessalonians, Philippians, Galatians, and 1 Corinthians," in *Society of Biblical Literature 1989 Seminar Papers* (ed. David J. Lull; Atlanta: Scholars Press, 1989) 417–20.

which all of the language of 2 Thessalonians is refracted" (p. 62). It is, in short, the theological center from which the author works, and all the traditional doctrinal categories that Krentz surveys reveal its pervasive presence. According to Krentz, this intense focus on apocalyptic eschatology is a response to an intense crisis, for the church addressed by the letter is clearly undergoing persecution. But, apart from this crisis, the community is "shapeless," and the presumed pseudonymity of the letter does not permit mining 1 Thessalonians for clues to the social, theological, or even the geographical situation of the church (see above, p. 53 n. 5). The result for Krentz is that the letter, though filled with dramatic imagery, is theologically rather "flat." It is a letter with only one theme, a theme strongly played, to be sure, but without evidence of Paul's complexity of thought.

For Jewett, on the other hand, 2 Thessalonians is a letter with remarkable complexity and subtlety of thought, and apocalyptic eschatology, though prominent, is not its *only* theme. In fact, according to Jewett the key to assessing the theology of the letter is the recognition that the apocalyptic emphases of the letter were part of an ongoing conversation. Thus they must be read against the background of assumptions that Paul shared with the church (which Paul rehearses briefly in the epistolary introduction) *and* as a deliberate corrective to the theological excesses of the church. The theology of the letter is thus one-sided in the direction of apocalyptic eschatology, but that one-sidedness represents a deliberate attempt to bring the community back to its Pauline center.[2] According to Jewett, then, the *context* of the letter generates the apocalyptic tension that is characteristic of Paul's theology. Viewed within this context, the letter's central theme is not apocalyptic eschatology per se. There are, in fact, two themes in the letter, the Christ-event and the parousia, and in the light of Paul's rhetorical strategy, the dominant theme — the one that serves as the basis or matrix for the contextual argument — is the message of salvation by grace (p. 65).

It is clear from this brief overview that different assumptions about the way the theology of the letter is to be defined have led these two scholars to radically different assessments of that theology. Krentz, with his understanding of theology in terms of doctrinal categories, focuses on the body of the letter and its strongly apocalyptic content while giving scant attention to the epistolary framework. He concludes that the apocalyptic eschatology of the letter overshadows the message of grace and that when grace is mentioned it is grounded in the character of God and not in the cross and resurrection of Jesus. Jewett, however, with his understanding of the indivisibility of the theology of the letter from the rhetorical and epistolary aspects of its

---

[2] See J. P. Sampley, "From Text to Thought World: The Route to Paul's Ways," p. 7 above.

communication, gives strong weight to the letter's framework and its formulaic references to grace, peace, faith, and love. Thus he finds a strong traditional message of grace undergirding the apocalyptic message, and that grace is both rooted in the past and pointed to the future, as it is in the other Pauline letters.

The approaches and conclusions of these two scholars are influenced by more than their different definitions of the theology of the letter. Their different presuppositions of who is—or who is not—writing this letter seem also to have played a strong role in determining which words of the text are to be considered and how they are to be evaluated. It is only, I think, under the presupposition of Pauline authorship (and under the influence of the great law-gospel antithesis of Romans and Galatians) that Jewett can find in the letter's refutation of ἀνομία (2:3, 7, 8) an early conservative affirmation of the value of the (Jewish) law instead of a reference to the generally chaotic conditions that were expected to characterize the period before the Day of the Lord (p. 66).[3] Likewise, it is only under the controlling presupposition of Pauline authorship that he can find hidden in the reference to traditions (τὰς παραδόσεις, 2:15) that crucial component of Paul's theology that is otherwise sorely missing in this letter: Christ crucified and resurrected (p. 68).[4] And it is, I think, primarily because of his presupposition of Pauline authorship that Jewett allows the formulaic passages, with their references to faith and grace, to control the interpretation of the body of the letter instead of vice versa.

Krentz, on the other hand, is probably led by his own quite different presuppositions essentially to *ignore* these formulaic passages. He concludes, for example, that in 2 Thessalonians God's fundamental character is justice, which it is in the *body* of the letter. In the epistolary framework and benedictions, however, God is hailed as Father (1:1; 2:16), as giver of grace and peace (1:2; 2:16), and as the source of the community's faith and love (1:3–4, 11; 2:13). Indeed, God is rather emphatically defined in terms of love (2:13[?], 16; 3:5) and election (1:11; 2:13–14). The theology of the letter may not be as thickly textured as that of Romans, but Krentz's presuppositions have led to a reading of the letter that flattens its theology beyond that suggested by the text itself.

---

[3] See, e.g., I. H. Marshall, *1 and 2 Thessalonians* (NCB; Grand Rapids: Eerdmans, 1983) 189: "We should take the term [ἀνομία] . . . with particular reference to rebellion against the will of God as it is manifested in the last days. The motif of 'law' has been submerged below the general concept of opposition to God." See also W. Trilling, *Der zweite Brief an die Thessalonicher* (EKKNT 14; Neukirchen-Vluyn: Neukirchener Verlag, 1980) 84.

[4] It seems to me much more likely that the author had moral or ethical "traditions" in mind, not the theology of the cross. Note, e.g., the direction of the argument in 2:16–17 and 3:6.

Each of these scholars has proceeded with inexorable logic from different presuppositions to different conclusions, and each has illuminated the letter in a different way. Indeed, their interpretations are mutually corrective: Jewett's forces us to deal honestly with the more formulaic elements of the letter, whereas Krentz's brings home the overwhelming presence of apocalyptic eschatology. What is needed to complement these two readings, however, is a reading that makes *no* presuppositions regarding authorship. Such a reading would illuminate the text in a third way and perhaps permit through triangulation a better approximation of the letter's theology.

"Is exegesis without presuppositions possible?"[5] I do not mean to imply, when I borrow this phrase from Bultmann's well-known essay, that Krentz's and Jewett's analyses of 2 Thessalonians presupposed the results. I *do* think, however, that their differing presuppositions inevitably caused them to evaluate the data differently. Because he assumes that Paul wrote the letter, Jewett can presuppose a concrete social and historical context that brings the theology of the letter into harmony with the theology of the uncontested letters. Because he assumes Paul did *not* write the letter, Krentz can dismiss the theological language of the epistolary framework as conventions appropriated in order to convey the *illusion* of Pauline authorship, not serious signals of a deeper theological matrix. This is not the same as presupposing the results of the analyses of the theology of the letter, but it does have an unmistakable influence on the directions those analyses take. Thus I raise the question of how it might be possible to assess the theology of this letter without being influenced by presuppositions concerning authorship. One must not pretend to be genuinely neutral about the authorship of the letter. The question is how to undertake a reading of the theology of the letter that effectively brackets out the authorship question.

Such an approach cannot, of course, presuppose a concrete historical situation: that would be tantamount to a presupposition concerning authorship. Nor can the approach screen out any statements as formulas borrowed without content. That, too, implies a presupposition concerning authorship. On the other hand, I do not mean to say that we must read the text "flat," with every theological statement given equal weight. The quest for the letter's theology is in large part a quest for the pattern and texture of the letter's theological statements. The text itself—and not our assumptions about its author—must suggest the weighting that we give to the various statements. The approach that I am suggesting, then, is one that is literary in nature, one that considers the shape of the document as a whole and the

---

[5] R. Bultmann, "Is Exegesis Without Presuppositions Possible?" in *New Testament and Mythology and Other Basic Writings* (ed. S. M. Ogden; Philadelphia: Fortress, 1984) 145–53.

relationship of the parts to the whole, of the frame to the body, and of each part to the others. Such an approach, which deliberately ignores the historical and social context, is antithetical to everything we have learned about how to read the letters in the New Testament canon, and I do not mean to challenge that wisdom.[6] Yet when two readings of a text, based on different assumptions about context, contradict each other as fundamentally as Jewett's and Krentz's do, perhaps a third reading of the text, based on no assumptions about context, will help resolve the contradiction.[7]

I begin, then, with the basic, literary observation that the letter opens and closes with references to grace and peace (1:2; 3:16, 18). It is interesting — but ultimately not relevant to the analysis here — that this *inclusio* is found in most of the Pauline letters, though rarely with the formal precision of 2 Thessalonians. All of the uncontested letters except 1 Thessalonians[8] open with the same greeting formula: "Grace to you and peace from God our Father and the Lord Jesus Christ." And all contain at or near the end of the letter a benediction that repeats the reference to grace: "The grace of our Lord Jesus Christ be with you." All save Philemon also contain at or near the end of the letter, but without the same formulaic precision, a reference to the God of peace (Rom 15:33; 16:20; 1 Cor 14:33; 1 Thess 5:23), or a statement (prayer or command) about peace (Gal 6:16), or both (2 Cor 13:11; Phil 4:7, 9).

In fact, in 2 Thessalonians the *inclusio* has an *abb'a'* pattern with particular emphasis on *b'*, the closing peace wish: "*Grace*[a] to you and *peace*[b] from God the Father and the Lord Jesus Christ," "Now may the *Lord of peace*[b'] himself give you *peace*[b'] at all times in all ways . . . the *grace*[a'] of our Lord Jesus Christ be with you all." Both God and the Lord Jesus Christ are presented as the sources of both grace and peace in the opening formula; only the Lord, however, is mentioned in the closing phrases.[9] Grace appears in the body of

---

[6] I fully agree, then, with V. P. Furnish's comment that "the real challenge for interpreters of Paul's thought lies just here: to find ways of respecting the situational and dialogical character of his theology without abandoning the attempt to understand its most fundamental convictions and its most pervasive concerns" ("Pauline Studies," in *The New Testament and Its Modern Interpreters* [ed. E. J. Epp and G. W. MacRae; Atlanta: Scholars Press, 1989] 338). It is out of a concern to isolate the letter's "most pervasive concerns" that I set aside for the moment questions concerning authorship, audience, and situation.

[7] The inspiration for this derives from the last of the thirteen *Middoth* of R. Ishmael: "When two verses contradict one another, the contradiction is removed by a third verse"; see H. L. Strack, *Introduction to the Talmud and Midrash* (New York: Atheneum, 1974) 95.

[8] The manuscript evidence is divided on this point. The full greeting formula, attested by B F G Ψ 629. 1739. 1881 *pc*, probably arose through harmonization with 2 Thess 1:2; א A (D) I and other constant witnesses contain the shorter formula, "Grace to you and peace," which is generally acknowledged as the better reading.

[9] In this regard 2 Thessalonians is distinctive. All other references in the Pauline corpus are

the letter in 1:12 (as the basis for a prayer that God will make them worthy) and in 2:16 (as the basis for a prayer that God will comfort and establish them). There are no explicit references to peace (εἰρήνη) in the body of the letter. I would argue, however, that the main sections of the letter (1:3–12; 2:1–3:5; 3:6–15) are, in fact, concerned with peace and that peace in its eschatological, ecclesiological, and social dimensions is the theological goal of this letter.

1:3–12. In this section of the letter,[10] statements about the community's steadfastness and faith (vv. 3–4a) soon yield to statements about the persecution the community is enduring (vv. 4b–5) and then to statements contrasting the eschatological fates of the persecutors and the persecuted (vv. 6–10). It closes with a prayer for the church, that its actions and attitude in the time of crisis might result in the glorification of God's name and of the community (vv. 11–12). Apocalyptic imagery is very strong,[11] yet here, as elsewhere in the canon, this imagery serves a clear and concrete function: to contrast the present persecution, affliction, and suffering of the community of the faithful with the rest (ἄνεσις, 1:7) that is promised to them.[12] The fundamental meaning of peace in the Greek tradition is precisely this notion of a state of rest following war, strife, or tribulation (θλίψις).[13]

There is a second contrast as well, the contrast between the eschatological rest of the faithful and the suffering and affliction that will be the ultimate fate of the church's oppressors. God's righteous judgment and the apocalypse of the Lord Jesus thus have as their common goal the reversal of the present circumstances: the present afflictors will face affliction, and the afflicted community will be granted rest. Although the message of the apocalyptic destruction of the oppressors seems to dominate the argument here, this serves primarily as a foil for the real emphasis: the promise of peace/rest to the afflicted saints. It is for their faith and steadfastness in persecution that the author gives thanks and boasts and it is for them that he prays. Though the Lord Jesus will prove to be an agent of terrible vengeance for those who have persecuted the church, he will be a "Lord of peace" for the faithful,

to the *God* of peace; 2 Thess 3:16, however, mentions the *Lord* of peace, and the context makes it clear that this refers to the Lord Jesus Christ (3:12, 18).

[10] There is general agreement that vv. 3–12 constitute a unified section of the letter, its (first) thanksgiving period. The unusual aspects of this letter's thanksgiving need not concern us here.

[11] See Krentz's "Through a Lens," pp. 52–62 above.

[12] See A. Yarbro Collins, *Crisis and Catharsis: The Power of the Apocalypse* (Philadelphia: Westminster, 1984) 141–63.

[13] W. Foerster and G. Delling, "εἰρήνη," *TDNT* 2. 401, 407, 409.

granting them the eschatological peace of the kingdom of God, which includes most concretely *rest* from their present tribulations.

2:1-3:5. Though the apocalyptic discourse of 2:1-12 is often treated in isolation from the verses that follow,[14] it seems clear to me that the argument that opens in 2:1 continues through 3:5. The most interesting part of the argument, at least as interest is measured in commentary pages, is the apocalyptic scenario that the author unfolds in 2:3-12. Yet this scenario is not presented for its doctrinal content but in response to the shaken minds and excited state of the ἀδελφοί, who have become convinced "by spirit or by word, or by letter purporting to be from us" that the Day of the Lord had come (2:1-2). Thus, after describing an apocalyptic scenario that proves that the Day of the Lord has *not* come and that the Day, when it does come, will bring destruction on all who do not believe the truth, the author turns to address the community directly. *They* have been chosen for salvation, so they are to stand firm (στήκετε [2:15], the opposite of σαλευθῆναι in 2:2). In the face of misleading and frightening messages concerning the Day of the Lord, they are to hold to the traditions taught by the author, "by word of mouth or by letter" (2:15; cf. 2:2). The author then prays that this disturbed and shaken church (θροεῖσθαι, 2:2) may be comforted and established (2:17).

In 3:1-2 the author seems to shift to a concern about his own fate, but he quickly returns to the topic of real concern—the situation in the church. How little the author is concerned with his own situation and how much he is concerned with that of the church are shown by the abrupt shift in the argument here: "Pray for *us* . . . that *we* may be delivered from wicked and evil men; for not all have faith. But the Lord is faithful; he will strengthen *you* and guard *you* from evil" (3:1-3). There follows a statement of confidence about the community and a prayer that God will direct them to the love of God and steadfastness of Christ (εἰς τὴν ὑπομονὴν τοῦ Χριστοῦ).

This whole section, then, from start (2:1-2) to finish (2:13-3:5) is concerned with calming those shaken in mind and excited by a strange message. The apocalyptic scenario that the author describes is itself the very antithesis of peace. There will be rebellion, lawlessness, the activity and power of Satan, signs and wonders, violent confrontation between the Lord Jesus and the lawless one, deception, and destruction. But the turbulent chaos of this

---

[14] See, e.g., W. Marxsen, *Der zweite Thessalonicherbrief* (Zürcher Bibelkommentar 11.2; Zurich: Theologischer Verlag, 1982) 76-98, where 2:1-12 is treated under the doctrinal heading "Der Ort der Gegenwart im Apokalyptischen Fahrplan," and 2:13-3:5 is treated separately under the heading "Verschiedene Ermahnungen." See also Marshall, *1 and 2 Thessalonians,* 205. W. Trilling treats 2:13-14 as part of the discussion of "Der 'Tag des Herrn'" (2:1-14) in his commentary, but all the subsequent verses (up to 3:16) are assigned to a separate "Ermahnender Teil."

apocalyptic drama must not obscure for us the reason that it was presented: to calm and comfort an agitated church—in short, to bring peace to their excited minds.

3:6–15. The final section of the letter addresses a social problem within the community: behavior characterized by the author as ἀτάκτως. Both Krentz and Jewett correctly understand this as a description of disorderly, and not idle, conduct, a state of "busy unrest" that precludes useful labor.[15] The author addresses a command first to those thus far untouched by the disorderly behavior and then to the ἄτακτοι themselves. The first group is enjoined to avoid contact with the disorderly (3:6; see also v. 14), but without generating an attitude of enmity (μὴ ὡς ἐχθρὸν ἡγεῖσθε, 3:15). The second group, the disorderly themselves, are exhorted to ἡσυχία (3:12). Both admonitions converge toward εἰρήνη, whether through the absence of hostility or through the presence of a state of quietude that is synonymous with peace.[16]

Summary. It is impossible to deny that apocalyptic imagery and thought dominate this letter, but to conclude, as Krentz does,[17] that this apocalyptic thought *defines* the theology of the letter is to overlook the function of this thought within the letter. The letter is directed toward *peace.* References to peace form an *inclusio* about the body of the letter, and the arguments within each section of the letter's body—though couched heavily in apocalyptic terms—have peace as their common goal. The apocalyptic judgment proclaimed in chap. 1 has as its primary outcome peace (ἄνεσις) for the suffering community. To be sure, this peace stands in stark contrast to the fate of the oppressors that is so vividly portrayed, but *for the community* the outcome is peace. The lively description of apocalyptic activity is presented in chap. 2 for the express purpose of achieving peace of mind in the face of the disturbing misinformation that is shaking the community. And the exhortations in the final section are designed to restore social peace (ἡσυχία) to the community. In every instance a peaceful attitude or existence is contrasted with a state of disorder or turmoil, whether inflicted from without or experienced within the minds and the social world of the community's members. Peace

---

[15] See above p. 61 (Krentz) and p. 69 (Jewett); see also G. Delling, "ἄτακτος" (s.v. "τάσσω"), *TDNT* 8. 48. The RSV, NRSV, NIV, and NEB all refer to "idleness" in 2 Thess 3:6–7; the NJB, however, refers to "undisciplined behavior" and the NAB speaks of "disorder."

[16] On the frequent connection established between εἰρήνη and ἡσυχία, see Foerster, "εἰρήνη," *TDNT* 2. 401.

[17] "The epistle deals with one theme consistently spun out—fidelity to the apocalyptic tradition" (see p. 62 above).

is a significant theological component of all the Pauline letters,[18] but rarely does it appear with such structural and thematic clarity as in this letter.

Krentz is quite correct, then, when he says that "all the resources the author uses . . . stress future salvation and are directed to the life of waiting under pressure" (p. 61), but that does not say quite enough. It does not indicate that all the argumentative energy of this letter is devoted to achieving peace. This includes, of course, eschatological peace, but it also includes the present emotional and social status of the saints. The really striking thing, for example, about the christology of *this* letter is not simply its apocalyptic coloring,[19] but that the Lord of the apocalyptic drama, the Lord of vengeance (1:8) and death and destruction (2:8) is, for the community, the Lord of peace, the one who will grant eschatological peace and who desires now peace within the community.

Jewett has identified the peace wish as important in the theology of this letter (p. 70), but he does not give it a broad enough reference and he does not quite define it correctly when he refers to it as "the constant gift of divine grace that provides sustenance for a beleaguered congregation." Peace is the constant *goal* of the letter's various arguments and exhortations, and as such it is rhetorically distinguishable from divine grace; the latter forms—in a vague sort of way—the grounds for the hope that lies behind the arguments and exhortations. We can confirm this by looking briefly at the role grace plays within the argument.

If the *inclusio* formed by the references to peace in 1:2 and 3:16 (*bis*) defines the pastoral, social, and theological goal of the various apocalyptic and hortatory arguments, this *inclusio* is embraced by yet another, the references to grace which formally open and close the letter. Though, like peace, grace forms an *inclusio*, it plays a different role in the body of the letter. It does not define the goal of the letter's various arguments but appears in the petitions and prayers that conclude the first two sections. Thus, having proclaimed that the Lord Jesus will come and be glorified in all his saints, the author prays that the name of Jesus may be glorified in the saints "according to the grace of our God and the Lord Jesus Christ" (1:10–11). Later, after presenting a description of apocalyptic events that is intended to calm the shaken church, the author prays that the Lord Jesus Christ and God might comfort their hearts, and God and Christ are defined as having already given them "eternal comfort and hope through grace" (2:16). This grace is not clearly linked to a specific event, but it serves here as the norm and means for the peaceful resolution of the turmoil presently afflicting the church. Thus grace

---

[18] See, e.g., the recent article by K. Haacker, "Der Römerbrief als Friedensmemorandum," *NTS* 36 (1990) 25–41.

[19] See Krentz, "Through a Lens," pp. 56–57 above.

is in a very general way the matrix of the letter's arguments; peace in various guises is the goal of these arguments; and apocalyptic eschatology is the primary theological resource out of which they are constructed. Therefore, I would not define the letter's theology exclusively in terms of apocalyptic convictions, nor would I promote grace as its defining theological character- istic. Both are present, but both serve a common goal. It is the same goal that the author asks the "Lord of peace" to grant: "peace at all times and in all ways." All things in this letter work toward that theological goal.

II. 1 THESSALONIANS:
SANCTIFICATION AND PEACE

Earl Richard's discussion of the theology of 1 Thessalonians poses a some- what different challenge. Authorship is not an issue here, for although Richard breaks with the prevailing consensus in asserting the composite character of this letter, he does affirm (with the exception of 2:14–16) the Pauline authorship of both letters that, according to his analysis, make up the canonical document. Regarding 1 Thessalonians as composite does, of course, affect the assessment of its theology, for each missive contained in it is assumed to be addressed to a different situation (though to the same com- munity) and thus each contains a different theological emphasis. Given the assumption of the letter's composite character (an assumption I do not share but one which I also do not want to debate here), this conclusion poses no methodological difficulties. More problematical, however, is the assumption implicit in the arrangement of the paper: that Paul's theological presupposi- tions — the language and concepts he shares with his audience — can *and should* be separated from the documents' explicit messages. Indeed, Richard argues that "the distinction between theological background and theological focus is *crucial, in methodological terms,* when examining the thought of a particular letter" (p. 50; my emphasis).

I would argue that the opposite is true, that Paul conveys his message by *using* shared or traditional theological concepts and that the *way* Paul uses these concepts in formulating and structuring his message to a particular community provides clear insight into Paul's theologizing and into the "theology" of (or in) a particular letter. Thus I do not think one has com- pletely grasped Paul's theology in 1 Thessalonians (or, if one follows Richard's analysis, in the longer missive contained in 1 Thessalonians) when one notes, for example, that Paul shares Israel's concept of God as a God of peace and then notes separately that a major emphasis in the parenesis of this letter is the emphasis on God's will for holiness (p. 43). What is distinctive is that in this letter these two concepts are brought together (5:23). It is precisely the God *of peace* who is petitioned to sanctify the community, so Paul clearly sees peace and sanctification as related concepts. Determining what that relationship is will move us closer to an understanding of the theology of this letter.

Richard does not, of course, make an *absolute* distinction between the theological "background" and the theological "focus" of the letter(s). Though he claims they can and should be distinguished, he recognizes their inherent interconnectedness in the argument of the letter. Thus he notes that Paul appeals to traditional formulations of both theology and christology (background) to support his exhortations (focus) (p. 44) and notes further that the apostle "is more interested in the theological motivation for action and behavior than in particular acts" (p. 49). Thus he concludes that "both of these [background and focus] form part of Pauline theology or thought; their relative importance depends on the role they play in Pauline thought generally or the extent to which they are developed or rhetorically engaged" (p. 50). This I agree with, but I also maintain that one will not be able to *see* their relative importance or the way they are rhetorically engaged if one analyzes them separately. As a case in point let us look at the phrase that I have identified as thematic in 2 Thessalonians, "the God of peace." How is this traditional theologoumenon brought to bear on the contextual argument of 1 Thessalonians?

1 Thessalonians, like so many letters in the Pauline corpus, closes with a reference to peace.[20] Here it takes the form of a petition to the "God of peace": "May the God of peace himself sanctify you wholly" (5:23a RSV). Several times Paul refers in his letters to the God of some attribute ("of steadfastness and encouragement" [Rom 15:5], "of hope" [Rom 15:13], "of all comfort" [2 Cor 1:3], "of love and peace" [2 Cor 13:11], and "of peace" [Rom 16:20; 1 Cor 14:33; Phil 4:9]) and then either petitions God to create that attribute in the community or exhorts the community to strive for that attribute themselves. One would expect to find the God *of holiness* petitioned here in 1 Thessalonians, but it is the God *of peace* who is asked to sanctify the community. One can thus conclude that Paul saw an inherent connection between "peace" and "sanctification," but only an analysis of his argument in 1 Thessalonians will reveal the nature of that connection and thus the specific contextual significance of the familiar theologoumenon ("God of peace") in this letter.

The full statement of the petition establishes the eschatological dimension of this peace, for the sanctifying actions of the God of peace will bear their fruits at the parousia of Christ: "May the God of peace himself sanctify you

---

[20] See above, p. 76.

wholly; and may your spirit and soul and body be kept sound and blameless at the coming of our Lord Jesus Christ" (v. 23). Thus here, as often in the New Testament, peace signifies salvation in its fullest possible sense.[21] Yet the preceding exhortations also pick up the language of sanctification and peace and demonstrate that peace has a temporal, social face as well.

The concept of sanctification (ἁγιασμός), for example, is intimately connected with the marriage instructions presented in 4:3–8.[22] The section opens by stating that God's will for the Thessalonians is ἁγιασμός (v. 3) and concludes by affirming that God had called them ἐν ἁγιασμῷ (v. 7) and that to disregard Paul's instructions in this matter is to disregard the God who gives the Holy Spirit (τὸ πνεῦμα τὸ ἅγιον, v. 8). The Thessalonians are thus specifically admonished to acquire a wife in holiness (ἐν ἁγιασμῷ, v. 4).[23] The emphasis here on holiness/sanctification is clear, yet when Paul defines more precisely what this means, it also becomes clear that actions that lead to holiness *also* lead to peace.

Holiness in marriage involves the usual concept of separation from "uncleanness" (v. 7), but it involves also attributes of inner and social harmony that can be defined in terms of peace. Thus, to acquire a wife *in holiness* is to avoid the passion of lust (μὴ ἐν πάθει ἐπιθυμίας), and Paul here refers not just to the stereotypical Jewish view of Gentiles (Rom 1:24–28) but also to one of the cardinal passions defined by Stoic philosophy. This disorder of the soul, like the other three (λυπή, φόβος, ἡδονή), was condemned by the Stoics because it was antithetical to ἀταραξία, the calmness and freedom from passion that characterized the ideal sage.[24] Thus, taking a wife in holiness will not only distinguish the Thessalonians from the heathen, who do not know God; it will also encourage an inner calm that can be defined in terms of peace. It will also lead to peace in the community, for taking a wife in holiness means not wronging a brother—a fellow Christian—through acts

---

[21] See Delling, "εἰρήνη," *TDNT* 2. 411.

[22] Whether one takes 4:1–2 as the superscription for the entire hortatory section (4:1–5:24), as most commentators do, or assigns these verses with Richard to the earlier missive, 4:3–8 emerges as a clearly defined segment of Paul's argument.

[23] On the difficulties posed by this verse and the justification for interpreting it this way, see O. L. Yarbrough, *Not Like the Gentiles: Marriage Rules in the Letters of Paul* (SBLDS 80; Atlanta: Scholars Press, 1985) 68–76.

[24] For a description of the Stoic evaluation of the passions, see J. H. Neyrey, "The Absence of Jesus' Emotions—The Lucan Redaction of Lk 22,39–46," *Bib* 61 (1980) 154–57. A. J. Malherbe argues that 1 Thessalonians is particularly rich in examples of Paul's appropriation of philosophic commonplaces; see, e.g., " 'Gentle as a Nurse': The Cynic Background to 1 Thessalonians 2," "Exhortation in 1 Thessalonians," and "Paul: Hellenistic Philosopher or Christian Pastor?" now collected in his *Paul and the Popular Philosophers* (Minneapolis: Fortress, 1989); see also his *Paul and the Thessalonians: The Philosophic Tradition of Pastoral Care* (Philadelphia: Fortress, 1987).

of adultery.[25] Taking a wife in holiness also leads to eschatological peace, whereas transgression in this matter will result in a confrontation with the avenging Lord (v. 6).

In the next section (4:9–12) Paul argues more directly for peace within the social fabric of the community. The church is admonished to continue to demonstrate mutual love and affection within the community, but they are specifically exhorted to live quietly (ἡσυχάζειν), and here as elsewhere ἡσυχία is a synonym for peace.[26] One can also argue that peace in the form of the absence of grief (ἵνα μὴ λυπῆσθε, v. 13) is promoted in vv. 13–18, where Paul emphasizes the eschatological hopes of the community — the sure promise of eschatological peace, if you will — in order to bring peace of mind to those who are grieving over the deaths of some members of the community.

Paul is also concerned, however, to avoid any misunderstanding that would interpret his words as an encouragement for complacency. Peace and sanctification may have temporal components, but their full realization lies in the future. Thus Paul assiduously avoids the conclusion that the fullness of eschatological peace is a present reality (5:1–11). He warns against those who proclaim peace as security (εἰρήνη καὶ ἀσφάλεια, 5:3) and advocates instead a sober watchfulness that will be enhanced by social peace but will not confuse the present social reality with its coming eschatological fullness.

The closing admonitions (5:12–22) not only work for blameless behavior but also — indirectly or directly — for peace: respect your leaders (vv. 12–13a), be at peace (v. 13b), admonish the disorderly (ἄτακτοι, v. 14),[27] do not repay evil for evil (v. 15). Thus when Paul closes this section of the letter — and the letter as a whole — in 5:23 with his petition to the "God of peace" to sanctify the community for the coming parousia, he is bringing together and highlighting the connection between various concerns that have surfaced in his exhortations: sanctification, peace in both its social and eschatological manifestations, and salvation. It is precisely in the interconnectedness of these concepts — and others — that we can begin to define the distinctive edge of Paul's theology in this letter.

Jewett, Krentz, and Richard have presented penetrating and challenging analyses of the theology of the Thessalonian correspondence. Each was influenced by different presuppositions to approach the task in a different way, and this resulted in rather different assessments of the theologies of

---

25 For a discussion of this interpretation, see Yarbrough, *Not Like the Gentiles,* 75–76.
26 See n. 16 above.
27 See n. 15 above.

these letters. In this essay I have offered my own assessments, not as a substitute for theirs but as a contribution to an ongoing conversation. The dialogue partners in this conversation may disagree on details of interpretation, but we all share a common fascination with the apostle Paul and a common desire for greater clarity about Paul's thought.

Part III

The Theology of Philippians

8 Philippians

Theology for the Heavenly Politeuma

Pheme Perkins
Boston College

PHILIPPIANS POSES THE PROBLEM of the context, underlying structure, and content of Paul's theology even in the questions about origin, setting, and composition that every interpretation must resolve. Scholarly literature on Philippians has been preoccupied with three issues: the integrity of the letter,[1] the various forms of opposition mentioned in the letter,[2] and the Christ hymn of Phil 2:6–11.[3] Before turning to an analysis of the theological reflection in Philippians, we will set out our working hypothesis in each of these areas.

The Integrity of Philippians. The canonical epistle appears to be composed of sections from as many as three letters: a receipt for aid received (4:10–20); a letter on the impending disposition of Paul's case (1:1–3:1; 4:2–7, [8–9]); and a warning against judaizing preachers (3:2–4:1, 8–9). Documentary papyri show that letters could be appended to one another.[4] Since Phil 2:19–24 envisages some time before Paul can dispatch Timothy, the warning

---

[1] See the discussion in R. Jewett, "The Epistolary Thanksgiving and the Integrity of Philippians," *NovT* 12 (1970) 40–53.

[2] R. Jewett, "Conflicting Movements in the Early Church as Reflected in Philippians," *NovT* 12 (1970) 362–90.

[3] J. Gnilka, *Der Philipperbrief* (HTKNT 10/3; Freiburg: Herder, 1968) 111–47.

[4] See J. L. White, *Light from Ancient Letters* (Philadelphia: Fortress, 1986) 35–36, 40–43, 217–18. In the case of administrative chain letters, the opening conventions can be reduced to "To X" and the closing omitted. In some cases the contents of an appended letter may be referred to, with the original attached for the recipient's information. A similar combination might have been true of the Philippian correspondence. Phil 4:10–20 may have been dispatched with the letter about Paul's case. Formally, this section fits the style of a receipt for aid.

against judaizing may have been sent with Timothy after the other two letters. There would have been no need to inform the recipients about Paul's situation in that letter, since Timothy could bring news about the apostle. This understanding of the divisions in Philippians presumes that the place of Paul's imprisonment was close enough to Philippi to permit exchange of information and aid, something not possible if the setting were Rome.[5] This assumption also situates the Philippian correspondence prior to Paul's deliverance from mortal threat in Asia (2 Cor 1:8–10) but after Timothy's return to Ephesus from the Corinthian visit mentioned in 1 Cor 4:17 and 16:10–11.[6] Consequently, the apparent shift in eschatology between the emphasis on Christians being "with Christ" at his parousia (1 Thess 4:13–18) and the apostle's expectation that he will be "with Christ" if this imprisonment leads to his death (Phil 1:21–26) cannot be resolved by appealing to changes in the apostle's thought over a period of time.

Opposition in Philippians. Three sources of opposition are clearly indicated in the letter. (1) Tensions among Christian preachers exist both in the city of imprisonment and in Philippi (1:15–18). These tensions are connected with the fact that the apostle is imprisoned.[7] Though Paul takes pains to stress the fact that his chains are "in Christ" and advance the gospel, others apparently held a different view.[8] (2) Non-Christians are responsible for the apostle's imprisonment and the hostility experienced by the Philippians as well (1:27–30). Paul takes θλῖψις of this sort as a given in Christian life (see 1 Thess 1:6–7).[9] (3) There is also a group of judaizing Christian missionaries, who do not appear to have an established base in the Philippian community or to be

---

[5] R. P. Martin, *Philippians* (NCB; London: Oliphants, 1976) 49–55. The references to Paul's trials in proconsular Asia and the danger to his life provide a strong case for such an imprisonment (2 Cor 1:8–10; 4:8–12; 6:4–10; Rom 16:3–4), even if the reference to fighting with beasts in Ephesus (1 Cor 15:32a) is a scribal allusion to a later legend about the apostle.

[6] See V. P. Furnish, *II Corinthians* (AB 32A; Garden City, NY: Doubleday, 1984) 122–25.

[7] They may reflect the social structure of the Pauline mission. If it was organized as a *societas* (so J. P. Sampley, *Pauline Partnership in Christ: Christian Community and Commitment in Light of Roman Law* [Philadelphia: Fortress, 1986] 14–16), Paul's death would dissolve the consent to a common endeavor that bound persons together in the missionary association.

[8] K. Wengst, *Pax Romana and the Peace of Jesus Christ* (Philadelphia: Fortress, 1987) 74.

[9] W. A. Meeks, *The First Urban Christians: The Social World of the Apostle Paul* (New Haven: Yale University Press, 1983) 174. The appearance of such hostility confirms the apostle's prediction of suffering and the solidarity of Christians in their common plight. Paul can point to the fact that persecutions attended the birth of the communities in both Thessalonica and Philippi (see R. Jewett, *The Thessalonian Correspondence: Pauline Rhetoric and Millenarian Piety* [FFNT; Philadelphia: Fortress, 1986] 93–94).

as consistently organized an "anti-Paul" group as one finds in 2 Corinthians (Phil 3:2–3).[10]

The divisions among persons who are preaching the gospel do not appear to be theologically motivated. The appeal for reconciliation between two women missionaries (4:2–3) probably represents the outcome that Paul expects from the exhortation to community harmony (2:1–5).[11] The grounds for the external opposition that led to the apostle's imprisonment are also unclear. Since others apparently preach unopposed, some interpreters have suggested that Paul's message must have been disturbing to the civic order.[12] Scholars have frequently read the polemic against "the dogs" in the light of the controversies in either Galatians or 2 Corinthians.[13] However, the unusual emphasis on the Christian *politeuma* in heaven may indicate that this exhortation should be linked to the situation of the community in the Roman colony of Philippi.[14]

The Christ Hymn. Phil 2:6–11 is taken from a pre-Pauline hymn, which the apostle has glossed[15] and used as a central piece in the exhortation to the Philippians. The basic pattern of the hymn reflects Paul's view of the principles that are evident in his present situation: surrendering divine existence

[10] G. Friedrich, *Der Brief an die Philipper* (NTD 8; Göttingen: Vandenhoeck & Ruprecht, 1985) 131–34. There is no reason to assign gnosticizing traits to these opponents or to presume that another group is introduced in Phil 3:18. Phil 3:19 reflects the sloganizing attack on opponents typical of Pauline rhetoric (e.g., 1 Cor 6:13; 15:32b). Though we disagree with Martin's argument for gnosticizing traits among the opponents, he has correctly identified the sloganizing character of the expression "their god is their belly," a proverbial description of persons preoccupied with material concerns (Martin, *Philippians*, 144–45).

[11] The language of the appeal picks up the exhortation in 2:1–2. The dispute is clearly one that affects the community or the Pauline mission; it is not just private animosity (so Gnilka, *Philipperbrief*, 166).

[12] So Wengst, *Pax Romana*, 202 n. 11.

[13] Gnilka, *Philipperbrief*, 185–206. Connections with Galatians are made on the basis of the contrast between Christians as the "true circumcision" which is linked to the Spirit and those who "trust in the flesh" (vv. 3–4), Paul's strong affirmation of his Jewish past as surpassing any claims by his adversaries (vv. 4–9), the contrast between "righteousness from the law" and "through faith of Christ" (v. 9), and the apparent imposition of kosher rules (v. 19). Connections with 2 Corinthians are predicated on the eschatology of the heavenly *politeuma* and the emphasis on the trials of the apostle. Furnish uses the Philippians passage to argue that 2 Cor 5:1–10 should not be interpreted as a statement about individual, bodily eschatology, but in terms of the heavenly "home" toward which the Christian community looks (*II Corinthians*, 295).

[14] Gnilka, *Philipperbrief*, 206.

[15] Though many scholars presume that the hymn originated in Greek-speaking circles, J. A. Fitzmyer has shown that a retroversion into first-century CE Aramaic is possible. In this retroversion, the only phrase that is certainly Pauline is θανάτου δὲ σταυροῦ (v. 8c) ("The Aramaic Background of Phil 2:6–11," *CBQ* 50 [1988] 470–83).

to the lowliness of humanity (vv. 6–7b), obedience even to death on a cross (vv. 7c–8), and exaltation as God's response (vv. 9–11).[16] Verse 5 tells the readers that they should τοῦτο φρονεῖν as Christ. This theme recurs throughout the letter (1:7; 2:2 [bis], 5; 3:15, 19; 4:2, 10).[17]

I. THE APOLOGETIC CONTEXT
OF PHILIPPIANS

Instead of using hypothetical reconstructions of the judaizers of Galatians or of the Hellenistic Jewish propaganda used by charismatic Christians in Corinth to describe the context of Paul's reflection in Philippians, we will rely on the correspondence itself. Since Paul refers to support that he had received from Philippi while he was working in Thessalonica (4:15–16), we may also refer to 1 Thessalonians for information about the Pauline mission in this period. Though we accept the hypothesis that canonical Philippians comprises three separate letters, we will argue that they all address the same religiocultural dilemma: the need to understand the social situation of the Christian community in the Greco-Roman *polis* in the light of the persistent fact of persecution. Finally, we will suggest that the theological understanding of the Christ-event reflected in the hymnic section shaped both Paul's self-understanding as one imprisoned and facing death (including his refusal to exercise the "rights" of Roman citizenship)[18] and his "political theology," which prohibited Christians from taking advantage of the earthly *politeuma* of the Jewish community. It is this issue, not a concern about the conditions of righteousness before God, that motivated the "dogs" in Philippians 3 to advocate circumcision and kosher observance.[19]

---

[16] On the parenetic schema in this section, see U. B. Müller, "Der Christushymnus Phil 2:6–11," *ZNW* 79 (1988) 17–44.

[17] Sampley emphasizes the importance of such a common agreement about the purpose of a *societas* to its continuation (*Partnership,* 15). Phil 2:12 defines the Philippians' obedience to Paul's exhortation when he is absent as part of God's cosmic plan. H. Giesen plays down the apocalyptic overtones of "fear and trembling" by insisting that Paul is not thinking of the Christian before God but of the trials Christians will face in this life ("'Furcht und Zittern'—vor Gott? Zu Philipper 2,12," *Theologie der Gegenwart* 31 [1988] 86–94). Paul uses a similar expression for his own ministry of preaching Christ crucified among the Corinthians (1 Cor 2:3) and of Titus's reception by them (2 Cor 7:15).

[18] Scholars have been so perplexed over this facet of Paul's behavior that they have concluded either that Luke was wrong to claim that Paul was a Roman citizen or that Paul's failure to make such a claim was due to his desire not to abandon fellow Christians suffering imprisonment with him (Martin, *Philippians,* 55).

[19] Public confusion over the identification of Christians and Jews and ambiguity in Paul's own appeal to the privilege of Roman citizenship are evident in the account of Paul and Silas in Philippi in Acts 16:19–40.

Philippians establishes an apologetic context by claiming that Paul's imprisonment has created a unique occasion for the defense of the gospel before the Praetorian Guard (1:13). Phil 4:22 returns to this theme, with an implied assertion of its success, by including greetings from the Christians of Caesar's household. Inscriptional evidence from Asia Minor confirms the existence of a proconsular headquarters as well as a fiscal staff (members of Caesar's household) in charge of the imperial bank.[20] The conversion of Onesimus, a fellow prisoner, whom Paul sends back to his master, Philemon, confirms the fact that Paul's imprisonment did not exclude the possibility of winning converts.[21] Paul may have converted some slaves or freedpersons attached to the imperial fiscus. This historical possibility does not, however, exhaust the rhetorical function of these references in the correspondence, where they serve as evidence for Paul's claim that his imprisonment is an opportunity for the gospel.

Scholars who rely on Acts 16:11–40 to reconstruct the conflict that led Paul to leave Philippi for Thessalonica (1 Thess 2:2; Phil 1:30) conclude that charges of civic disturbance must have led to Paul's imprisonment.[22] This disturbance may have been fairly widespread. Christians in Philippi also face the possibility of persecution (1:28–30), and 1 Thessalonians emphasizes the apostle's prophetic word that Christians there should anticipate persecution (1 Thess 1:6; 2:14; 3:1–5). The reason for this disturbance and persecution was probably related to the imperial cult. Numismatic evidence for Thessalonica shows that civic virtue was expressed in cultic devotion to the Augustan house.[23] Similar sentiments may have been common at Philippi, which was also a Roman colony. Christians could hardly offer such honors to the city's imperial benefactors. If conversion led to their withdrawal from such participation, they would easily be suspected of subversive activity.[24]

Christ's appearance from heaven with those Thessalonians whose death may have resulted from persecution evokes the symbolism of an imperial visit (1 Thess 4:16–17).[25] A similar terminological conjunction occurs in Phil 3:20: Christians have a heavenly *politeuma,* from which they await the Lord as σωτήρ.[26] Since Paul does not normally use σωτήρ of Christ, the term may

---

[20] Martin, *Philippians,* 51.

[21] Philemon would appear to postdate the Philippian correspondence, since the apostle suggests that he will soon be released (v. 22).

[22] See, e.g., F. B. Craddock, *Philippians* (Atlanta: John Knox, 1985) 12–13.

[23] See Jewett, *Thessalonian Correspondence,* 123–25; K. P. Donfried, "The Cults of Thessalonica and the Thessalonian Correspondence," *NTS* 31 (1985) 341–46.

[24] Jewett, *Thessalonian Correspondence,* 125.

[25] Donfried, "Cults," 344.

[26] Gnilka, *Philipperbrief,* 207.

have been derived from the language of the imperial cult. The political expressions in Phil 3:20–21 may have been taken from those whose views Paul opposed. Paul's "true circumcision" and heavenly *politeuma* reverse positions that can be ascribed to the Jewish community. Richard Stoops, for example, has shown that an apologetic appeal for Jewish privileges, especially those garnered by Jewish communities who had formed their own organization as a *politeuma*, underlies Luke's account of the episode at Ephesus in Acts 19:23–41. He notes that Luke's argument follows a pattern evident in Philo and Josephus: Roman officials should uphold the privileges of those who are innocent victims of a mob incited to riot. In fact, a number of the imperial decrees gathered by Josephus concerning Jewish privileges are directed to Ephesus.[27] Suspected by the local populace for their withdrawal from common pieties, Gentile converts to Christianity could seek to identify with the local Jewish community.[28]

Within this context, Paul's emphasis on his prior status as a member of Israel and the reversal that has resulted from coming to know Christ (3:4–11) has striking consequences. It may even increase his chances of sharing the sufferings of Christ (v. 10). Paul's own credentials as a Jew are clearly superior to claims advanced by his opponents, who may have been Gentile Christians seeking to share Israel's heritage.[29] Rather than elevating a person's status, Paul argues, conversion implies an "emptying" analogous to that of Christ. This process anticipates the Christian's eventual participation in the exaltation/resurrection of Christ (3:11, 21). Christians are not to seek their *politeuma* on earth, since it is a heavenly, not an earthly, reality. As a consequence, Christians will remain vulnerable to suffering that results from their confession that Christ is κύριος. The hymnic section in Phil 2:6–11 also undercuts claims that any earthly powers might make for honors or allegiance,[30] just as it sets the pattern for Paul's own shift from privilege to the abandonment of all that he held valuable and then to imprisonment and suffering. Christ's exaltation supports Paul's confidence that he will also share the resurrection of Christ.

---

[27] R. F. Stoops, "Riot and Assembly: The Social Context of Acts 19:23–41," *JBL* 108 (1989) 73–91.

[28] Gnilka notes that *politeuma* language is unique to Philippians but was used for Jewish diaspora communities (*Philipperbrief*, 206). White argues that the official Roman attitude toward Jews was colored by the civil discord between Jews and the various groups of the populace in Alexandria (*Letters*, 17).

[29] So Gnilka, *Philipperbrief*, 186–89.

[30] E. Schüssler Fiorenza, "Wisdom Mythology and the Christological Hymns of the New Testament," in *Aspects of Wisdom in Judaism and Early Christianity* (ed. R. Wilken; Notre Dame: University of Notre Dame Press, 1975) 17–41.

II. THE CHRIST HYMN AS
GOVERNING METAPHOR

Theological interpretation of the Christ hymn has been preoccupied with the problem of whether or not it presupposes a preexistent Christ who surrendered equality with God upon assuming humanity.[31] The language of the passage is ambiguous, though μορφή θεοῦ would commonly suggest the "appearance" or "shape" of God, an identification somewhat different from the divine "image" attributed to Adam.[32] At the same time, the concluding exaltation is described as a new response of God's saving power, not the return of a heavenly redeemer figure to his former place of glory.[33] Pauline additions to the hymn emphasize the degradation of the human death, death on a cross (v. 8c), and the exaltation of Jesus as Lord over all the powers of the cosmos (v. 10c).[34] Since the operative elements in the hymn involve self-emptying to the point of death on a cross and subsequent exaltation by God, the nature of Christ's relationship to God prior to the cross/exaltation remains unspecified. Scholars have been unable to find decisive evidence to determine whether or not the expression οὐχ ἁρπαγμὸν ἡγήσατο τὸ εἶναι ἴσα θεῷ describes a simple condition of preexistent equality with God or an activity of grasping or attempting to exploit an equality with God, which would suggest some form of rebellion against God.[35]

In its immediate context, Paul almost seems to forget about the sweeping theological metaphors of the hymn. The exhortation in Phil 2:12–18 looks to blameless behavior by the Philippians even in the event of the apostle's death.[36] Paul and the Philippians will be able to rejoice together in the fruits

---

[31] Gnilka, *Philipperbrief*, 111–31. J. D. G. Dunn adopts the view that the "likeness to God" represents the likeness attributed to Adam in Genesis. He interprets the hymn on the basis of an Adam typology derived from Romans and 1 Corinthians (*Christology in the Making: A New Testament Inquiry into the Origins of the Doctrine of the Incarnation* [Philadelphia: Westminster, 1980] 113–21).

[32] So D. Steenburg, "The Case Against the Synonymity of *Morphē* and *Eikōn*," *JSNT* 34 (1988) 77–86.

[33] This concern with God's activity evident in the life of a historical personage distinguishes Phil 2:6–11 from mythic patterns of expression that may be employed as the language of the hymn (so G. Barth, *Der Brief an die Philipper* [Zürcher Bibelkommentar NT 9; Zurich: Theologischer Verlag, 1979] 45–48).

[34] Though Fitzmyer proposes an Aramaic rendering for the phrase "of heavenly, earthly and chthonic," which would remove the necessity of treating it as a gloss ("Aramaic Background," 476), the phrase seems to intrude on the citation of Isa 45:23.

[35] Martin, *Philippians*, 96–97; idem, *Carmen Christi: Philippians ii. 5–11 in Recent Interpretation and in the Setting of Early Christian Worship* (SNTSMS 4; Cambridge: Cambridge University Press, 1967) 134–64.

[36] Barth, *Brief an die Philipper,* 48–51.

of his labor "in the day of Christ" (vv. 16–18). Is the hymn merely theological decoration for parenesis about the unity of the Philippians with one another and their fellowship in preaching the gospel after Paul's demise? The hymn suggests that renouncing at risk to one's life even the legitimate appearances of status and exaltation in order to identify with the lowly reflects God's saving activity. The truth of this claim, Paul suggests, can be verified in the experience of his own ministry as it is known to the Philippians.[37] Paul makes two such appeals to experience in Phil 1:1–3:1: (1) his own defense of the gospel even while he is imprisoned (1:7b, 12–20); (2) Epaphroditus's recovery from a life-threatening illness (2:25–30). This section has been linked to Paul's own uncertain fate through verbal repetition of the word λειτουργία, which represents both Paul's self-offering for the faith of the Philippians (2:17) and the service Epaphroditus has rendered to Paul on their behalf (2:25, 30).[38] Though Paul's own return to the Philippians remains in doubt, Epaphroditus's homecoming is to be a cause for rejoicing.[39]

If we accept the hypothesis that Phil 1:1–3:1 represents the thanksgiving, body, parenesis, and concluding travel plans of one letter, further symmetry in the construction of the letter highlights the Christ hymn. Paul's description of his own experience in defense of the gospel, with its allusions to the activities of other preachers and a reflection on the future "apostolic parousia," leads into exhortation to the Philippians about their own behavior (1:12–2:5). In the process Paul reminds them that they share the same ἀγών which they see him undergoing (1:30). Following the hymn, Paul returns to the theme of Philippian obedience in the absence of the apostle, whom they are nonetheless to consider very much present, and then moves from the possible future activity of Timothy among them to the experience of Epaphroditus's service and return (2:12–3:1).

The hortatory material in Phil 4:2–9 is divided among the letters in various ways by those scholars who accept the three-letter hypothesis. The urging that Euodia and Syntyche τὸ αὐτὸ φρονεῖν ἐν κυρίῳ falls most naturally into

---

[37] Meeks stresses the importance of experiential confirmation of Paul's "paradox of the cross" in Pauline communities: "Paul and others who are weak in terms of the dominant value system nevertheless do powerful things — for example, they survive despite the most extraordinary pressures and afflictions — therefore this power must not be their own, but God's" (*Urban Christians*, 183).

[38] W. Schenk notes the verbal links between this section and *peristasis* catalogues elsewhere in Paul (*Die Philipperbriefe des Paulus: Kommentar* [Stuttgart: Kohlhammer, 1984] 237–39).

[39] Timothy's relationship to the congregation if and when he arrives cannot fill this function of representing the joyous reception of the apostle whose defense of the gospel has brought him near death. See Schenk (*Philipperbriefe*, 230–34) on the verbal treatment of Timothy in the Pauline letters.

the general exhortation of 2:1–5.[40] The hortatory *sententiae* in 4:4–9 might all belong to a single letter or be divided at v. 8 with τὸ λοιπόν.[41]

If we understand theology to be exposition of, or reflection upon, central Christian topoi such as the saving effect of the cross, God's plan of salvation, the relationship of the community to Christ, Christ's relationship to God, or the future destiny of Christians, then we should admit that Phil 1:1–3:1; 4:4–7 is not theological in intent. To be sure, the Christ hymn at its center contains the metaphorical seeds for centuries of christological reflection, but Paul's rhetorical activity in the letter has not developed such suggestions. Instead, the hymn sets out the central Christian metaphor whose effects are to be detected in the experiences of Paul, Epaphroditus, and the Philippians as they serve the gospel. Though Paul never says so directly in this section, their "blamelessness in the Day of the Lord" guarantees an exaltation like that of Christ.

As F. Craddock has observed, Philippians plays on the problem of absence and presence. He describes Philippians as an epistle of "intimate distance."[42] The thanksgiving (1:3–11) and the letter acknowledging the Philippians' aid (4:10–20) evoke the time when Paul was present in Philippi. Yet each description of Christian life is marked with a reflection on the approach of death. Paul's expression of love for the Philippians in the thanksgiving is especially strong. He takes the unusual step of guaranteeing his feeling for them with an oath formula,[43] an expression otherwise reserved for affirmations of apostolic integrity (2 Cor 1:23; 1 Thess 2:5, 10).[44] Faced with the need to assure that the κοινωνία of the Philippians will endure despite his permanent absence, Paul exhibits the affection that will bind them together in their imitation of the apostle (1:29–30; 2:12; 3:17; 4:9a).[45]

Within this rhetorical context, we can understand the ambiguity of Paul's reference to his future "with Christ" in Phil 1:23, which is embedded in strong reassurances that it would be "better" if Paul remained to encourage the Philippians in the προκοπή and χαρά of their faith. Since Christ now reigns in heaven over the powers of the world, an apostle who is "with Christ" is not entirely separated from the addressees to whom he has been united by such bonds of love. Paul has rendered the issue of his own death or

---

[40] So Gnilka, *Philipperbrief*, 165.

[41] So Gnilka (*Philipperbrief*, 168–70), who finds the repetition of the peace wish (vv. 7, 9) an indication that this section contains two separate letter closings.

[42] Craddock, *Philippians*, 6.

[43] See also Rom 1:9, which is to a community that Paul does not know.

[44] J.-F. Collange, *The Epistle of Saint Paul to the Philippians* (London: Epworth, 1979) 46–48.

[45] So G. P. Wiles, *Paul's Intercessory Prayers* (SNTSMS 24; Cambridge: Cambridge University Press, 1974) 194–99.

life indifferent. This confidence in the saving power of Christ's exaltation does not imply that Paul is abandoning the images of resurrection, joyful reunion of believers, and judgment that he uses elsewhere.[46] For Paul the expression σὺν Χριστῷ εἶναι represents the goal of all Christian life.[47] Paul's eschatological perspective continues to be determined by the anticipation of Christ's coming, when the blamelessness and righteousness of the community will glorify God (1:10–11; 2:16; 3:21; 4:5).[48]

III. EXALTED LORD AND
THE HEAVENLY *POLITEUMA*

Scholars who identify the opponents in Phil 3:2–4:1 with charismatic missionaries of the type presupposed by 2 Corinthians think that Paul's insistence on qualifying the perfection reached in this life (3:12–16) counters an excessive emphasis on Christ as resurrection power.[49] Paul affirms that the power which enabled Christ to subdue "all things" will transform into the glory of his resurrected body those who share the lowliness of Christ's suffering (3:20–21). This possibility is grounded in the exaltation of Christ over all powers, but it does not apply to the life of Christians in this world, which remains marked by the cross.[50]

In the consolation letter (Phil 1:1–3:1) Paul used the image of the lowly one now exalted as Lord to overcome the distance and division that might be created by his absence. In the polemical letter (Phil 3:2–4:1), the figure of the lowly/exalted Lord plays a somewhat different role. As we have already suggested, Paul himself exemplifies the practical choice of "lowliness" in his rejection of the former marks of his status as a member of Israel in order to "know the Lord" (3:4–11). He insists that Christians cannot accept those who

[46] See the discussion of the relationship between Phil 1:23 and 1 Thess 4:17 in P. Siber, *Mit Christus Leben: Eine Studie zur paulinischen Auferstehungshoffnung* (Zurich: Theologischer Verlag, 1971) 86–94.

[47] So Gnilka (*Philipperbrief*, 75–93), who emphasizes the apocalyptic imagery of this passage, pointing to texts such as *1 Enoch* 103:2–4, where the fate of the righteous dead is preferable to that of the living.

[48] Phil 1:11 represents Paul's usual teaching on "righteousness": the community filled with the fruits of righteousness will stand blameless on the day of judgment (so J. Reumann, *"Righteousness" in the New Testament: "Justification" in the United States Lutheran–Roman Catholic Dialogue* [Philadelphia: Fortress; New York: Paulist, 1982] 63).

[49] Reumann, *Righteousness*, 62.

[50] Martin, who treats Philippians as a unity, rejects the suggestion that Phil 2:6–11 uses the example of Christ as parenesis, because Paul would then encourage Christians to think of themselves as exalted, an attitude typical of his opponents (*Philippians*, 99). We have argued, however, that Paul does wish to imply that there is a sense in which his departure to be "with Christ" will not cut him off from κοινωνία with the Philippians.

seek to reinstate the physical marks of belonging to the earthly *politeuma* of the Jewish community.

The carefully structured sentences in 3:2–11[51] use the rhetorical device of apologetic autobiography to ground the claim that "knowing Christ" reveals that all human signs of religious status are garbage. The contrasts that play such a prominent role in the polemical arguments of Galatians and Romans — flesh versus Spirit (3:3) and "my own righteousness through the law" versus "righteousness from God through faith of Christ" (v. 9) — appear in this section.[52] They are not, however, the governing metaphors in the passage.[53] The dominant image emerges in the chiastic pattern of vv. 10–11, where "knowing Christ" is specified as knowing the "power of his resurrection." The concrete effects of that power are defined as sharing in the present in the sufferings of Christ, even conforming to his death, in anticipation of sharing his resurrection. This expression recalls the imagery of Phil 2:6–11.[54] The antithetical structure of the passage leads the reader to presume that sharing the power of the risen Christ excludes participation or confidence in the patterns of righteousness characteristic of Judaism. Since the triad of phrases about Paul's own obedience to the law in v. 6 includes persecution of the church, one might presume an association between such righteousness and the persecution suffered by Paul and his associates.[55] The text itself does not, however, provide linguistic markers that would necessitate such a development of its argument.

Phil 3:12–16 introduces a new term into the discussion—"perfection." Scholars who equate those who consider themselves τέλειοι (v. 15) with an

---

[51] See Schenk, *Philipperbrief*, 250–52.

[52] The sarcastic or heavily ironic use of apostolic autobiography in passages like 2 Cor 11:21–29 need not be brought into the interpretation of this section. Paul's claim to have been blameless in righteousness (v. 6) should not be taken ironically (so Gnilka, *Philipperbrief*, 189–91).

[53] Reumann notes that "righteousness" appears in Philippians only in individual terms. It has none of the communal or cosmic overtones that one finds in Romans (*Righteousness*, 63). Since Paul apparently uses the contrast between the two types of righteousness in this apologetic autobiography without further development, "righteousness" does not appear to be a key element in the dispute between Paul and his Philippian opponents.

[54] Craddock, *Philippians*, 58–60. It is also characteristic of Pauline language about manifesting the death of Jesus in his flesh (2 Cor 1:5, 7; 4:10) and his expectation of future exaltation (Rom 8:29) (so Gnilka, *Philipperbrief*, 196).

[55] However, 1 Thess 2:14–16 makes the connection only by analogy. The suffering of the Gentiles from their own people gives them a place in the shared suffering of the churches of Judea. In Gal 1:13 Paul's persecution of the church is associated with his righteousness as a Jew in a way that makes the "blame" attached to such behavior more evident. 1 Cor 15:9–10 argues that the blame attached to Paul's career as persecutor of the church has been erased by his apostolic labors.

ideology like that of those Corinthians who made claims to wisdom, perfection, and "reigning as kings" (1 Corinthians 1–4) either presume that Paul has switched from the problem of judaizing to the dangers of libertinism or presume that the appeal of Judaism had been that persons would attain perfection through it.[56] Paul guards his claim to know the power of the risen Christ against the misconception that he has attained the goal of Christian life. The imagery of the passage recalls both the imperial cult and athletic contests of a Roman colony like Philippi. When Paul spoke of himself and the Philippians as participants in the same ἀγών (1:27–30) and now uses the imagery of running a race whose goal is set by the upward call of God in Christ (3:13–14), his readers may have been reminded of the games staged to honor members of the imperial family. When Paul equates his own success with that of his churches (2:16), he could also be referring to such images, for the patron of a runner, who has provided material support for his training, could be described as being crowned when his protégé became victorious.[57]

Perhaps we should not attempt to construe "perfection" in terms of the spiritual and ethical problems of 1 Corinthians, none of which are alluded to in Philippians, but rather in the context of the athletic image that Paul has introduced. Scholars have frequently noted that Paul's letter of acknowledgment (4:10–20) appears uneasy in its expression of thanks for the aid sent.[58] Documentary papyri show that thanks for gifts, solicitation of needed supplies, and even injunctions not to trouble oneself over unneeded gifts were commonplace. As a petitioner requesting aid, however, Paul might be seen as inferior to those from whom he receives it.[59] In Phil 4:10–20, Paul avoids the position of *client* by evoking the Stoic ethical theme of self-sufficiency and contentment achieved through adaptation to any circumstances (4:11–13). Moreover, Paul's special relationship with the Philippians may have mitigated somewhat the social consequences of such patterns of giving and receiving (4:15–16).[60] Yet Paul takes pains to avoid any appearance of subordination to the Philippians by emphasizing the occasional character

---

[56] Craddock, *Philippians,* 61–63. Schenk appeals to Jewish apocalyptic, Qumran, and Philo for indications that righteousness, perfection, and ascent into the heavenly world could have been combined in a Jewish framework (*Philipperbrief,* 291–304).

[57] See White, *Letters,* 38.

[58] Gnilka, *Philipperbrief,* 171.

[59] Sampley, *Partnership,* 52–58.

[60] Commenting on the opposition's charges that such aid received from Macedonia is evidence of Paul's deceit (2 Cor 11:7–11), Furnish points out that Paul would have become dependent on those who supported him (*II Corinthians,* 507–8). P. Marshall argues that the friendship between Paul and the Philippians removes any possibility of seeing Paul as inferior to or dependent on the Philippians who have supported him (*Enmity in Corinth: Social Conventions in Paul's Relations with the Corinthians* [WUNT 2/23; Tübingen: Mohr (Siebeck), 1987] 157–64).

of such gifts. He presents himself as independent of any need for aid. Instead, material assistance is subordinated to the true purpose of their fellowship, the fruit which comes from preaching the gospel and which represents a pleasing offering to God (4:17–18).[61]

Paul's allusion to his present circumstances as though he were expecting to be crowned as victor in the race once he had completed his training reaffirms his high "status" as apostle/contestant even though he is supported by the Philippians. Uncertainty about his position as τέλειος may have been generated by his continuing imprisonment. If Phil 3:2–4:1 was written sometime after the other two letters, neither the triumphant departure to be "with Christ" nor the preferable return of the apostle to nurture the faith of his converts has occurred. Paul's reflection on his present situation in vv. 12–16 enables him to incorporate this awkward delay into the schema he has established. He can then return to the autobiographical apologetic against his opponents with the appeal to become imitators of the apostle (v. 17).

The concluding section (3:17–4:1) distinguishes Paul and his imitators from the "many who walk as enemies of the cross of Christ." The only other reference to the cross in Philippians is the Pauline gloss on the Christ hymn (2:8). The contrasts between lowliness and glory as well as the reference to the power by which all things are subjected to Christ in vv. 20–21 also echo Paul's understanding of that hymn.[62] Once again, the rhetorical construction, using topoi designed to discredit the moral character of one's opposition (v. 19),[63] renders identification with the opponents absurd. Some of the terms of this polemic may derive from the pagan-Jewish polemics of the Greco-Roman period.[64] Josephus says of Apion that he "has the mind of an ass and the impudence of a dog, which his countrymen are wont to worship" (*Ag. Ap.* 2.7 §86).[65] Paul's opening salvo, "dogs, evil workers, mutilation" (3:2), has the

---

[61] The topos that God (the gods) will supply the needs of one who is generous (to them) recurs in the collection appeal of 2 Cor 9:6–12 (see H. D. Betz, *2 Corinthians 8 and 9* [Philadelphia: Fortress, 1985] 109–17).

[62] Martin, *Philippians*, 149–50.

[63] As Gnilka recognizes when he notes how difficult it is to reconstruct the preaching of the opposition (*Philipperbrief*, 211–18). Since Paul never attacks circumcision except in polemical contexts, some form of judaizing is involved, but the characterization of the opponents as persons whose "god is their belly" and who have their minds set on earthly things could as well be taken from Hellenistic Jewish preaching against pagans (so Barth, *Brief an die Philipper,* 67).

[64] See L. T. Johnson, "The New Testament's Anti-Jewish Slander and the Conventions of Ancient Polemic," *JBL* 108 (1989) 434–36. The same polemic is also reflected in intra-Jewish sectarian disputes, though our evidence is primarily from Josephus's treatment of the zealots and Qumran (ibid. 436–41).

[65] Cited in Johnson, "Slander," 435.

appearance of pagan anti-Jewish slander. Similarly, the depravity of opponents destined to destruction, "whose god is their belly and their glory, shame" (v. 19), could easily be at home in Jewish polemic against pagans. The reader of Philippians may have been somewhat shocked to hear Paul, a Jew, turn such rhetoric against fellow Christians. The pagan-Jewish polemic on which Paul draws was forged in the struggles of diaspora Jews to secure their position in the Greco-Roman cities and to counter the resentment, as well as the social conflict, that their claims often provoked.[66]

Though Paul's own difficulties might suggest that Christians ought to seek to establish a secure place for themselves within the diverse communities of the city, Paul's response denies them that option. They cannot invoke the links between Christianity and Judaism to establish their claim to a place within the city. Instead, this section summons Christians to see themselves as members of a heavenly *politeuma,* awaiting the arrival of their Lord and σωτήρ much as members of the earthly city anticipated imperial visitations.[67] Both the *politeuma* and the body which is marked as belonging to the Christian community are "from heaven." They cannot be attained by earthly means.

Is it merely religious status as members of the Jewish community that the enemies of the cross of Christ held out? Such a struggle might, in itself, create dissension such as the rioting caused by Christian preaching in the Jewish community in Rome under Claudius (Suetonius, *Claudius* 25). Or was their religious posture one which also carried with it some form of integration into the earthly society, a *politeuma* that Paul considers incompatible with the lordship of the crucified Christ? In that case, we might suppose that such persons became enemies of the cross of Christ by exercising a zeal similar to that which had made Paul himself a persecutor. Though they may not have persecuted fellow Christians, they could have agreed that some of their number, like the imprisoned apostle, deserved punishment for disturbing civic order.[68]

---

[66] Alexandrian evidence shows that the struggles among various groups in the city to establish their status led to social conflict. Claudius's decree in 41 CE rejected Jewish attempts to move into the class of Greek citizens. The Greek populace, on the other hand, was denied the right to form an independent council — a privilege which the Jews, organized as a *politeuma,* did enjoy (see the discussion in White, *Letters,* 16–19). A petition from a resident of Alexandria against being forced to pay the poll tax on the grounds that his parents were Alexandrians and that he had received a Greek education may have failed, since a scribe has noted that the petitioner was a Jew (ibid., 128). Claudius also prohibited Jews from forcing their way into athletic contests presided over by *gymnarchoi.* Nor were they to admit to their community any Jews from the outside, whether from Egypt or Syria (ibid., 135–36).

[67] Gnilka, *Philipperbrief,* 207.

[68] This hypothesis coheres with the suggestion that Paul's defense in Phil 1:12–30 hints at the fact that some Christians use Paul's imprisonment as evidence against the divine character of

Paul's exhortation to the Thessalonians in 1 Thess 4:9–12 advocated a posture of withdrawal from public affairs. At the same time, Paul had to defend this posture against the common perception that those who advocated withdrawal from civic life were freeloading, meddlesome Cynics or atheistic Epicureans. He does so by advocating a self-sufficiency grounded in manual labor, which is to commend the Thessalonian Christians to outsiders. Though manual labor was held in contempt by the aristocracy, this advice may have been intended to indicate that Christians would "stick to their place" in the social order.[69] Philippians does not contain such direct advice about the social place of Christians. Perhaps this difference indicates that the socioeconomic makeup of the Philippian community differed from that in Thessalonica. Or perhaps the difference occurs because Paul himself had not set an example by laboring to supply his needs in Philippi as he had in Thessalonica (1 Thess 2:9) and Corinth (1 Cor 9:4–27) but had depended on the Philippians to supply them.[70] The exhortation in Phil 4:5 and 8 assumes that the Christians will commend themselves to outsiders by exhibiting those virtues conventionally attributed to good persons.

Paul's brief comment, "The Lord is near" (4:5), raises the question of how such eschatological statements functioned in his discourse. Is reference to the impending Day of the Lord merely a motivational stimulus to the life of virtue? Or is it central to the apostle's evident determination to keep Christians from involving themselves in the conflicts of the earthly city? In the Philippian letters, Paul has drawn definite, practical conclusions from the governing metaphor for Christian belief set forth in Phil 2:6–11. His particular fate as imprisoned apostle marks him as one who shares the sufferings of Christ[71] and may anticipate resurrection transformation as well. Consequently, his imprisonment serves to advance and defend the gospel rather than to hinder it. Since Christ rejected equality with God for the slavelike

---

the apostle's mission. It also suits the suspicion of the author of 2 Tim 4:16–18 that Paul was abandoned in making his first *apologia*. Further hints that Paul's imprisonment led Christian leaders to abandon him might be found in the disappearance of Jerusalem Christians from the narrative about Paul's imprisonment there in Acts 21:27–26:32 (see P. J. Achtemeier, *The Quest for Unity in the New Testament Church* [Philadelphia: Fortress, 1987] 42, 55, 60).

[69] See A. J. Malherbe, *Paul and the Thessalonians: The Philosophic Tradition of Pastoral Care* (Philadelphia: Fortress, 1987) 99–107.

[70] A fact represented in the tradition of Paul's relationship with the purple cloth merchant, Lydia, in Acts 16:14–15.

[71] J. H. Schütz notes that Paul speaks of Christ's sufferings only when they are represented in the experience of the suffering apostle; he does not establish an independent image of the suffering Christ (*Paul and the Anatomy of Apostolic Authority* [SNTSMS 26; Cambridge: Cambridge University Press, 1975] 243–45).

humiliation of the cross, all forms of human status and every attempt to secure one's social or religious position by gaining status is rejected. In the Philippian context, this conviction finds its most striking representation in the opposition of those who await their σωτήρ from the heavenly *politeuma* to any attempt to secure status through the "righteousness" of the Jewish community. The rhetorical strategy of Philippians is not to argue the case for "faith of Christ" and Spirit over against the law as Paul does in Galatians and Romans but to tar the opponents with polemical topoi drawn from pagan–Jewish conflicts. Within the Philippian community itself, Paul applies the governing metaphor to relationships. The harmony and devotion to a common purpose, which are critical to the mission of testifying to the gospel, will be fostered if the Philippians follow the example of Christ in surrendering their self-interests to those of others (2:1–5). If they imitate the apostle, the Philippians will share his struggle, his willingness to count all human social and religious distinctions as nothing compared with knowing Christ, and his efforts to finish the race that has been initiated by the divine call from above.

9 FRIENDS AND ENEMIES IN THE POLITICS OF HEAVEN

Reading Theology in Philippians

Stanley K. Stowers
Brown University

ALTHOUGH PHEME PERKINS and I agree in many areas, our chapters illustrate rather different approaches to Paul's letters and "theology." I consider such contrast a useful display of interpretive options. Both Perkins and I agree that Paul's theology cannot be considered in separation from readings of particular letters. Like all readers, we also proceed by constructing what literary theorists call "metatexts."[1] Metatexts consist of the causalities, metaphors, and metonymies that readers construct in the process of reading.[2] We differ most in the ways in which we go about creating those metatexts.

Perkins proceeds by first establishing her position on three traditional issues: the integrity of the letter, the nature of the "opposition in Philippians," and the assumption that 2:6–11 is based on a pre-Pauline hymn. From these assumptions about *events behind the text,* she proceeds to construct an account of historical events and social circumstances that serve as both causal and contextual explanations for particular linguistic features of the text. With this metatext, she then focuses her exposition on themes that Christianity has come to categorize as theological. The whole is skillful and illuminating.

I proceed somewhat differently. My initial questions signal a different starting point: What kind of literature is Philippians, and what cultural codes and texts constitute it? In my view, an adequate reading of Philippians would begin with a "thick description" of these codes, followed by an exposition of how in complex ways these varied codes and generic conceptions find a particular historical instantiation in Philippians. As the words of Robert Scholes

---

[1] Robert Scholes, *Protocols of Reading* (New Haven: Yale University Press, 1989) 1–50.

[2] Hume pointed out that the figures of resemblance, contiguity, and causality are the only three principles of connection between "ideas"; see Scholes, *Protocols,* 18, 50.

suggest, this approach is even more necessary since Paul's letters belong to a very different culture, and one distant in time:

> *Reading* is possible only to the extent that the actual reader shares a semantic and syntactic field with the writer. A "field" in this sense is a set of codes and paradigms that enable and constrain meaning. The further estranged the reader is from the writer (by time, space, language or temperament) the more *interpretation* must be called upon to provide a conscious construction of unavailable or faded codes and paradigms.[3]

The questions of integrity, the nature of opposition in Philippians, and the significance of 2:6–11 will be answered in the process that I have suggested above, but they cannot be answered first.

I will also be explicit about my understanding of theology in Paul's letters. Theology is not a timeless universal set of categories and schemes of meaning so that, for example, a Greek-reading Buddhist or even a traditional Jew would simply *see* theology in Paul's letters. Theology is a method of organizing religious knowledge that arose at a particular time in the history of Christianity and that presupposes a class of knowledge producers, knowledge consumers, and certain institutions. The Buddhist or the Jew might well understand the text and yet simply neither focus on what Christians have come to value as significant nor relate and organize features of the text in a "theological" way. This lack of universality is difficult for Christian interpreters to understand, since Christianity has viewed other religions as shadows or *simulacra* of Christianity, the universal religious experience. Since Paul, the Jewish follower of Christ, deserves to be considered at most only a precursor of Christian theology, we risk distortion in reading his letters for theology. But reading always looks in two directions: not only back toward the original context, but also forward to the reader's own situation, own concerns, and own cultural codes and texts.[4] As Roland Barthes says, all of us, including the sternest historians, rewrite "the text of the work within the text of our lives."[5] This is what we do when we find theology in Paul's letters. This activity need not viciously distort a historical reading, however, if one reads with an awareness of what she or he is doing. Constructing theology out of Paul's letters is even more legitimate, because we can genuinely consider Paul a precursor of theology.

The question of genre and cultural codes in Philippians confronts the reader with a massive, almost overwhelming number of connections with

---

[3] R. Scholes, *Textual Power* (New Haven: Yale University Press, 1985) 48.

[4] Scholes, *Protocols,* 7.

[5] R. Barthes, "Day by Day with Roland Barthes," in *On Signs* (ed. M. Blonsky; Baltimore: Johns Hopkins University Press, 1985) 101.

ancient, especially Greek, friendship motifs. The more particularly Jewish and early Christian codes—often allusions to what God has done, is doing, and will do—also prominently manifest themselves. I avoid the usual temptation of emphasizing only these more particularly Jewish and early Christian codes and of ignoring the rest, since that tactic can only lead to anachronism. Rather, the more interesting question concerns the relationship between the two and the reasons why the "Christian material" lies so deeply imbedded in the language of friendship. As Perkins properly emphasizes, Philippians also displays a significant vocabulary of politics. Her main thesis attempts to explain this political language as part of a warning for the Philippians not to avail themselves of the earthly Roman or Jewish commonwealths in times of persecution. I think this question of political language also is significant, but I will forward a different solution.

I. A HORTATORY LETTER
OF FRIENDSHIP

Scholars of ancient letter writing have long identified Philippians as a letter of friendship (φιλικὸς τύπος).[6] This essential fact has gone virtually unnoticed in the commentaries on Philippians.[7] The letter is so densely packed with the motifs of friendship that it lies far beyond the scope of this chapter to comment on each section. I will attempt, however, to outline the essential features and logic of the ancient Greek institution of φιλία as reflected in the letter.

Ancient friendship has very little in common with the modern institution of private or personal friendship.[8] Indeed, the ancient institution of friendship encompassed both politics and business. Greek and Roman writers frequently pointed out that friendship is the basis for both political and economic activity and institutions. Although Greek friendship as depicted by

[6] Heikki Koskenniemi, *Studien zur Idee und Phraseologie des griechischen Briefes bis 400 n. Chr.* (Helsinki: Suomalainen Tiedeakatemia, 1956) 115–27; Klaus Thraede, *Grundzüge griechisch-römischer Brieftopic* (Zetemata 48; Munich: Beck, 1970); Stanley Stowers, *Letter Writing in Greco-Roman Antiquity* (Library of Early Christianity 5; Philadelphia: Westminster, 1986) 50–70.

[7] The only commentator I have discovered who emphasizes friendship in Philippians is L. Michael White, "Morality Between Two Worlds: A Paradigm of Friendship in Philippians," in *Greeks, Romans and Christians: Essays in Honor of Abraham J. Malherbe* (ed. D. L. Balch, E. Ferguson, and W. A. Meeks; Minneapolis: Fortress, 1990).

[8] On ancient friendship, see G. Hermann, *Ritualized Friendship and the Greek City* (Cambridge: Cambridge University Press, 1987); R. Saller, *Personal Patronage under the Early Empire* (Cambridge: Cambridge University Press, 1982) 1–40; Horst Hutter, *Politics as Friendship* (Waterloo, Ont.: Wilfrid Laurier University Press, 1978); P. Marshall, *Enmity in Corinth: Social Conventions in Paul's Relations with the Corinthians* (WUNT 2/23; Tübingen: Mohr [Siebeck], 1987). My account of Greek and Roman friendship draws on these sources.

Aristotle and others found its ideal in the friendship between aristocratic males of equal social status, Aristotle readily admits that ordinary usage also employed φιλία and φίλος for relationships between parents and children and close kin (*Nichomachean Ethics,* book 8). Thus, friendship in its broadest sense was a structure of overlapping relationships and institutions. One can aptly speak about "types" of ancient friendship while recognizing some common features.

The sample of a friendly letter in the epistolary handbook of Pseudo-Demetrius provides a useful starting point for discussing friendship in Philippians.

> Even though I have been separated from you for a long time, I suffer this in body only. For I can never forget you or the impeccable way we were raised together from childhood up. Knowing that I myself am genuinely concerned about your affairs, and that I have worked unstintingly for what is most advantageous for you, I have assumed that you, too, have the same opinion of me and will refuse me in nothing. You will do well, therefore, to give close attention to the members of my household lest they need anything, to assist them in whatever they might need, and to write to us about whatever you should choose (*Epistolary Types* 1).[9]

In introducing this epitome of a friendly letter, Demetrius notes that people in public office especially employ such letters and that not only equals use friendly letters but also superiors writing to inferiors. "Superiors" could be such not only in status or office but also in character or experience. In giving exhortation, a more experienced friend wrote to a less experienced friend.[10] According to Greco-Roman thought, then, friendship provided the context for moral instruction, including exhortation by letter. The classic case is Seneca's letters to Lucilius. Seneca, the more experienced friend, takes the role of psychagogue to Lucilius, trying to guide his progress in development of character so that both will be equals.[11] Seneca writes letters that display models of character for Lucilius, often presenting himself as the model.

We can best understand Philippians as a hortatory or psychagogic letter of friendship. It differs from Seneca's letters in being addressed to a community of friends rather than an individual. Paul aims for the Philippians to become people of a certain quality or type, but not as isolated individuals. He describes his role as a psychagogue for the Philippians when he says, "But to remain in the flesh is more necessary on your account. . . . I shall remain

---

[9] Trans. A. J. Malherbe, *Ancient Epistolary Theorists* (SBLSBS 19; Atlanta: Scholars Press, 1988) 33.

[10] On exhortation, see A. J. Malherbe, *Paul and the Thessalonians: The Philosophic Tradition of Pastoral Care* (Philadelphia: Fortress, 1987) 69–78; Stowers, *Letter Writing,* 91–106.

[11] I. Hadot, *Seneca und die griechisch-römische Tradition der Seelenleitung* (Berlin: de Gruyter, 1969).

and continue with you all, for your progress and joy in the faith" (1:24–25).[12] Similarly, he prays that "your love may abound more and more, with knowledge and all discernment, so that you may approve what is excellent" (1:9–10). Throughout the letter, Paul presents himself as a model of one who is struggling in this process. He presses on toward the goal and strains forward toward the prize (3:12–14).

The first line of Demetrius's sample letter illustrates one of the stock motifs of the friendly letter, the theme of presence and absence.[13] The sample letter in the handbook of Pseudo-Libanius consists of only two sentences, and the second again displays the presence–absence motif: "For it is a holy thing to honor genuine friends when they are present, and to speak to them when they are absent."[14] These handbooks merely suggest a theme that could be worked out in complex ways in letters of friendship.

Paul artfully develops the motif in Philippians. He is faced with the alternatives of being with Christ or remaining with the Philippians for their benefit (1:19–26). Paul then uses the theme to frame the exhortation in 1:27–2:13, including the so-called Christ hymn, with the ethos of friendship.

> Only let your manner of life be worthy of the gospel of Christ, so that whether I come and see you or am absent, I may hear . . . (1:27). Therefore, my beloved, as you have always obeyed, so now, not only as in my presence but much more in my absence, work out your own salvation with fear and trembling (2:12).

Ancient writers on friendship say that one of its requirements is that friends spend time together and be present for one another. The letter of friendship claimed to be a substitute for actual presence and a medium for dealing with the problem of absence.[15]

Expressions of affection and longing to be with one's friends were considered appropriate for letters of friendship and manifest themselves in commonplace phraseology and topoi.[16] Paul thinks it "just" (δίκαιον) to regard the Philippians so highly since they are "in his heart" (1:7) and he "yearns for" (ἐπιποθῶ) all of them with "the affection (σπλάγχνα) of Christ Jesus" (v. 8). In 4:1 he declares that he loves and longs for the Philippians. Epaphroditus, who has been separated from his fellow Philippians, "longs for them" and is distressed at the knowledge that the Philippians have worried about him (2:26).

---

[12] Unless otherwise specified, translations are from the Revised Standard Version.

[13] The motif is discussed by Koskenniemi (*Studien*) and Thraede (*Grundzüge*).

[14] Trans. Malherbe, *Theorists*, 75.

[15] See, e.g., Cicero, *Ep. ad. Fam.* 2.4.1; *De Amic.* 44; Seneca, *Ep.* 75.1; Ps.-Libanius 2.58.

[16] A. M. Guillemin, *Pline et la vie littéraire de son temps* (Paris: Les Belles Lettres, 1929) 3–28; Koskenniemi, *Studien*, 35–37; Hadot, *Seneca*, 65–70.

The Greeks and Romans, above all, emphasized that friendship was a kind of oneness, of sharing, of reciprocity between individuals. Friendships sought "to effect a thorough-going likeness in characters, feelings, language, pursuits and dispositions."[17] Here the concept of people working together for common goals or common projects is absolutely central. Such projects prominently included politics and economic activity, making ancient friendship quite different from modern. Philippians exhibits the classic vocabulary of friendship in highlighting the common project that Paul and the Philippians share. The apostle is thankful for their partnership (κοινωνία) in the gospel from the very beginning of their relationship to the present (1:5). They are so closely involved with Paul in his work that they share as partners (συγκοινωνός) both his trials and his achievements (1:7). They rejoice together (2:17–18) and share in his sufferings (4:14).

For ancient friendship, it was never enough merely to share leisure activities and thoughts and feelings. Friendship meant that one shared in practical activities of life and that there would be concrete mutual assistance and reciprocity.[18] Note how Demetrius's letter focuses on offers of concrete assistance:

> I myself am genuinely concerned about your affairs. . . . I have worked unstintingly for what is most advantageous to you. . . . [Y]ou too have the same opinion and will refuse me nothing . . . therefore give close attention to the members of my household lest they need anything, to assist them in whatever they might need. . . .

Greek and Roman writers speak of "giving" and "receiving" as one of the basic obligations of friendship.[19] Paul writes that only the Philippians "entered into a partnership (κοινωνεῖν) with me in giving and receiving" (4:15). After an intensive study of this passage, P. Marshall concludes: "But given the financial basis of the majority of friendships and the common use of commercial language and ideas in describing them, it is fair to suggest that the entire phrase, κοινωνεῖν εἰς λόγον δόσεως καὶ λήμψεως, is an idiomatic expression indicating friendship."[20] The next verses go on to mention specific gifts Paul has received from the Philippians.

In Philippians the discourse of friendship and sharing goes far beyond what one would expect in a friendly letter. Paul's exhortations dwell on the nature of the community in terms of ideal friendship and make the community

[17] Marshall, Enmity, 71.
[18] Ibid., 21–23.
[19] Ibid., 1–12.
[20] Ibid., 163.

itself the goal of Paul's work, to be delivered to Christ at his return (1:6, 9–11). This makes Paul's discourse resemble Greek and Roman discussions of utopian communities, the ideal alternatives to the *polis*. Not surprisingly, such discussions revolve around friendship as the basis for the just society. According to the popular ancient cliché, a friend is a second self. Plutarch writes, "In the symphony and harmony of friendship no element must be unlike, uneven, or unequal, but all must be like to create agreement in word, thought and feelings; it must be as if one soul were distributed among two bodies" (*De Amic. Mult.* 96E).[21] Cicero writes that friendship is "the most complete agreement in policy, in pursuits and in opinions" (*De Amic.* 4.15). Further, it consists of "accord in all things human and divine, conjoined with mutual goodwill and affection" (*De Amic.* 6.20) and "equality and perfect reciprocity in all things" (*De Inv.* 2.66).

Almost all of our sources stress that friendship consists of agreement and equality. Most admit that the reality is not the ideal. Writers who consider φιλία fundamental to the ideal ordering of society take different positions on the relationship between φιλία and the tendency toward inequality in society.[22] In his shorthand definition of friendship, Aristotle says that "friendship is κοινωνία" (*EN* 1171b33), and Plato says that "it is ὁμόνοια" (*Alcib.* 126–27). Both terms, but particularly the latter, play their roles in social theory.[23] Ὁμόνοια (literally, "the same mind") means "agreement," "concord," or "harmony." For these two philosophers, only the true and noble could be friends. These aristocratic friends would rule the lower classes in the ideal society. When the inferior classes submit to the rule of the upper class of "good men," who naturally have ὁμόνοια in their souls, there is also ὁμόνοια in the society as a whole.[24]

The early Stoics took a different position and had a somewhat different conception of friendship. The Stoic definitions of friendship describe it as a sharing (κοινωνία) and an agreement (ὁμόνοια) in living (*SVF* 3.24.22; 3.27.3; 3.161.16; 3.166.17). "We treat our friends as we should ourselves" (Diogenes Laertius 7.124). In language borrowed from the Stoics, Clement of Alexandria defines love (ἀγάπη) as "agreement (ὁμόνοια) in reason, life and habits, or, in short, sharing (κοινωνία) in life or earnest friendship (φιλία) and affection (φιλοστοργία) with right reason concerning the enjoyment of companions" (*SVF* 3.292 = Clement of Alexandria, *Strom.* 2.9).[25] In *Politeia*, his

---

[21] My translation.

[22] Andrew Erskine, *The Hellenistic Stoa: Political Thought and Action* (Ithaca: Cornell University Press, 1990) 19–25, 58–60.

[23] Ibid.

[24] Ibid., 30–33.

[25] My translation.

work on the ideal society, Zeno closely associates friendship and ὁμόνοια and advocates that all would be free and equal in the ideal commonwealth.[26] Such friendship is possible when there is agreement about what is good.

In Philippians, that behavior which the Christ hymn warrants is described in the traditional language of ideal friendship. As befits the gospel, the Philippians are urged (1:27) to stand firm in one spirit (ἐνὶ πνεύματι) and one soul (μιᾷ ψυχῇ). Already Aristotle explicitly calls μιά ψυχή a common "proverbial" expression about friendship (EN 1163b6–7; cf. Euripides, Orest. 1046). The Acts of the Apostles employs the expression in its idealized description of the Jerusalem community (Acts 4:32).[27] Paul encourages the Philippians to find love, κοινωνία in the spirit, affection, and sympathy in Christ (Phil 2:1).

The exhortation to community continues with the expression τὸ αὐτὸ φρονεῖν, "to think the same thing" (2:2). This expression serves as a synonym for ὁμόνοια and can be found in discussions of the concept.[28] The remainder of v. 2 piles up synonyms and near synonyms: "having the same love" (ἀγάπη), "united in soul" (σύμψυχος), "one in thinking" (τὸ ἓν φρονοῦντες). In 4:2 he exhorts Euodia and Syntyche to agree (τὸ αὐτὸ φρονεῖν), that is, to become friends. The accumulation of the language of ideal friendship is unmistakable.

Again, Paul's language fits the pattern when he opens his exhortations on friendship in Christ with πολιτεύεσθαι: "Live as citizens in a way that is worthy of the gospel of Christ" (1:27). In 3:20 he speaks of a "state" or "commonwealth" (πολίτευμα) that is in heaven. Andrew Lincoln's understanding of 3:20 is convincing, since it places Paul's own views among those of contemporary Jews and resists the assimilation of 3:20 to later Christian conceptions of the end-time: "It is not, as has often been thought, that heaven as such is the homeland of Christians to which they, as perpetual foreigners on earth, must strive to return, but rather that since their Lord is in heaven, their life is to be governed by the heavenly commonwealth." Moreover, "Paul often conceives of objects and events normally associated with the end-time as existing already in heaven (e.g., the Jerusalem above in Galatians 4:26)."[29] Thus, for example, we should probably understand paradise, which according to Paul is now in the third heaven (2 Cor 12:3), to be like the New

---

[26] On Zeno's *Politeia*, see Erskine, *Hellenistic Stoa,* esp. p. 59.

[27] L. T. Johnson, *The Literary Function of Possessions in Luke-Acts* (SBLDS 39; Missoula, MT: Scholars Press, 1977) 2–3 and esp. p. 3 n. 1.

[28] See, e.g., Dio Chrysostom, *Or.* 34.20; Dionysius of Halicarnassus, *Ant. R.* 4.20.4.2; 7.59.7.4, 9; 8.15.1.8.

[29] Andrew Lincoln, *Paradise Now and Not Yet* (SNTSMS 43; Cambridge: Cambridge University Press, 1981) 193, 63.

Jerusalem in Rev 21:2–3, which God has prepared in heaven to be put in its proper place for humans (earth) at the end of time.

Here one should remember that Plato's and Zeno's discussions of friendship occur in works on the ideal society. The Epicureans also understood their communities of friends as alternatives to the social order of the Greek city.[30] Numenius aptly combines the language of friendship and social-political organization in describing the Epicurean communities (Eusebius, *Praep. Ev.* 14.5): "The school of Epicurus resembles a true commonwealth (πολιτεία), altogether free of factionalism, sharing one mind and one disposition, of which there were and are and, it appears, will be willing followers." Paul's language of ideal society characterized by ideal friendship more than suggests that he understood his ministry with the Philippians as one of forming them into such a community in and through Christ.

My sketch of major features of friendship in Philippians lacks one essential element: Greek friendship was highly agonistic, that is, competitive.[31] As the proverb "he who has no enemies, has no friends" suggests, the Greeks—and to a lesser extent the Romans—could not conceive of friendship without enmity. Plutarch writes, "Enmities follow close upon friendships, and are interwoven with them, inasmuch as it is impossible for a friend not to share his friend's wrongs or disrepute or disfavor" (*De Amic. Mult.* 96A–B). In the Greco-Roman social system, there are no neutral parties; only friends, enemies, and people you do not know. Again, "enmity" has no modern counterpart. Enmity, like friendship, was an ordered set of conventions and relationships with rules of reciprocity and patronage.

The importance of enmity for Paul's ministry has been ably demonstrated by Peter Marshall in his book on the Corinthian letters. Understanding ancient institutions like friendship and enmity allows the interpreter to see why explaining a letter by "events" suggested by the letter itself is never sufficient. All of the important elements for understanding go unnoticed in such a case. The "events" approach allows the reader too easily to read with modern suppositions and institutions in mind instead of ancient cultural codes. One has the same problem when the project consists of "reconstructing" Paul's theology.

Another Greek proverb states that "friends share one's joy while enemies gloat over one's misfortunes" (Dio Chrysostom, *Or.* 3.103). Constant attention to friends meant constant watchfulness of enemies (Plutarch, *De Cap.* 87B). The ancients consistently claimed that the motivation for enmity was

---

[30] Reimar Müller, *Die Epikureische Gesellschaftstheorie* (Studien zur Geschichte und Kultur des Altertums 5; Berlin: Akademie-Verlag, 1972).

[31] For a thorough discussion of enmity, see Marshall, *Enmity,* 35–67.

envy. Your enemy's goal was to discover a weakness or misfortune and to use such a circumstance as an occasion to shame you publicly.[32]

Philippians is exactly the sort of letter one would expect a leader in the Greco-Roman world to write to his friends when in a vulnerable situation. Paul must deal with the misfortune of his imprisonment in the light of both his friends and his enemies. Since ancient friendship is by nature agonistic, Paul's discourse of friendship must emphasize the common struggle against enemies. The common project is like an athletic competition or a military campaign. Again, Philippians contains the classic vocabulary:

> Live as citizens . . . so that you may stand firm in one spirit, with one soul struggling together (συναθλεῖν) by the faithfulness of the gospel (1:27). . . . For the sake of Christ you should believe into him but also suffer for his sake engaged in the same conflict (ἀγών) which you saw in me and now hear to be mine (1:29–30).[33]

In his situation of great vulnerability, Paul must first convince his friends and enemies that his misfortune is, in reality, good fortune: "I want you to know, brethren, that what has happened to me has really served to advance the gospel" (1:12). Using typical vocabulary of friendship and enmity, 1:15–18 compares (i.e., a σύγκρισις) the reactions of friends and enemies to his misfortune: "Some indeed preach Christ from envy and rivalry, but others from good will" (1:15).[34] The enemies are motivated by envy (φθόνος), rivalry (ἔρις), and partisanship (ἐριθεία); the friends by love (1:16–17). The enemies want to afflict Paul in his imprisonment (1:17). In urging the Philippians on in the struggle (1:28), Paul exhorts them not to be frightened by their enemies (τῶν ἀντικειμένων). The Philippians are to stand united against the opposition. Paul's recommendation of Timothy presents that fellow worker as a true and trustworthy friend, in contrast to false friends (2:19–24).

II. FRIENDS, ENEMIES, AND THE ARCHITECTURE OF PHILIPPIANS

An understanding of ancient friendship and the hortatory rhetoric employed in its context allows a solution to the problems that Perkins treats in the beginning of her essay. The language of opposition to Paul is not merely a matter of bashing one's enemies; it is a fundamental element of the kind of friendship letter that Philippians is. References to one's common

---

[32] Ibid., 49–69.

[33] Adapted from the RSV.

[34] For the use of σύγκρισις in the treatment of friends and enemies, see Marshall, *Enmity*, 53–55.

enemies frequently play a prominent role in friendly letters. But Philippians is also hortatory and psychagogic. Paul's use of his own example constitutes one of Philippians' most prominent hortatory features.

Philippians manifests a well-known hortatory strategy in its use of contrastive models.[35] The fundamental architecture of the letter is one of antithetical models, most often contrasting Paul and his enemies.[36] The letter urges the reader to emulate one kind of behavior and avoid or oppose another kind. The comparison of Paul's friends and enemies and their opposing motivations (1:15–17) occurs within a discussion of Paul's handling of his imprisonment (1:12–14, 19–26). He has made his misfortune into an opportunity for the gospel. He wants only to honor Christ. When faced with the possibility of being with Christ, Paul instead chooses not his own interest but that of his friends, the Philippians. The self-seeking envy of the enemies stands in contrast to Paul's unselfishness.

Just as Paul seeks not his own good but that of his friends, so the Philippians are to stand united against the opposition (1:27–2:4), "doing nothing from selfishness" (2:3) and "looking out not for their own interests but that of others" (2:4). At this point comes the narrative of Christ's giving up his own advantage to serve and die for the benefit of others (2:5–11). As Christ was ultimately victorious, so shall the Philippians prevail against their enemies (1:28). Paul contrasts the Philippians with the current evil generation and urges the readers to follow the sacrificial pattern of his competitive struggle (2:14–18). Timothy will look out for the interests of the Philippians, in contrast to competitors who "look out for their own interests" (2:19–24). Paul similarly emphasizes Epaphroditus's self-sacrifice (2:30). The antithetical pattern of contrastive models should be clear.

Because interpreters have missed this pattern of contrasting the behavior of friends and enemies, 3:2 has appeared such an abrupt change in tone that it has been imagined to be the beginning of another letter clumsily edited together with some other letter fragment or fragments.[37] Commentators have equally puzzled at 3:1b, "to write the same things is not irksome to me, and is safe for you." In the traditional manner of reading the letter, 3:1b connects neither with what precedes nor with what follows. But the sentence

---

[35] L. T. Johnson, "II Timothy and the Polemic Against False Teachers: A Re-Examination," *JRelS* 6 (1978) esp. pp. 13–22; Benjamin Fiore, *The Function of Personal Example in the Socratic and Pastoral Epistles* (AnBib 105; Rome: Biblical Institute Press, 1986).

[36] For σύγκρισις, see Marshall, *Enmity*, 53–55.

[37] For discussion of the issues, see Robert Jewett, "The Epistolary Thanksgiving and the Integrity of Philippians," *NovT* 12 (1970) 53–61; D. Garland, "The Composition and Unity of Philippians: Some Neglected Literary Factors," *NovT* 27 (1985) 141–73; Duane F. Watson, "A Rhetorical Analysis of Philippians and Its Implications for the Unity Question," *NovT* 30 (1988) 57–88.

should be recognized as a hortatory idiom of parenetic letters. One of the conventions of parenesis is to assure readers that they do not really need the advice being proffered. What they are being told is not new, and it does not imply that they are uninstructed.[38] Rather, the advice is a reminder. In a classic parenetic letter, Isocrates admits to Nicocles "Do not be surprised that in what I have said there are many things which you know as well as I" (*Nicocles* 40). Dio Chrysostom apologizes to his audience for repeating that which they have heard before (*Or.* 17.1–2). In 1 Thessalonians, Paul repeatedly uses expressions such as "you remember" and "as you know" in a similar way (e.g., 1:5; 2:1, 2, 5, 9, 11; 4:1, 2, 6, 11; 5:2). He also employs the formula, "concerning X, you have no need that anyone write to you" (1 Thess 4:9; 5:1; see also 2 Cor 9:1; Cicero, *Ep. ad. Fam.* 1.4.3; 2.4.2; Isocrates, *Philip.* 105). The expression in Phil 3:1b assures readers that the contrasting models that are about to follow contain nothing surprising but are reminders to ensure that the Philippians "keep on doing what they are already doing" (see 1 Thess 4:1, 10; 5:11). Such parenetic features give little reason to think that the Philippian community was deeply divided or ravaged by "false teachers."

A common mistranslation of βλέπετε as "beware" (3:2) makes the section appear less hortatory than it actually is.[39] Most translations render the word as "look out for" or "beware of," but for this meaning the verb must be followed by μή and the aorist subjunctive or by the preposition ἀπό. When a direct object follows, βλέπετε means "consider" or "reflect upon." Thus Phil 3:2 does not warn of imminent dangers from judaizers or allude to current events but asks the readers to reflect upon the negative example of judaizing missionaries. The Philippians may well have never seen judaizers, but in Paul's rhetoric of friendship/enmity and antithetical exhortation, the Philippians have indeed *heard* about them.

To these missionaries, Paul again contrasts his own example (3:4–17). He makes this tactic quite explicit in 3:17–18: "Brethren, join in imitating me, and mark those who so live as you have an example in us. For many, of whom I have often told you and now tell you even with tears, live as enemies of the cross of Christ." Note that v. 18 contains the same hortatory idiom as 3:1b: they have already heard what they are being told. The verses provide an explicit call to imitation and an explicit reference to the example of Paul's behavior (τύπος) in contrast to that of the enemies (οἱ ἐχθροί). The judaizing missionaries will not accept the redemptive sufficiency of God's grace through Christ for the Gentiles but want to exalt their own Jewishness by

---

[38] Malherbe, *Paul and the Thessalonians,* 70–72.

[39] G. D. Kilpatrick, "ΒΛΕΠΕΤΕ, Philippians 3:2," in *In Memoriam Paul Kahle* (ed. M. Black and G. Fohrer; BZAW 103; Berlin: Töpelmann, 1968) 146–48; Garland, "Composition."

demanding certain works from the law for Gentiles. In contrast, Paul has given up all of the truly great benefits that were his as a faithful Jew in order to obey God's call to live and work with the Gentiles. In a pattern like Christ's in the "hymn" of chap. 2, he has given up his own advantage but will experience an even greater one (3:10–11).[40] The enemies' self-seeking behavior stands in opposition to the way of life in the commonwealth which is directed from heaven.

III. FRIENDSHIP AND THEOLOGY

A series of positive and negative models of how friends behave versus how enemies behave constitutes the core of the letter and is the key to its architecture. What I have until now left out of the account, however, are references to the activity of God and Christ, that is, theology. How do the cultural codes of friendship, ideal community, and enmity relate to statements about God and Christ? Or are they unrelated? As some have imagined, do the "genuinely Christian" elements of the gospel stand apart from the time-bound and culture-bound features of the letter?

The fundamental theological tactic of the letter's discourse interprets the Philippians' experience by means of a larger narrative about God, Christ, and Paul. The experience of community resulting from Paul's missionary work is part of a grand drama beginning with Christ's decision to live as a servant and reaching its goal with Christ's return. The letter treats the experience of the Philippian community as a process and holds forth a clear goal that coincides with the resolution of the grand narrative. Paul describes the Philippian community as a good work that will be brought to completion on the day of Jesus Christ (1:6). He prays that the Philippians may develop certain virtues and capacities—love, knowledge, and discernment—so that they will be "pure and blameless for the day of Christ" (1:9–10). The Philippian community itself is the goal of Paul's work, for which he will be proud on the day of Christ (2:16).

The active agents of this process are God and Paul, but not Christ. The possible exception is 1:11, which speaks of the fruit of righteousness through Christ (διὰ Ἰησοῦ Χριστοῦ).[41] God began the good work of creating the Philippian community and *he* will bring it to completion (1:6). Therefore Paul thanks God for the Philippians. They are to work out their own salvation, since God is at work among them (2:13). In a similar paradox, Paul proclaims his self-sufficiency (αὐτάρκης), since he can do all through God's

---

[40] White, "Morality."
[41] One might add also 1:19, which speaks of the Spirit of Christ saving Paul.

strength (4:11–13). Verses 11–12 could have been said by a Cynic philosopher, but v. 13 then subverts them. God will save the Philippians from their enemies (1:28) and will supply their needs (4:19).

The language about Christ fits a quite different pattern with two poles: Christ as sovereign ruler and Christ as friend. A few texts leave no doubt that Christ stands over the Philippians, and even the whole world, as some sort of ruler. Paul, of course, is a servant of Christ (1:1). Recognition of Christ's lordship over the cosmos will come only in some indefinite future (2:9–10). Paul and the Philippians, however, already call him "Lord" and acknowledge his exaltation by God (2:9). In contrast to the narrow view of the enemies, Paul urges his readers to recognize that their commonwealth, their ideal society, rests in heaven. Andrew Lincoln convincingly argues that this urging means that Christ, the ideal ruler of the ideal society, now resides in heaven.[42] The *telos* will occur when ruler and ruled are united on the day of Christ. In the meantime, Paul as community psychagogue works to prepare the Philippians for that day.

Another set of texts employs language proper to friendship in connection with Christ. At first sight, these texts might seem in tension with the language of Christ as sovereign, but in Paul's day, key elements of friendship and patron/client relations had been assimilated to one another.[43] A faithful client of the emperor was called a "friend of Caesar." Pseudo-Demetrius's discussion of the friendly letter stresses that although friends in theory ought to be or become equals, rulers and government officers frequently employed friendly letters in communicating with those under them. Peter Marshall gives a prominent place in his study to what he calls "patronal friendship."[44] I suggest that, for Paul, Christ embodies in one personage the ideal qualities of both a superior and a friend.

The apostle yearns for the Philippians with the affection of Jesus Christ (1:8). Paul exhibits this characteristic of friendship as Christ does. Paul's circumstances in regard to the presence/absence motif are typical in that he has friends in different places. If he is with one, he will be away from others. Strikingly, however, one friend is Christ. He yearns to be with Christ (1:23). Without actually calling Christ a friend, as the Gospel of John does, Paul nevertheless employs friendship topoi and language concerning Christ. The Philippians will suffer for Christ (1:29). Friends suffer and, if need be, even die for their friends. Suffering can be expected, since friends struggle together in a common ἀγών. Paul exhorts his audience to the sharing and

---

42 Lincoln, *Paradise*, 193.
43 Saller, *Personal Patronage.*
44 Marshall, *Enmity*, 143–47.

unity of friendship, *since* "in Christ" there is encouragement, the consolation of love, the sharing of the spirit, affection, and sympathy (2:1). The predicates of friendship are part of the relationship with Christ.

Christ also has enemies, who stand against his act of suffering for others (3:18). Paul gave up his normal life as a Jew to go to the Gentiles. The enormous sacrifice was worth it, however, because he came to know Jesus Christ, his Lord (3:8). A relationship of "knowing" another goes hand in hand with the intimacy of friendship, *not* with the typical relationship of a subject to a sovereign. Similarly, Paul wants to "gain" Christ (3:8). Reflecting the reciprocity that characterizes friendship, Paul can say that "Christ Jesus has made me his own" (3:12). As I have already shown, Paul presents himself as a model for the Philippians to follow in chap. 3. The letter displays a remarkable symmetry between the relationship of Paul and the Philippians, the relationship the Philippians are to have with one another, and the relationship both have with Christ. Christ is both Lord and friend.

In the light of what I have argued, the so-called Christ hymn allows us to see what is most typical and atypical about Paul's adaptation of the concept of Greek friendship.[45] This text serves as a hortatory model illustrating the virtues of friendship advocated in 1:27–2:4.[46] Most directly, the "hymn" constitutes a narrative modeling of the exhortation in v. 4: "Let each of you look not only to his own interests, but also to the interests of others." I believe that we can say without hesitation that the hymn would have recalled to its ancient readers stories about those who gave up their own lives for their friends.

L. Michael White has made a strikingly illuminating comparison of the hymn with a story in Lucian's *Toxaris*.[47] In this work, two men compete in telling the best stories about the ideal of friendship. In one story, the slave of a young aristocrat is wrongfully imprisoned. His master, Demetrius, displays his true friendship by attending to his slave in the wretched prison. When the guards no longer allow Demetrius to visit, he gets himself arrested so that he can be with his beloved slave. Demetrius thus demonstrated the highest ideals of Greek friendship by giving up his status, honor, wealth, and

---

[45] The fact that Paul does not use the words φιλία or φίλος in the letter should not be a matter for surprise. Often one finds friendship discussed without these words. Philippians is clearly a letter of friendship even without these direct terms. After all, how many business letters use the word "business" or explicitly state, "this is a business letter"? On the other hand, the virtual absence of these words from the whole Pauline corpus is a bit more surprising and may indicate that Paul was deliberately trying to avoid certain associations, as, e.g., with Epicureanism.

[46] I consider the debate about whether the "hymn" is moral or soteriological to be misguided. See White, "Morality," for a discussion of the issues.

[47] Ibid.

freedom for a slave. As in the Christ hymn, Demetrius lowers himself to a humble status for the sake of another.

Readers of Aristotle on friendship might wince at this story and proclaim it "un-Greek." Although friends were to suffer and die for friends, Greek writings usually suppose that such comrades will be social and moral equals. Nonetheless, φιλία did allow for circumstances in which unequal relationships were genuine friendships. A judicious judgment would recognize that both Lucian's and Paul's stories stretch to the limit but do not break the logic of Greek friendship. E. A. Judge has argued that, although Paul fully moves in the world of Greco-Roman friendship and patronage, he differs in consciously choosing language from the lower end of the status spectrum, for example, that of servants or slaves.[48] Thus we see friendship in Paul, but with a novel twist.

Missing from Philippians is any form of the later orthodox narrative of salvation, that is, the view that humans have an ontological and/or moral flaw due to a primordial fall that only the incarnation of divinity into humanity or the substitutionary sacrifice of an adequate offering for sin can erase. If we had only Philippians, we could never construct such a narrative. Rather, Christ acted so as to make the Philippians into his friends, and thus into friends and sons of God, and he will finally bring all enemies into subjugation. Above all, however, Christ serves as a warrant and model for the kind of friendship which constitutes his community and which Paul attempts to instill, so that ruler and ruled will also be friends when Christ returns.

A confirmation of this understanding can be found in the carefully crafted parallelism between Christ and Paul. Paul's dictum "imitate me as I imitate Christ" (1 Cor 11:2) appears worked out in the form of hortatory rhetoric more clearly in Philippians than anywhere else. According to the hymn, Christ either had some sort of exalted status or the opportunity for an exalted status, but he surrendered vast privileges in order to serve and suffer for others. God rewarded Christ's faithfulness to this mission with resurrection from the dead and sovereignty over the cosmos. Paul truly had great benefits in his life as a faithful Jew but surrendered that life in order to be faithful to his call to be an apostle to the Gentiles. In spite of suffering as Christ suffered (3:10) and facing death, Paul is confident that he will also be raised like Christ (3:11). Paul's narrative no more regards his past Jewish life as worthless than the exalted prerogatives that Christ gave up should be regarded as worthless. Rather, the first pales in comparison with the second.

An extremely influential line of modern interpretation has regarded Paul's language about righteousness or justification by faith in chap. 3 as in one way

[48] E. A. Judge, "Paul as Radical Critic of Society," *Interchange* 16 (1974) 191–203. Marshall develops Judge's insight (*Enmity*).

or another central to the theology of Philippians.[49] This reading is predicated on the translation of διὰ πίστεως Χριστοῦ in 3:9 as "through faith in Christ." In my estimation, however, recent scholarship has conclusively shown that the phrase should be rendered "through Christ's faithfulness."[50] "Christ's faithfulness" serves as shorthand for "Christ's obedience unto death, Christ's servanthood and self-giving in obedience to God." Reconciliation, the transformation of enemies into friends, constituted a regular part of the institutions of friendship and enmity.[51] One of Paul's deepest convictions was that God had regarded Christ's faithfulness as an act of reconciling those who were enemies to him.

IV. CONCLUSIONS

Pheme Perkins and I come up with differing constructions of theology in Philippians because we read the letter in different ways. She reads statements and exhortations as reactions to specific incidents and circumstances outside the text that scholars must re-create by imagining the reverse of Paul's language. Thus, for example, if Paul says that he has not yet reached perfection, Perkins speculates that it must be because charismatic missionaries placed excessive emphasis on Christ's resurrection power (p. 98). If Paul says that the Philippian commonwealth is in heaven, it must be to counter those Philippians who wanted to rely on earthly governments. One problem with such mirror reading is that it begs the genre question. All human utterances are not polemical or apologetic reactions.

I have tried to show that Philippians is best read as a hortatory letter of friendship. When it is read in this way, one does not so easily see a deeply divided community or a church ravaged by missionaries with theologies opposite to Paul's. Mostly, I have tried to parse the logic of the text according to those Greco-Roman cultural codes that seem to best fit the language. This approach yields not only a plausible literary integrity to the letter but also a theology in conceptualities we know Paul's readers were likely to have understood.[52]

---

[49] On this tradition of interpreting Paul, see Krister Stendahl, "The Apostle Paul and the Introspective Conscience of the West," *HTR* 56 (1963) 199–219, reproduced in *The Writings of St. Paul* (ed. W. A. Meeks; New York: Norton, 1972) 422–34.

[50] For arguments and bibliography, see Richard Hays, *The Faith of Jesus Christ: An Investigation of the Narrative Substructure of Galatians 3:1–4:11* (SBLDS 56; Chico, CA: Scholars Press, 1983); Sam K. Williams, "Again *Pistis Christou*," *CBQ* 49 (1987) 431–47; Morna D. Hooker, "ΠΙΣΤΙΣ ΧΡΙΣΤΟΥ," *NTS* 35 (1989) 321–42.

[51] Marshall, *Enmity*, 42–44.

[52] I would like to thank Katherine Eldred for invaluable last-minute assistance in the preparation of this chapter.

Part IV

The Theology of Galatians

10 THE THEOLOGY OF GALATIANS

The Issue of Covenantal Nomism

James D. G. Dunn
University of Durham

MY THESIS IS THAT Galatians is Paul's first sustained attempt to deal with the issue of covenantal nomism. His argument is basically (1) that the outworking of God's saving power will be consistent with its initial decisive expression, (2) that that initial expression of God's covenant purpose was in terms of promise and faith and always had the Gentiles in view from the first, and (3) that the law, where it is understood in a way which conflicts with that initial expression, has been given a distorted role.

I will begin by recalling what "covenantal nomism" means and why it was so important at the time of Paul. Then I will attempt to demonstrate exegetically that covenantal nomism is the issue underlying Paul's argument in Galatians and how Paul deals with it in what I see to be his three-stranded argument. Finally, I will try to indicate why I think that Galatians is Paul's first full-scale attempt to deal with this issue. In all this I take it for granted that, however else we may want to speak of "the theology of Galatians," we must at least start by asking what Paul was saying within the context of his times and of his mission and in relation to the specific situation in Galatia, and what he wanted his Galatian readership and audience to hear and to understand in what he wrote. In the spirit of the seminar I will confine my discussion to Galatians itself and not attempt to underpin or develop the main part of the thesis by reference to any other Pauline text.[1]

[1] This is a reworked version of the paper delivered to the Pauline Theology Group of the SBL at its Chicago meeting in 1988. I wish to express my appreciation to members of the group for a most valuable discussion of the first draft, particularly to J. Louis Martyn, the chief respondent. The revision, I hope, reflects something of the benefit I derived from that discussion. A fuller version appears in *Jesus, Paul and the Law* (London: SPCK; Philadelphia: Westminster, 1990).

I

"Covenantal nomism," as coined by E. P. Sanders, is a phrase well fitted to characterize Jewish self-understanding or, more precisely, the understanding of the relation between God and his people Israel as it comes to expression consistently (though not uniformly) within Jewish literature, particularly from Deuteronomy on.[2] Fundamental to Judaism's sense of identity was the conviction that God had made a special *covenant* with the patriarchs, the central feature of which was the choice of Israel to be God's peculiar people (e.g., Deut 4:31; 2 Macc 8:15; *Pss. Sol.* 9:10; CD 6:2; 8:18), and had given the *law* as an integral part of the covenant both to show Israel how to live within that covenant ("This do and you shall live" [Deut 4:1, 10, 40; 5:29–33; 6:1–2, 18, 24; etc.]) and to make it possible for them to do so (the system of atonement).[3] Thus in the phrase "covenantal nomism," the former word emphasizes God's prevenient grace, and the latter cannot and should not be confused with legalism or with any idea of "earning" salvation.

The typical mind-set of covenantal nomism included a strong sense of special privilege and prerogative over against other peoples (e.g., Bar 3:36–4:4; *Pss. Sol.* 13:6–11; Philo, *Vit. Mos.* 2.17–25; Josephus, *Ag. Ap.* 2.38 §§277–86). But it also and inevitably meant a reinforcing of the sense of national identity and separateness from other nations (e.g., *Jub.* 22:16; *Ep. Arist.* 139, 142; Philo, *Vit. Mos.* 1.278).[4] This was evidently a major motivating factor in the reconstitution of Judea after the exile (Ezra 9–10), and the same sense of a basic need to remain loyal to the covenant obligations was obviously one of the most powerful factors in the Maccabean attempt to restore national integrity and to retain national identity. At that time, the obligations of covenantal nomism focused on those features of national and religious life which marked out the distinctiveness of the Jewish people— circumcision and food laws (1 Macc 1:60–63). This was because these demands of the law had become a principal target of Syrian persecution— and for the same reason, namely, that they prevented assimilation and integration into a larger international and religious whole. At the same time "Judaism" first appears in our literature precisely as a protest against such hellenizing pressure (2 Macc 2:21; 8:1; 14:38), that is, as a way of marking off the entity of Jewish self-identity from a Hellenism that had swamped and threatened to obliterate such national distinctives. The verb "to judaize" is

---

[2] E. P. Sanders, *Paul and Palestinian Judaism* (Philadelphia: Fortress, 1977) 75, 420, 544; J. J. Collins, *Between Athens and Jerusalem: Jewish Identity in the Hellenistic Diaspora* (New York: Crossroad, 1983); see index, under "covenantal nomism."

[3] Rightly emphasized by Sanders (*Paul and Palestinian Judaism,* 422).

[4] See further my *Romans* (WBC 38; Dallas: Word, 1988) lxvii–lxxi.

coined to indicate those Gentiles who choose to live their lives in accord with the ancestral customs and practices distinctive of the Jewish nation (Esth 8:17 LXX; Josephus, *J.W.* 2.17.10 §454; 2.18.2 §§462–63).[5]

Equally it is evident that these concerns shaped so clearly by the Maccabean national crisis continued to be a dominant factor in the following period. All the literature from then on through the next two centuries bears testimony to a concern to assert, define, and defend the boundaries of the covenant, as different groups claimed that *their* understanding and practice were the *proper* covenantal nomism, that they (alone) were the "righteous" and "devout," and that the other nonpractitioners were "sinners," disloyal to the covenant—if not apostates—by their failure to keep the law as it should be kept (e.g., Wisdom of Solomon 2–5; *Jub.* 6:32–35; *1 Enoch* 1:1, 7–9; 1QS 2:4–5; *Pss. Sol.* 3:3–12; 13:5–12).[6] In this period circumcision and food laws, together with other specific commandments like sabbath and festivals, remained the clearest identity and boundary markers of Judaism as a whole, as indicated by evidence both within and without the corpus of Jewish writings.[7]

All this is more or less noncontroversial: the evidence is clear and consistent. I emphasize it by way of introduction to the particular study of Galatians for the obvious reason that the thrust of Paul's argument regarding these same two features, covenant and law, is unlikely to be understood without an adequate grasp of *the taken-for-granted nature of covenantal nomism within Jewish circles.* The extent to which Paul is actually addressing covenantal nomism has, of course, yet to be established, but where such a fundamental mind-set was involved, any discussion of covenant and law in relation to Judaism was bound to be influenced in greater rather than lesser degree by that mind-set and its taken-for-granteds.

More controversial, I suppose, may be two specific claims that I have already advanced elsewhere, even though they seem to me to follow inevitably from the above.[8] The first claim is that covenantal nomism was so

[5] Texts cited in my "Incident at Antioch (Gal 2.11–18)," *JSNT* 18 (1983) 26–27, reprinted in my *Jesus, Paul and the Law,* chap. 6.
[6] See further my "Pharisees, Sinners and Jesus," in *The Social World of Formative Christianity and Judaism: Essays in Tribute to Howard Clark Kee* (ed. J. Neusner et al.; Philadelphia: Fortress, 1988) 264–89, reprinted in *Jesus, Paul and the Law,* chap. 3.
[7] See, e.g., the texts cited in my "New Perspective on Paul," *BJRL* 65 (1983) 107–10, reprinted in *Jesus, Paul and the Law,* chap. 7.
[8] "New Perspective" and "Works of the Law and the Curse of the Law (Galatians 3:10–14)," *NTS* 31 (1985) 523–42, reprinted in *Jesus, Paul and the Law,* chap. 8. The points have been well grasped by J. M. G. Barclay, *Obeying the Truth: A Study of Paul's Ethics in Galatians* (Studies of the New Testament and Its World; Edinburgh: T. & T. Clark, 1988) 78, 82.

tightly bound up with a sense of national or ethnic identity that the law became coterminous with Israel, marking out the Jews in their distinctiveness as God's people and in their distinctiveness from others (Gentiles = not God's people).[9] That is to say, however universal the claims made for the law might have been,[10] it never ceased to be the Jewish law; its religious appeal (evident in the many God-fearers who attached themselves in differing degrees to the diaspora synagogues)[11] was never such as could be divorced from its national function as the civil and criminal code of the Jews as a distinct ethnic entity. This "social function of the law" I believe to be important for our fuller understanding of the mind-set with which Paul is engaging in Galatians.

The second claim is that the phrase "works of the law" was a way of describing the same covenantal-nomistic mind-set; that is, "works of the law" refers to the praxis which the law of the covenant laid upon the covenant member. This is borne out by the use of an equivalent phrase, "deeds of the law," in the Dead Sea Scrolls, where it describes the obligations laid upon the sectarian by his membership in the Qumran community (1QS 5:21, 23; 6:18; 4QFlor 1:1–7; and an unpublished text from Cave 4), though whether it was of wider currency or simply a natural way of expressing covenantal obligations we cannot say. In particular, such a sense of obligation probably came to particular expression in those commandments that focused on the distinctiveness of the claim to be a people set apart by the one God. In the Maccabean crisis that meant specifically circumcision and the food laws, and there are sufficient indications thereafter that wherever Jewish identity came into question the issue of covenantal nomism would focus on these same commandments and on any others that reinforced Jewish distinctiveness. Such deeds/works of the law became the test cases for Jewish faithfulness.[12]

With one of our key terms thus clarified, we can now turn to Galatians and attempt to explicate the line of argument and emphases Paul employs to meet the challenge confronting his understanding of the gospel among his Galatian converts.[13]

---

[9] See also T. D. Gordon, "The Problem at Galatia," *Int* 41 (1987) 32–43, esp. p. 38, and those cited by him; and P. Alexander, "Jewish Law in the Time of Jesus: Towards a Clarification of the Problem," in *Law and Religion: Essays on the Place of the Law in Israel and Early Christianity* (ed. B. Lindars; Cambridge: James Clarke, 1988). Alexander notes that "the centrality of the Torah of Moses to Judaism was the centrality of a national flag" (p. 56).

[10] See N. A. Dahl, "The One God of Jews and Gentiles," in *Studies in Paul* (Minneapolis: Augsburg, 1977) 178–91.

[11] For details, see my "Incident at Antioch," 21–23; see also my *Romans*, xlvii–xlviii.

[12] Note the clarification of my earliest statement of this conclusion in *Jesus, Paul and the Law*, particularly chap. 7, Additional Note 6.

[13] This is not to say that Paul accepted his Galatian opponents' frame of reference (a criticism

II

Paul was concerned with the issue of covenantal nomism as it was affecting his converts in Galatia. This becomes clear in Paul's consistent focus on what we might call the "second phase." It is most explicit in 3:3: What follows from the beginning they have made? How do they think the completion of God's saving work will be achieved? The same concern lies behind almost every paragraph of the letter, in a whole sequence of variations. What follows from the gospel and its acceptance (1:6–7; 2:14)? What is the outworking of the grace of God (1:6)? For Paul it was apostleship to the Gentiles (1:16; 2:9); for those he opposed it was evidently the law (2:21; 5:4). If the issue of circumcision for Gentiles had been settled (2:1–10), what about the issue of continuing life-style, as focused (as also with the Pharisees)[14] in table fellowship (2:11–14)?

Most persistent of all is the argument regarding the relation of faith and the law. How is (the initial expression of) faith to be correlated with "works of the law"? The implication of the ἐὰν μή of 2:16a, especially in its context as referring back to the issue of food laws at Antioch (2:11–14), is that Jewish Christians thought works of the law (like observance of the dietary laws) were quite compatible with faith in Christ and still a necessary (covenantal) obligation for Jewish believers in Messiah Jesus.[15] But Paul drives that distinction (faith in Christ and works of law) into an outright antithesis (2:16bc;[16] 3:2, 5, 10–12): to regard the law (covenantal nomism) as the outworking of faith is retrogressive, a stepping back from the freedom of the children of God into immature childhood and slavery (3:23–4:11; 4:21–31). The outworking of faith has to be conceived in different terms from works of the law (circumcision, etc.): that is, in terms of the Spirit as against works of the flesh (5:16–26; 6:7–9), a focusing on physical features which would include a nationalistic evaluation of circumcision (3:3; 4:21–31; 6:12–13). This outworking may be conceived in terms of the law, but not the law focused in such Jewish distinctives as circumcision, but focused rather in love of neighbor (5:6, 13–14) as exemplified by Christ (6:1–4).[17]

---

made of the first draft of this paper by J. L. Martyn at the SBL seminar in Chicago), but simply to say that the teaching in Galatians had set an agenda and posed an issue to which Paul had to respond; see section III below.

[14] J. Neusner, *From Politics to Piety* (Englewood Cliffs, NJ: Prentice Hall, 1973); see also his *Judaism, The Evidence of the Mishnah* (Chicago: University of Chicago Press, 1981).

[15] See my clarification of the exposition of Gal 2:16 in *Jesus, Paul and the Law*, chap. 7, Additional Note 9.

[16] See further below; see also *Jesus, Paul and the Law*, chap. 7, Additional Note 3.

[17] See particularly Barclay, *Obeying*, 125–42.

The issue underlying all this is covenantal nomism, that is, the issue of whether those Gentiles who had come to faith in the Messiah of the Jews and who thus claimed a share in the benefits of God's covenant with Israel needed to live in accordance with the law of Israel—either by following Jewish customs ("to judaize") or by becoming proselytes—in order to sustain that claim.[18] That this is the issue has been obscured by several factors. One is the fact that covenantal nomism was such a taken-for-granted for the typical Jewish mind-set that it did not need to be spelled out any more clearly than it is.[19] A second is that "works of the law" have for too long been understood as "good works by which individuals try to gain acceptance by God." This fundamental misunderstanding has skewed the whole exegesis of the letter, distorting or concealing the Jewish (as well as Christian) recognition of the priority of God's grace and losing sight of the corporate dimension of the discussion in its focus on an individualistic doctrine of justification by faith.[20] Third, Sanders's own rebuttal of that misplaced emphasis in turn clouded the issue by making too sharp a distinction between entry into the covenant and continuance or maintenance of status within it. "Justification" (being "righteoused") was classified as "transfer terminology,"[21] with the implication that that was also where Paul's emphasis on faith belonged, that is, only with the question of entry and not with that of continuance. (Yet Gal 5:4–5 indicates that justification has much to do with continuance and final outcome!) Consequently, *the issue of the continuum between faith and its outworking/corollary was obscured:* Does (covenant) faith (necessarily, inevitably?) come to expression in (covenant) works of the law or continue to be the basis of continuance as well as of entry, or what?[22] This last confusion has been the more plausible since so much of the issue in Galatians focuses on circumcision, which seems to reinforce a distinction between "entry into covenant" and "maintenance of status." But the issue of works of the law first comes to expression as a result of the Antioch incident (2:11–16), where the concern was clearly the maintenance of covenant status on the part of the Jewish Christians in Antioch through faithful observance of the food laws. Moreover, it was not merely circumcision which the Galatian converts were being exhorted to undergo, but circumcision as the beginning of that law

---

[18] I had formulated this thesis before reading C. K. Barrett, *Freedom and Obligation: A Study of the Epistle to the Galatians* (Philadelphia: Westminster, 1985) 10: The theology of the judaizers "seems to me to tally in some remarkable ways (though not in every way) with the covenantal nomism of E. P. Sanders."

[19] See pp. 126–27 above.

[20] See further *Jesus, Paul and the Law*, chap. 7.

[21] E. P. Sanders, *Paul, the Law, and the Jewish People* (Philadelphia: Fortress, 1983).

[22] See further *Jesus, Paul and the Law*, chap. 7, Additional Note 8.

observance which was expected of all devout covenant members (4:10; 5:3). At this point it is well to recall that circumcision was not typically thought of within Judaism as a rite of entry into the covenant but as one of the commandments by obeying which one expressed one's status as a Jew (or proselyte)[23] — the first act, we may say, of covenantal nomism.

III

The main thrust of Paul's argument against covenantal nomism has three strands. (1) *The expression of life within the covenant should be consistent with its beginning.* This is evident from Paul's initial appeal to his readers: what they are doing is abandoning the grace of God, which first brought them to faith, in favor of a different gospel (1:6–9). The appeal is regularly repeated throughout the rest of the letter (3:1–5; 4:8–11; 5:1–12). It was by faith that they became participants in the promises of God; their continuing status as such would be maintained in the same way. Paul sees his own experience of being commissioned with the gospel in the same light (1:11–2:10; 2:18–20). Whatever his relationship with Jerusalem after his conversion, and whatever may have passed between himself and the pillar apostles on his two visits there, the crucial fact is that they added nothing to him but gave full recognition to the grace of God which was the manifest proof of his original commissioning (2:6–9). Similarly, he is concerned to make it clear that to have resumed a full-scale observance of the food laws in table fellowship would have been equivalent to his building again what Christ's death and commissioning had pulled down for him (2:14–21). The same point is found at the heart of his argument in chap. 3: the law neither annuls nor alters the terms of the original covenant promise to Abraham (3:15–20). That is to say, the original promise to Abraham, as given to faith, continues to characterize the covenant and the relationship with God which it sustains; to insist that covenantal nomism with its now traditional checkpoints was the only way to live for heirs of the promise was to make the promise void. It is still, of course, necessary to know how faith will work out in practice. Guidance on life-style and praxis is still necessary: hence the final exhortation in 5:13–6:10. There Paul clearly shows that he sees the law as still having a function. He still believes in a kind of "covenantal nomism"! But it has markers

---

[23] P. Borgen, "Observations on the Theme 'Paul and Philo,'" in *Die paulinische Literatur und Theologie* (ed. S. Pedersen; Teologiske Studier 7; Aarhus: Aros, 1980) 85–102. Borgen notes that "Philo's and Hillel's understanding has thus been that bodily circumcision was not the requirement for entering the Jewish community, but was one of the commandments which they had to obey upon receiving status as a Jew" (p. 88).

different from the ancestral customs of the Jews—love and Spirit, not circumcision.[24]

Paul's argument is thus clear. *Ongoing praxis must be a continuing expression of the faith by which his readers first began to function within God's covenant promise and purpose*—a beginning whose divinely given character was self-evident both to Paul and to his readers. Stated thus, the argument is certainly open to sharp criticism: The law was also given by God; why should works of the law be regarded as an antithesis to faith? We hardly need Jas 2:18–26 to spell this line of criticism out for us. But at least Paul's logic is clear, and it is only part of the complete argument.

(2) The second strand of Paul's argument is that *God's promise always had the Gentiles in view from the beginning.* This is obviously the point of 3:6–9, where the gospel is focused in the original promise to Abraham, "In you shall all the nations be blessed" (3:8 LXX).[25] The point is clear: the promise is to be offered to those originally in view in it and on the original terms—to the Gentiles, by faith. The covenant promise was not intended solely for Jews.[26]

The verses that follow (3:10–14) have been much disputed and much misunderstood, but they are most obviously to be taken as speaking of a curse on lawlessness, and therefore as a curse which the law has interposed between the Gentiles (lawless) and their share in the promise. Thus the whole thrust of the paragraph is the opening up of the blessing of Abraham to the Gentiles which Christ achieved by removing that curse in his death (3:13–14). Therefore, whatever else is in view, Paul almost certainly has in mind the law's function in branding the Gentile per se as "sinner" (2:15)—outside Israel, outside the law, therefore sinner and transgressor, and under a curse. *The curse of the law on the Gentile as Gentile is precisely that corollary of covenantal nomism as it had come to be understood in the nationalistic presumption* (we are the "righteous"; they the "sinners") *and ethnic restrictiveness* (inheritance is limited to the Jews and proselytes—οἱ ἐξ ἔργων νόμου) *which Paul now contests.*[27]

---

[24] See particularly the central thesis of Barclay, *Obeying:* that Paul addresses both the issue of identity and that of behavioral patterns, that "a major ingredient in the Galatian dispute is the question of how the members of God's people should live," and that the exhortation of 5:13–6:10 "develops out of and concludes his earlier arguments" (p. 216). See also my *Romans,* 705–6.

[25] See F. F. Bruce, *Galatians* (NIGTC; Exeter: Paternoster, 1982) 156–57.

[26] J. L. Martyn, in his response to the Chicago version of this paper, largely ignored and indeed discounted this horizontal *Heilsgeschichte* dimension of the whole discussion. Contrast B. R. Gaventa, "The Singularity of the Gospel: A Reading of Galatians" (p. 159 below) and R. B. Hays, "Crucified with Christ: A Synthesis of the Theology of 1 and 2 Thessalonians, Philemon, Philippians, and Galatians" (pp. 231–34 below); see also the essays by R. Scroggs and D. J. Lull in this volume.

[27] For a fuller exposition, see *Jesus, Paul and the Law,* chap. 8 and Additional Note 1. See also the main thesis of G. Howard, *Paul: Crisis in Galatia* (SNTSMS 35; Cambridge: Cambridge

We see a similar pattern in the argument about Christ as Abraham's "seed" according to the promise (3:16). The whole point of this argument is to enable Paul to make the claim that Gentiles have become partakers of the promise "in Christ" (3:14, 28–29),[28] through the Spirit (3:14). Paul evidently does not need to debate more fundamental issues of christology. The centrality of Christ and his death for the gospel (1:4; 2:19–21; 3:1; 4:4–5; 6:12) and the necessity for faith in him (2:16; 3:22–24, 26) were emphases he shared with his readers and indeed with the "judaizers."[29] What Paul needed to emphasize was what we might call the Gentile dimension of his christology and his gospel (1:15–16; 2:2–5, 7–8, 15–17; 3:8, 13–14, 16, 27–29; 5:6, 11; 6:14–15), that faith in Christ *continues* to be the means through which *continued* participation in the promise and inheritance of Abraham is maintained. What Paul was concerned about was that the gospel which they took as their common starting point was actually distorted in its fundamentals if these emphases, which were outworkings of the gospel and christology, were not followed through. For the Galatian believers to accept the covenantal nomism which reclaimed the Jewish Christians at Antioch (2:12–14) would be to lose the gospel and Christ (1:6–9; 5:4).

So too Paul evidently felt no need to justify the assumption that the gift of the Spirit was the fulfillment of the promise to Abraham. This must be because the gift of the Spirit to Gentiles was both recognized among the first Christians and acknowledged as the sure indication of God's acceptance/ justifying act (so Gal 3:2–5; 4:6, 29; 5:5; see also Acts 10:44–48; 11:15–18; Rom 8:9, 14).[30] "This reception of the 'Spirit' is the primary datum of the Christian churches in Galatia."[31] Here too what Paul needed to emphasize was the gift and continued experience of the Spirit as operating independently

---

University Press, 1979), though I disagree with several subsidiary aspects of Howard's argument.

[28] See J. C. Beker, *Paul the Apostle: The Triumph of God in Life and Thought* (Philadelphia: Fortress, 1980) 50–52, 96; J. L. Martyn, "Paul and His Jewish-Christian Interpreters," *USQR* 42 (1987–88) 3–4.

[29] R. B. Hays rightly notes that in Galatians christology is "not the issue" ("Christology and Ethics in Galatians: The Law of Christ," *CBQ* 49 [1987] 276).

[30] See further my *Baptism in the Holy Spirit: A Reexamination of the New Testament Teaching on the Gift of the Spirit in Relation to Pentecostalism Today* (SBT 2/15; London: SCM, 1970).

[31] H. D. Betz, "Spirit, Freedom, and Law: Paul's Message to the Galatian Churches," *SEÅ* 39 (1974) 145. See also D. J. Lull, *The Spirit in Galatia: Paul's Interpretation of Pneuma as Divine Power* (SBLDS 49; Chico, CA: Scholars Press, 1980); S. K. Williams, "Justification and the Spirit in Galatians," *JSNT* 29 (1987) 91–100; idem, "*Promise* in Galatians: A Reading of Paul's Reading of Scripture," *JBL* 107 (1988) 709–20. Williams argues that the promise to Abraham is the promise of the Spirit.

of the law and ethnic (fleshly) considerations (3:2–5; 4:3–7, 29; 5:5–6, 18; 6:8).[32] In both cases, the christology and pneumatology of the letter presuppose a richer and fuller theology as fundamental, but in the letter itself Paul develops only those aspects of immediate importance to the situation of the readers.

We might simply note also how much of Paul's own self-understanding of his commission (that is, of his whole existence as a Christian) was bound up with the conviction that it was now time to reach out to and bring in the Gentiles on equal terms with the Jews (that is, without their ceasing to be "Greeks" as distinct from "Jews"). Hence he emphasized in his description of his conversion and calling that he was "called . . . to preach God's Son among the Gentiles" (1:15–16).[33] Clearly, his conviction that he had been called from the first to go to the uncircumcision was bound up with his understanding that the Gentiles were in view from the first expression of the covenant promise. Which of these two came first and gave rise to the other it is not possible now to say.

(3) What then was *the purpose of the law?* The question arises inevitably from the line of argument outlined above. The fact that it also arises in 3:19 and 21 may be taken as at least some confirmation that our analysis of Paul's argument so far is on the right lines. The question arises, obviously, because Paul's treatment of the law as so far outlined has had strongly pejorative features. "Works of the law" he regards in a very negative light (2:16; 3:2, 5, 10). It is the law which is understood to condemn Gentiles as "sinners" (2:15), to place a curse on the lawless which prevents them from participating in the covenant promise (3:10–14). But he does see a positive role for the law, at least in that he speaks of love of neighbor as fulfilling the whole law (5:14). What then is Paul objecting to so strongly?

The answer has already been suggested in the treatment of the curse of the law: Paul objects to covenantal nomism understood as it then was consistently throughout Judaism — covenantal nomism as restricting the covenant to those within the boundaries marked by the law, that is, to Jews and

---

[32] See now Barclay, *Obeying,* particularly chap. 4, "The Sufficiency of the Spirit."

[33] See further my "'A Light to the Gentiles': The Significance of the Damascus Road Christophany for Paul," in *The Glory of Christ in the New Testament: Studies in Christology in Memory of G. B. Caird* (ed. L. D. Hurst and N. T. Wright; Oxford: Clarendon, 1987) 251–66, reprinted in *Jesus, Paul and the Law,* chap. 4. See also Gordon, "Problem at Galatia," 35. A corollary of this is that Paul's principal concern in Galatians 1–2 was not to defend his apostleship or apostolic authority as such (so still G. Lüdemann, *Paulus, der Heidenapostel: Band II, Antipaulinismus in frühen Christentum* [Göttingen: Vandenhoeck & Ruprecht, 1983] 145); see B. R. Gaventa, "Galatians 1 and 2: Autobiography as Paradigm," *NovT* 28 (1986) 309–26; and B. Lategan, "Is Paul Defending his Apostleship in Galatians?" *NTS* 34 (1988) 411–30.

proselytes.[34] This is confirmed by his emphasis on another word used with strong negative overtones—"flesh" (3:3; 5:19, 24; 6:8). "Flesh" also marks out a misunderstood relationship with Abraham, or rather a relationship with Abraham in which the emphasis has been misplaced. Hence the allegory of 4:21–31: There is a line of descent from Abraham understood in terms of the flesh—a racial or ethnic or national identity—and that is not the line of promise.[35] To limit participation in the promise to a relationship κατὰ σάρκα is to misunderstand the promise.[36] Hence too the point of 6:12–13: the glorying in the flesh which Paul condemns is a glorying not in human exertion or in ritual action, but in ethnic identity.[37] To insist that Gentiles must be circumcised is to assume that God's purpose means the triumph of Israel as a nation state, whose supremacy is acknowledged by those who seek to become part of it by crossing the ritual boundaries which divide Gentile from Jew.[38]

I suspect this also provides the key to the puzzling statement in 3:19: the law was given through angels ("in hand of mediator" is probably in apposition to "ordained through angels," in the light of the next clause). Anyone familiar with the Jewish understanding of the one God's ordering of his

---

[34] See also Paul's argument in 2:21: If righteousness was still in terms of the law and still included a covenantal nomistic "us and them" distinction between Jews and Gentiles, then Christ's death was "in vain" since it had not ended the covenantal nomistic function of the law as a dividing line that excluded Gentiles as such from the blessings of the covenant promise.

[35] The fact that Paul speaks of *two* covenants in Gal 4:21–31 is an interesting variation on the continuity/discontinuity Paul sees in salvation history. Strictly speaking, the "covenantal nomism" to which Paul objects refers only to the covenant of slavery; the correlative of the covenant of promise is the freedom of the Spirit (3:2–5; etc.).

[36] See particularly J. L. Martyn, "A Law-Observant Mission to Gentiles: The Background of Galatians," *Michigan Quarterly Review* 22 (1983) 221–36, esp. pp. 231–32; reprinted in *SJT* 38 (1985) 307–24, esp. pp. 318–20; idem, "Apocalyptic Antinomies in Paul's Letter to the Galatians," *NTS* 31 (1985) 410–24. My exegesis does not exclude the possibility that Paul was reacting to his "opponents" at this point (so advocated by Martyn, Barclay [*Obeying*, 91], and earlier by C. K. Barrett ["The Allegory of Abraham, Sarah, and Hagar in the Argument of Galatians," in *Essays on Paul* (London: SPCK, 1982) 154–70]). Barrett appositely cites *Jub.* 16:17–18 as an indication of the sort of exposition they would probably have used (note also 1 Macc 2:16). See now particularly G. Bouwman, "Die Hagar- und Sara-Perikope (Gal 4:21–31)," *ANRW* II.25.4 (1987) 3135–55; and more generally J. M. G. Barclay, "Mirror-Reading a Polemical Letter: Galatians as a Test Case," *JSNT* 31 (1987) 73–93.

[37] W. Schmithals's threadbare hypothesis falls apart here in his argument that the "glorying in the flesh" is expressed in a gnostic "contempt for the flesh" ("The Heretics in Galatia," in *Paul and the Gnostics* [Nashville: Abingdon, 1972] 55). Not gnostic but ethnic identity is the issue at this point.

[38] This false evaluation of circumcision and flesh means also a failure to recognize the proper function of the law (3:19; 4:8–10) and so also to keep it (3:10; 6:13; see also Rom 2:17–29). See also *Jesus, Paul and the Law,* chap. 8 and Additional Note 1.

creation and of the nations within it would be familiar also with the idea of God having appointed guardian angels for each state (Deut 32:8–9; Sir 17:17; *Jub.* 15:31–32; *1 Enoch* 20:5; *Tg. Ps.-J.* Gen 11:7–8).[39] The usual corollary in Jewish thought was that God, having appointed angels over other nations, kept Israel for himself, with no mediator interposing. The point Paul is probably making is that to treat the law in such an exclusive, restrictive way is equivalent to treating the law as though it was given through Israel's guardian angels or, indeed, as though the law itself was Israel's guardian angel (the implication of 4:8–10, coming as it does at the end of 3:23–4:10; hence also the definition of the characteristic state of the Jews as "under the law" as a ruling power [3:23; 4:4–5, 21; 5:18]).[40] To thus regard the law as a national identity marker, as a boundary dividing Jew from Gentile, is in effect to deny the oneness of God.

Even this treatment of the law is not unreservedly negative. There was a positive side to this giving of the law to Israel. It gave the covenant people a way of dealing with sin in the period of time prior to the coming of Christ (3:19).[41] The law (guardian angel) served to direct, govern, and protect Israel

---

[39] R. Meyer, "λαός," *TDNT* 4. 39–41. See also T. Callan, "Pauline Midrash: The Exegetical Background for Gal 3:19b," *JBL* 99 (1980) 549–67.

[40] Here I dispute such views as those of J. W. Drane that 3:19 amounts to "a categorical denial of the divine origin of the Torah" (*Paul: Libertine or Legalist?: A Study in the Theology of the Major Pauline Epistles* [London: SPCK, 1975] 34) or of H. Hübner that 3:19 means that the law "is the product of demonic angelic powers" (*Law in Paul's Thought* [Edinburgh: T. & T. Clark, 1984] 24–36), both of whom read too much into the text and ignore the context of Jewish thought, where the association of angels in the giving of the law was quite familiar and unthreatening (Deut 33:2 LXX; *Jub.* 1:29ff.; Philo, *Somn.* 1.143; Josephus, *Ant.* 15.5.3 §136; see also Acts 7:38, 53; Heb 2:2); see also S. Westerholm, *Israel's Law and the Church's Faith: Paul and His Recent Interpreters* (Grand Rapids: Eerdmans, 1988) 176–79. A. J. M. Wedderburn chides me for denying that Paul is opposed to the law *per se*, referring to Gal 3:19, which he thinks does "seem to express opposition to the law per se," though without further explanation ("Paul and the Law," *SJT* 38 [1985] 618 n. 11). So too I must register my dissent with Howard (*Paul*, 60–61) and L. Gaston ("Paul and the Torah," in *Antisemitism and the Foundations of Christianity* [ed. A. T. Davies; New York: Paulist, 1979] 62–64), who maintain that "under the law" could include, or even specifically designate, the Gentile situation, and with Martyn, who maintained in the Chicago seminar that the phrase "to be under" meant to be "under the tyrannical power of something." But see n. 42 below.

[41] I see no grounds within this phase of Paul's argument to interpret 3:19 ("the law was added for the sake of transgressions") in terms of *multiplying* transgressions (so, e.g., Barrett, *Freedom*, 33; Westerholm, *Israel's Law*, 178, 182). That reads Gal 3:19 too much through the differently slanted and more careful argument of Rom 5:20. Here Paul is explaining the positive side of covenantal nomism in the period before Christ (see further below n. 42). Likewise, the point of 3:21 is not totally to dismiss the law; the mistake Paul objects to is the assumption that the law fulfills the role of the promise (*giving* life) as well as its own role (*regulating* life within the covenant [2:12], particularly in the period before Christ).

until the promise could be fulfilled in Christ (3:23–4:7).[42] But now that Christ has come, the promise is open to Gentile as well as Jew on the original conditions. Consequently, to return under the oversight of the law in its role as guardian of national rights and prerogatives is to return to childish subserviency and servility and to deny the fullness of the promise. The upshot is that Paul is able to pose a different alternative from that usually posed by Judaism. Judaism asserted: within the law = within the covenant. Paul in contrast asserted: within Christ = within the covenant; within the law = outside Christ (5:4).[43]

In short, Paul's attitude to the law in Galatians has regularly been misperceived as more unyieldingly negative than it is. The misunderstanding has been based on a misperception of "works of the law" as "good works," and of 3:10 as requiring perfect compliance with the law.[44] But once the point has been grasped that Paul's chief target is a covenantal nomism understood in restrictively nationalistic terms —"works of the law" as maintaining Jewish identity, "the curse of the law" as falling on the lawless so as to exclude Gentiles as such from the covenant promise — then it becomes clear that Paul's negative remarks had a more limited thrust and that so long as the law is not similarly misunderstood as defining and defending the prerogatives of a particular group, it still has a positive role to play in the expression of God's purpose and will.[45]

---

[42] See particularly D. J. Lull, "'The Law Was Our Pedagogue': A Study in Galatians 3:19–25," *JBL* 105 (1986) 481–98; N. H. Young, "*Paidagogos:* The Social Setting of a Pauline Metaphor," *NovT* 29 (1987) 150–76; T. D. Gordon, "A Note on ΠΑΙΔΑΓΩΓΟΣ in Galatians 3:24–25," *NTS* 35 (1989) 150–54. Young sees the emphasis of 3:23–24 as falling "on the confining and restrictive rather than either the corrective or protective functions of a pedagogue" (p. 171). He concludes: "Thus the law is 'our pedagogue' in the sense that the restrictive regulations which separated Jew and Gentile, which Sinai epitomized, were only temporary. Just as a pedagogue's guardian role finished when the child arrived at maturity, so the legal separation of Jew and Gentile ended with the coming of the new age in Christ" (p. 176). Gordon sees the *paidagogos's* function as guarding and protecting Israel "from the defiling idolatry of the Gentiles, preserving a community which propagated faith in the God of Abraham until the promise made to Abraham became historical reality" (p. 154).

[43] See J. H. Neyrey, "Bewitched in Galatia: Paul and Cultural Anthropology," *CBQ* 50 (1988) 72–100, esp. pp. 80–83.

[44] This is the nub of Hübner's consistent misinterpretation of Paul's treatment of the law in Galatians. His insistence that 3:10 has in view "the primarily *quantitative* demand of the law that all . . . its stipulations be followed out, so that whoever transgresses against even a single one of these stipulations is accursed" (*Law,* 38) ignores the facts that "doing what the law requires" includes the provision of atonement for failure (see above n. 3), and that Paul equally expects "the whole law" to be "fulfilled" by believers (5:14). See also Barclay's critique of Hübner at this point (*Obeying,* 136–37). Hübner's, of course, is a variant of the normal interpretation of 3:10 (see *Jesus, Paul and the Law,* chap. 8 n. 38).

[45] F. Watson turns Paul's concerns upside down. Far from objecting to a covenantal nomism

IV

The last main part of my thesis is the claim that *Galatians is Paul's first sustained attempt to deal with the issue of covenantal nomism within the new movement we call Christianity.* The main ground for the claim is that covenantal nomism does not seem to have been an issue before the Antioch incident (2:11–14). Here the relation between 2:1–10 and 2:11–14 is important. What had been settled at Jerusalem (2:1–10) was the issue of circumcision. What emerged at Antioch (2:11–14) was a different issue—food laws. Just how different these issues were lay at the heart of the disagreement.

If we assume that the "certain individuals from James" (2:12) had accepted the Jerusalem agreement not to require circumcision of Gentile converts (however unwillingly, perhaps), then it follows that they must have regarded the agreement as permitting a concession rather than as conceding a principle. They may well have regarded it as simply extending the degree of hospitality to God-fearers which diaspora Judaism had hitherto regularly practiced (not least in Syria; see Josephus, *J.W.* 2.18.2 §§462–63; 7.3.3 §§50–51). That they did not think the principle of covenantal nomism had thereby been conceded is probably indicated by 2:10: almsgiving was such a fundamental expression of covenantal righteousness (Dan 4:27; Sir 29:12; 40:24; Tob 4:10; 12:9; 14:10–11)[46] that Paul's ready agreement to maintain the practice could easily be read as an expression of his own readiness to maintain the principle of covenantal nomism. Moreover, since the tradition of Gentile sympathizers willingly embracing the ancestral customs of the Jews ("judaizing")

---

which inevitably means a reinforcement of the boundary between Jew(ish Christian) and Gentile (Christian), Watson thinks Paul's objective was that "the church should separate from the Jewish community" (*Paul, Judaism and the Gentiles: A Sociological Approach* [SNTSMS 56; Cambridge: Cambridge University Press, 1986] 64). This thesis recognizes only the discontinuities in Paul's view of *Heilsgeschichte* (promise/law, two covenants) and fails to recognize the continuity of Abraham's seed, of the "we" which includes Jew and Gentile (3:14; 4:5), of a sonship coming to maturity (3:23–4:5), and of the law fulfilled with faith and in love (5:6, 14). The other major flaw in Watson's thesis is that he uses "Jewish community" in a too undifferentiated and all-inclusive sense. There were Jews for whom Paul's argument and gospel would mean total separation, but there were others—Jewish Christians still functioning as Jews in synagogue service—who would go along with Paul (himself a Jewish Christian). And there were no doubt still others, Jews and Jewish Christians, with ambivalent views in between. It was not a case of Paul accepting the boundaries (circumcision, food laws, etc.) as immovable and simply stepping outside of them (contrast 1 Cor 9:20–21); he was attempting to redraw the boundaries with Gentile Christians inside! See also my critique of Watson in *Romans,* see index, under "Watson"; also my responses to P. F. Esler and H. Räisänen in *Jesus, Paul and the Law,* chap. 6, Additional Note 10, and chap. 7, Additional Note 4, respectively.

[46] See further K. Berger, "Almosen für Israel: Zum historischen Kontext der paulinischen Kollekte," *NTS* 23 (1976–77) 180–204.

was so well established,[47] the men from James may well have assumed that the table fellowship in Antioch was on a judaizing basis. This would be sufficient to explain why the issue did not emerge earlier from the Jerusalem side.[48]

On Paul's side, the agreement at Jerusalem was probably taken as a point of principle. Paul understood circumcision in what we would now call covenantal nomistic terms: it was not simply a rite of entry, but the first act of a continuing compliance with the law. The agreement in Jerusalem would be understood by him as providing a precedent for playing down other boundary-defining, Gentile-excluding commandments. If, however, 2:10 is once again anything to go by, the issue was not yet so clearly defined for him. He warmly agreed to a continuing emphasis on almsgiving without seeing it as a qualification of the agreement on circumcision. Perhaps the relief at winning the day on his principal objective made him eager to assent to this one request (requirement?) without sufficient thought for how it would be understood in Jerusalem. Or perhaps the connection between covenantal nomism and Jewish ethnic identity had not yet become sharply focused for him; after all, any almsgiving by Gentile to Jew could be readily understood within such a mind-set as part of Gentile acknowledgment of Jewish hegemony (Isa 45:14; 60:5-17; 61:6; Mic 4:13; Tob 13:11; 1QM 12:13-15).

Whatever the precise facts on either side, and whatever the shared or differing understandings of the Jerusalem agreement,[49] the Antioch incident itself seems to have come as a surprise to both sides—the men from James surprised at Jewish Christians' disregard of the food laws to such an extent and Paul surprised that there still was an issue here. In any event, the Antioch incident seems to have been the first major dispute on the issue of food laws or, in more general terms, on the issue of whether covenantal nomism as hitherto understood was still binding on Jewish Christians.

Gal 2:14-16 does look as though Paul is marking out a step beyond a previously agreed position. To be more precise, in these verses Paul seems to be making explicit a theological logic which he may well previously have taken for granted (and so not previously formulated), but which others (even

[47] See n. 5 above.

[48] For the pressures leading to the demand of the men from James, see my "Incident at Antioch," §2.2, with particular reference to R. Jewett, "The Agitators and the Galatian Congregation," *NTS* 17 (1970-71) 204-6.

[49] I question whether it is right to speak of a "unilateral reversal of the earlier agreement" on the part of James (so P. J. Achtemeier, *The Quest for Unity in the New Testament Church* [Philadelphia: Fortress, 1987] 54; see also Watson, *Paul*, 53-56). Barrett's formulation is probably nearer the mark: "What agreement there was had probably been inadequately thought through" (*Freedom*, 12).

close associates) had not recognized or agreed to, as the Antioch incident demonstrated. What he now saw with clarity was that the gospel relativized the nationalistic expression of covenantal nomism, and it is this which he (quite possibly for the first time) expressed at Antioch to Peter. Since Peter and the other Jewish Christians at Antioch probably did not accept Paul's argument at that time,[50] Paul uses the opportunity of this letter to Galatia to restate, and presumably to strengthen, the argument used then.

The issue is clearly posed in ethnic terms—Jew and Gentile, "living like Gentiles," "judaizing" (2:14). Here the traditional parameters of covenantal nomism are in view: they can be defined simply as "not living like the Gentiles" (see, e.g., *Jub.* 6:35; 15:34; *Pss. Sol.* 8:13). Likewise, the traditional life-style of the God-fearer—"judaizing"—is evident. The assumption of the men from James and of Peter and the other Jewish Christians is clearly implied: in order for the Jew(ish Christians) to continue to practice their covenantal nomism, the Gentile God-fearers/Christians should be prepared to judaize, to live like Jews. What Paul cannot stomach, however, is that this should be made a requirement for faith. The use of the same verb in 2:3 and 2:14 ("compel") is not accidental. What Paul objects to is that the agreement made in Jerusalem is being set at naught by the de facto compulsion of the Jewish Christians' behavior in regard to table fellowship at Antioch.

The sense of ethnic boundary and distinctiveness is again to the fore in v. 15—"Jews by nature," "Gentile sinners." And since "sinner" indicates the lawless person (see, e.g., Ps 27:2; 54:3; 1 Macc 1:34; 2:44), again the implication is clear that the issue focuses on the function of the law as defining the Gentile per se as "sinner" (Ps 9:17; 1 Macc 2:48; *Pss. Sol.* 1:1; 2:1–2; Luke 6:33/Matt 5:47).[51] To be noted is the fact that Paul expresses himself in traditionally Jewish terms ("we are Jews by nature"). *He speaks as one who is consciously within Judaism* and conscious of his distinctiveness from the Gentile; he speaks as one within the law, who has traditionally seen the Gentile as outside the bounds marked out by the law—and so by definition a "sinner." Since it is this very distinction that he will be going on to question, it must be that Paul is trying to argue from an agreed position and perspective within Judaism to a new position and perspective. It is probable also that the movement in self-understanding which he is thereby trying to encourage was a

---

[50] That Paul's plea to Peter was unsuccessful is now accepted by most commentators. See, e.g., Achtemeier, *Quest,* 59 and those cited by him in nn. 8–9; and see further below.

[51] A. Suhl completely ignores this whole dimension of the historical context when he attempts to defend the paraphrase, "We, of course Jews by nature and not stemming from the Gentiles, are nevertheless sinners (as much as them)" ("Der Galaterbrief—Situation und Argumentation," *ANRW* II.25.4 [1987] 3102–6).

reflection of his own changed self-understanding. But he remains a Jew; *it is still an inner-Jewish dispute.*[52] He is still able to identify himself with the older mind-set, which suggests that the full implications of his own changed perspective are still only becoming clear to him.

This sheds light on the much misunderstood opening to 2:16, which I still think has to be read as follows: "We are Jews by nature . . . knowing that someone is not justified by works of law except [*or,* but only] through faith in Jesus Christ. . . ."[53] Paul continues to locate himself within the Jewish mind-set, but now the traditional Jewish perspective is qualified by giving "faith in Christ" the decisive role.[54] *What is expressed here is the viewpoint of Peter and the other Jewish Christians at Antioch.* They are all at one so far as the gospel's call for faith in Jesus Christ is concerned. The Jewish Christian understanding is that although this is a fundamental redefinition of covenantal nomism, the life of righteousness *within* the covenant is still defined by works of the law. But that, the Jewish Christians now believe, is not decisive for acceptance by God and final acquittal. Faith in God's Messiah is the primary necessity. "No one is justified by works of law unless they also believe in Messiah Jesus."

This is Paul's starting point, as his own Jewish identity was in v. 15, but he goes on from that to underline the equally evident fact that faith in Christ Jesus has been exercised and has been fully effective *without* works of the law.

---

[52]See further K. Haacker, "Paulus und das Judentum im Galaterbrief," *Gottes Augapfel: Beiträge zur Erneuerung des Verhältnisses von Christen und Juden* (ed. E. Brocke and J. Sein; Neukirchen-Vluyn: Neukirchener Verlag, 1986) 95–111; and W. D. Davies's critical review of H. D. Betz, *Galatians: A Commentary on Paul's Letter to the Churches in Galatia* (Hermeneia; Philadelphia: Fortress, 1979) in *Jewish and Pauline Studies* (London: SPCK, 1984) 172–88.

[53] See further my "New Perspective," in *Jesus, Paul and the Law,* with Additional Notes 3 and 9; and Watson, *Paul,* 197 n. 73.

[54] I remain quite unconvinced by the now renewedly popular argument that "the faith of Christ" means "Christ's faith" rather than "faith in Christ." The latter is wholly in line with the sustained thrust of the letter, including the fundamental distinction between (human) faith and (human) works, whereas the former introduces a quite different tack. R. B. Hays, for example, in the fullest recent treatment, finds himself drawn into arguing that effectively all the key πίστις references in Gal 3:1–14 denote the faithfulness of Christ (*The Faith of Jesus Christ* [SBLDS 56; Chico, CA: Scholars Press, 1983] chap. 4). But the relevant πίστις references of 3:7–9 are bracketed by talk of Abraham's believing and Abraham's πίστις (vv. 6, 9) and are more naturally understood as carrying the same sense of πίστις. Further, 3:14 is more naturally understood to speak of the mode of *receiving* ("through faith") than of the mode of bestowing. The problem with "the faith of Christ" interpretation is that to be sustainable it must draw in most other πίστις references, leaving the verbal reference to human believing without a noun counterpart at important points in the argument, the mode of human reception thus unspecified, and references like Gal 5:5–6 in some confusion. The debate on this phrase was postponed at the Chicago meeting till the Pauline Theology Group reaches Romans. But see also now Barclay, *Obeying,* 78 n. 8; and Westerholm, *Israel's Law,* 111–12 n. 12.

Experience has demonstrated that God's acceptance is not conditional on covenantal nomism, certainly as that is usually understood. Experience of grace has given sufficient proof that "no one will be justified before God" (Ps 143:2), and that must include all who depend on their Jewish status and praxis for justification or who think of themselves as righteous because they live in accordance with the ancestral customs. Jewish Christians and Galatians should carry this basic insight through in their continuing life together and not return to questions of ethnic ("flesh") and religious ("sinners") distinctions.

Here again, therefore, the very structure of the argument seems to indicate a transition in Paul's own thinking and perspective. We seem to see Paul working through the implications of his understanding of the gospel, Paul forced by the turn of events in Antioch to bring to clear expression consequences and corollaries which he had previously practiced without having had to spell out their full theological rationale.

A further indication that there has been some development in Paul's own position, or at least in his articulation of it as it related to more traditional Jewish perspectives, is the change in Paul's attitude toward the Jerusalem apostles as it becomes evident in 2:1–10. In this passage the tension between a readiness to accept their authority and a clear distancing of himself from them is quite evident.[55]

On the one hand, he readily acknowledges that their reception of his understanding of the gospel would determine whether his work had been or was in vain (2:2). He expresses himself with great care when he describes the actual encounter in Jerusalem (2:3ff.), but the implication of v. 3 is that Paul recognized the Jerusalem authorities' right to require circumcision, if they so chose. His relief that they did not "compel" Titus to be circumcised is fairly evident, as is his relief that they "added nothing to him" (2:6) so far as his understanding and preaching of the gospel was concerned. But the implication is the same: he acknowledged thereby that they had a right to make such stipulations. Indeed, this may lie behind his readiness to accept the obligation that was actually laid down in v. 10, to remember the poor. There is even an implication that he recognized the pillar apostles' authority to confirm his mission to the Gentiles. Such, at any rate, seems to be the significance of the right hand of fellowship given in order that Barnabas and Paul should go to the Gentiles, just as Peter and the others should go to the circumcised (2:9).

At the same time, Paul also clearly wants to distance himself from the

---

[55] In the following paragraphs I draw on my "Relationship between Paul and Jerusalem according to Galatians 1 and 2," *NTS* 28 (1982) 461–78, reprinted in *Jesus, Paul and the Law*, chap. 5.

Jerusalem authorities. He describes them as "those reputed to be of some account," "those regarded as pillars" (2:6, 9), phrases neatly chosen to indicate that they were highly esteemed, but not necessarily by him. In v. 10 he coyly omits the verb that would have been most appropriate to describe the obligation laid upon him by the pillar apostles, lest, presumably, it seem that he had agreed to an element of traditional covenantal nomism at their behest. Clearest of all is the parenthesis inserted into v. 6: "what they [the pillar apostles] once were matters nothing to me; God takes no account of human evaluation of status." Here Paul is almost explicit in his implication that he had once accorded the Jerusalem apostles an authority which he no longer recognized and to which he was no longer willing to submit.

The best way to explain the tension between these rather different attitudes to the Jerusalem authorities is that they reflect different stages in Paul's own career and mission. There was a period when he acknowledged and would have been ready to defer to the authority of Peter and the others. Presumably this was the period when he was active as a member of the church in Antioch, that is to say, during his time both as a teacher in Antioch (if we follow Acts 13:1), and as a missionary commissioned by Antioch (Acts 13:2–3).[56] The decisive factor here, presumably, would be that Antioch saw itself as a daughter church of Jerusalem. Consequently, Paul probably attended the Jerusalem consultation (Gal 2:1–10) as a delegate from Antioch. All during this period, and immediately thereafter, he recognized and operated within the terms of Jerusalem's authority. The degree of mutual acceptance implies that covenantal nomism as such had not yet become an issue.

That issue only came to the surface in the Antioch incident (2:11–14). Whether it would have exploded into outright disagreement at Jerusalem if the pillar apostles had after all tried to "compel" Titus to be circumcised we cannot tell. Quite likely the answer is yes. Paul was sufficiently clearheaded on the circumcision issue to fight his corner with the utmost resolution (2:5). *But the acceptance of his argument at that time was probably enough to prevent the issue emerging in terms of mutually exclusive possibilities: either* covenantal nomism *or* faith. What is clear enough is that when such compulsion was exerted by the men from James, and when Peter and the other Jewish Christians acquiesced to what they demanded, at that point Paul drew the line (2:14ff.). His rejection of the demands of covenantal nomism as they affected the Gentile Christians was at the same time a rejection of the Jerusalem authority

---

[56] I take "apostles" in Acts 14:4, 14 in the sense of emissaries or missionaries of Antioch (see 2 Cor 8:23; Phil 2:25), since according to Acts 1:21–22 neither Paul nor Barnabas could be accounted apostles in the sense of witnesses of Christ's resurrection (as claimed by Paul for himself in 1 Cor 9:1; 15:7–11).

which laid them down. Here again, therefore, is sufficient indication that the Antioch incident was a decisive factor in the development of Paul's under-standing of the gospel, both of how it related to covenantal nomism and what that meant for Gentile believers in relation to the hitherto unquestioned assumption that covenant membership was bound up with Jewish ethnic identity.[57]

To complete the argument I include a brief response to those who claim that Paul's attitude to the law (and so also to covenantal nomism) was a more or less immediate consequence of his Damascus road conversion.[58]

In the first place, I find no evidence to indicate that the Hellenists had already "abandoned" the law. The only material that explicitly claims to express Hellenist views (Acts 7) is directed against the temple and not against the law. In Acts 7 the attitude to the law is positive (7:38, 53). That temple and law were tightly bound together is, of course, true (the laws of sacrifice, etc.), and hence the accusation against Stephen in Acts 6:14 is formulated in terms of both. But it requires no argument to claim that the law could be held in high esteem even when the temple was heavily criticized or, subsequently, when the temple ceased to be a factor in the life and praxis of Judaism. We cannot assume therefore that what Paul was converted to was a Hellenist rejection of the law.

Paul's persecution of the church was certainly an expression of his zeal for the law (Gal 1:13–14; Phil 3:6). This should not be taken as implying a wholesale rejection of the law by the Hellenists who were being persecuted. The key word here is "zeal." It indicates the attitude of a zealot, one who wanted to define the boundaries around the covenant more sharply, to mark off the righteous more clearly from the sinner. It expresses an attitude evident in such writings as *1 Enoch* 1–5, the *Psalms of Solomon,* and the Dead Sea Scrolls, and also, it would appear, among the Pharisees—a factional or even sectarian attitude that was prepared to condemn and even to persecute fellow

---

[57] Watson argues that the Gentile mission began as a response to the failure of the Jewish Christian congregation of Antioch in its preaching among the Jews and that it "involved a more or less complete separation from the Jewish community" (*Paul,* 31–32, 36–38). This ignores the evidence of Gal 2:9 that there was a conjoint mission to Jews and Gentiles and of Gal 2:12a that there was at least initially in Antioch a continuum of Jew, Jewish-Christian, and Gentile Chris-tian. It also treats 1 Cor 9:21–22 (present tense) and 2 Cor 11:24 in a highly tendentious way, not to mention the primary thrust of Romans 9–11. The implication is that Paul continued to operate within the context of the synagogue so far as possible and sought to maintain the continuum. See also n. 45 above.

[58] Particularly S. Kim, *The Origin of Paul's Gospel* (WUNT 2/4; Tübingen: Mohr [Siebeck], 1981); and C. Dietzfelbinger, *Die Berufung des Paulus als Ursprung seiner Theologie* (WMANT 58; Neukirchen-Vluyn: Neukirchener Verlag, 1985). What follows supplements the discussion of *Jesus, Paul and the Law,* chap. 4.

Jews whose loyalty to the ancestral traditions was not so firm and whose practice seemed to question and so to threaten these more tightly drawn boundaries.[59] Thus we should probably envisage a persecution by Paul of Jews who *in their own reckoning* were being properly observant of what the law required—a condemnation of fellow Jews equivalent to that of the Pharisees by the Qumran covenanters, or of the Sadduccees by the *Psalms of Solomon,* or subsequently of the fainthearted by the Zealots.[60]

Paul's own view of his conversion is not of a *conversion* as such—not a conversion in his attitude to the law and far less a conversion *from* Judaism— but of a commissioning to go to the Gentiles (Gal 1:15–16).[61] His acknowl-edgment of the crucified as Lord did not lead him at once to the conclusion that the law which counted the crucified as accursed was wholly discredited and disowned by God. Such a line of reasoning appears nowhere in Paul's writings. The theological logic focuses rather on the relation between the curse of the law and the Gentile. For Christ to have died as one cursed by the law meant that he had been put outside the covenant, had become, in effect, like a Gentile. For God to have vindicated this Christ therefore meant that that boundary line between Gentile and Jew no longer counted with God. God accepted the outsider; his promise could now be accepted by the Gentiles without their coming within the boundary of the law (3:13–14).[62] The seed and principle of Paul's full-blown theology of justification was thus given him from the first, which is why he puts so much emphasis on the "revelation of Christ" (1:12) in the letter. But evidently the full implications of it were not worked out and did not become clear in these early years, presumably because the ambiguity of God-fearers and proselytes both believing in Jesus *and* willing to judaize to some extent (as they had done before they heard about Jesus) meant that the issue had not yet come into focus. Certainly it is hard to believe that Jew and Gentile believers in Messiah Jesus had completely abandoned the law in Antioch for a decade or more before it came to the attention of the more conservative brothers in Judea or caused any kind of surprise or comment.[63]

In short, the evidence of Galatians seems to indicate that an evolving

---

[59] See Haacker, "Paulus und das Judentum," 104–7; my *Romans,* 586–87; and *Jesus, Paul and the Law,* chap. 4, Additional Note 1. Despite Sanders's rejection of the claim that Paul's persecution of the church was tied up with his convictions as a Pharisee, it must be significant to the contrary that Paul uses the same word, "zeal," to characterize both his commitment to the ancestral customs of his people (that is, as a Pharisee [Gal 1:14]) and his energy in persecution (Phil 3:6).

[60] See also *Jesus, Paul and the Law,* chap. 3.

[61] Ibid., chap. 4 n. 1.

[62] See the fuller exposition in *Jesus, Paul and the Law,* chap. 4 and chap. 8 n. 56a.

[63] Ibid., chap. 6, Additional Note 1.

situation in Antioch and a double confrontation with what had hitherto usually been regarded as central in covenantal nomism brought home to Paul what he now saw always to have been implicit in his initial commissioning to the Gentiles. It is this implication for covenantal nomism which he works out, probably for the first time in such detail, in his letter to his converts in Galatia.

11 THE SINGULARITY OF THE GOSPEL

A Reading of Galatians

Beverly Roberts Gaventa
Columbia Theological Seminary

IN HIS LETTER to Galatian Christians, Paul responds to a problem that has arisen because, subsequent to his initial preaching and teaching in this region, other Christians have offered a different interpretation of the gospel. Those who have entered the Galatian churches after Paul insist that circumcision and keeping of (at least portions of) the Law of Moses are necessary for full membership in the people of Israel. The advent of Jesus Christ means that Gentiles may become full partners in Israel, but it does not in any way call into question the law itself. Paul's letter responds in the sharpest manner to those who find this "other gospel" attractive, arguing that Gentile Christians *must not* take on the observance of the law. Paul's strategy in dealing with this problem is to argue both from the experience of believers and from the interpretation of scripture that the law belongs to a past age and *must not* be observed by Gentiles who are "in Christ." Although one could scarcely speak of a consensus among Pauline scholars, this scenario is typical of the ways in which Galatians is read.[1]

For the purpose of identifying the theology reflected in this particular Pauline letter, it is important to ask whether Paul's response to the problem in Galatia constitutes the theology of the letter. That is, in order to discern

[1] For discussions of the situation behind the letter, see J. B. Tyson, "Paul's Opponents in Galatia," *NovT* 4 (1968) 241–54; R. Jewett, "The Agitators and the Galatian Congregation," *NTS* 17 (1970–71) 198–212; J. Eckert, *Die urchristliche Verkündigung im Streit zwischen Paulus und seinen Gegnern nach dem Galaterbrief* (Biblische Untersuchungen 6; Regensburg: Pustet, 1971); W. Schmithals, *Paul and the Gnostics* (Nashville: Abingdon, 1972); G. Howard, *Paul: Crisis in Galatia* (SNTSMS 35; Cambridge: Cambridge University Press, 1979) 1–19; B. H. Brinsmead, *Galatians: Dialogical Response to Opponents* (SBLDS 65; Chico, CA: Scholars Press, 1982); J. Louis Martyn, "A Law-Observant Mission to Gentiles: The Background of Galatians," *SJT* 38 (1985) 307–24; T. David Gordon, "The Problem at Galatia," *Int* 41 (1987) 32–43.

the theology of Galatians, do we primarily look at Paul's response to the stated problem? Apparently H. D. Betz would answer that question in the affirmative. His discussion of the theology of Galatians focuses on the problem, which he takes to be the threat posed to the freedom of the Galatians by outsiders who are insisting that Gentile believers in Christ must submit to the Law of Moses if they are to be full members of the people of Israel. Betz's presentation of the theology of the letter thus delineates Paul's arguments against the position of his opponents, identifying as central Paul's concept of freedom.[2]

Despite his careful articulation of the relationship between coherence and contingency in Paul's letters, J. Christiaan Beker's interpretation of Galatians appears to tip the balance toward contingency by identifying the theology of this letter with the argument Paul makes against the position taken by his opponents.[3] Because his Jewish Christian opponents have presented a version of salvation history that stresses the continuity between Abraham, the law, circumcision, and Christ, Paul is forced to insist on the disjuncture between law and Christ, between law and faith. Although Beker insists that the function of Paul's discussion about Abraham and the law in Galatians 3 can be understood only within the "total context of the letter,"[4] he follows the conventional wisdom in distinguishing between the "personal" part of Galatians (chaps. 1–2) and the "material considerations" in 3:1–5:25.[5]

It is worth noting that both these understandings of the letter focus almost exclusively on chaps. 3–4. Indeed, analyses of Galatians almost universally identify chaps. 3–4 as the theological center of the letter. Since the first two chapters are regarded as a defense of Paul's apostleship, they do not enter the discussion of "theology." Similarly, the last two chapters are frequently bracketed off as parenesis, which, by virtue of its traditional character, is not regarded as shedding light on Paul's theology. The result of this analysis of the letter is that discussions about the theology of Galatians take chaps. 3–4 as their starting point and then move backward to chaps. 1–2 and forward to chaps. 5–6.

Such a reading of Galatians has the effect of virtually ignoring chaps. 1–2 (with the possible exception of 2:16–21). These chapters enter the picture when the goal is to reconstruct something of a "life of Paul" or the history

---

[2] H. D. Betz, *Galatians: A Commentary on Paul's Letter to the Churches in Galatia* (Hermeneia; Philadelphia: Fortress, 1979) 28–33.

[3] Beker himself acknowledges that this is the case (*Paul the Apostle: The Triumph of God in Life and Thought* [Philadelphia: Fortress, 1980] 56–58).

[4] Ibid., 41.

[5] Ibid., 47. Elsewhere I have attempted to show the problems with this conventional notion that Galatians 1–2 deal entirely with matters of self-defense; see "Galatians 1 and 2: Autobiography as Paradigm," *NovT* 28 (1986) 302–26.

of early Christianity, but not when the issue is assessing the theological argument of the letter.[6] Similarly, chaps. 5–6 are bracketed off as pragmatic advice of a traditional character that bears no material relationship to the preceding chapters.[7]

If we attend not simply to chaps. 3–4 but to the whole of the letter,[8] an alternative possibility emerges, namely, that although the letter arises out of the issue of the law, the underlying theological convictions that shape Paul's response to the problem derive not from his interpretation of the law but from his christology. The theology reflected in Galatians is first of all about Jesus Christ and the new creation God has begun in him (1:1–4; 6:14–15), and only in the light of that christocentrism can Paul's remarks concerning the law be understood.[9] The word "christocentrism" is the right word, in that Paul presupposes from beginning to end that there is only one gospel (1:6–9), the singularity of which consists of the revelation of Jesus Christ as God's son whose crucifixion inaugurates the new age. This singular gospel results in a singular transformation for those called as believers, who are themselves moved into a new identity in Christ alone (2:19–21; 3:26–29) and new life in the Spirit (3:1–4; 5:16–25).[10] The new creation results in the nullification of previous identifications, whether these come from within the law (1:11–17) or from outside it (4:8–11). The position to be argued here, then, is that the governing theological antithesis in Galatians is between Christ or the new creation and the cosmos; the antitheses between Christ and the law and between the cross and circumcision are not the equivalent of this central premise but follow from it.

[6] Gaventa, "Autobiography as Paradigm," 311–13.

[7] On the relationship between the exhortations of Galatians 5–6 and the theological argument in chaps. 1–4, see Richard B. Hays, "Christology and Ethics in Galatians: The Law of Christ," *CBQ* 49 (1987) 268–90.

[8] I take this methodological point to be consistent with George Kennedy's comment that Paul's audience would have anticipated that the argument in the letter would develop in a linear manner (*New Testament Interpretation through Rhetorical Criticism* [Chapel Hill: University of North Carolina Press, 1984] 5, 146).

[9] So also J. Louis Martyn, who writes: "And even in the parts of Galatians that are heavily concerned with the Law, it is clear that Paul's theological point of departure is not the Law, but rather the advent of Christ, and specifically Christ's faithful death" ("Paul and His Jewish-Christian Interpreters," *USQR* 42 [1987–88] 4).

[10] The phrase "the singularity of the gospel" comes from John Schütz's discussion of Galatians in *Paul and the Anatomy of Apostolic Authority* (SNTSMS 26; Cambridge: Cambridge University Press, 1975) 121. In my judgment students of Paul have seriously neglected that work, in part at least because Schütz was several years ahead of the discussion of Paul in the context of the social sciences. On the issue of transformation in Paul, see John T. Koenig, "The Motif of Transformation in the Pauline Epistles: A History-of-Religions/Exegetical Study" (Ph.D. diss., Union Theological Seminary, 1970); B. R. Gaventa, *From Darkness to Light: Aspects of Conversion in the New Testament* (OBT 20; Philadelphia: Fortress, 1986) 40–46.

Three initial objections to this approach require brief comment. First, it may be thought that the argument that the theology of the letter is to be found elsewhere than in Paul's problem-solving strategy is tantamount to the view that Paul's theology is a timeless essence expressed differently in different contexts. That is not my intent. Indeed, a sidelong glance at Romans reveals the dramatic difference between the christocentrism of Galatians and the theocentrism of Romans. My argument is not that Paul takes from his theological storehouse the appropriate response for this setting, but that we may not arrive at the theology expressed in the letter by merely adding up responses to a particular problem. Just because the *present problem* concerns the law does not mean that, in Paul's perspective, the *central theological issue* at stake is the law. It is entirely possible that the Galatians themselves did not see the need to submit to the law as a theological issue. For them, it may have been an act of social identification or a pragmatic response to the demand of the outsiders. Whatever their view of the nature of the demand for circumcision, *Paul* sees in it the symptom of a critical theological problem.

The second objection arises as a result of introducing the term "christology," which we customarily associate with the systematic tasks of Christian theology in later periods. I am not suggesting that Paul's view of the relationship between divinity and humanity in Christ or his view of the relationship between Christ and God dictates his argument in Galatians. Nevertheless, it is his understanding of who Jesus Christ is and what he has inaugurated and accomplished, in other words *christology,* that stands as the focus of this letter.

Third, it may be objected that it is true but not important to say that Galatians is primarily to be understood as a christological statement. Paul makes use of traditional christologoumena (e.g., in 1:4), but—so the objection goes—those are only gestures to common tradition that have no impact on his argument and no significance for reading the letter itself. It will be my objective to show that these traditional expressions are not mere concessions to Paul's intended audience, but that they constitute an important part of the argument itself.[11]

I. WHY *NOT* OBSERVE THE LAW?

For heuristic purposes, we begin with a question that might be addressed to Paul in response to a reading of Galatians. Perhaps a group of believers

---

[11] This is consistent with the methodological procedure employed by Jouette Bassler in her study of Paul's use of the axiom of divine impartiality (*Divine Impartiality: Paul and a Theological Axiom* [SBLDS 59; Chico, CA: Scholars Press, 1982]). Bassler rightly contends that instead of assuming that traditional formulations reveal nothing of Paul's own thought, students of Paul need to attend to the way in which he uses those traditional affirmations.

from among the Galatians approach Paul, eager to find a solution that will satisfy both Paul and their more recent visitors. The question from this imaginary "compromise party"[12] runs as follows:

Why make such a point of saying that Christians *must not* follow the law? Perhaps the Gentiles will benefit from keeping some portions of the law. It surely cannot adversely affect their Christian lives, and it might help to restrain their enthusiastic or libertinistic tendencies. Would not the external sign of circumcision ensure that Gentile Christians identified themselves with the people of Israel and their God? You are perhaps right to contend that Gentiles are not *obliged* to follow the law, but why do you insist that they *must not* do so?

What arguments might be inferred from the letter in response to this imaginary proposal for a reasonable compromise between the two conflicting positions? Several possibilities can be considered and discarded. As is widely recognized, Paul's initial argument against the law is that it does not justify. Justification comes about only ἐκ πίστεως Χριστοῦ (2:16–21). To this may be added his reminder to the Galatians that they received the Spirit ἐξ ἀκοῆς πίστεως and not ἐξ ἔργων νόμου (3:1–5). Such statements do not adequately respond to the compromise position, however, since the compromise does not propose that the law saves or that the Galatians came to faith through the law, but only that the law might be profitable for identifying Gentiles with Israel and for curbing the temptation to sin.

A second kind of argument Paul employs is the priority of faith over the law in the course of Israel's history. Here, of course, Abraham enters the discussion, since God grants righteousness to Abraham on the basis of faith, not on the basis of observance of the law (3:6–9). Indeed, the law comes into the world some 430 years after the promise to Abraham, a promise made to faith (3:15–18). Again, this argument does not meet the position of the compromisers, who suggest (somewhat more emphatically this time) that even if the law is historically secondary to faith and the promise made to Abraham, it still has the important functions, given by God, of setting Israel apart from the rest of the world and protecting Israel against evil.

Paul also claims that all who are ἐξ ἔργων νόμου are under a curse (3:10–14) and that Christ's death on the cross, itself resulting in the law's curse, removes believers from that curse. Contrary to the way in which this passage is sometimes read, Paul does not conclude that Christ therefore nullifies or curses the law. The compromisers still have room to suggest that even if

---

[12] I want it to be clear that I introduce this scenario entirely for heuristic purposes. It is not my intention to suggest that a "compromise party" ever existed, but I contend that the question I ascribe to such an imaginary group does logically follow from the letter itself.

Christ's death removes believers from the law's curse, its power to discipline and direct the behavior of believers remains in force and remains necessary. These aspects of Paul's argument about the law do not seem effective as a response to the hypothetical question, Why *not* observe the law? One remaining feature of his argument even serves to reinforce the reasonableness of the compromisers' position, and that is Paul's contention that the law was intended as a protection (παιδαγωγός) against sin.[13] To be sure, Paul introduces this claim in connection with the argument that the law was a temporary measure, superseded by Christ, but even *in* Christ the law might be understood as a curb against sin. To our sense that Paul's argument so far is something less than satisfying we may add George Kennedy's observation that Paul might easily have employed more common arguments against circumcision as unaesthetic and unnatural.[14]

I have deliberately omitted from this imaginary exchange the dominant thread in Paul's comments about the law in order to highlight the fact that the argument regarding the law in Galatians 3–4 consists of statements used to bolster a previously chosen position.[15] That is, these are arguments which reinforce a position already taken, and it is that position, rather than these subordinate arguments, which leads us to understand what Paul's primary response to a compromise party would be.[16]

What the imaginary exchange deliberately omits is the antithesis Paul perceives between Christ and the law. Turning back now to Paul's comments about the law, we see that as early as the letter's first reference to the law in 2:16, it stands in direct opposition to Christ. One is either justified ἐξ ἔργων νόμου or διὰ πίστεως Ἰησοῦ Χριστοῦ (2:16). The same kind of antithesis dominates much of the argument in chap. 3. The Spirit came to the Galatians

---

[13] This understanding of the παιδαγωγός image in Galatians 3 is influenced by the work of David J. Lull in "'The Law Was Our Pedagogue': A Study in Galatians 3:19–25," *JBL* 105 (1986) 481–98. See also Norman H. Young, "*Paidagogos*: The Social Setting of a Pauline Metaphor," *NovT* 29 (1987) 150–76.

[14] Kennedy, *Rhetorical Criticism*, 151.

[15] In his essay in this volume, N. T. Wright helpfully distinguishes between the way in which an individual arrives at a conclusion and the arguments that same individual may employ when demonstrating that conclusion to others (see below, pp. 192–94). Of course, Paul would insist that he did not choose this position; it was chosen for him (1:11–17).

[16] Here I am clearly influenced by the argument of E. P. Sanders that for Paul the solution precedes the problem (*Paul and Palestinian Judaism* [Philadelphia: Fortress, 1977] 442–47). To put it as Sanders does elsewhere: "Paul's various statements about the law are not the result of theoretical thought about the law as such, but spring from and serve other convictions. The main lines of his discussions about the law are determined by christology, soteriology (especially their universal aspects), and what we may call Christian behavior" (*Paul, the Law, and the Jewish People* [Philadelphia: Fortress, 1983] 143).

either through faith *or* through the law (3:1–5). The extremely complex section 3:10–14 turns on this opposition, since Paul sets over against each other Hab 2:4 ("the righteous one will live by faith" [v. 11b]) and Lev 18:5 ("the one who does these things will live by them" [v. 12b]) in order to show that the law is not from faith.

The baptismal formula employed in vv. 26–29 makes it clear that Paul is not simply arguing *against* some defect in the law but *for* the conviction that those who are baptized are baptized into Christ. That identification is not only primary; it is exclusive. There can be no identification both in Christ and under the law — not even under some portion of the law understood as an aid for those in danger of succumbing to temptation in the form of libertinism.[17] Paul's response to the compromisers' proposition is clear: There can be no compromise between Christ and the law. Compromise is the thing Paul cannot do — and that not for psychological or social reasons but for profoundly theological reasons.[18] There can be no compromising of the gospel's singular and exclusive location in Jesus Christ alone.

This antithesis between Christ and the law becomes explicit in 5:1–6. To receive circumcision means that one derives no benefit from Christ (5:2). Circumcision obligates one to the whole law, which means that one is set apart from the grace of Christ. Again we find the expression "in Christ" positioned antithetically over against circumcision (5:6). One may be under the law or one may be in Christ, but it is impossible to be both.[19]

II. THE SINGULARITY OF THE GOSPEL

We have seen that the antithesis between Christ and the law dominates Paul's argument regarding the law in Galatians 3–4, and the question arises

---

[17] It has, of course, been argued that νόμος Χριστοῦ refers to just such a law, appropriate for the messianic age (C. H. Dodd, "ENNOMOS CHRISTOU," in *More New Testament Studies* [Manchester: Manchester University Press, 1968] 134–48; W. D. Davies, *Paul and Rabbinic Judaism* [4th ed.; Philadelphia: Fortress, 1980] 142–45). The expression is better understood, however, as an ironic formulation designed to counter Paul's opponents (Hays, "Christology and Ethics," 275).

[18] To some this will appear to be an exaggerated statement. It may be that Paul was himself psychologically constructed such that he could not compromise, or it may be that he perceived a threat to the boundary of the community and hence would not compromise for a social reason. I do not imply that such investigations are inappropriate; however, the reasoning that Galatians 3 makes available to us is theological reasoning.

[19] In a recent article, T. L. Donaldson revives the thesis that Paul's understanding of the incompatibility between Christ and the law may be traced to the period prior to his conversion ("Zealot and Convert: The Origin of Paul's Christ-Torah Antithesis," *CBQ* 51 [1989] 655–82).

whether this same pattern holds in the remainder of the letter. Since the term νόμος does not appear until 2:16, the letter does not begin with an explicit antithesis between Christ and the law. Instead of an attack on the law, here we find an assertion about the singular character of the gospel and its claims.

The letter opens with a salutation that immediately focuses on Jesus Christ. Although it is customary to see in 1:1 the beginnings of Paul's defense of his apostleship, even on this reading of the verse Paul points immediately to the source of his apostleship: "Jesus Christ and God [the] father who raised him from [the] dead." The grace reverses this order of "Jesus Christ and God" and introduces a more extended formula: "God our father and Lord Jesus Christ, who gave himself on behalf of our sins, in order that he might deliver us from the present evil age according to the will of God and our father. . . ."[20] It is worth noting how much we learn from these few lines. Already we know that Paul's apostleship comes from Jesus Christ. Jesus is identified as one who gave himself for "our" sins. This act had as its goal "our" deliverance from the present age, which Paul identifies as evil. God, who is designated as father, not only willed the action of Jesus Christ but raised him from the dead. The fact that Paul may be using traditional language here does not diminish the importance of this opening statement. The common "story" to which he refers is one about Jesus Christ and his actions, in accordance with God's will and as a result of God's power, as savior ("on behalf of our sins," "to deliver us").[21] Since the letter lacks the traditional thanksgiving, in which we would expect to find indications of the subject of the letter, the suspicion arises that in Galatians the salutation itself introduces the main issue to be addressed.[22]

What Paul wishes to say about Jesus Christ becomes more focused in vv. 6–9. The Galatians have turned away from the one who called them and are turning to "another gospel." With a variety of expressions, Paul insists that there is no second gospel: ὃ οὐκ ἔστιν ἄλλο . . . μεταστρέψαι τὸ εὐαγγέλιον τοῦ Χριστοῦ . . . εὐαγγελίζεται παρ' ὃ παρελάβετε. For Paul, it is essential to understand that the gospel is singular and the Galatians may have left its sphere for that of "another" gospel, which does not exist. Little in vv. 6–9 allows us to identify the content or character of this singular gospel. Paul

---

[20] Unless otherwise indicated, translations of biblical texts are my own.

[21] On the issue of the "story" of Jesus that underlies Galatians, see Richard B. Hays, *The Faith of Jesus Christ: An Investigation of the Narrative Substructure of Galatians 3:1–4:11* (SBLDS 56; Chico, CA: Scholars Press, 1983). Jouette Bassler has drawn attention to some limitations of this term ("Paul's Theology: Whence and Whither? A Synthesis (of sorts) of the Theology of Philemon, 1 Thessalonians, Philippians, Galatians, and 1 Corinthians," *Society of Biblical Literature 1989 Seminar Papers* [ed. D. J. Lull; Atlanta: Scholars Press, 1989] 412–23).

[22] So also Hays, "Christology and Ethics," 277 n. 28.

identifies it only with the word "of Christ" and with the indication that he ["we"] preached it among the Galatians. Paul does not say that this gospel brings freedom, that it has to do with justification by faith, or that it pertains to membership in Israel. It is simply the "gospel of Christ." That formulation points back to the language identifying Christ in vv. 1–5.

If we read no further than vv. 1–9, we would surely conclude that what motivates Paul's letter to the Galatians has to do with a differing understanding of the gospel, one introduced by those who "trouble" the Galatians. Although Paul does not specify the source of the difference, the identification of the gospel he preached as the "gospel of Christ" suggests that the difference concerns the understanding of Christ.

The passage often regarded as Paul's defense of his apostleship, 1:10 (or 1:11)–2:14 (or 2:21), also insists on the singular and exclusive nature of the gospel's claims. In Paul's retrospective account, he makes a sharp and uninterpreted transition from his former life (1:13–14) to his apostolic call (1:15–17). The two parts of his life, standing next to each other as they do here, support his conviction that the gospel comes from God alone and that it demands a singular and exclusive response.[23] Paul illustrates his own singular response to that gospel in 1:16b–2:21.

We have already seen the christocentrism in the central portion of the letter (chaps. 3–4), but it might be objected that the ethical exhortations of the last part (5:13–6:10) derive little from the christological perspectives of chaps. 1–4. Certainly it is true that the name of Christ appears seldom in this section, and commentators have often concluded from this that Paul's ethics have little material connection with his christology. Before we agree to this partitioning, we need to look at the kinds of exhortations presented here. Richard B. Hays has recently argued that Paul's exhortations in this part of the letter are largely concerned with issues of freedom and slavery and address those issues within the context of communal responsibility. Although Paul does not directly invoke the name of Christ (but see 5:6, 24; 6:2), the exhortations correspond to Paul's claims about the actions of Christ, whose crucifixion resulted directly from his obedience and love.[24]

The conclusion of the letter (6:11–18) confirms the impression left by its opening that Paul is preoccupied in this letter with the Christ-event, particularly with the exclusive nature of its claim upon believers. Here, where the argument of the letter culminates,[25] the antithesis between Christ and the

---

[23] More extensive discussion of this reading of 1:11–17 may be found in Gaventa, *From Darkness to Light*, 22–28; idem, "Autobiography as Paradigm," 314–16.

[24] So also Hays, "Christology and Ethics," 276–83, 289–90.

[25] Kennedy notes that in the epilogue Paul sums up what he believes he has demonstrated

law is first focused and then radicalized. In vv. 12–13, Paul takes up the Christ–law antithesis, but in what appears to be a highly focused way, for he contrasts a specific law, that of circumcision, with the cross of Christ. Those who urge circumcision do so only in order that they will not be persecuted because of the cross (6:12). They wish to boast in the flesh, while Paul boasts only in the cross (6:14a). It is at this point that Paul radicalizes the contrast: in the cross of Christ, the whole cosmos has been crucified to Paul, and Paul to the cosmos (6:14b). Therefore, the primary antithesis is not Christ–law, or cross–circumcision. These are but subsets of the more fundamental antithesis, which is between Christ/new creation and cosmos.[26]

III. ELEMENTS IN THE CHRISTOLOGY OF GALATIANS

We have seen that in Galatians Paul responds to a claim that believers must also observe the law, or at least parts of the law, by insisting that an antithesis exists between Christ and the cosmos (which, of course, includes the law). Can we be more precise about the content of the christology of Paul's letter to the Galatians and therefore about this antithesis? What is the nature of this opposition? Is it moral, philosophical, apocalyptic?

It is clear, first of all, that Christ is viewed by Paul as an agent of God. The dominance of language about Christ and the scarcity of language about God here could cause us to miss this point, but 1:1–4 and 4:3–5 make it clear that it is God who acts to send Christ and to raise him from the dead. The dominance of language about Christ should not lead us to read christomonism in Galatians, for Christ is clearly subordinate to God. It is God who reveals Christ, who calls Paul to proclaim Christ as God's son (1:15–16), and who calls the Galatians (1:6; see also 3:5).

Although the letter refers to Christ's resurrection, it is the crucifixion that dominates Paul's christology in Galatians. Paul sharply reminds the Galatians that Christ was presented to them publicly as "crucified" (3:1). Paul allows himself to boast only in the cross (6:14). This crucifixion results from Christ's own act of self-giving (1:4; 2:20). Because in the crucifixion the law placed Christ under a curse, that event purchased freedom from the law for those who are in Christ (3:10–14). This freedom is not merely freedom from the

---

with these words: "neither circumcision counts for anything nor uncircumcision, but a new creation" (*Rhetorical Criticism,* 151).

[26] On the conclusion of Galatians, I have been greatly helped by the paper my colleague Charles B. Cousar presented at the 1989 SBL meeting, "Galatians 6:11–18: Interpretive Clues to the Letter."

law (circumcision) but also from uncircumcision (5:6). In other words, the freedom Christ brings is not merely freedom from certain practices legally understood but freedom from all things—save Christ himself.

Here Betz's discussion about freedom in Galatians makes an important point, namely, that the preaching of those who followed Paul in the Galatian churches was attractive precisely because it offered a means to "protect the new Christian life from deterioration and destruction."[27] By being both "in Christ" and "under law," believers could be certain that they were full members of God's ἐκκλησία. At some level, they saw in Paul's preaching a threatening claim that they must live in—and only in—the gospel of Jesus Christ. The uncertainty of that claim and the perceived inability of this gospel to offer them concrete instructions for living out their faith made them willing to undertake the more secure avenue of the law.

Do Paul's references to the cross carry an implicit reference to resurrection as well, as is sometimes suggested? The answer to that question, at least in Galatians, must surely be no. Paul's references to the cross or crucifixion or death of Christ are multivalent in that they carry within them references to God's action in sending Christ, to Christ's love and faithfulness in the cross, and to the curse of the law; but that multivalence does not mean that cross for Paul includes resurrection. Although the formula of 1:1 refers to Christ's having been raised from the dead, most of the references to Jesus' death/cross in Galatians are sufficiently specific to exclude our attaching to them allusions to resurrection.[28]

More significant in Galatians is what the crucifixion expresses or reflects about Christ. One explanation Paul gives is that Christ's crucifixion stems from his self-giving love, as noted earlier. Paul also affirms that what has brought about the salvation of the Galatians is the πίστις Χριστοῦ. Although scholarly consensus has long understood this expression to refer to faith *in* Jesus Christ, recent studies of πίστις Χριστοῦ argue persuasively for the translation "faithfulness of Christ" or "obedience of Christ."[29] This interpretation means that the references to Jesus' self-giving love in 1:4 and 2:20

---

[27] Betz, *Galatians,* 29.

[28] To be sure, both 2:20 ("Christ lives in me") and the numerous references to the activity of the Spirit reflect Paul's conviction about the resurrection of Jesus, but the letter makes few explicit references to the resurrection. Beker notes "the virtual absence of the resurrection of Christ" in this letter (*Paul the Apostle,* 58).

[29] G. M. Taylor, "The Function of PISTIS CHRISTOU in Galatians," *JBL* 85 (1966) 58–76; George Howard, "On the Faith of Christ," *HTR* 60 (1967) 459–84; idem, "The 'Faith of Christ,'" *ExpT* 85 (1974) 212–15; L. T. Johnson, "Romans 3:21–26 and the Faith of Jesus," *CBQ* 44 (1982) 77–90; Hays, *Faith of Jesus Christ,* 139–76; Sam K. Williams, "Again *Pistis Christou,*" *CBQ* 49 (1987) 431–47; Morna D. Hooker, "ΠΙΣΤΙΣ ΧΡΙΣΤΟΥ," *NTS* 35 (1989) 321–42.

ought not be sentimentalized, for the self-giving of Jesus stems from his faithfulness to God's will (1:4). Jesus does not act out of an individualized affection for believers, as a reading of 2:20 out of context might suggest,[30] but out of faithful obedience to God's intent.

In what has been said thus far there is little indication that this understanding of Christ has anything to do with Israel, but that is to neglect an important though elusive feature of Galatians. Although Christ is not confined to history, it is clear that Christ belongs to history. Born of a woman (4:4), Christ enters history. It is precisely within history, in the person of a son of woman, in the person of one crucified, that God reveals the end of history's distinctions between and among peoples. Although Christ is born under the law, his cross brings to an end both law and what we might call "unlaw." His birth under the law (4:4) means also that he is born into Israel's particular history of relationship with God. Christ is *the* offspring of Abraham (3:16), and as such he represents God's intervention in a particular history, now radicalized to include all humankind.

This observation returns us to the question raised earlier: What is the character of the antithesis between Christ and the law or, more properly, between Christ and all things? We may immediately rule out both the philosophical and the moral as descriptions of the antithesis. In Galatians, the historical locus of the Christ-event means that Christ is not some eternal aeon that exists in contrast to the realm of the flesh. Neither does Paul interpret Christ and the law as ontological opposites. Similarly, Christ does not represent the moral good in contrast to evil. It is not as the good person that Christ is crucified, but as the faithful, loving son of God.

That the underlying antithesis in Galatians between Christ and the law stems from Paul's apocalyptic convictions has recently been forcefully argued by J. Louis Martyn.[31] Because what is said above about this antithesis bears a striking similarity to Martyn's arguments and is indeed informed by them, his proposal warrants particular attention. My reluctance to identify the antithesis (or, to use the term Martyn uses, antinomy) as apocalyptic stems in part from the confusion that surrounds that word. Does apocalyptic refer to a movement, to a general thought world, or to a body of literature? In Martyn's work, apocalyptic seems to refer to none of these but rather to God's ἀποχάλυψις of Jesus Christ and to the new creation. Martyn does identify certain of the motifs related to the Christ–cosmos antithesis with motifs found also in apocalyptic literature, but the question remains whether the use

---

[30] The first person singular here refers not only to Paul but to believers in general.

[31] J. L. Martyn, "Apocalyptic Antinomies in Paul's Letter to the Galatians," *NTS* 31 (1985) 410–24.

of similar motifs makes Paul's thought apocalyptic.[32] Given the confusion that continues to surround the term "apocalyptic," it obscures at least as much as it clarifies.

A second, more substantive disagreement with Martyn's proposal has to do with the relationship between the in-breaking character of the gospel in Galatians and its continuity with Israel. Martyn rightly draws attention to the way in which the gospel invades the old age,[33] but, as noted earlier, in Galatians Paul also identifies Christ as the seed of Abraham and therefore interprets him in the context of Israel's history. Moreover, Paul constantly uses biblical interpretation and imagery, not only in response to his opponents' claims about the law but in reference to his own apostolic role (1:15). This absorption in scripture indicates that the gospel's invasion does not negate the place of Israel (see 6:16). An adequate statement of the theology of this letter requires attention to the elements both of continuity *and* of discontinuity.[34]

The characterization of the Christ–cosmos antithesis in Galatians as either philosophical or moral is untenable. While the term "apocalyptic" captures part of the antithesis in Galatians, the many problems surrounding the term itself render it less than adequate. At present, I shall resist the temptation to create a new phrase for describing the Christ–cosmos antithesis. It is, at any rate, more important to identify the antithesis and its function in Galatians than to give it a name.

The following may be offered by way of conclusion: Although the issue that prompts Paul to write to Galatian Christians arises from a conflict regarding the law, in addressing that problem Paul takes the position that the gospel proclaims Jesus Christ crucified to be the inauguration of a new creation. This new creation allows for no supplementation or augmentation by the law or any other power or loyalty. What the Galatians seek in the law is a certainty that they have a firm place in the ἐκκλησία of God and that they know what God requires of them. It is precisely this certainty, and every other form of certainty, that Paul rejects with his claim about the exclusivity and singularity of Jesus Christ.

---

[32] Ibid., 416–20.

[33] "For Paul there are no through-trains *from* the patriarchal traditions and their perceptive criteria — whether Jewish or Greek — *to* the gospel of God's Son" (Martyn, "Paul and His Jewish-Christian Interpreters," 6).

[34] In my judgment this issue in Pauline theology (the relationship between continuity and discontinuity) cries out for extended discussion.

12 EVENTS IN GALATIA

Modified Covenantal Nomism versus God's
Invasion of the Cosmos in the Singular Gospel:
A Response to J. D. G. Dunn and B. R. Gaventa

J. Louis Martyn

I. PRELIMINARY REMARKS:
DEFINITION

ONE HARDLY NEEDS TO SAY that the definition of the subject—the theology of
Galatians—is crucial to a discussion of it and thus to an assessment of the
labors of colleagues who have directed several thoughtful studies to it. In
J. D. G. Dunn's essay for the present volume one finds the assumption that
the theology of Galatians is the *argument* that Paul crafted in order to *respond*
to developments in his Galatian congregations. That is a venerable definition,
and much is to be said for it, especially in the light of Dunn's rigorous
attempt to analyze the Galatian argument as the culmination of a sequence
of events, beginning with the Jerusalem meeting and the incident in Antioch
(pp. 138–40).

In my opinion, however, the definition of *the theology of Galatians* as *a responsive argument* crafted in the light of previous developments, while helpful,
does not reach all the way.

Let me begin with the term "argument." It is one of the helpful contributions of B. R. Gaventa to point out (vis-à-vis the labors of H. D. Betz and
J. C. Beker) that concentration on this word inclines the interpreter to read
in a less-than-adequate way the earlier and later chapters of the letter and to
underestimate the role of christology in the document (Gaventa, pp. 147–50).

There is also the plain fact that Paul sent the letter because he could not
go himself.[1] To be sure, considered alone, that fact—true of all the letters—

[1] See the valuable study of R. W. Funk, "The Apostolic *Parousia:* Form and Significance," in

could mean no more than that circumstances required Paul to rely on a written argument instead of an oral one; the theology of the letter would be considered, again, this written argument. But if in reading Galatians one concentrates one's attention on what might be called *the letter's work,* one may be led to a rather different definition of the letter's theology.

Paul wrote Galatians in the confidence that *God* intended to cause a certain event *to occur* in the Galatian congregations when Paul's messenger read the letter aloud to them. Let me suggest, then, that the theology of Galatians is focused on that *aural event, as it was intended and actively anticipated by Paul,* an event closely related to what one may call the letter's argument, but not identical with it. It follows that one is dealing with the theology of Galatians *first* insofar as one is able to take one's seat in a meeting of a Galatian congregation and thus to hear the letter with the ears of the Galatians themselves, and *second* insofar as one is able to move chronologically backward from that hearing, so as to look over the shoulder of the author and to enter into *his active anticipation of it.* The order of these two steps is as important as the steps themselves.[2] The author we see in the course of reading Galatians is a man who *does* theology by writing in such a way as *to anticipate* a theological *event.*

If the theology of the letter cannot be fully comprehended in the word "argument," surely the term "response" must be retained, in the sense that the anticipated aural event is responsive in nature. One would agree that Paul wrote this extraordinarily angry letter because his Galatian churches had been invaded by traveling evangelists teaching a theology he considered to be untrue and thus lethal.[3] Paul knows that the Galatians will hear his letter with the Teachers' words still ringing in their ears, indeed with the Teachers themselves sitting in their midst, doubtless more than ready to assist them in interpreting the missive.[4] Knowing that the Teachers are still there, still speaking regularly to the Galatians, knowing their major motifs, even some of their favorite locutions and scripture texts, Paul can anticipate how the Galatians will hear his words when he borrows elements of the Teachers'

Christian History and Interpretation: Studies Presented to John Knox (ed. W. R. Farmer et al.; Cambridge: Cambridge University Press, 1967) 249–68.

[2] One recalls the emphatic insistence of Matthäus Flacius Illyricus, as paraphrased by W. G. Kümmel, *Das Neue Testament* (Freiburg: Alber, 1958) 23 (emphasis added): "Flacius erkennt auch ganz genau, dass zur Ermittlung des wörtlichen Sinnes eines biblischen Textes nötig ist, den Text im Sinn seiner ursprünglichen Leser zu verstehen *und darüber hinaus* das Ziel zu erkennen, das der biblische Schriftsteller im Auge hatte. . . ." Oral tradition (Göttingen, 1957) ascribes the same interpretive rule to Walter Bauer.

[3] Henceforth I will refer to these people as "the Teachers"; see J. Louis Martyn, "A Law-Observant Mission to Gentiles: The Background of Galatians," *SJT* 38 (1985) 307–24.

[4] See J. Louis Martyn, "Paul and His Jewish-Christian Interpreters," *USQR* 42 (1987–88) 1–15.

vocabulary and when he gives his own exegesis of their texts. Is it not obvious, then, that the letter is a response?

What seems obvious is seldom so. Ponder for a moment Paul's understanding of the *relationship* between the anticipated aural event and the message he knows the Galatians to be hearing from the Teachers. Respecting this relationship, three major possibilities arise: (1) Paul could accept the Teachers' questions and even their basic frame of reference in order to formulate an argument designed to correct them on their own ground. He could accept, for example, as his fundamental category "covenantal nomism," in order to correct the Teachers' too-narrow view of it (Dunn). (2) Paul could commence his witness at a different point, unfold a basically different world of discourse, march to an utterly different drum, and arrive at a conclusion having neither linguistic nor conceptual connection with the message of the Teachers. (3) Or he could begin his argument at a different point, unfold it, however, in ways that make contact with the Teachers' message, only to modulate the terms of that message onto a radically new level of discourse consonant with his different point of depa. ture, doing all of that, finally, in order to arrive at a conclusion that ultimately silences the Teachers' themes not by contradicting them, properly speaking, but rather by being composed, as it were, on a radically different musical scale.

Trying to listen to the letter with the Galatians' ears has convinced me that Paul traveled the third route. Along the way he makes *contact* with the Teachers' theology, but he does not begin with it; he does not accept its frame of reference; he does not even correct it in the proper sense of that expression. Vis-à-vis the Teachers he begins, as it were, on a different planet, argues, therefore, with a different frame of reference even while making linguistic connections, and ends his argument by anticipating that through it God will bring the Galatians to that strange and wondrous land that served as his point of departure. The letter, therefore, contains an argument, but that is not the end of the matter, for Paul anticipates that when the argument is read aloud, God will re-preach his gospel to the Galatians.[5]

Given this reading of Galatians, I have to say that the term "response" is woefully inadequate, leading inevitably to a domesticated interpretation of

[5] Regarding Paul's conviction that God insists on being present, thus being himself the proclaimer of the gospel, see E. Käsemann's comments on the inseparability of gift and Giver ("'The Righteousness of God' in Paul," in *New Testament Questions of Today* [Philadelphia: Fortress, 1969] 168–82), the genitive of authorship in Rom 1:1 ("the gospel of which God is the author"), and the cogent comments of J. M. Bassler on the importance of the presence of God in Paul's theology ("Paul's Theology: Whence and Whither? A Synthesis (of sorts) of the Theology of Philemon, 1 Thessalonians, Philippians, Galatians, and 1 Corinthians," in *Society of Biblical Literature 1989 Seminar Papers* [ed. D. J. Lull; Atlanta: Scholars Press, 1989] 420–23).

the letter. Specifically, to define the theology of Galatians as an argumentative response involves running the risk of confusing the Teachers' definition of the issues and their frame of reference with Paul's definition of the issues and his frame of reference. In writing this document Paul remains what he was when he first came to Galatia, not fundamentally a rhetorical responder, but rather the situational proclaimer of the gospel, the word that is at its heart *invasive* rather than responsive. We do well, then, to speak not of an argumentative response but rather of a situational proclamation focused on the anticipated aural event in which God will cause the gospel to invade the edition of the present evil age that is current in Galatia.[6]

A few comments, section by section, will indicate some of the ways in which this definition leads me to agree and not to agree with the labors of Dunn and Gaventa.

II. CRITIQUE

1:1-2:21

The major thesis of Dunn's essay is that, when Paul was confronted in Galatia with a modified form of covenantal nomism combining allegiance to Christ with observance of the national and ritualistic aspects of the Law, he formulated and argued for a still more modified form of the same: faith in Christ accompanied by observance of the Law relieved of its restrictive national and ritualistic aspects.[7] In writing to the Galatians, Paul speaks several times of "works of the Law" and of "the curse of the Law," expressions indicating, according to Dunn, his central concern with the Law. The fundamental issue of Galatians, then, is taken to be "covenantal nomism, that is, the issue whether [as Paul's opponents would have it] those Gentiles who had come to faith in the Messiah of the Jews and who thus claimed a share in the benefits of *God's covenant with Israel* needed to live in accordance with the law of Israel . . ." (p. 130, emphasis added).

Having to deal with this distortedly strict form of covenantal nomism, Paul reclaims his commission to preach to the Gentiles, in order to secure for them "their share in the promise . . . ," that is "to reach out to and bring in the Gentiles on equal terms with the Jews" (p. 134). The promise, Dunn

---

[6] See B. Barbara Hall, "Battle Imagery in Paul's Letters" (Ph.D. diss., Union Theological Seminary, 1973).

[7] Dunn borrows the expression "covenantal nomism" from E. P. Sanders (*Paul and Palestinian Judaism* [Philadelphia: Fortress, 1977]), who uses it to characterize not Paul's own theology but rather major elements in Palestinian Judaism at the time of Paul.

continues, is "open to Gentile as well as Jew on the original conditions" [i.e., on the condition of faith, not on the condition of observance of the national and ritualistic dimensions of the Law] (p. 137).

Attempting to hear Gal 1:1–2:21 with the ears of the Galatians, one is reminded—vis-à-vis Dunn's essay—that they will have listened to rather more than a quarter of the letter before hearing the expression "works of the Law," and to more than a third of it before encountering "the curse of the Law." Given the extraordinarily attractive nomistic instruction they were currently receiving from the Teachers, we can be confident that they will have waited with keen anticipation for Paul's word on the subject of the Law. He makes them wait.

The attentive ones among them will have noted, then, that *instead* of speaking about the Law (the Teachers' major theme), Paul gives concentrated attention to Christ, to the gospel of Christ, and to the apocalypse of Christ in which God caused that gospel to happen to him, calling him to preach Christ among the Gentiles. Here one thinks of a major emphasis in the essay of Gaventa, written independently of Dunn's piece but nevertheless, in my judgment, corrective of it at a number of points. Gaventa charts a helpful course when she finds in Paul's christology the major clue to his insistence on the singularity of the gospel, devoid of even the most "reasonable" admixture of Law observance.[8] "The word 'christocentrism' is the right word, in that Paul presupposes from beginning to end that there is only one gospel (1:6–9), the singularity of which consists of the revelation of Jesus Christ as God's son whose crucifixion inaugurates the new age" (Gaventa, p. 149).

From the remarkable narrative stretch of 1:11–2:14, then, the Galatians will have seen that Paul has taken as his leading subject not the Law but rather the gospel of Christ and the history that this gospel has created and continues to create.[9] From all of this they will have sensed that Paul's theological point of departure is not a modified edition of covenantal nomism but rather the apocalypse of Christ and *the power of that apocalypse to create a history.*

What Dunn says, then, about covenantal nomism seems fundamentally appropriate to the position of *the Teachers.* They are indeed addressing these

---

[8] In a significant section of her essay, Gaventa imaginatively brings on stage a "compromise party," internal to the Galatian congregations and intent on insisting that Christians, although not *obliged* to observe the Law, *may* do so nevertheless, finding it "profitable for identifying Gentiles with Israel and for curbing the temptation to sin" (p. 151 above). It is a heuristic exercise, not tied to the historical setting of the letter but helpful in that it places in relief aspects of Paul's position that have proved difficult to discern.

[9] See B. R. Gaventa, "Galatians 1 and 2: Autobiography as Paradigm," *NovT* 28 (1986) 310–26; Paul "offers himself as a paradigm of the *work* of the gospel . . . an example of the gospel's *power*" (ibid., 326; emphasis added).

issues: How wide is the circle of the covenant, and on what conditions can Gentiles get into it? As Gaventa puts it, they are concerned to communicate to the Galatians the steps that are necessary "for full membership in the people of Israel" (Gaventa, p. 147). As she also points out, however, the first two chapters of Galatians show *Paul* to be marching in a different direction. His fundamental concern is the singularity of the gospel, as he focuses his attention specifically on what the gospel of Christ has done and is doing to the world. The Teachers' fundamental issue is covenantal nomism, if you like; Paul's is evangelical, cosmic, history-creating christology.

Returning to 1:1–2:21, we can also suggest that especially attentive Galatians will also have seen in this section Paul's tendency to refer to antinomies, beginning with the venerable one between the actions of human beings and the action of God, and including the application of that fundamental antinomy not only to his own apostolate (1:1) but also — in the form of the human activity of traditioning versus the divine activity of apocalypse — to the gospel itself (1:11–16).[10] When, then, they first hear about Law observance (ἔργα νόμου), they see (1) that (in mixed churches) the truth of the gospel declares Law observance to be playing a negative role in the history elicited by the gospel and (2) that that same truth of the gospel shows *Law observance to be on the human side of the divine–human antinomy.* Law observance is merely a *human* activity, whereas what makes for the rectification of human beings is the activity of *God* in Christ's faith:

> We . . . , knowing that God has elected to rectify human beings not by something they themselves do — observe the Law — but rather (ἐὰν μή) by something he has done in the faithful death of Christ Jesus, even we who are Jews by birth have believed in Christ Jesus, in order that we might be rectified by that deed of God, Christ's faith, and not by our own deed, observance of the Law, for by observance of the Law not a single person will be rectified. (Gal 2:15–16)[11]

In a word, by coming to the matter of Law observance *in* the context of gospel-created history, Paul sees an antinomy between Law observance and the faithful death of Christ: they are opposites in the sense that the former is a human deed, impotent to rectify, whereas the latter and the latter alone is God's active power to set things right.[12]

---

[10] Regarding the use of the term "antinomy" to refer to one of the fundamental building blocks of Paul's theology, see J. Louis Martyn, "Apocalyptic Antinomies in Paul's Letter to the Galatians," *NTS* 31 (1985) 410–24.

[11] On ἐὰν μή in Gal 2:16, see H. Räisänen, "Galatians 2.16 and Paul's Break with Judaism," *NTS* 31 (1985) 543–53, esp. p. 547.

[12] The fact that Galatians does not contain the expression "the rectification *of God*" says nothing against the major thesis of Käsemann's seminal essay, "'The Righteousness of God' in

There are a few remarks in Dunn's paper that could suggest a similar analysis, but fundamentally the point gets repeatedly lost, I think, as the result of two closely related assumptions, the first of which is sustainable, the second not so: (1) the assumption that, like Peter, the Teachers ("Antiochenes" in Dunn's nomenclature) held covenantal nomism as the primary given, its being only "qualified" by faith in Christ (p. 141); (2) the assumption that Paul also held covenantal nomism to be the primary given, going only *further* in qualifying it than did Peter and others.[13]

Paul does not present to the Galatians a more fully modified and corrected view of the Law in the context of an old and unacceptably narrow view of it. On the contrary, to say it again, he makes his point of departure clear by considering the Law in the context of the history of the gospel, speaking indeed of Law observance as the human side of a divine–human antinomy that has arisen with the advent of the gospel. The Galatians will have sensed his doing that; he will have anticipated their doing so; he will have intended them to do so.

3:6–4:7

Paul has now laid the foundation for the theological event that God will cause to happen when the letter is read aloud in the Galatian churches. He has spoken repeatedly of the truth of the gospel by tracing events in the history created by the gospel, including the genesis and sustenance of the Galatian churches themselves (3:1–5). Having laid this foundation, Paul can now make direct contact with one of the Teachers' major themes—the blessedness of Abraham's children—even citing several of their favorite texts (Gen 12:3; 18:18; Deut 27:26).[14] His contact with this theme, however, shows extraordinary sophistication, as he anticipates with great finesse the way in which the Galatians' ears will relate his words about Abraham to the Abraham sermons they are presently hearing from the Teachers.[15]

Paul," *pace* R. B. Hays ("Crucified with Christ," p. 257 below). The study of Paul's letters may pose no issue more important than the question whether the gospel has fundamentally to do with possibility (and human decision) or with power (and divine invasion). See Martyn, "Paul and His Jewish-Christian Interpreters," 12 n. 17; and consider Martinus C. de Boer's extraordinarily perceptive analysis of two strains in Jewish apocalyptic, one primarily forensic, the other primarily cosmic: "Paul and Jewish Apocalyptic Theology," in *Apocalyptic and the New Testament* (ed. J. Marcus and M. L. Soards; Sheffield: JSOT Press, 1989) 169–90. Paul's fundamental perception of δικαιοσύνη is that of God's powerfully invasive deed in making the whole of the cosmos right.

[13] Note "relativized" (p. 140) and "he goes on from that . . ." (p. 141).

[14] See Martyn, "Law-Observant Mission," 317–20.

[15] Had the Teachers not had such extraordinary success with their Abraham sermons, we

In broad terms one can say that although Paul accepts descent from Abraham as his connecting theme, he develops it in such a way as to compel it to take a distinctly secondary place, serving a theme that is far more basic—descent from God (4:6–7).[16] Gal 3:6–4:7 presents us, therefore, with a prime example of Paul's way of making contact with a theme of the Teachers without accepting the frame of reference in which they interpret that theme.[17] If, dangling the values of Abrahamic descent before the Galatians, the Teachers have spoken of incorporation into Abraham (the ἐν σοὶ of Gen 12:3) and thus of entry into the nomistic covenant via circumcision, Paul will speak fundamentally of incorporation into Christ, emphasizing that that incorporation has as its necessary corollary the obliteration of the distinctions between Jews and Gentiles (3:26–28). Again, then, christology proves to be the fulcrum on which Paul turns a theme introduced into the Galatian setting by the Teachers, that of descent.

Returning to the essay of Dunn, I have to say that it strikes me as more than strange—indeed as reductionistic—to credit Paul with composing Galatians 3 and 4 in order to correct a too-narrow view of covenantal nomism. In three crucial regards this reading of Galatians seems to me to go wrong: (1) in line of movement; (2) in the matter of faith, the cross, and the Law; and (3) with regard to covenant and seed in Galatians 3.

Line of movement. An example of Dunn's picture of the dominant line of movement, as we have seen, is his crediting Paul with the conviction "that it was now time to reach out to and *bring in* the Gentiles" (p. 134; emphasis added). Gentiles should and do *come into* the covenant. But this way of perceiving the dominant line of movement is characteristic of the Teachers, not of Paul. It is they who hold that Gentiles *can move,* by Law observance, *into* the covenant community.[18]

---

would probably know nothing of Paul's interpretation of the patriarch, for Romans 4 is clearly a reworking of Galatians 3.

[16] See J. Louis Martyn, "Galatians," in *The Books of the Bible* (ed. B. W. Anderson; 2 vols.; New York: Scribner's, 1989) 2. 271–84, esp. pp. 272–73, 276.

[17] Bassler raises an exceedingly important question when she asks whether the *universalizing* implications of the Abrahamic promise were part of the pre-Pauline tradition or a *proprium* of Paul ("Paul's Theology," 417). My own answer: (a) the *opportunity* for universal descent from Abraham by Law observance was a central tenet of the Teachers, being in fact fundamental to their own Gentile mission; (b) Abraham *began* to figure in Paul's theologizing when the apostle had to deal with the work of the Teachers; (c) the universal dimensions of Paul's gospel were brought *from* his view of Christ *to* his references to Abraham (Gal 3:29).

[18] Here one can scarcely avoid thinking of the questions of E. P. Sanders: How does one get in, and how does one stay in? Dunn makes a critique of the overuse of these questions, but in my opinion he falls victim to them nevertheless. What I have in mind should become clear when I say that the chart on p. 7 of Sanders's *Paul, the Law, and the Jewish People* (Philadelphia: Fortress,

For Paul, the dominant line is the one along which God *has* moved *into the cosmos* in the invasive sending of Christ and in Christ's faithful death for all (note the verbs in 3:23, 25; 4:4, 6, etc.). The difference between these two lines of movement is monumental: that difference is the major reason for Paul's being unwilling (unable) to accept the Teachers' frame of reference in the writing of his letter; that difference is not at all grasped by the distinction between two different conditions for entry into the covenant community—in Dunn's terms, the post-Maccabean and too-narrow one of observing the ethnic and ritual Law, and the original (Abrahamic) and proper one of believing and loving—for that distinction remains in the Teachers' frame of reference; the difference between human movement into the covenant and God's movement into the cosmos is, in the terms of Galatians, the watershed distinction between religion and ἀποκάλυψις, which is one way of encapsulating the subject of the letter.

Faith, the cross, the Law. The matter of faith is an issue in regard to which I find myself, once again, agreeing with Gaventa (p. 157) and disagreeing with Dunn (n. 54). Much of what is at stake here can be seen when one considers the expression πίστις Χριστοῦ 'Ιησοῦ, and notably when one asks oneself how that expression is likely to have struck the Galatians as they heard Paul's messenger read 2:16. If one takes it to mean "faith in Christ Jesus," then one makes two highly unlikely assumptions: (1) One assumes that Paul intends the antinomy between ἔργα νόμου and πίστις Χριστοῦ to refer to two human alternatives: should one observe the Law, or should one have faith in Christ? I have already addressed this matter above; let me now add that all of the other antinomies Paul displays in the letter, beginning with the one in the first verse, place over against one another a deed of God and a deed of the human being, not two alternative acts of human beings. (2) One assumes that having established the antinomous pattern indicated by ἄνθρωπος/θεός, Paul can expect the Galatians to know that he intends to depart from that pattern in the case of ἔργα νόμου/πίστις Χριστοῦ, even though he gives them no signal of such a departure. Dunn has pondered the various arguments of Taylor, Howard, Hays, Hooker, and others and finds himself unconvinced, referring to "the sustained thrust of the letter" as something that included "the fundamental distinction between (human) faith and (human) works" (n. 54).[19]

1983), a book from which I have learned a great deal, seems to me to have much more to do with the theology of the Teachers than with that of Paul. The crucial difference between the two is the matter under discussion above: the identification of the dominant *line of movement*. For the Teachers that line is the one along which Gentiles *can* move, by Law observance, *into the covenant community* (note the uppermost arrow on p. 7).

[19] The works of Taylor et al. are listed in Gaventa, p. 157 n. 29 above; see also the references to Barclay and Westerholm in Dunn, p. 141 n. 54 above.

There could scarcely be a point on which Dunn and I are in greater disagreement, precisely as regards "the sustained thrust of the letter." Let me mention two points. (a) The issue is not whether Paul ever speaks in Galatians about human beings having faith. Clearly he does. The issue can be grasped — at least in large part — when we ask whether he has an interest in the question of faith's genesis. His use in 3:2 and 3:5 of the expression ἀκοὴ πίστεως (the message that elicits faith) answers this question decisively in the affirmative: faith is kindled, incited, elicited by the proclamation of Christ's death, and it is to that inciter, Christ's faithful death, that Paul refers when he speaks of πίστις Χριστοῦ.[20] (b) It follows that Paul's argument is fundamentally misconstrued when the faith of human beings is identified as the "original conditions" of God's promise. To be sure, one might fault Paul for laying out the two clauses of Gen 15:6 as he does, leaving the verse open to the interpretation that the first move was Abraham's (he had faith), so that, when that condition was met, God made the second move, responding to Abraham's faith by rectifying him. As the development of the argument in Galatians 3 makes plain, however, Paul always presupposes that God's promise anteceded (and indeed elicited) Abraham's faith. Thus, nothing could be clearer in Galatians than Paul's conviction that what overcomes the Law's power to pronounce a curse is not something that human beings can do but rather something that God has already done. In a word, the "initial decisive expression" of "God's saving power" (Dunn, p. 125) is not faith but rather that which awakens it.[21] Nothing Paul says about faith gives so much as a hint that it is the condition for entrance into the covenant.

From these two points one can see that Paul is very far indeed from merely modifying the Teachers' view of covenantal nomism. And there is more. One thinks of the weighty role Paul gives to the matter of enslavement. It is scarcely his intention to equate enslavement with the view of covenantal nomism in which the Gentile is excluded as Gentile (Dunn). On the contrary, for Paul enslavement is the monolithic state of affairs in which the elements

---

[20] It is important to note one juncture in Dunn's articles at which he reflects Paul's interest in faith's genesis: the highly welcome reference to "faith . . . brought about by the word of preaching" in "Works of the Law and the Curse of the Law (Galatians 3:10–14)," *NTS* 31 (1985) 535. It follows, however, as I have said above, that faith is scarcely human in Paul's sense of the phrase κατὰ ἄνθρωπον.

[21] The tendency to credit Paul with the view that faith is a human deed prerequisite to redemption spreads far beyond the realm of television evangelists; it is astonishingly widespread even among talented exegetes. J. Paul Sampley, e.g., after noting correctly that in Galatians "faith [is] linked directly with the coming of Christ," adds that "decision has become the criterion of admission, not ancestry, and not the keeping of certain ritual performance [*sic*]" ("Romans and Galatians: Comparison and Contrast," in *Understanding the Word: Essays in Honor of Bernhard W. Anderson* [ed. J. T. Butler et al.; JSOTSup 37; Sheffield: JSOT Press, 1985] 325, 327–28).

of the cosmos hold in bondage *all human beings* and in which the Law functions as one of these universally enslaving elements.[22] Indeed, apart from
Christ's faithful death, it is τὰ πάντα that is enslaved (3:22), and liberation is
equally cosmic (καινὴ κτίσις).

   In the course of saying all of this, Paul takes his bearings from the conviction that in the event of the crucifixion there was a collision between the Law
and God's Christ (3:13).[23] That conviction is surely reflected in the fact that
in this letter Paul never refers to the Law as God's Law (contrast three
instances in Romans [and one in Matthew]). The intended effect of Gal
3:19–20 (with its partial syllogism) is to distance God from the Law as far
as possible without declaring an absolute divorce between the two. The
extraordinarily dangerous implications of 3:19–20 become doubly clear
from the fact that in 3:21 Paul has to curb them by quickly and explicitly
insisting that the divorce between God and the Law is not absolute.

   As regards the Law itself, the truly crucial point is that its collision with
God's Christ has revealed — or opened up — an antinomy that is *internal* to the
Law, an antinomy reflected in 3:14–29 by the way Paul uses the words
"promise" and "Law," and even more fully displayed in 4:21–5:1.[24] Again,
however, one has to say that this antinomy which the cross has opened up
internal to the Law is hardly grasped when Paul is credited with the intention

---

[22] Recalling that Paul puts Jew and Gentile together (e.g., employing the plural pronoun in
both 4:3 and 3:13), one notes also his striking use of the expression ὑπό τινα εἶναι (and equiva-
lents) in 3:10, 22, 23, 25; 4:2, 3, 4 (*bis*), referring in each instance to the universal experience of
being imprisoned as slaves under a tyrannical power. See BAGD, s.v. ὑπό 2b; and note the verbs
Paul employs in 3:22, 23; 4:3, 4. The parallelism between μορφὴν δούλου λαβών and ἐν ὁμοιώματι
ἀνθρώπων γενόμενος in the Philippian hymn (Phil 2:7) is only one of many data showing Paul's
assumption that to be a human being — of whatever race or religion — is to be a slave in the
cosmos (cf. *Poimandres* 14–15; prior to the development of apocalyptic theology, Hebraic traditions give no instance of the thought that one is a slave simply by being a human being). This
assumption permeates the whole of Galatians and indicates the fundamental import of Paul's
reference in 3:24 to the Law as an enslaving pedagogue.

[23] Robert G. Hamerton-Kelly has recently explored in a helpfully provocative way Paul's
perception of the relationship between the death of Christ and the Law: "Sacred Violence and
the Curse of the Law (Galatians 3:13): The Death of Christ as a Sacrificial Travesty," *NTS* 36
(1990) 98–118.

[24] The antinomy internal to the Law is one of the most subtle and complex elements in Paul's
thought. In the limits of the present paper I can say only (a) that it has no genuine parallel in
Jewish traditions, the thought of there being inconsistencies in the Law proving to be something
quite different; (b) that it is very far indeed from the theory of false pericopes developed by the
Gnostics and by some Jewish Christians of the second century; and (c) that it is not grasped
any better by the distinctions that are sometimes drawn between laws ritual and ethical, between
laws God-and-human and human-and-human, between *haggadah* and *halakah,* between *mythos*
and *ethos.* Regarding the theories of development in Paul's thought, it will not do to say that
in Romans Paul has given up the view of an antinomy internal to the Law; see, e.g., Rom 3:21.

of correcting a mistaken *view* of the Law or with holding to a certain kind [doubtless a new kind] of covenantal nomism himself (Dunn, p. 131).[25] On the contrary, in Galatians 3 Paul compels his Galatian hearers to risk a brief trip into territory later explored (wrongly in important regards) by Marcion. Attentive Galatians will have noticed that in 3:14–29 Paul consistently credits the promise to God, whereas in 3:19–20 he paints a picture of the Law's genesis from which God is absent. He also speaks in an astonishing way of the covenant.

Covenant and seed in Galatians 3. It is, in fact, Paul's use of the word "covenant" in Galatians 3 that compels me to a truly significant point of disagreement with both Dunn and Gaventa. The three of us might well agree that, in all probability, the Galatians have heard from the Teachers some extraordinarily powerful things about God's covenant with Israel (spoken to Abraham and ratified at Sinai). When we turn, however, to the way in which Paul employs the venerable term "covenant" in Gal 3:15–18, we arrive at significantly different readings; for it seems clear to me that what Paul sees and affirms is a divorce of the covenant from the Law. In Paul's picture— contrary to that of the Teachers—the covenant is tied *exclusively* to the Abrahamic promise, and it is emphatically *divorced* from the Law.[26]

On the basis of Gal 3:15–18 one can speak, indeed, of the *identity* of the covenant and, to some extent, of the identity of the Law: in this passage the covenant *is* exclusively the promise, spoken to Abraham and thus ratified ahead of time by God himself, whereas the Law is the product of angels acting in God's absence. Separating covenant and Law in this radical manner, then, Paul is scarcely pursuing a line of thought that moves within the frame of reference properly identified as covenantal nomism. On the contrary, it explodes that frame of reference by a bill of divorce, the divorcing of covenant from Law.

The motif of a divorce—of a radical separation—may remind one of Gaventa's emphasis on exclusivity as it emerges in the contrasting statements about Christ and the Law. "Those who are baptized are baptized into Christ. That identification is not only primary; it is exclusive. . . . There can be no compromising of the gospel's singular and exclusive location in Jesus Christ

---

[25] Cf. Gaventa's remark, "Paul is not simply arguing *against* some defect in the law . . ." (see p. 153 above).

[26] At several points the paragraphs immediately following reflect things I have learned from the first essay in E. Grässer, *Der Alte Bund im Neuen* (Tübingen: Mohr [Siebeck], 1985). One of the significant contributions made by Grässer is that of showing that the term "covenant" does not itself point to a fundamental element of Paul's theology. With few exceptions, Paul employs the term only when one of his churches has become enamored of the use being made of it by traveling evangelists who stand in opposition to his mission (Galatians 3–4; 2 Corinthians 3).

alone" (Gaventa, p. 153). What I have now to suggest is that *additional aspects of the motif of exclusivity* emerge in Paul's divorcing of covenant from Law in Galatians 3, and emphatically in his use of the word "seed."

Consider the emphatic way in which Paul goes about his exegesis of Gen 13:15 and 17:8. I give first a somewhat paraphrastic translation of Gal 3:16:

> Now, the covenantal promises were spoken by God to Abraham "and to his seed." The text does *not* say "and to his seeds," as though it were speaking about many people, but rather, speaking about one, it reads "and to your seed," and that seed is Christ.

Again, the implications for the word covenant are staggering, and they seem to pass by Gaventa's otherwise percipient and persuasive essay. One recalls her insistence that Christ belongs to history, his having been "born *into Israel's particular history* of relationship with God" (p. 158, emphasis added). Similarly, she says that in Galatians 3 Paul argues for "the priority of faith over the law *in the course of Israel's history*" (p. 151, emphasis added). In this view of things she is joined by Dunn (see pp. 136–37 and nn. 26 and 42) and, with variations, by the authors of the essays in the last section of the present volume. The result is a basically *heilsgeschichtlich* reading of Paul advanced by a sizable group of highly competent exegetes.[27]

It is a matter to which we will return in commenting below on Gal 4:21–5:1 and in the conclusion. For the moment I have only to say that the data in Galatians 3 seem to me to lead in a quite different direction. Not only does Paul see a divorce between the promissory covenant and the Law of Sinai; but also, at least by implication, he excludes a connection between that promissory covenant and what he must have known to be the specific history of corpus Israel: ". . . the text does *not* say 'and to his seeds,' as though it were speaking about many people. . . ." Thus, the covenantal promise uttered by God to Abraham — as Ulrich Luz correctly put it some time ago — remained in a sort of docetic state until the advent of the singular seed, Christ.[28] By implication the corporate people of Israel was a dance sat out by the covenantal promise as it waited for its true referent, the Singular Seed.

One would be quick to add that Gaventa's references to "history," and specifically to "the history of Israel," have the very welcome effect — intended, no doubt — of posing one of the truly crucial issues of the Pauline letter that

---

[27] One notes also that the admirable concentration on apocalyptic in the book of J. Christiaan Beker (*Paul the Apostle: The Triumph of God in Life and Thought* [Philadelphia: Fortress, 1980]) is coupled with the giving of a remarkable role to *Heilsgeschichte,* a matter discussed critically in my review (*WW* 2 [1982] 194–98).

[28] U. Luz, "Der alte und der neue Bund bei Paulus und im Hebräerbrief," *EvT* 27 (1967) 318–36, esp. p. 322.

has frequently been read as anti-Judaic.[29] Her use of these expressions, that is to say, is one way of pointing to the matter of continuity and discontinuity, a matter she addresses when she insists that the motif of the gospel's discontinuity is significantly qualified when Paul "identifies Christ as the seed of Abraham and therefore interprets him in the context of Israel's history" (p. 159).

But here again Paul's use of the term "covenant" in Galatians 3 proves to be a kind of wild animal that cannot be so easily tamed. For in this text the covenantal promise is precisely *not said* to have commenced a history that subsequently served as the context into which Christ was born. That covenantal promise did not at all found its own epoch. Indeed, because of the docetic state of the covenantal promise prior to Christ's advent, there is no indication in this passage that before that point there was something that could be identified as the history of a corporate people of God created by the power of that promise.

The resultant picture presents, therefore, neither a modified form of covenantal nomism nor an edition of *Heilsgeschichte* properly equipped with the pre-Christ linearity necessary to a meaningful use of that term.[30] In Galatians, Abraham is distinctly a punctiliar figure rather than a linear one. The recipient of God's promise, he is not at all the beginning of a line that can be traced through something properly called history, for he does not have "seeds," but rather a "singular seed." Thus neither history nor story is a word well linked with Paul's portrait of Abraham in Galatians.[31]

Let me put the matter in yet another way. As I have noted, Gaventa's essay, true to its title, is most helpful in its exploration of the motif of the

---

[29] One thinks of the understandable, and unfortunate, tendency in current discussions of the relations between Christians and Jews to silence the voice of Galatians in favor of that of Romans. See, e.g., the resolution on the renovation of the relationship of Christians and Jews issued by the Rheinland Synod in 1980, a resolution that has loosed a veritable flood of literature. One aspect of the Rheinland resolution is discussed in J. Louis Martyn, "The Covenants of Hagar and Sarah," in *Faith and History: Essays in Honor of Paul W. Meyer* (ed. John T. Carroll et al.; Atlanta: Scholars Press, 1991) 160–92.

[30] The anti-Enlightenment pietists in eighteenth-century Germany who coined the term *Heilsgeschichte* certainly had in mind a *linear history,* beginning (if not with Adam) with Abraham, and including *the history of Israel* on its way to Christ and to his parousia.

[31] The use of the word "story" in Richard B. Hays's essay for this volume is, I think, a helpful reflection of the linear and dynamic character of Paul's theology, so long as one is referring explicitly to *the history of Jesus Christ* (one thinks foremost of 1 Corinthians 15, and also of references to Jesus Christ and his future in Jürgen Moltmann, *Theology of Hope* [New York: Harper & Row, 1967]). When, however, Hays says that Paul sees in the Galatians' desire to be under the Law "a regression to an earlier phase of the story" (p. 233 below), he credits the apostle with a pre-Christ linearity nowhere evident in Galatians.

singularity of the gospel vis-à-vis the Law. But from Galatians 3 one can see that that singularity involves another — the singularity of the Seed — and this other singularity is as *anti-linear* as it is anti-plural. The singularity of the Seed spells, in fact, the end of *Heilsgeschichte* as a view that encompasses a linear history of a people of God prior to Christ. For Christ was born not into the context of "Israel's history" but rather "under the dominance of the Law" and thus, as we have already seen, into a context marked by a sort of covenantal docetism and by universal enslavement.

Is the letter, then, an absolute foreigner to history? By no means. I have already noted that 1:11–2:14 (plus 3:1–5) is a narrative in which Paul traces the power of the gospel to create a history. Were one allowed a side glance at Philippians, one would note there the expression προκοπὴ τοῦ εὐαγγελίου (1:12), thus underlining the fact that Paul understands the gospel to be on a victorious — one can even say linear — march through the world.[32] In Galatians there is, however, not the slightest hint that this march has a linear *pre*-history, a linear *praeparatio evangelica*. In a word, there is no affirmation of a salvific linearity prior to the advent of Christ.

At the same time, Gaventa's analysis serves to remind one that the true voice of Paul, even in Galatians 3, is worlds away from that of Marcion. Paul is emphatic about what one may term in the restricted sense of the word "*theological* continuity," namely, the continuity provided by the consistent identity of the one God (3:20). The God who is now rectifying the Gentiles by eliciting their faith is the same God who, in the voice of scripture, promised Abraham long ago that he would do that. Moreover the picture Paul paints in Galatians 3 is quite different from the one in which the church is thought to replace Israel as God's people. Here there simply *is* no indication of a covenant-created people of God during the time of the Law.

4:21–5:1

In this passage the antinomy internal to the Law enables the Law to testify against itself, lifting its voice to say that in the Law-observant mission to Gentiles it is bearing children into slavery, while in the Law-free mission the Spirit is bearing children into freedom.[33] The resulting line of thought is

---

[32] The history created by the gospel's victorious march through the world may prove to be a consistent Pauline *proprium* from 1 Thessalonians to Romans. For reasons displayed in nn. 30 and 31, however, it is a mistake to speak of this gospel-created history as *Heilsgeschichte*.

[33] Paul takes the radical step of mentioning *two* covenants in this passage in order to refer in a mutually exclusive way to the two Gentile *missions* that have crossed paths in Galatia, one Law-free and one Law-observant. See Martyn, "Covenants of Hagar and Sarah."

complex; here we can note only a few ramifications of Paul's use for a second time of the term "covenant."

We have already observed that in the earlier covenant passage Paul divorced the covenant (the Abrahamic promise) from the Law. A first glance at the present passage might suggest that he is now in retreat from such radicality, for he does reunite the terms, referring in fact to the covenant of Sinai. A closer look reveals, however, anything but a retreat: Here, for the first time, Paul takes the unprecedented step of placing opposite one another *two* covenants, one the promising covenant of Sarah, the covenant that liberates, the other the Sinai/Law covenant of Hagar, the covenant that enslaves.

When Paul refers to these two covenants, he marches clean off the theological map of the Teachers, refusing their frame of reference altogether. He is not agreeing that Gentiles should be allowed to get into the Sinai covenant while disagreeing only on the means of their getting in (by faith rather than by works of the Law). *When Paul contemplates Gentile entry into the Sinai covenant, he sees only enslavement under the power of the Law.* The farthest thing from his mind is to argue for the Gentiles' right to claim "a share in the benefits of God's covenant with Israel" (Dunn, p. 130). The Sarah covenant (the Law-free mission to Gentiles) stands entirely distinct from and in opposition to the Sinai covenant (the Law-observant mission to Gentiles).

It will not suffice, therefore, to say that Paul's unprecedented reference to two covenants points to "an interesting variation on the continuity/discontinuity . . . *in salvation history*" (Dunn, n. 35, emphasis added). On the contrary, Christian interpreters will begin to grasp the true radicality of this reference when they listen carefully to their Jewish colleagues, for Paul's willingness to speak of two covenants and to link the Sinai covenant with enslavement is something to which Jewish interpreters of Paul have been exquisitely sensitive. Schalom Ben-Chorin, for example, understandably speaks of Gal 4:21–31 as "eine völlige Umdrehung der Vätersage."[34] The Teachers in Galatia will scarcely have been less sensitive. They will have seen that, far from modifying their covenantal nomism, Paul posits a second covenant *over against it* in order to deny that it is God's intention to bring the Gentiles into the Sinai covenant on any conditions.

Once again we see the cogency of Gaventa's emphasis on the singularity of the gospel: the gospel reaches out into the world *only* in the pattern of Isaac and *not* in the pattern of Ishmael. Having asked the Galatians whether they have really heard the voice of the Law, Paul shows that a witness to the gospel-covenant can indeed be found in scripture (4:21 recalls 3:8). That is to say, given the advent of Christ's Spirit, one can *look back* to Isaac's birth

---

[34] Schalom Ben-Chorin, *Paulus: Der Völkerapostel in jüdischer Sicht* (Munich: Paul List, 1970) 132.

The Theology of Galatians

to Sarah (Genesis 21), thus seeing a type of the birth of Gentile congregations by the freeing power of that Spirit.[35]

By this same looking back *from* the singular gospel, however, Paul sees that Gentile congregations born in the Law-observant mission correspond to Ishmael, born to Hagar, the slave (Genesis 16). Must we not say, then, that for Paul it is precisely the singularity of the invasive gospel that creates the singularity of the liberating covenant? By that same token, the unqualified opposition between the two covenants shows that a continuity is to be found only in *God* and in God's salvific deed, not in the creation of a historical linearity. In a word, Paul's radical reading of the birth stories in Genesis 16–21 is anthropologically discontinuous in order to be theologically continuous (see Gal 1:1). It passes clean by both covenantal nomism and the history of Israel in order to speak of the eschatological purpose of God.

Vis-à-vis Dunn's essay, then, one has to say that Paul's exegesis in Gal 4:21–5:1 is very far indeed from reflecting an attempt "to redraw the boundaries with Gentile Christians inside" (Dunn, n. 45). Pondering the essay of Gaventa, one must ask yet again whether her helpful emphasis on the word "singular" does not necessarily bring with it *an opposition to both "plural" and "linear."* Paul's startling reference to two diametrically opposed covenants in Galatians 4 does not bear witness to the occurrence of a new event "in the context of Israel's history" (Gaventa, p. 159) any more than did his reference to "seeds" and "seed" in Galatians 3. Indeed, one has to say that *throughout* Galatians, far from proposing a linear history that begins with Abraham, Paul stands in opposition to such a view. Given the work of the Teachers, Paul's insistence on the singularity of the gospel has necessarily to be anti-*heilsgeschichtlich.*[36]

5:16–6:18

The full implications of Paul's taking the gospel of Christ as his sole point of departure will have been brought home to the Galatians only by their

---

[35] The motif of *looking back* is one of the keys to Paul's interpretation of scripture, for in his view of things the gospel cannot be made "subject to criteria of perception that have been developed apart from the gospel. . . . [The cross makes clear that] there are no through-trains *from* the patriarchal traditions and their perceptive criteria . . . *to* the gospel of God's Son" (Martyn, "Paul and His Jewish-Christian Interpreters," 6). Taking this comment about Paul's backward hermeneutical look as a caveat, one will find, I think, numerous insights in the perceptive book of Richard B. Hays, *Echoes of Scripture in the Letters of Paul* (New Haven and London: Yale University Press, 1989).

[36] The history of the interpretation of Paul's letters includes a number of instances in which exegetes have unwittingly attributed to Paul aspects of the theologies he was in fact strenuously opposing.

hearing several times the entire letter. We may ask, finally, then, how they would have heard the closing paragraphs. Several points stand out: (1) When they heard Paul mention the ἐπιθυμία σαρκός, they would almost certainly have recognized a reference to one of the Teachers' favorite topics: the Evil Impulse.[37] They would also have seen that, unlike the Teachers, Paul speaks here of a *new* pair of opposites. It is not the Law but rather the Spirit (of God's Son) that functions in their corporate life in such a way as to hold the Impulse in check. Again, they would not have thought that Paul was about the business of modifying a too-narrow view of the Law, as though that view were impotent to check the Impulse whereas true covenantal nomism were up to the task. They would have seen that, taking his bearing once again from the advent of Christ and of his Spirit, Paul is speaking of *a new state of affairs,* the state of affairs resulting from Christ's crucifixion (5:24; 6:14) and from the arrival of the Spirit that bears the communal fruit of love, joy, peace, etc. In this new state of affairs a community led by the Spirit does in fact fulfill the Law of love, the Law of Christ.[38] Paul considers that affirmation to be of great importance. The way in which he puts it, however, would have caused the Galatians to sense its christological basis and thus to know that the heartbeat of the letter is not about Law observance and not even about the Law. As we have repeatedly noted, it is about the gospel of Christ's cross that—without setting conditions of any sort—has brought about the death (paradigmatically) of Paul's cosmos and thus (paradigmatically) of Paul himself, in order to commence the new creation.

(2) How would the Galatians have heard the word "cosmos" in 6:14? The attentive ones would have noted that the cosmos that has suffered crucifixion is the order of things in which circumcision and uncircumcision, Law and not-Law, were opposites. With the death of this order one sees that the opposite of Law is the same as the opposite of not-Law, namely, the καινὴ κτίσις.

(3) But in saying this, Paul has once again refused the Teachers' definition of the issue at stake and their entire frame of reference, *both* covenantal nomism and *Heilsgeschichte.* Having as its primary focus not the issue of the Law but rather the cross of Christ, this letter, as I have said above, marches clean off the map of the Teachers' theology.[39] For the Jew/Gentile issue, the Law/not-Law issue, the included/not-included issue have all of them been transfigured in the event of the crucifixion.

---

[37] See Joel Marcus, "The Evil Inclination in the Letters of Paul," *IBS* 8 (1986) 8–21.

[38] See Richard B. Hays, "Christology and Ethics in Galatians: The Law of Christ," *CBQ* 49 (1987) 268–90.

[39] Note Gaventa's argument that christology dominates the letter and that the crucifixion dominates the letter's christology, without including in itself Christ's resurrection (pp. 156-57 above). See also the emphasis on crucifixion in the essay of Richard B. Hays in this volume.

Precisely in this connection I am reminded that Gaventa and I clearly agree on the deep import of the expression "new creation" *and* on the use of the term "invasion" to speak of the way in which God has begun this newly creative act.[40] We do not always agree, it seems, on the identity of that which has been invaded and on the implications of the invasion for Paul's view of Israel. In my understanding, the motif of *invasion* involves that of *warfare;* hence one must ask both what it is that is invaded and who it is against whom war is declared. As far as I can see, these are matters with respect to which Paul gives no role at all to Israel. Certainly Christ does not come as the liberating warrior into *Israel.* God's act in Christ is invasive, rather, of the *cosmos* that, from one end to the other, had fallen prey to *malignant powers,* the cosmos that was, for that reason, in all essential regards a monolith prior to Christ.[41]

What does it mean, then, to say that "the gospel's invasion does not negate the place of Israel (see 6:16)" (Gaventa, p. 159)?[42] We should obviously agree that in Gal 6:16 Paul refers to the Israel *of God,* but that is an expression by which I take him to speak—in writing to the Galatians—of those *former* Jews and *former* Gentiles who live in the new creation, because in the singular gospel God has liberated them from that form of enslavement that previously differentiated them from one another.[43] It may very well be that Paul's reference to Israel in Gal 6:16 was as opaque to the Galatians as it has proven to be to later interpreters. It may also be that part of Paul's motive for writing

[40] Invasion is also closely connected to divine election, a motif that plays a weighty role in Galatians, God himself being identified as ὁ καλῶν. God's election is powerfully invasive of "the present evil age."

[41] Christ's being born "under the Law" refers to his real entry into the human state of enslavement, not to his coming into the history of Israel (see comments on ὑπό τινα εἶναι in n. 22 above). The resulting picture is, I think, apocalyptic. Gaventa, agreeing on the use of the term "invasion," says that she wishes to avoid reference to apocalyptic because it is a matter clouded by imprecise and debated definition. The issue of definition is indeed thorny, and in that regard, as in others, I am instructed by Gaventa's critique of my suggestions. For the time being I can only say that I have tried to make clear the basic dimensions of apocalyptic *as I use the term:* see Martyn, "Apocalyptic Antinomies," 417–18; see the six points developed, especially the fourth—warfare.

[42] I agree with Gaventa, if she means that the invasive character of the gospel does not negate the place of Israel *by transferring it to the church.* What I have said above, however—about the implications of Paul's references to "covenant" and "seed" in Galatians 3 and about his essentially monolithic view of the cosmos prior to Christ—will indicate that I think Paul, in writing to the Galatians, had no intention of reserving a *heilsgeschichtlich* place for Israel.

[43] One might recall that attempts to differentiate Jews from Gentiles *within the church* became a pressing issue when the so-called Arian paragraph was introduced into church life on 6 September 1933 by the Generalsynode of the Evangelische Kirche der altpreussischen Union. See most recently Andreas Lindemann, "Neutestamentler in der Zeit des Nationalsozialismus; Hans von Soden und Rudolf Bultmann in Marburg," *WD* 20 (1989) 25–52, esp. p. 31.

Romans 9–11 was to clarify—perhaps even slightly to modify—that cryptic reference. Certainly no segment of the synthetic road, the first part of which is traveled in the last section of the present volume, is more treacherous than the one in which the interpreter, attempting to speak of Paul's understanding of Israel, seeks to honor both Galatians and Romans.[44] In any case, read by itself, Galatians presents, as we have seen, a cosmic story in which Paul attributes a salvific role only to the Singular Seed.

III. CONCLUSION

Let me close, then, by suggesting that Galatians shows us a Paul who does not accept "covenant" as a term indicating a fundamental building block of his theology. However disappointing it may be to have to say so, this apostle is not a covenantal theologian and thus scarcely one for whom covenantal nomism—however construed—constitutes a frame of reference within which he can preach and re-preach the gospel. Neither does he present as his theology a form of *Heilsgeschichte* in which Christ is interpreted in line with Israel's history. Indeed, both covenantal nomism and *Heilsgeschichte* are characteristic of the message presented to the Galatians by the Teachers.

In stark contrast, Paul's theological horizon is given by the motif of God's warlike and liberating invasion of the cosmos in Christ's cross and in Christ's Spirit, coupled with the bold assertion of the new creation inaugurated by that invasion. Because of developments in Galatia, Paul can re-preach this good news only by specifying the collision between that cruciform invasion and the Law. But just in this way he shows that in that collision the cosmos that one might call "human-entry-into-the-covenant-of-Israel-on-condition" is eclipsed by the new creation born in the divine-invasion-of-the-cosmos-on-no-conditions. It is in the singular gospel that this redemptive invasion is announced and performed.

[44] The bibliography on Romans 9–11 is endless. Let me mention one article that seems to me to be unusually percipient (and largely overlooked in studies written in English): N. Walter, "Zur Interpretation von Römer 9–11," *ZTK* 81 (1984) 172–95.

Part V

Partial Syntheses
of Paul's Theology

13 PUTTING PAUL TOGETHER AGAIN

Toward a Synthesis of Pauline Theology
(1 and 2 Thessalonians, Philippians, and Philemon)

N. T. Wright
Worcester College, Oxford

THE PROBLEM ADDRESSED in this paper has the air of those slightly unreal examination questions that devious-minded professors set from time to time: "Consider justification as a major theme in John's gospel" or "Does Jude have a christology?" I mean this: that to talk about Pauline theology, and a synthesis thereof in particular, while imposing a self-denying ordinance that will keep one bound to these four letters, might be thought an artificial and recondite task. The matter is made worse for me because I do not believe that these four letters were the first to be written of those we now possess. I date Galatians early, and though I agree with H. Koester and others in putting Philemon, and probably Philippians, during a hypothetical Ephesian imprisonment,[1] I also think that Colossians was written, by Paul, at the same time, and I put 1 Corinthians before this imprisonment and 2 Corinthians shortly afterward. The current selection has for me, therefore, an arbitrary feel. Nevertheless, I remain enthusiastic about the project of which this paper is a constituent part: to explore the theology of the letters one by one, stopping as we go to see what sort of picture has been constructed so far. Yet I need to proceed with some caution upon my task, which has both an absurd and an exciting flavor to it. I want to do so in the following manner.

First, I shall offer some reflections on the aims and methods of the task. This exercise seems to be the more necessary in the light of some recent work and is intended as a contribution to the ongoing methodological discussion in the papers of J. C. Beker and J. P. Sampley.[2] It may be of some use as the

---

[1] See, e.g., H. Koester, *Introduction to the New Testament:* Vol. 2, *History and Literature of Early Christianity* (FFNT; Philadelphia: Fortress, 1982) 130–35.

[2] See above, pp. 3–14 (Sampley) and 15–24 (Beker).

project addresses other letters in future years. However, this section could be skipped by anyone eager to get on to the "real" issues. Second, I shall highlight some issues from the work done thus far on the project and offer my own reflections on the nature and shape of Pauline theology as I see it emerging from these four very different letters.

I. AIMS AND METHODS

What is "Pauline Theology"?

Since those who look for nothing often find it, it may be as well to say briefly what this entity, "Pauline theology," may be conceived to be. I take the phrase to refer to that integrated set of beliefs which may be supposed to inform and undergird Paul's life, mission, and writing, coming to expression in varied ways throughout all three. If we were to specify the content of this set of beliefs, it would be natural, since Paul by his own admission continued to understand his work from the standpoint of one who had been a zealous Pharisaic Jew, to group them under the twin heads of Jewish theology, namely, monotheism and election, God and Israel. Indeed, I shall argue in the second section that Paul's theology consists precisely in the redefinition, by means of christology and pneumatology, of those two key Jewish doctrines. Those familiar with recent discussions may conclude that I am not far, formally, from J. C. Beker's "coherence and contingency," and in some senses, though not all, I shall suggest that my proposal is also not so far from his in terms of substance as might at first appear.[3] That is to say, what I see as Paul's redefinition, via Christ and the Spirit, of the Jewish doctrines of monotheism and election corresponds quite closely, when its eschatological implications are explored, to what Beker and others mean by his christological redefinition of apocalyptic.

There are two obvious problems, of course, about saying anything like this today. First, *are* Paul's beliefs really integrated? Second, are Paul's beliefs, whether integrated or not, the real heart and driving force of his writing and work? Several scholars, notably H. Räisänen, have recently answered no to both questions, arguing some form of the thesis that Paul's theology is full of rank inconsistencies, best explained on the hypothesis that what appears to be theological argumentation in Paul is merely secondary rationalization of positions reached on quite other grounds.[4] These two charges must be

---

[3] In addition to Beker's essay in this volume, see *Paul the Apostle: The Triumph of God in Life and Thought* (Philadelphia: Fortress, 1980) esp. pp. 23–36.

[4] See H. Räisänen, *Paul and the Law* (Philadelphia: Fortress, 1986).

dealt with at more length in the next two sections, but before we turn to them specifically we may enter another observation that leads initially in a different direction.

Wayne Meeks has pointed out, as the result of his sociological inquiry into the Pauline churches, that the boundary marker of these early Christian communities was the confession that we find in 1 Cor 8:6: One God, one Lord.[5] This confession, as I have suggested elsewhere, is itself a rewriting, whether by Paul or by some other early Christian, of the Jewish confession of faith, the *Shema*.[6] This, in fact, I believe to be the heart of the Pauline doctrine of justification by faith: that the community of the people of God, those declared in the present to be *dikaios*, are those whose faith is defined thus. They are marked off from pagan polytheists on the one hand—since the formula, in its context in 1 Corinthians 8, is clearly monotheistic in intent— and from Jews on the other by the radical and startling christological redefinition of Jewish monotheism. Rather than move with E. P. Sanders to neologism, therefore, and use the noun "faith" as a verb,[7] I propose that we use the noun cognate with "believe" to express the status of this confession within the Pauline communities: justification by *belief*, that is, covenant membership demarcated by that which is believed.

If I am correct in that suggestion, which I am well aware will be frowned on by some (despite my redefinition of what "justification" actually *means*), then a corollary follows. The nature of that faith—not in the sense of the analysis of the act of believing but in the sense of an analysis of the thing(s) believed (in)—is of vital importance to Paul in his work. This is so not because he is an idealist wishing to achieve a coherence of abstract thought for its own sake but because he is anxious about the boundary markers of the communities he believes himself called upon to found and nurture. Classically, he is anxious in positive and negative ways. On the one hand, the boundary marker must be faith in Christ, and those who do not confess Christ (whether by their behavior or by their speech) are to be regarded as outsiders. On the other hand, the boundary marker is faith in Christ and *not* Jewish race, with its badges of circumcision, kosher laws, sabbath observance, and—in and through all—the possession of or attempts to keep Torah. Pauline theology thus has, if you like, a sociological cutting edge: it leads Paul into action in relation to his communities, just as modern study of those

---

[5] W. A. Meeks, *The First Urban Christians: The Social World of the Apostle Paul* (New Haven: Yale University Press, 1983) 164–70.

[6] See N. T. Wright, "'Constraints' and the Jesus of History," *SJT* 39 (1986) 189–210, esp. pp. 208–9.

[7] See E. P. Sanders, *Paul, the Law, and the Jewish People* (Philadelphia: Fortress, 1983) 39–40.

communities leads inexorably—as in the case of Meeks—back to the study of theology, of that which is believed and confessed.

It is not enough, however, merely to consider the specific topics treated by Paul at this or that point in his letters. It is also important to ask questions about the underlying structure of his belief system. What options were open to him at this level, and which (if any) did he take up? Here we have to do with issues too large to be seen frequently on the surface: questions of monism and dualism; of paganism, pantheism, and polytheism; of monotheism, its alternatives and its implications. It is my conviction that if we are really studying Pauline theology these issues must at least be on the table, if we are not to condemn ourselves ultimately to shallowness. Ultimately, theology is all about the great wholes, the single worldviews that determine and dominate the day-to-day handling of varied issues. Most, perhaps all, great thinkers and writers can in the last resort be studied at this level. It thus becomes all the more important to ask: what about the supposed "inconsistencies" in Paul?

Contradictions, Tensions, Inconsistencies, Antinomies, and Other Worrying Things

To call someone inconsistent seems today a somewhat two-edged compliment. S. Schechter's dictum is often quoted to the effect that, whatever faults the rabbis may have had, consistency was not among them.[8] It is implied that watertight consistency is the province of small minds and that awareness of larger truth, or readiness to be open to different aspects of the situation, will lead inevitably to a healthy inconsistency, which is a sign not of mental laziness or sloppiness but of continual growth in stature. Thus Paul is declared "gloriously" inconsistent, and it is somehow implied that he ought to be pleased with the compliment. Who wants to be rigidly dogmatic?

The appearance of inconsistency, nevertheless, presents a problem for students of any abstract thinker or writer. An apparent inconsistency in Plato, say, is a cause for scholarly questioning. Did he change his mind? Was he aware of the problem? Is there a third passage that reconciles the two? Are we forcing his ideas into the wrong mold? This problem increases when the text in question forms part of a corpus regarded by some as in some sense authoritative—which is still the case among many Pauline scholars, including some who expose his apparent inconsistencies. Do we set up a scheme of textual surgery?[9] Or postulate development of thought?[10] Or situation

---

[8] See S. Schechter, *Some Aspects of Rabbinic Theology* (London, 1909) 46.

[9] So J. C. O'Neill, *Paul's Letter to the Romans* (Harmondsworth, Middlesex: Penguin, 1975).

[10] So H. Hübner, *Law in Paul's Thought* (Edinburgh: T. & T. Clark, 1984); and J. W. Drane,

ethics?[11] Or suggest using *Sachkritik?*[12] Or do we carefully expound the passages in question so that one set is allowed to dominate and the others apparently made to harmonize with it?[13] Or should we have part of the cake and eat the other part, dividing it up into "coherence" and "contingency"?[14] Or should we simply give up and say that Paul contradicts himself on major matters, that the impression of profundity is simply the result of this confusion,[15] and that many of his arguments are not real arguments but psychologically explicable secondary rationalizations?[16] At this point the compliment seems to be wearing a little thin, but Paul is still left in the position of being unable to reply to the charges laid against him, since (it is implied) he ought to be flattered rather than threatened by them.

It is of course pleasantly easy to produce apparent self-contradiction in almost any writer. Ronald Knox had no difficulty in proving the existence of different hands in the Sherlock Holmes corpus or in demonstrating that the second half of *Pilgrim's Progress* was written by a middle-aged Anglo-Catholic woman (Deutero-Bunyan, of course).[17] If we imagine the sort of reply Bunyan himself would have made to this happy nonsense we may well be able to imagine also potential replies that Paul might make. The way to produce inconsistency is to ask a sharp question (especially on a subject not central to all the writings in question) and to insist on a yes-or-no answer. Is Montreal a hot city, yes or no? Is Greek an easy language to learn, yes or no? Was Jane Austen in favor of repentance, yes or no? Is the Bible the word of God, yes or no? Is the Torah abolished, yes or no? We surely want to reply "It all depends . . . ," but the words are scarcely out of our mouths before our questioner interrupts: don't prevaricate, don't try to evade with cheap quibbles — I only asked a simple question. When we meet this sort of thing in real life, we smile and explain the problem or simply change the subject. When we meet it in scholarship we allow ourselves to be browbeaten, to be threatened by the implied rebuke that if you manage to answer yes *and* no, you're just a harmonizer, flattening out Paul's craggy contours, denying the

Paul, Libertine or Legalist? A Study in the Theology of the Major Pauline Epistles (London: SPCK, 1975).

[11] So P. Richardson and P. W. Gooch, "Accommodation Ethics," *TynBul* 29 (1978) 89–142.

[12] So E. Käsemann, *Commentary on Romans* (Grand Rapids: Eerdmans, 1980).

[13] So C. E. B. Cranfield, *A Critical and Exegetical Commentary on the Epistle to the Romans* (2 vols.; ICC; Edinburgh: T. & T. Clark, 1975, 1979). Cranfield gives priority to Romans; many Lutherans, however, make Galatians the yardstick.

[14] So Beker, *Paul the Apostle.*

[15] So Sanders, *Paul, the Law, and the Jewish People.*

[16] So Räisänen, *Paul and the Law.*

[17] Ronald Knox, *Essays in Satire* (London: Sheed & Ward, 1928).

poor apostle the fun, and the scholarly prestige, of his own splendid inconsistency.

If harmonization is disallowed in principle, as a means of dealing with Pauline contradictions, or at least (the softer version of the same point) inconsistency, a more philosophical counterattack suggests itself. How could the charge of contradiction be either proved or falsified? If neither is possible, the charge hangs in the air as a fairly worthless hypothesis, creating a fog perhaps, but not deserving to arrest our forward progress. What will count as contradiction? What will count as a refutation of the charge? I suggest that we should operate with a fairly tight definition of contradiction: it is present when two passages in which the same subject is being discussed make irreconcilable assertions on the same point. This of course leaves open the question whether the same subject, or the same point, is in fact at issue in the two passages in question—and for that matter what counts as irreconcilability—but these are matters of detail. Conversely, I suggest that the charge of contradiction can in principle be falsified by old-fashioned hypothesis and verification. Is there a larger category, preferably one that Paul somewhere spells out explicitly, which sets up a framework within which the two things thought of as irreconcilable are in fact held together? A good historical example of this would be the replies, by the early English reformers, to the charge that they, following Luther, were proposing a scheme in which faith and works were mutually exclusive. Their replies (I am thinking particularly of William Tyndale) consistently spell out a larger doctrine of salvation in which the respective places of faith and works are explicated and correlated. Whether or not they were successful is not my point; the method they used, of widening categories to show consistency between apparently opposed claims, is what is needed.

Literary criticism (if one may generalize so sweepingly) would provide another possible line of counterattack. In some recent writing on Paul, one gets the impression that he is contradictory until proved otherwise; the irreconcilable material is so obvious that one starts from the presupposition that nothing can be done about it and then rejects, or scorns, all attempts to solve it. But the literary critic would be inclined to proceed in the opposite direction, to start with the assumption of coherence and only relinquish it when forced to do so, having tried all reasonable hypotheses to save it. This method is taken in principle by, for instance, Ernst Käsemann in his commentary on Romans: "Until I have proof to the contrary I proceed on the assumption that the text has a central concern and a remarkable inner logic that may no longer be entirely comprehensible to us."[18] Käsemann, of course, does not

---

[18] Käsemann, *Romans*, viii.

allow himself to be thereby prevented from using *Sachkritik* to relativize certain aspects of the letter, but in his hands *Sachkritik* is a method not so much of exegesis as of hermeneutics: this is how we find not only the "real center" of Paul's thought (though he would hope for that too) but the real center of his message for the church. The same sort of move is made by C. H. Dodd.[19] For those who are not so concerned with making such a herme-neutical move, the problem thereby solved is not so pressing. If we are interested in Paul simply as a historical figure of some importance for the history of first-century religion, we can leave him as inconsistent or self-contradictory as we like. Indeed (though this is not so often noticed), to leave him self-contradictory may often be a subtle way of arguing that he is best left in his own century and should not be allowed to roam free and weave his confusions in the modern world too. He must be kept in his place.[20]

Within the attempt to find a hypothetical larger model, the softer cate-gories of inconsistency, tension, and antinomy may well find a place. Theo-logians love to point out the antinomy between waves and particles in physics; nobody doubts that both are in some sense true and important, but nobody can reconcile them within present models of understanding. Tensions are present in every interesting writer on every subject and are indeed exploited deliberately by any good writer as a way of teasing the reader into thinking harder about the subject. Neither, then, is sufficient ground for predicating contradiction. Inconsistency is a slippery category, sometimes meaning "apparent contradiction," implying that given time and/or more papyrus Paul could and perhaps would have reduced the apparent contradiction to a mere tension or antinomy. A further similar category would be incoherence, in which the implied assertion would be that Paul (or whoever) was struggling to say something clearly (and perhaps that we can say it more clearly on his behalf) but that he just failed to attain clarity in his actual expression. This charge, even more than the others, rebounds too often on its proposers for any cautious critic to be utterly happy about using it. I suggest that care be taken in discussing Paul lest we use these various words too loosely or without sufficiently recognizing the baggage which some of them carry.

I suggest, to take one example of considerable importance for Pauline theology in Philippians at least, that Paul's treatments of Torah are in fact not self-contained but that they form part of a larger whole, or indeed several

---

[19] See his comment on Rom 9:20–21: "Man is not a pot" (*The Epistle of Paul to the Romans* [MNTC; New York and London: Harper, 1932] 159).

[20] See F. Watson, *Paul, Judaism and the Gentiles: A Sociological Approach* (SNTSMS 56; Cambridge: Cambridge University Press, 1986).

larger wholes. They cannot be isolated from, for instance, his treatment of justification, his discussions of Israel, his christology and theology of the cross, his pneumatology, even his view of baptism. And it is my contention that, when even some of these contexts are taken seriously as the matrix of his various remarks about Torah, some at least of the contradictions (and other unpleasant things) which are often, and sometimes too gleefully, found in his writings will be discovered to be illusory. When that happens we will be forced to think again about the nature of his theological method, which is often currently dismissed by the charge of "rationalization." What do such charges involve?

Proofs, Arguments, Assertions, Rationalization, and Excuses

Another area in which scholars use a set of terms without proper distinctions being drawn is the description of what Paul is doing in any particular passage. "Paul proves this point by arguing . . ."; "The apostle here argues that . . ."; "Paul attempts to demonstrate . . ."; "Paul rationalizes this by asserting . . ."; such phrases, the stock-in-trade of writers about Paul, are often used almost interchangeably as a way simply of introducing the next verse under discussion. But there are, in fact, several quite different things which Paul does in his letters. He is quite capable of arguing a point millimeter by millimeter from first principles, but he certainly does not employ this method for all, or even most, of the time. Nor should he be criticized for illogicality if on occasion it can be shown that what he has done is not argue but assert, not prove but rationalize. Thus, for instance, he sometimes merely asserts a point, without attempting to argue it: "The sting of death is sin, and the power of sin is the Torah" (1 Cor 15:56). Paul does in fact argue this fully in Romans 6–7, but in context it is a bald, and provocative, assertion. Sometimes he argues in regular syllogistic form: if a then b, if b then c, so if a then c — leading either to the conclusion "and a is in fact true" (an assertion within an argument) "therefore c is also true," or to a *reductio ad absurdum*, "and c is absurd, therefore a, which would have led to it, is untrue." An example of the first would be Rom 8:9–11, analyzed into its effective component stages:

a If you belong to Christ, the Spirit dwells in you:
b The Spirit is the one who raised Jesus from the dead:
c Therefore if you belong to Christ, the Spirit will raise you too.
Practical conclusion: Since you do in fact belong to Christ (an assertion, here unsupported, within an argument), the Spirit will in fact raise you too.

Properly speaking, this requires a further premise, *b2:* the Spirit will do for Jesus' people, those who are in Christ, what he did for Jesus. Paul is able to assume this from his previous statements in, for example, chap. 6. An example of a *reductio ad absurdum* would be Rom 6:15–23, similarly analyzed:

a If you yield yourselves to sin, you become the slave of sin:
b Slavery to sin leads to death:
c Therefore yielding oneself to sin leads to death.
Practical conclusion: Death is the wrong place to end up; therefore, yielding oneself to sin is the wrong place to begin.

It must be stressed that in syllogisms like these, or indeed in almost any form of argument, the terms of the syllogisms are not themselves argued for. While Paul is arguing from *a* and *b* to *c,* he is not usually at the same time arguing for the truth of *a* and *b* themselves. Confusion often arises at this point. Scholars frequently attempt to read Paul as if he were actually arguing for every line, as if (for instance) the sentence "I through the law died to the law" in Gal 2:19 were the result of, or even part of the flow of, a consecutive argument. It is in fact a fresh assertion introduced to bring a *new* point *into* an argument. It thus becomes part of the argument but is not itself here argued for. (In this particular case, it could be suggested that Paul argues the point fully in Romans 7, the same place, in fact, where he argues fully the tendentious assertion of 1 Cor 15:56.)

A further variant on the syllogism may also be noted here. Paul sometimes reverses the order of minor premise and conclusion, *b* and *c:*

a Torah, sin, and death are the problem analyzed in Romans 7:
c Therefore there is no condemnation for those in Christ Jesus (8:1):
b Because God has solved the problem of Romans 7 (8:2–11).

There are thus different, interlocking types of writing in Paul. Although we use the word "argument" loosely, referring to almost anything that Paul says, we should (I suggest) restrict it more carefully to passages where Paul actually *is* arguing and note carefully those sentences within an argument which are not themselves there argued for. This will have the effect of restricting the ambitions of exegesis, placing bounds on the desire to extract, say, a full doctrine of Torah from every passage in which it is mentioned. It will also, I believe, help in the task of identifying, in relation to my previous section, places where the charge of contradiction has even any plausibility.

One final kind of argument should be noted here in passing. In his stimulating monograph *The Faith of Jesus Christ,* Richard B. Hays suggests that we can trace a narrative substructure underneath Paul's argument at key points in Galatians 3–4 and that this substructure carries its own kind of narrative logic on the basis of which certain things can be regarded as proved, not by regular formal argument but by appeal to the known story.[21] This possibility must at least be borne in mind as a useful, perhaps sometimes even necessary, tool for exegesis in certain passages (perhaps, e.g., Phil 3:2–11).

What, then (to return to our earlier point), is a rationalization? An argument, presumably, designed to lead to a conclusion already reached by the writer or speaker on different grounds. When put like that, "rationalization" seems clearly a term of abuse, strong enough indeed to knock down an entire line of thought: "You only say that because you want to remain a good Calvinist/Lutheran/liberal." But this weapon has too light a trigger. Unless we are simply arational beings, in which case we might as well stop talking altogether, there will always be reasons for what we say, and having such reasons can hardly be in every case an argument against saying anything at all. One is reminded of C. S. Lewis's *reductio ad absurdum* for this sort of thing:

> "Now tell me, someone, what is argument?"
> There was a confused murmur.
> "Come, come," said the jailor. "You must know your catechisms by now. You, there, what is argument?"
> "Argument is the attempted rationalization of the arguer's desires."
> "Very good," replied the jailor, "but you should turn out your toes and put your hands behind your back. That is better. Now: what is the proper answer to an argument proving the existence of the Landlord [God]?"
> "The proper answer is, 'You say that because you are a Steward [Priest].'"
> . . . .
> "Good. Now just one more. What is the answer to an argument turning on the belief that two and two make four?"
> "The answer is, 'You say that because you are a mathematician.'"
> "You are a very good boy," said the jailor. "And when I come back I shall bring you something nice."[22]

Not only is the cry "rationalization" likely to prove too much. It frequently invokes a quite unwarranted slur on an argument. If something is true, it is likely *a priori* that there will be more than one valid argument by which it can be proved. Thus, if I wish to know the height of the fir tree I can see from my study window, I have more than one option. I can climb the tree clutching a long piece of string attached to the base, mark the height, return

---

[21] R. B. Hays, *The Faith of Jesus Christ: An Investigation of the Narrative Substructure of Galatians 3:1–4:1* (SBLDS 56; Chico, CA: Scholars Press, 1983).

[22] C. S. Lewis, *The Pilgrim's Regress* (New York: Sheed & Ward, 1944) 69–70.

to the ground, and measure the string. I can conduct comparatively sophisticated geometrical experiments with vertical poles placed some distance from the tree, measuring angles and poles instead of the tree itself. I can even take a reading of the ground-level height above sea level with an air-pressure gauge, fly in a helicopter to a point level with the treetop, take another reading, and subtract *a* from *b*. And — and this is the point that really matters for the study of Paul — there is no reason why the argument I give to demonstrate that the tree is, say, forty-five feet high should be any particular one of these; no reason, moreover, why it should be *the same argument by which I myself arrived at the information*. It is, indeed, more likely to be directly related to my perception of the sort of argument likely to be accepted as valid by the person whom I wish to convince. I may have arrived at the conclusion in the first instance by any one of a variety of routes. I may have guessed; I may have believed the guess of a friend with a practiced eye; I may have compared it with the building next to it, whose height I happen to know. Especially in the first case (the guess), there will be a need to provide what are in fact rationalizations: reasoned-out demonstrations of a point reached by other, perhaps even nonrational, means. *Such a process does not discredit the rationalizations. It requires them.* In Paul's case, it is clear that the resurrection, faith in which came to Paul in, or shortly after, his Damascus road experience, was his actual starting point. But, once having come to believe in Jesus as the risen Messiah, he was at liberty to see the scheme whole, with the resurrection as climax, not ground, and to start at another point in any given actual debate.

There is, in fact, every likelihood that some people will find some sorts of arguments convincing, and others, others. A good arguer will appeal to the ones deemed likely to convince this audience in particular. Thus, when Paul argues a point about the Torah, it is quite illegitimate to respond, "But, Paul, that's not how *you* came to your view." Did he ever claim that it was? (Possible answer: no, but several of his interpreters have.)

Almost all scientific arguments are secondary rationalizations designed to argue inductively for a conclusion reached originally by a leap of imagination. A great many well-accepted scholarly arguments in the biblical field are of this type. Consider, for instance, Julius Wellhausen's own account of his instant acceptance of K. H. Graf's hypothesis about the lateness of P: "Wellhausen tells us, when he heard of Graf's conclusion, in a private conversation with Albrecht Ritschl, he sensed immediately that it was right, even though he could not at the time examine Graf's reasons."[23] That is, he reached

---

[23] R. E. Clements, *A Century of Old Testament Study* (rev. ed.; Guildford, Surrey: Lutterworth, 1983) 9.

in a flash of intuition an idea that was only subsequently filled out by the mass of detail which was then presented, and quite properly so, as argument for the benefit of those who could not come by the intuitive leap—the Damascus road experience in which the four sources appeared in glory—made by the master. Nearer home, I am skeptical, in a friendly sort of way, of Cranfield's suggestion that his theological essays at the end of the Romans commentary are to be seen as the result of the detailed exegesis that has preceded them.[24] The fullest is in fact a reworking of his famous essay on Paul and the law, first printed many years before, which has at point after point influenced the actual course of exegesis.[25] I do not say, influenced for the worse. I do not think, and this in fact is my main point here, that the detailed argument which provides reasons for a hypothesis is any the worse for having that status. If it is, Einstein falls along with Cranfield. Thus, while there is no need to doubt Räisänen's protestations that *he* did not come to *his* research with a fixed notion of the results he eventually found,[26] there was in fact no need for him to be so sensitive about the possibility.

Why, then, have rationalizations had such a bad press? Why did Räisänen want to avoid the charge himself? Because, clearly, they are very often illegitimate as arguments in their own right, and Räisänen, who is about to use this as his principal charge against Paul, is obviously warding off in advance any chance of a *tu quoque*. But the charge is only worth making under the following circumstances. It is possible that a writer or speaker will advance, as a supposedly valid argument for a position reached on other grounds, a line of thought which is in fact *not* valid but which gains its apparent force simply from rhetorical skill or emotive pressure. When subject to the light of day, the argument turns out to be spurious, an *invalid* secondary rationalization of a position reached on other grounds. But it is the invalidity of the argument itself, not the fact that it is a secondary rationalization, which renders it invalid. A better word for such a process would be "excuse," though even that does not of itself carry the negative force required; "invalid excuse" would be better.

It is only in such cases that the question of motive—of the psychological and sociological factors with which Räisänen makes so much play, which are to my mind the principal weaknesses of his book—even needs to be raised. If we can see that the argument is invalid, we are entitled to ask, why then did somebody who gives the appearance, if not necessarily of actually being rational, at least of desiring to be thought so, make them in the first place?

[24] Cranfield, *Romans*, 1. 1.
[25] C. E. B. Cranfield, "St. Paul and the Law," *SJT* 17 (1964) 43–68.
[26] Räisänen, *Paul and the Law*, v.

I am not saying that we can give satisfactory answers to such questions. Psychologists and therapists have a hard enough time answering them when the patient is sitting still in the same room and cooperating. How ancient historians can hope to have any success in the same process with fantastically small evidence is beyond my comprehension.

All of the above serves as a major premise to a syllogism of my own, whose minor, like some of Paul's, cannot for reasons of space be argued, but merely stated:

a Only some rationalizations are invalid:

b Räisänen (and others) argue as if all rationalizations are invalid:

c Therefore the question remains open whether Paul's actual arguments, even if demonstrably rationalizations, are in fact invalid.

Were there space, it would have been fun to examine Galatians 3, one of the passages most affected by this argument, and see what would happen. I am not, of course, suggesting that there are no problems in Paul's arguments, only that the problems do not lie just where they are commonly thought to.

What method, then, is appropriate to use when dealing with questions of Pauline theology? Unquestionably the right starting point is exegesis. But we cannot come to exegesis pretending to be neutral. We join the hermeneutical spiral, traveling (we may hope) in an upward direction as we go round from text to hypothesis, or vice versa, and back again. We need at least some preliminary questions to ask, and their choice is far from neutral. The questions I have to offer are the result of several trips round the spiral. I do not pretend that they are not, in the sense described above, part of a process of rationalization. I do claim that they are advanced genuinely as questions. One of the tests of whether a rationalization is valid or invalid is whether, in the course of making it, its proponent is prepared to modify the position being rationalized. If so, then the scientific model of hypothesis and verification is being followed, and there is no need to grumble.

The Preliminary Questions

I have suggested that Paul's Jewish background makes it natural for us to approach him with certain theological questions in mind, though not the ones we normally bring to him: What was his view of God and the people of God? Monotheism and election served not so much as abstract beliefs, mere propositions to which intellectual assent should be given by the thinking Jew, but as truths to be celebrated, as boundary markers round the community, as symbols of national and racial solidarity. It is natural to ask, then, what, if anything, did Paul do with these beliefs? Did they change through his becoming Christian, and if so in what way? Could we, from what we know of first-century Pharisaism, have "predicted" (in the scientific sense) these modifications? These questions break down into subsidiary ones: In what did Paul's critique of Israel and, within that, of the Torah consist? What is the basis of it? Did he begin with a "problem" about Judaism to which he received a solution or, discovering a solution in Christ, did he suddenly realize that all along he had had a problem?[27] To what extent does he maintain, despite all this, a positive view of Torah? What is his view of the church? How (to put that another way) has he modified the Jewish doctrine of election? In particular, how has the Pharisaic attitude to the Gentiles — more specifically, to their place in God's purposes for the age to come — been taken up and reshaped, and why has it been done like this?

Questions such as these, I take it, are the stock-in-trade of what "Pauline theology" is all about. (Questions of rhetorical style, of social setting, of literary structure, and so forth are, to be sure, vital matters, but they are not exactly the same thing. I am not suggesting that one is more important than the other, merely that they are different, and that it is on theology that this paper is focused.) They form appropriate starting points for discussions of Pauline theology. This is not to deny, of course, the very important point that every text must be allowed to suggest its own questions and to answer them in its own way and time. Not every text that appears to deal with God can be pressed for a fully blown theological statement of Paul's "position," nor every text about the Torah for a final word about "Paul and the law." But they provide at least an initial sense of direction.

They also do more: they indicate or at least provide clues to the theological "deep structure" of Paul's thought, that is, where he is to be located on the spectrum of worldviews, of dualism, pantheism, etc. Pauline theology has not often dealt with issues such as these, because they are not themselves dealt with on the surface of the letters; but at many points (e.g., 1 Corinthians 8, Romans 14) a case could be made for seeing them as the real underlying issues, perhaps even as the "core communication."[28] What I am arguing for is an approach to Pauline theology that will neither reduce it on the one hand to a mere function of social forces or rhetorical conventions nor subsume it

---

[27] These, of course, are the suggestions of R. Bultmann (*Theology of the New Testament* [2 vols.; New York: Scribner's, 1951, 1955] 1. 190–352, esp. p. 301); and E. P. Sanders (*Paul and Palestinian Judaism: A Comparison of Patterns of Religion* [Philadelphia: Fortress, 1977] 442–47), respectively.

[28] Can we *know, pace* Sampley (pp. 6–8 above), that the model of what Paul is communicating *must* be like two electromagnetic poles with tension between them? I think this model is helpful in some ways, but we should beware of imposing it from without.

on the other hand under the traditional loci of a different age (whether the sixteenth or any other century), but will grapple with the task of understanding Paul's own thought forms and thought patterns, as a Pharisee and then as a Christian, and attempt to restate them coherently in such a way as to show their proper interrelation within a total worldview without doing violence to them en route. It is with this intention as the long-term goal that the rest of this paper, with all its obvious inadequacies, is offered.

II. THE STORY SO FAR:
1 AND 2 THESSALONIANS,
PHILIPPIANS, PHILEMON

From the papers we have seen so far on the theology of these letters, certain themes have emerged explicitly, and others implicitly, which indicate directions of thought that can usefully be pursued within the task of synthesis. We may introduce them under four headings — apocalyptic, covenant people, Jesus Christ, and eschatology and mission — offering some comments on each as we do so. (The fourth is actually not a summary of work done but simply some reflections of my own.)

Apocalyptic

There is a growing consensus that Paul's thought can be seen as, in some sense, the reworking of a Jewish apocalyptic framework of thought. This is clearly so for the Thessalonian correspondence and emerges also at the end of Philippians 3; that Philemon is apparently innocent of it is hardly relevant, given its small size. It is perhaps a particularly helpful move to draw attention to the problem underlying 1 Thessalonians as that of persecution consequent upon state suspicion of early Christianity and thereby to present Paul's argument as in some significant ways parallel to the martyr ideology of that Judaism in which apocalyptic seems to have flourished.[29] This points quite clearly to the similar themes in Philippians 1. The consequent theme of the vindication of the church in 1 and 2 Thessalonians and Philippians 3 thus takes the place, within this scheme, of the vindication of Israel/the righteous/ the martyrs. To think this through further may take us quite a long way.

But there is not, perhaps, sufficient exploration as yet of what precisely this might mean in terms of the structure or detail of Paul's theology. Beker's bold

---

[29] See K. P. Donfried, "The Theology of 1 Thessalonians as a Reflection of Its Purpose," in *To Touch the Text: Biblical and Related Studies in Honor of Joseph A. Fitzmyer, S.J.* (ed. M. P. Horgan and P. J. Kobelski; New York: Crossroad, 1989) 243–60; and J. S. Pobee, *Persecution and Martyrdom in the Theology of Paul* (JSNTSup 6; Sheffield: JSOT Press, 1985).

thesis still needs filling in and elucidating, and perhaps correcting.[30] Does Paul pour Jewish apocalyptic into a new mold, that, for example, of christology, or does he pour the church's christology into the apocalyptic mold? It seems to me that there are six things to be said here, which together lead naturally into the next major category to be studied.

(1) It can be argued that Jewish apocalyptic has its home base in the covenantal hope of Israel. Some insist that "apocalyptic" has as its basic referent the imminent expectation of the end of the space-time universe. Others see it as a form of esoteric speculation about manifold mysteries normally kept hidden. I think it is better to see the main aim of apocalyptic as being to articulate, and give theological depth to, the hope of Israel that, because Israel was the covenant people of the one God of all the earth, this God would eventually vindicate Israel as his people by delivering it from its oppressors. This theme of covenant vindication, whose roots go back to Daniel and beyond, emerges very clearly in 4 Ezra and *2 Baruch* and in the other major apocalypses that help create what we think of as the regular apocalyptic corpus. This fact—as I believe it to be—should modify quite drastically the idea that all that apocalyptists looked for was the end of the world and/or a heavenly haven for the righteous. Apocalyptic hope is perfectly consistent with the idea of a continuing this-worldly order, and it is indeed this that necessitates (where it occurs) a doctrine of resurrection, so that earlier martyrs may share the this-worldly inheritance of the still-living righteous.

(2) The language of apocalyptic must therefore be read as a highly charged metaphorical/mythical manner of speaking about God and his plans for his covenant people, not—or not automatically—as a "literal" or one-dimensional description of space-time events. It is perhaps surprising that, in an age when we have learned to read so much of the Bible nonliterally, some scholars should still read apocalyptic language, whose nonliteralness is almost as obvious as that of *Pilgrim's Progress,* in this fashion. Following the work of G. B. Caird on biblical language and M. J. Borg on the end-of-the-world language in the gospels, I propose that we see this language system as the appropriate language, developed within a Jewish context which lent it a carefully shaded set of overtones borrowed from creation and exodus, for referring to this-worldly events and investing them with their theological significance.[31] This is not to say that no Jew, or Christian, ever thought of or referred to the actual end of the space-time universe; but it should cause

---

[30] Beker, *Paul the Apostle,* esp. pp. 23–36; see also Beker's essay in this volume.

[31] G. B. Caird, *The Language and Imagery of the Bible* (Philadelphia: Westminster, 1980); M. J. Borg, *Conflict, Holiness and Politics in the Teachings of Jesus* (New York: Mellen, 1984).

us to pause and reexamine many cases where we have been led to assume that people were doing just that. The "end-of-the-world Paul" is as overdue for review as the "end-of-the-world Jesus." As an example of this we cite 2 Thess 2:1–2: If the "Day of the Lord" were what has been commonly thought of as an "apocalyptic event" involving the end of the space-time universe, it would be odd, to say the least, to imagine that news of this event would be brought to the Thessalonians by letter.

(3) This emphasis means that "apocalyptic" cannot be divorced from several other aspects and expressions of Israel's life, belief, and hope. In particular, there is no clear line to be drawn between those who expressed the national aspiration in this literary fashion and those who were prepared to engage in violent demonstrations or protests on the basis that Israel should have "no king but God" (see, e.g., Josephus, *J.W.* 2.8.1 §§117–18) or to die rather than see the law transgressed (*J.W.* 1.33.2 § 648, etc.). This does not mean that all apocalyptists were proto-Zealots or vice versa, but merely that, by invoking "apocalyptic" as Paul's background, we have not placed him in one tidy little corner of the Jewish world but right at its confused and turbulent heart. An emphasis on Paul's apocalyptic theology does not therefore relativize, but rather creates a natural context for, other essential elements of the same Jewish picture, such as justification (see below).[32]

(4) Paul's apocalyptic theology is in fact thus much more specifically Israel-oriented than is usually supposed. The fact of his polemic against the Jews of his day (which I believe we should distinguish carefully from anti-Judaism per se, and still more from anti-Semitism) does not mean that his theology somehow ceases to be "Jewish," and the fact that he has radically redefined what the covenant is all about does not mean that he is not therefore "covenantal." As we will see below, the language of Phil 3:2-11 is the most obvious evidence for this: we are the περιτομή (not the "true" circumcision, but just the circumcision). Paul's redrawn apocalyptic schema has Jesus, and then his people, occupying the roles which in Jewish writings of this type would invariably be taken by Israel itself or a representative figure standing for the whole nation. We may for various reasons shy away from speaking of a "replacement" of Israel by the church, but in terms of the structure of Paul's apocalyptic thought that is exactly what has happened.

(5) The other revisions of the apocalyptic scheme that are evident, particularly in these four letters, point in the same direction and indicate more specifically where the major theological emphases that result from Paul's

---

[32] This means that Beker was too hasty in agreeing with Martyn's objection that in Galatians the apocalyptic theme is suppressed (see above, p. 18). The question of Israel, its definition and its hope, is still the main item on the agenda.

redefinition of apocalyptic may be said to lie. The salvation that Paul expects is not from an external enemy (namely, Rome or "the Kittim"), but from the wrath of God (1 Thess 1:10, etc.). Evil is not "out there" in the world beyond the pale of ethnic covenant membership, but a matter of the καρδία, and thus found within Israel itself. As a result, this "wrath" appears to include the coming judgment on ethnic Israel (1 Thess 2:14–16). I accept this passage as genuine and suggest that, like a certain amount of other material in 1 and 2 Thessalonians, it has quite close links with the so-called Synoptic apocalypse.[33] This in turn suggests that Paul may well have been familiar with the early Christian notion, which I believe goes back to Jesus himself, that refusal to heed the dominical message would bring inevitable doom on the city and temple. As I shall argue below, I think this notion may have played a far more important role in Paul's thought than we usually realize. Here my point is to note the way in which the apocalyptic scheme is revised: the "enemy" is defined as those who reject and oppose the Christian message.

(6) The apocalyptic expectation is focused on the coming future vindication of those who belong to Jesus (1 Thessalonians 4; Phil 3:21). By characterizing these passages as "apocalyptic" we do not shift attention away from the doctrine of justification which Paul has articulated in Phil 3:2–11, but rather underline its basic characteristic as *eschatological vindication*. What has happened is that the hope of Israel—that God would vindicate Israel over its enemies—has been transposed. The real enemies are now sin and death.[34] The coming vindication—the resurrection, in which, just as for Pharisaic Judaism, God would make it clear once and for all who his people really always were—will not be that of Israel over its enemies, but the people of God in Christ over sin and death. Those who have opposed the gospel (both Jew and Gentile) will find themselves on the side of that sin and death and therefore subject to wrath, a wrath that will work itself out first, and perhaps foremost, in terrible events within history. Justification is therefore to be seen—as we will argue more fully presently—as the eschatological vindication of the people of God, and thus as a proper theme within the apocalyptic/covenantal scheme which Paul is reworking.

In thus agreeing with the emerging consensus that redrawn apocalyptic characterizes Paul's theology in the four letters under review, we have also suggested some ways in which this insight might be developed if it is to be

---

[33] See D. Wenham, *The Rediscovery of Jesus' Eschatological Discourse* (Sheffield: JSOT Press, 1984).

[34] Although reference to the Corinthian correspondence is "off limits" in the present discussion, one cannot fail to note how "death" turns up, in the role of the archenemy, in that typically Pauline reworked apocalypse, 1 Cor 15:20–28, followed at once by the reference to Ps 8:7, which matches that in Phil 3:21.

fully understood. What we have said so far points naturally to the redefinition of the people of God as a major focus of Paul's thought here.

The Covenant People

These four letters make it clear in a whole variety of ways that Paul is transferring to the people of Christ attributes and characteristics of Israel. Paul deduces the ἐκλογή of the church in Thessalonica from the fact that the Spirit enabled the Thessalonians to receive his words in their proper power (1 Thess 1:4–5). He desires their ἁγιασμός (4:3), bringing them under what looks like a revision of a purity code. More particularly, he transfers to them, as we saw above, the typically Jewish idea that on the Day of the Lord the people of God would be vindicated, exalted. The description of the Day in 4:13–18, though frequently referred to as though it were basically *about* the parousia, is in fact more particularly about the vindication of God's people, their exaltation "on the clouds," and the resurrection of those who have already died. Paul has, I think, combined here the Jewish martyr theology, with resurrection as its concomitant, with the idea, as in Daniel 7 (controversial though this point will inevitably be), of the vindication of the people of God after their suffering at the hands of the enemies of God's people. A similar point could be made in connection with 2 Thess 1:3–12, where typical Jewish apocalyptic descriptions of the coming judgment in which God's people will at last be vindicated and their enemies judged—even though things seem to be delaying at the moment—are once more transposed into the specifically Christian key.

It is of course in Philippians 3 that this point is most fully set out, and indeed this chapter is in my view one of the clearest statements anywhere in Paul of the belief that those who belong to Christ form the covenant people of God. "We are the circumcision," explicitly (and rudely) contrasted with the κατατομή, the "mutilation," whose implications are well enough known (Phil 3:2). As P. Perkins says, what we see here is Paul abandoning a Jewish sociocultural status in favor of a different one.[35] We may fill this out further: the entire passage from v. 2 to v. 11 consists of a statement that covenant membership is demarcated not by the old badges of race and Torah and all that goes with them, but by Christ and by faith in him. I suggest that in 3:9, and elsewhere where it refers to a status accorded to human beings, δικαιο-σύνη is best translated as "covenant membership" or "covenant status," with all the sociocultural overtones that this will imply. Certainly there can be no gainsaying the fact that what Paul is talking about is the transfer from one

---

[35] See above, pp. 89–104, esp. p. 98.

community to another; and the badges of the former community, that of Pharisaic Judaism, are precisely those badges which demarcate the covenant people. We have thus arrived by an unusual route at what is usually known as the Pauline theology of justification, and we may be in a position to understand it better than is often done by coming from Romans or Galatians. Covenant membership is defined in the present age for the Jew by means of the "works of Torah," specifically those things that mark him/her out from his/her pagan neighbors: circumcision, food laws, etc. For the Christian covenant membership is defined by Christ, with membership in Christ evidenced by faith. In both schemes the doctrine is completed by eschatological vindication, namely, resurrection. For the Jew the resurrection will make it evident who was really within the covenant (with the Torah providing advance information on the matter), and for the Christian it serves the same function (3:10–11), with faith as the present evidence of that covenant membership which will be openly ratified on the last day. The same contrast informs 3:17–21.[36]

This suggests a rather different picture of "righteousness" and "justification" in Paul from that proffered in many recent works, though space forbids debate.[37] It suggests, in fact, that the *content* of faith — the *fides quae* more than the *fides qua,* though the latter is obviously fully involved as well — is what Paul is talking about when, in this passage in Philippians 3, he is defining the Christian community over against the Pharisaism he once practiced. It is in believing *these things* (one God; one Lord; Jesus is Lord; God raised him from the dead; etc.) that the community is marked out rather than by its racial origin, its dietary customs, its physical badges.

"Justification" (a word, of course, that Paul seldom uses, talking instead usually about "righteousness") may then be seen not as the means or mode of entry into the people of God (see below) so much as the declaration that one already is a member. The forensic nature of the metaphor, we may suggest, derives from the apocalyptic/eschatological scenario envisaged within the covenantal theology of Second Temple Judaism. Here one regular image for God's final act was the lawcourt with God, the judge, vindicating Israel, the beleaguered and helpless defendant. The verdict of the last day will take the form of resurrection; the verdict in the present, anticipating this, is the welcome into the covenant community of those who believe. It is only in this sense that "justification" is "transfer" or "entry" terminology; more technically, it refers to the declaration that someone is already a member of the

---

[36] See particularly Watson, *Paul,* 73–80.

[37] Suffice it to say that this view coheres well with the point made by Meeks about the Christian confession of faith serving as a boundary marker; see p. 185 above; and Meeks, *Urban Christians,* 164–70.

covenant, though naturally enough it comes then to refer—as in classical Christian theology—to the means and mode of entry itself.

Philippians 3 thus constitutes a major statement of what is implicit in the apocalyptic scenario of 1 and 2 Thessalonians: those who belong to Christ are the covenant people who, marked out in the present by their faith, will be vindicated when God raises them from the dead. A preliminary statement of this doctrine of covenant membership present and future may be found in Phil 1:6, which helps to explain how the logic works: he who began a good work in you will bring it to completion at the day of Christ Jesus. The "beginning of the good work," on the analogy of 1 Thessalonians 1, is presumably the work of the Spirit by which the Philippians believed Paul's gospel when it was preached to them, thus giving evidence that they were indeed the people of God; the "completion" is clearly the resurrection.

So far in this section we have seen evidence in three of the letters under consideration that Paul, as part of his Christian redrawing of apocalyptic theology, has used of the church not only language but also whole blocks of ideas that belonged to Israel according to the flesh. A further aspect of his ecclesiology, commented on in other papers, must also be brought into the picture: his passionate desire for unity and κοινωνία. This is where the letter to Philemon comes into its own.

As I have argued elsewhere, Philemon 6 is the driving heart of the letter.[38] Space forbids a full discussion of this very difficult verse. I offer as a possible paraphrase, "I am praying that the mutual participation which is proper to the Christian faith you hold may have its full effect in your realization of every good thing that God wants to accomplish in us to lead us into the fullness of Christian fellowship, that is, into Christ." Those familiar with the technicalities of the debate will see easily enough the moves necessary to reach this conclusion, which (I believe) does justice to the actual words Paul uses in a way no other option can do. For our present purposes there are two important things to note. (1) The idea of κοινωνία is not merely that of business partnership, but that mutual participation, that "exchange" or "interchange" in Christ which will then form the subtle basis of the argument Paul uses to bring Philemon round to welcoming Onesimus. Paul is identified with Onesimus; Paul is identified with Philemon; therefore in *Paul* Onesimus is identified with Philemon, and the whole fellowship "grows up in every way . . . into Christ" (Eph 4:15; if by an imitator, one who understood exactly what Paul was talking about here). (2) The use of "Christ" to mean "the mature people of God (who find their identity in Christ)" is a highly

---

[38] N. T. Wright, *The Epistles of Paul to the Colossians and to Philemon* (Grand Rapids: Eerdmans, 1986) 175–78.

significant occurrence; though it would take us too far afield to explore its ramifications elsewhere in the corpus, I may perhaps simply record my conviction that this "incorporative" use finds its origins in the idea of the messiah as the representative of the people of God—hence, another thoroughly Jewish idea reworked into the Christian scheme.

The theology of Philemon as a whole, then, is the outworking of the nature of κοινωνία, the unity which the church must express because it has it already in Christ; and the *modus operandi* of that unity and participation is the apostolic ministry of Paul, "in whom" the two divergent parties may be reconciled. These two themes point to major theological motifs that must be integrated into our overall synthesis. First, the church is the true humanity which cannot but transcend all known human barriers if it is not to lose its very raison d'être.[39] This, again, goes back to a Jewish perception of Israel's vocation: Israel would be the true Adam, God's true humanity.[40] Second, the apostolic ministry (here including the writing of letters itself) is God's intended means of furthering and producing this genuine humanity. This is not an incidental aside or tailpiece to Paul's theology, as we will see when discussing the underlying missionary theology of these letters.

This theme of unity and κοινωνία finds a further classic exposition, of course, in Phil 2:1–5, and it is in the service of this cause that the poem of 2:5(6?)–11 is introduced. The unity of the church is not a negotiable point for Paul but is of its essence, being stressed every bit as much as correct doctrine or behavior. Paul, perhaps especially when in prison, viewed with horror the prospect that his churches might become fissiparous. He had already seen signs of this in Corinth, and without his being able to visit the churches he was always anxious that old sociocultural distinctions might rear their heads and create division within the community that was intended, by its very unity, to witness to the world that the one God of all the world had here created a people of his own—in other words, to demonstrate in practice the Christian versions of the Jewish doctrines of monotheism and election.

We have seen that the church is regarded in these letters as the covenant community, which in several quite different but complementary ways is regarded by Paul as heir to the titles, prerogatives, and role in God's plan that had been taken by Israel (or the righteous within Israel) in standard Jewish thought. This ecclesiology is thus an integral part of that redrawn apocalyptic of which we spoke earlier and contains within itself, in miniature though perfectly consistently, that theology of righteousness and of Torah which we

---

[39] See Meeks, *Urban Christians* (esp. chap. 6), for the enormity of this idea.

[40] See N. T. Wright, "Adam in Pauline Christology," in *Society of Biblical Literature 1983 Seminar Papers* (ed. K. H. Richards; Chico, CA: Scholars Press, 1983) 361–65, with references.

see fully elaborated, in the face of two very different situations, in Galatians and Romans. We must now look at the underlying factor in Paul's thought that caused him to modify his apocalyptic framework in the first place and gave his ecclesiology its particular pattern.

Jesus Christ, the Lord

It would be absurd to propose here a full discussion of the christology even of these letters. Philippians 2 would be enough for several papers of its own.[41] But there are some themes which have been highlighted in certain ways in the papers already before us and which deserve to be set within the context of the overall synthesis at this point.

As has often been noted, the christology of Phil 2:5–11 forms the ground plan for the covenant theology of 3:2–21. (This says nothing about the prehistory of the former passage, of course, only about its role in its present context. It does imply, however, that whenever chap. 3 was written it was intended to stand in parallel with chap. 2.) Christ, though possessing equality with God, does not regard this status as something to take advantage of but makes himself as nothing in order to fulfill the real meaning of divine equality. This is why God then bestows on him the supreme name, *Kyrios,* and shares with him the glory he has sworn to share with no one beside himself (2:11, comparing Isa 45:23 in context). So Paul in 3:2–11, and the Christian in 3:20–21, find that as they abandon the false badges of covenant membership, making themselves as nothing for the sake of Christ, they are reaffirmed as covenant members after all, their only present badge being their faith, and are assured of a share, themselves, in the glory of Christ's resurrection.

This parallel—which is also, of course, a sequence—is scarcely to be regarded as simply a rhetorical flourish. It bears witness again to a fundamental feature of Paul's view of the people of God, namely, that they (in some sense) *consist of* Christ, that they are "in" him such that what is true of him is true of them.[42] But behind this again there is a more fundamental point yet. If Philippians 3 offers us a redefined Jewish covenant theology—a reworked doctrine of election, if you like—and if Philippians 2 offers us the model upon which that redefinition of election is built up, we should *expect,* on the basis of the vital interrelation between the two Jewish doctrines of election and monotheism, mutually defining and interpreting as they are, that

---

[41] See, e.g., N. T. Wright, "ἁρπαγμός and the Meaning of Philippians 2.5–11," *JTS* n.s. 37 (1986) 321–52, on which I draw for the implied interpretation below.

[42] See my comments above on the "incorporative" use of "Christ," p. 204.

Philippians 2 would offer us a redefinition of monotheism such as would undergird this revision of election. That, I suggest, is precisely what we do find. Monotheism, like election, has been redefined christologically: one God, one *Kyrios* (to the glory of the Father), and this *Kyrios* is one who from all eternity, prior to becoming human, was "in the form of God" and "equal with God."

Thus, even before we add in the scandal of the cross, we are here faced with one of the most highly striking and original moves in the whole history of theology. "It is the contention of [the New Testament writers] that with the coming of Jesus the whole situation of mankind has so altered as to change the semantic content of the word 'God.'"[43] This contention is directly correlated—as it should be, considering where it has come from—with a parallel and directly derived change in the semantic content of the phrase "people of God." Christological monotheism underlies christological ecclesiology, both being shaped and directed by the fact that the Christ is none other than the Jesus who was crucified. This most Pauline of emphases means that christological monotheism is all about a God of incredible self-giving love and that christological election is all about a people delivered from captivity at great cost. It is also a further vital link between the two chapters, for just as the self-giving of the cross lies at the heart of the hymn's parenetic significance (the appeal for unity and κοινωνία of 2:1–5), so this κοινωνία is effected in practice by the renunciation of human privilege and status, the equivalent of the cross in the life of the Pharisee (3:2–11). That is why those who oppose the message and who seek to perpetuate the former divisions are "enemies of the cross of Christ" (3:18).

To call Jesus *Kyrios*, however, is not uncomfortable merely for the Pharisee. As Philippians 1 makes clear, and as has emerged in other papers, the proclamation of Jesus as Lord brought trouble in its wake. The Macedonian churches were faced from the start with a gospel that was likely to land them in jail or in the grave. To announce that Jesus is Lord is, quite simply, to imply that Caesar is not. "Another King" is being heralded, whose followers are not bound by the δόγματα of Caesar. (Acts 17:7 seems to be on target for the situation of Thessalonica, and perhaps for Philippi too.) The three longer letters under consideration here are thus bound together by the themes of persecution and martyrdom. These are Jewish themes, and the reason underlying them is likewise very Jewish, though of course redefined christologically. "No δεσποτής but God," cried Judas the Galilean; and though the application of the principle varied considerably in the first century, the basic monotheistic claim of Israel, with its thinly veiled political threat, remained

---

[43] Caird, *Language*, 51.

constant. If the Christians were indeed announcing a monotheistic gospel with Jesus at its center—and that is indeed the implication not only of Philippians but also of 1 Thessalonians 1—they are offering a threat to the established religious, and hence political, powers.

This may help us, within the overall synthesis, to make sense of the otherwise very difficult passage Phil 1:15–18. As long as we take "proclaiming Christ" in 1:15 and 17 (the verbs are different—κηρύσσω and καταγγέλλω—but the sense is surely the same) to mean "preach" in the sense of "invite people to respond," the passage remains opaque. But if "announce Christ" could mean to say, in effect, "This man Paul is going around saying that Jesus, the Jewish Messiah, is Lord of the world," then the passage becomes clear. Paul's opponents are revealing the content of his message, knowing that it will get him into trouble. From Paul's point of view, as long as people hear the news, even from people who disbelieve it, he is content.

This theme of the gospel inevitably attracting adverse attention not only from Jews but also from Gentiles emerges also, of course, in 1 Thess 2:14–16. That passage—and indeed the whole theme—indicates a point of considerable importance in current debate, namely, that Paul's polemic against Judaism, though often violent, sarcastic, and even coarse, does not indicate that he regarded Jews as any worse off ultimately than Gentiles who rejected the absolute claim of Christ. He spends more time attacking Jewish opponents partly, no doubt, because they were often the immediate problem, but also because, theologically, it is they who need bringing down to the level of the Gentiles, who need to be convinced that the Jewish message of the crucified Messiah does not after all contain a clause in which they receive special automatic favor. The unity of the new humanity could scarcely be built on a foundation in which one race had a special reserved place.

The christology of these letters thus reinforces and further interprets the reworked apocalyptic and the ecclesiology we have already observed. We must now turn, finally, to Paul's eschatology itself, which will turn out to be another variation on the same theme.

Eschatology and Mission

I confess to feeling less secure on this ground than on some of the previous issues. My attempts to understand the intention of Jewish apocalyptic, its function within the determinative monotheism and election of mainline Judaism, and its reworking in Pauline thought have left me with as many puzzles as answers. What I have to offer here is therefore even more tentative than the reconstructions suggested above. I wish to suggest the following hypothesis for consideration.

In 1 and 2 Thessalonians, the meaning of the "wrath" that is coming on
Israel and the meaning of the "Day of the Lord" (1 Thess 2:16; 2 Thess 2:2)
are not, or at the very least not primarily, either the return of Jesus to earth
or the end of the space-time order. As we have already pointed out, the latter
would hardly need announcing (let alone debating) in correspondence. (I am
not sure that Paul used all the relevant terms univocally either, which may
produce more confusion.) Rather, the likelihood is that they refer to the
imminent destruction of Jerusalem, the time when Jesus would be vindicated
over the city that had rejected him. This view, which accords well with
Jewish prophecy and apocalyptic, in which judgment upon Jerusalem is
frequently the referent of such language, depends on more detailed argument
than can here be stated and has to do (among other things) with that newer
understanding of the judgment tradition in the Synoptics associated particularly with M. J. Borg, the fresh understanding of the Synoptic apocalypse
in, for instance, R. T. France's commentary on Matthew, and the detailed
tradition history of D. Wenham.[44] Though there may well have been all sorts
of confusion in the early church (presaging that among critical scholars!) as
to the meaning of the apocalyptic language in both the gospels and the
Thessalonian correspondence, I think there is a good *prima facie* case to be
made for saying, against the majority, that the anti-Jerusalem and anti-
temple traditions we meet in, say, Stephen's speech were widely known in
early Christianity, were themselves part of the basic proclamation and are
naturally referred to when Paul is talking of the judgment to come on those
who have rejected the gospel message. The language of Jesus' eschatological
victory and vindication (the "coming" of the Son of Man) may just as easily
refer not to his *return* to earth—though Paul speaks of that too, just as Acts
does in 1:11, alongside the description of his exaltation—but to his vindication through the visible destruction of the city and temple which he had
prophetically predicted.

   If this is so, it is easier to see that, when Paul *is* talking of the return to earth
of the ascended Lord (as he clearly is, for instance, in 1 Thess 4:13–18; Phil
3:20–21), he is (a) stressing the vindication of believers rather than the return
of Jesus and (b) emphasizing that there will be no signs for the return. It will
be, as Jesus had said, like a thief in the night, unexpected and unheralded. It
might occur at *any* time; hence, constant vigilance is needed, but no alarm
need be occasioned if it is later rather than sooner. Christians are already
children of the day and will not therefore be surprised (as will the rest of the

---

[44] Borg, *Conflict;* R. T. France, *The Gospel according to Matthew* (Grand Rapids: Eerdmans,
1985); Wenham, *Rediscovery.*

world, asleep as it is) when the day itself dawns.[45] (There may be some mileage to be gained, in terms of development in Paul's expectation, in the reflection that in Philippians Paul still expects to live until the parousia, despite his desire not to do so, thus perhaps putting this letter with 1 Corinthians and 1 Thessalonians, and before 2 Corinthians. But this takes us too far afield.)

If Paul was aware of the imminent destruction of Jerusalem and had given it theological significance in his mind, a new possibility is opened up for the interpretation of the urgency within his mission. The theories of Paul's going to Jerusalem to bring about the end of the world by the conversion of the Jews have long struck me as unworkable either exegetically, historically, or theologically. How much better to suggest that he hopes "by all means to save *some*," that is, to persuade some Jews, while there is yet time, to join the new movement and so to escape (i.e., find "salvation" from) the "wrath" that is about to come on the city and the temple. In the meantime he is concerned as a matter of great urgency not to save a few representative Gentiles before the end of the space-time world but to *plant churches on Gentile soil before Jerusalem is destroyed,* before, in other words, the mother church (which he still regards as such, Rom 15:19) is taken away. The significance of this is surely clear. While Jerusalem stands, the churches of the Gentile world will still look to it as the center. Paul has lived with the problems thereby created, as we can see in various letters. He is now determined that, by the time the city falls, the church will have been securely planted in such a way as to be able to continue in existence and mission.

Not only so. Paul's whole theme of the unity of the church, the new humanity in which the walls of racial separation are broken down, demands that the churches he plants on Gentile soil should, as far as is possible, be composed of Jews and Gentiles together. "The gospel is . . . for Jew first and also Greek": the crucial announcement to the Roman church (which was in danger of anticipating some modern scholarship and insisting that Pauline churches should be composed of Gentiles only) reflects the agenda of Paul's mission in the eastern Mediterranean, as it indicates his program for the west. If such churches are founded before Jerusalem is destroyed, the church will be in a strong position to grow from there; if not, then the fall of the mother (and Jewish Christian) community could presage a split in which Jewish Christian and Gentile Christian will go their separate ways, undoing precisely that work which Paul, as we saw, was most anxious about, reflecting

---

[45] See Caird, *Language,* 269-71, in relation both to the specific point and to the whole argument.

as it did the christological monotheism which was at the center of his revised-apocalyptic thinking. The collection is clearly of importance here too. By giving money for the Jerusalem church, the predominantly Gentile churches are reminded that they are wild branches grafted in; by accepting it, the Jewish church in Jerusalem will be realizing humbly that Jesus' welcome to sinners has now been extended to a great multitude of ἁμαρτωλοί which no one can number. But this has already taken us far afield, and it will be as well to draw back from speculation and assess the positive gains of our synthesis.

III. CONCLUSION

I have suggested, in relation to these four letters, what I would wish to argue in relation to Pauline theology as a whole: that it may be understood as the redefinition, by means of christology in particular, of the Jewish and apocalyptic understanding of God and his people, that is, of the doctrines of monotheism and election. Were there space, and if we had had other letters, particularly 1 Corinthians and Romans, to attend to, it would have become clear that the redefinition of these two cardinal doctrines, forming in their new shape the heart of Paul's belief and consequently the distinguishing mark of the covenant family he believed himself called to plant, was achieved not only by christology but also, and equally importantly, by pneumatology. Of this we get only hints in the letters before us, but already there are some important conclusions that can be suggested.

(1) The "Jewishness" of Paul's basic scheme was never abandoned, not even when he included Gentiles within the family on equal terms. Paul remains emphatically a monotheist in the senses most important at this period; that is to say, he rejects totally any form of either dualism or paganism. This is, indeed, the key to his underlying worldview: the world is created by God and as such is good, only spoiled by human sin. This essential Jewishness means that we must reject, in the history-of-religions work that must accompany Pauline theology along the way, any suggestion that he abandoned Judaism as such and built up a scheme on pagan presuppositions, or that, if he found himself obliged to quote a "covenant" formula, he needed at once to add a few phrases to modify it. For Paul, the true interpretation of the covenant with Abraham *was* the Christian, worldwide, family-characterized-by-faith one.

(2) The unity of the church — unity within individual churches as well as unity between different churches — was a fundamental concern of Paul not merely because it was a function of that love which was the true outward mark of the church but, even more fundamentally, because he understood the

church as the elect people of the one God and therefore inevitably a single worldwide family. Barriers of all sorts, but especially those between Jew and Gentile, were to have no place, for the very highest of theological reasons, in the church.

(3) In his apocalyptic eschatology he by no means embraced the imminent-end-of-the-world view that has been foisted on him by post-Schweitzer scholarship. I have suggested that he believed in the imminent destruction of Jerusalem and have ventured to suggest that this belief colored his agenda for mission. Whether or not this is accepted, it is high time that, while affirming both that apocalyptic is the proper background for understanding Paul and that he retained the basic apocalyptic structure of thought even while modifying it consistently via his view of Christ and the Spirit, we released ourselves from the woodenly literal reading of apocalyptic language which has been such a strange characteristic of an otherwise linguistically sensitive age. "Weiss and Schweitzer were right in thinking that eschatology was central to the understanding of biblical thought, but wrong in assuming that the biblical writers had minds as pedestrian as their own."[46]

Finally, we may observe how remarkably large an area of Pauline theology, as traditionally discussed, we have traversed simply on the basis of four letters not normally regarded as entirely central. There are of course lacunas, but the impression of a coherent and consistent mind working with highly complex but carefully and properly interrelated ideas, and doing so under social and political pressures which are in their turn located on the same overall map, grows as we watch. If this is merely a brief summary and synthesis of Pauline theology in four of the apparently lesser epistles, how much more will there be when we advance to the rest?

[46] Ibid., 271.

14 SALVATION HISTORY

The Theological Structure of
Paul's Thought (1 Thessalonians,
Philippians, and Galatians)

Robin Scroggs
Union Theological Seminary, New York

I. PRESUPPOSITIONS AND ASSUMPTIONS

BEFORE I PERFORM my assigned task of surveying Paul's theology in three of his shorter letters, and in order to make my presentation intelligible, I set out here my own conclusions about issues that are fundamental to that task. My judgments are laid out tersely and without argument, since my purpose is not to convince but simply to prepare for what follows.

Paul's theology is what he thinks about the transcendent and its intervention into immanent reality. Since this intervention affects people in the totality of existence, this definition obviously includes ecclesiology and ethics as dimensions of theology. Indeed, since Paul views himself and all other people as centrally and consistently affected by that intervention (either positively or negatively), it might be legitimate to claim that *everything* Paul says in his letters is his theology. In order to achieve some limitation to the matter, however, for the purposes of this paper I will exclude all sentences about human reality that do not *directly* reflect judgments upon transcendent intervention.

With such a definition, I have no problem using either the term "Paul's theology" or "Paul's thought" to define our subject matter.[1] This is so because I take the search for Paul's theology to be a search for his *judgments,* not his argumentation or systematization. If and when Paul provides us with the

---

[1] For those who object to the idea of "Paul's theology," I am content to replace that with "Paul's thought" and will use the terms interchangeably in my paper. I agree with N. Peterson that the substitution of "gospel" for "theology" does not really change things (Peterson, "Response to J. Paul Sampley," an unpublished paper presented at the 1986 SBL Consultation on Pauline Theology).

latter, they are certainly to be included. As I think we all agree, coherent systematization of the apostle's ideas, insofar as anyone achieves that, is a scholarly reconstruction and can perhaps be labeled "Pauline theology."[2]

This raises the more complex issue of the triad formulated by J. P. Sampley—Paul's thought, thought world, and his communication of them.[3] I would like to begin with an obvious distinction—that between the general thought world *available* to someone like Paul and that part of the available thought world that has actually been appropriated, whether centrally or peripherally. Paul's thought world is obviously larger than that part of it which he appropriated, but *insofar as he appropriated it,* it becomes not just his thought world, but *his* thought. In fact, we know what was his thought world, by and large, because he does appropriate part of it and thus communicate it. He may, of course, communicate something of that world in order to reject it; such sentences are in their own way helpful for knowing his thought.

Although this reflection calls into question the practical usefulness (for our purposes) of the distinction between Paul's thought and his thought world, it does highlight the importance of the traditions incorporated by Paul into his letters. Whatever traditions Paul uses can and must be seen as part of his thought. For example, I agree with those who say that Paul cites formulas indicating the preexistence of Christ but does not use that topos in exploring his own matters of interest. Nothing, however, gives us the right to exclude the topos from "Paul's thought."

The potential distinction between his thought and his communication is even more problematic. Let me begin with this observation: We all have dimensions of our thought world that are operative in ways that other dimensions are not. These operative parts are our passion and, it is fair to say, are *central* to our thinking, are the *core* of our thought. It might seem obvious that we would then *communicate* this core more frequently, with more passion, and in greater detail than the less-operative dimensions.

Given a large number of communications, or even one or two of sufficient length, the balance among the various elements of our thought world would probably become clear. Any given communication, however, may well obscure the real balance because of the influence of the situation.[4] For

---

[2] R. Jewett, "A Methodological Suggestion Emerging out of the Beker-Sampley Session," an unpublished paper presented in response to the 1986 SBL Consultation on Pauline Theology.

[3] J. P. Sampley, "From Text to Thought World: The Route to Paul's Ways," pp. 3–4 above. This issue was highlighted in Peterson's response (see n. 1 above).

[4] See J. C. Beker, "Recasting Pauline Theology: The Coherence-Contingency Scheme as Interpretive Model," pp. 15–24 above; and Sampley, "From Text to Thought World," p. 7 above.

example, it is a common experience in lecturing to classes that student questions deflect our communication from what *we* consider important to matters of lesser concern, or perhaps even indifference, to us. We may even end up spending a large amount of time dealing with what for us are less operative (or even inoperative) parts of our thought world. If someone collected seven random transcripts of our class lectures, would we be happy to have them published so that posterity could argue about the core of our thought?

But this is precisely what we have as our data—a few accidentally preserved communications whose topics are in large measure determined not by Paul but by his congregations. This means that the communications we have may actually obscure, not clarify, Paul's thought. That is, quantitative measurements—whether of length of treatment or of repetition of idea—are not in any simple way a guide to the core of Paul's thought. This is my reason for coming to doubt our ability to decide on the "central" message of Paul. Sampley comes to the same conclusion because he does not think that Paul thought in terms of a core idea.[5] I do not know how one decides whether he could or could not have thought this way, but I do doubt that the nature of our evidence gives us confidence in deciding what was his core, even if he did think in such a pattern. As "Pauline theologians" *we* may find coherence in looking at his thought in such or such a pattern, but we should not claim that that coherence represents the core of Paul.

This leads me to what I think are important suggestions of Sampley.[6] He proposes a number of ways of getting at Paul's thought quite independently of the quantitative one of focusing on what Paul stresses or repeats. Often the things Paul says in passing can be important clues to what Paul thinks. That is, Paul's thought *has to be teased out* of his statements throughout his communications, not just derived from the quantitatively "heavy" parts. In fact, it might be appropriate, methodologically, to be at least initially suspicious of what seems important in the letters, because that "weight" may have been created by the situation, not by Paul's own internal emphases.

Yet I resist the skepticism that discounts what Paul says precisely when it occurs in a context of debate. As part of my hermeneutic I accord to Paul a basic integrity and assume, unless clear evidence indicates otherwise, that Paul means what he says, even when angry or otherwise disturbed. *For the purposes of this paper I try to give equal weight to all statements, provoked or not.*

Let me sum up by adding still another metaphor to those which are accumulating. Instead of that derived from physics (electromagnetic fields)

---

[5] Sampley, "From Text to Thought World," p. 6 above.
[6] Ibid., 9–14.

or optics (lenses), mine is a pictorial one. Let us assume that Paul's thought is a picture cut into jigsaw puzzle pieces.[7] Each letter we have presents us with a number of those pieces, but who would claim that when we put those together we have the whole picture? Many pieces are inevitably missing. But my metaphor is more discouraging still. Even when our puzzle is partially reconstructed, no piece is sufficiently sharp in line or color to allow us to see the emerging picture with the sharpness of focus that the original had. We have no chiaroscuro to guide us. That is, I think we must be more cautious than we have been in the past (I am as guilty as anyone) of being sure we know what is of greater or lesser importance to Paul, unless he tells us himself.

The above considerations guide the presentation that follows. I will use, moreover, an inductive approach, for I think that manner of teasing Paul's thought from his various statements is a more holistic and safer procedure than leaping to some focus that may reflect more Paul's situational needs or a scholar's predilections than the structure of Paul's theology.[8]

II. PAUL'S THOUGHT AS SALVATION HISTORY

When I look at each theological statement as of equal value to any other (that is, when I deliberately refuse to prioritize on the basis of some presuppositional stance), I am surprised at the overwhelming quantity of statements that fall into the often-maligned category of salvation history.

Let me try to define this term in a nondoctrinaire, neutral way: Paul is conscious of being a part of an ongoing history in which God, the central actor, relates to a people with an ultimate aim. One could perhaps rephrase this in terms of the now-popular "story theology." Paul knows himself to be part of a grand story, the past of which he reads out of the Torah (from the perspective of his present faith); the present, from his experience of the Christ-event and the church; and the future, from his hope in the constancy of the God he has come to know out of the past and present—that is, through the Christ-event. This does not mean that the term "salvation history" excludes "un-salvation history," that it necessarily involves triumphalism, or that it

---

[7] So also R. Morgan, *The Nature of New Testament Theology* (SBT 2/25; London: SCM, 1973) 15.

[8] I am in sympathy with the inductive procedures of J. Reumann, although I do not use his categories in what follows; see Reumann, "The Theologies of 1 Thessalonians and Philippians: Concerns, Comparison and Composite," in *Society of Biblical Literature 1987 Seminar Papers* (ed. K. H. Richards; Atlanta: Scholars Press, 1987) 521–36.

ignores the necessity of personal appropriation through faith. Such possibilities reflect some particular content rather than the structure itself of salvation history.

As I am using the term, salvation history refers simply to the *structure* of Paul's thinking. If we are searching for a structure that Paul himself would recognize and comprehend, this surely must be our choice. *To rethink Paul's theology within the structure of salvation history does the least violence, I believe, to his own conscious thought processes.*

Thus I begin with the fact that the vast majority of statements indicate that the apostle is constantly aware that the church and his role in it are guided by God toward an inevitable goal—inevitable because God's power and acts overwhelm any opposition. The *present* of this history is the present of the church (and of the apostle). The ultimate *future* is eternal life for believers. How far back the *past* is said to reach depends on the letter. In 1 Thessalonians and Philippians it extends back to the Christ-event; in Galatians, to Abraham.

Also impressive is the casualness of the apostle in denoting a specific agent for the events of divine intervention. God is obviously the ultimate source, and even in Galatians I think it fair to label Paul's thought theocentric.[9] But since the Spirit and Jesus Christ are "hands" of God, they also are said to be agents of various acts. That is, the subjects of the sentences about divine intervention have a great deal of fluidity.

For that matter, the predicate has great fluidity as well. That is, it is not clear that peace, joy, faith, etc., are separate realities. It is more likely that they are different ways of speaking about the single, intensely controlling conviction that the church is the focus of God's salvation and that that divine act changes the reality of those persons involved, individually and corporately.

My procedure is thus to record the basic outline of this salvation history. Accepting the fluidities in Paul's statements means accepting a certain amount of ambiguity. This is helpful in restraining us from imposing our modern penchant for precision on his thought. That is, *a thinker's ambiguity is precisely part of his or her thought structure.* For this reason I will not add sections attempting to summarize Paul's statements about God, Christ, etc.

Since Galatians suggests a different scope to the spread of history, I think it helpful first to describe salvation history as it is spoken of in 1 Thessalonians and Philippians. Then Galatians will be superimposed, indicating both points of overlap and differences. What I report is thus both simple and

---

[9] R. Scroggs, "A Paul for Unitarian Universalists," *The Unitarian Universalist Christian* 41 (1986) 26–31; idem, *Christology in Paul and John* (Philadelphia: Fortress, 1988) 110–12.

obvious. Hopefully it can provide a framework from which greater profundity can emerge.

III. 1 THESSALONIANS AND PHILIPPIANS

The Past

The event of Jesus Christ. Salvation history has its root and beginning point (as far as these documents are concerned) in the Christ-event. That Paul cites the hymn in Phil 2:6–11 is, I take it, evidence that he has no theoretical objection to its thought. Whether he is uncomfortable about its past (which I take to refer to the preexistent Christ) and present victorious implications is unclear. In the light, however, of the future orientation of his own language reflecting the theme (Phil 3:21), this possibility must at least be considered.

Christ became human and died on a cross (Phil 2:6–8); he died and rose, or was raised, from the dead (1 Thess 1:10; 4:14). His death is "for us" (1 Thess 5:10). It is a reality in which one can participate in the present (Phil 3:10). The resurrection is implied (but not stated) in the hymn. There Christ is enthroned as a result of his resurrection (Phil 2:9–11) and in his resurrection state he possesses a body of glory (Phil 3:21). That the death is "for us" and that believers will be changed by the resurrected Christ establish these events as salvatory (so also Phil 3:10–11).

Enthronement to cosmocrator is certainly the dominant motif of the hymn, and this seems to be a statement about the meaning of the Christ-event for the world, not just the church. Enthronement is, for the hymn at least, climactic and perhaps final, since no appeal to the future is made.

The founding of the church. Despite the importance of the Christ-event, the emphasis in these documents lies on the participation of the church and its members in salvation history. Statements are not always easily separable into those which speak of the founding of the church and those which speak of its present and continuing support and guidance. Thus the following attempt to make such a separation is at least partially artificial.

God has chosen the church (1 Thess 1:4), "begun in you a good work" (Phil 1:6), "calls you into his own kingdom and glory" (1 Thess 2:12; the present tense is probably correct), has placed (τίθημι) it for salvation (1 Thess 5:9). Members are "saints" (Phil 1:1; 1 Thess 3:13?) and "partakers of grace" (Phil 1:7). The power of the Spirit was involved in the founding of the community (1 Thess 1:5).

Δικαιοσύνη language, absent from 1 Thessalonians, appears in Philippians. As J. D. G. Dunn has argued, justification is not just entry language but also sustaining language. That is, it points to how one stays in just as much as it does to how one gets in.[10] The "righteousness from God" is that quality of relationship which is the reality of chosenness, the reality of present discipleship, and the reality of eternal life. Thus, it belongs as much in the category of founding act as sustaining power.

Indeed, in three of the four instances of the noun in Philippians (1:11; 3:9[bis]; 3:6 is a reference to false δικαιοσύνη under the law) the reference is oriented to the future — a δικαιοσύνη that is to be manifested in the eschaton. What is remarkable is the close association of ἐχ θεοῦ δικαιοσύνη with other pointers to the present and future culmination of God's design for believers: they are to "be found in him," to "know him and the power of his resurrection," and to become "like him in his death" (Phil 3:9–10). Yet, despite the consistent orientation to the future in the entire section (Phil 3:8–16), the conclusion points back to the present and past: "To that which we have reached, to that let us hold" (v. 16, my translation).

The Present

The church. Paul repeatedly suggests that the present reality of the church is positively grounded in and supported by God. Frequently he states that God witnesses to and reveals the truth to the communities (1 Thess 2:5, 10; 4:9; Phil 1:8; 3:15). God is at work in the believers (Phil 2:13). God wills purity (1 Thess 4:3, 7, 8; 5:23–24). God loves the church (1 Thess 1:4) and creates love within it (1 Thess 3:12; 4:9), causes peace (1 Thess 5:23), and inspires joy (1 Thess 1:6). Once members of the church are called "children (τέχνα) of God," but here as the object of a verb in the subjunctive (Phil 2:15).

Is the church Jewish or Gentile? As stated earlier, the references to salvation history in these letters do not go back behind the sending of the Christ. We presume that the recipients of 1 Thessalonians were Gentiles, and this is probably true. Paul does not use separation language, however, except in the disputed passage 1 Thess 2:14–16. Apart from that, references to Jew or Judaism do not appear in either letter, nor is either church addressed as Gentile. Although the Thessalonians have turned from idols (1 Thess 1:9) and thus are presumably Gentile in origin, later Paul contrasts the members with Gentiles, speaking to them almost as if they are Jews (4:5).

Even Phil 3:2–21 is ambiguous here. Sharp distinction is made between "we," the true circumcision, and those who mutilate the flesh. Yet the "we" includes Paul the Jew, and it is certainly possible that the "enemies" (v. 18) are believers in Christ. Thus, whether Paul thinks of the church as belonging

---

[10] J. D. G. Dunn, "The Theology of Galatians," p. 130 above.

to Israel cannot be ascertained with certainty. The least that can be said is that he does not say explicitly that the church is *not* part of Israel.

Paul believes that physical changes in members can be caused by divine intervention. God supplies needs (Phil 4:19), saves from illness (Phil 2:27), and influences legal decisions by secular courts (Phil 1:19—here the prayers of the church and the "Spirit of Jesus Christ" are the immediate agents). If 1 Thess 2:16 is authentic—a judgment I resist—Paul also thinks that the actions of God in the present can result in destructive physical acts on the persecutors of the church.

The apostle. Obviously Paul sees himself as part of God's interventions into the history of God's people. Statements to this effect in 1 Thessalonians and Philippians are, however, muted, and it is not entirely clear that what God does to and through Paul is not also applicable to other believers. Only in 1 Thess 2:7, for example, does the term "apostle" appear, apparently meant seriously as a plural, and with reserve. The one reference to a named "fellow worker of God" is to Timothy (1 Thess 3:2). Paul refers to his commission in 1 Thess 2:4; elsewhere, in a rhetorical turn of phrase he says that Christ has "claimed" him, but this is in a section in which it seems to me likely that Paul's discipleship is paradigmatic for that of all believers (Phil 3:12). Paul does believe that God tests him (1 Thess 2:4) and has confidence that God's intervention will lead to a judgment of acquittal in his trial (Phil 1:19).

Countervailing forces. Opposing God's powerful intervention is another spiritual force which also has invaded the present in order to frustrate God's intentions. Satan has hindered Paul on occasion from doing what he (and thus presumably God) wants (1 Thess 2:18). Paul fears that "the tempter" (presumably Satan) might lead the church to unfaith (1 Thess 3:5). In Philippians, however, where Paul agonizes about his incarceration and its implications for the progress of the gospel, he points only to human opposition and motivation.

The Future

The goal, of course, of God's intervention lies in the future culmination of the gathering of the saints in heaven. Ahead for all the world lies the threat of God's wrath. The faithful will be delivered from this wrath (1 Thess 1:10; Phil 1:28), but for their enemies ἀπωλεία is the future fate (Phil 1:28). Whether this ἀπωλεία is future nonexistence or eternal punishment cannot be determined.

In a context that points to the future and ultimate subjugation of the cosmos, the warrior Christ is given power by God to subject τὰ πάντα to himself or perhaps to God (Phil 3:21). (Is Paul correcting the present leanings of the hymn?) In Philippians this future event is labeled the "day of Christ" (1:6; 2:16). In 1 Thessalonians Paul describes it in terms of the coming of Christ (3:13; 4:16).

This future consummation has important meanings for the saints. The church is the fulfillment of that goal; one could say even that the fulfillment of the goal *is* the fulfillment of the church (Phil 1:6). The earthly σῶμα will be transformed into the glorious σῶμα of the resurrected Christ (Phil 3:21). In graphic terms Paul even describes how the "quick and the dead" in Christ will rise to be with him forever (1 Thess 4:13–17).

Notice needs to be taken of a suggestion made earlier, that the language of justification in Philippians has a future orientation. Paul's prayer is that the church in the day of Christ will be "filled with the fruits of δικαιοσύνη" (Phil 1:11). In a context that looks forward to the resurrection from the dead, the "righteousness from God that depends on faith" seems to be more an eschatological hope than a past or present reality (Phil 3:9).

IV. GALATIANS

The Past

Israel. The most obvious difference between Galatians and the letters discussed above is that the horizon of the past now includes God's dealings with Israel. Had we only the above letters, we could possibly give a Marcionite interpretation to Paul (even to the hymn). Even so, nothing is said in any of our letters about God as creator, but at least in Galatians God's intervention into history includes events prior to the coming of Jesus Christ, however much that past history reflects a deep ambiguity.

Perhaps here is a good time to raise the question about the importance that can be given to silence in an argument about Paul's theology. Are we to think that his basic theology did not include an interpretation of Israel's past, that the arguments in Galatians were "invented" *ad hoc* to deal with the situation? I find it incredible to imagine that Paul at the time of writing 1 Thessalonians had not wrestled in his own reflections and with his hearers about God and Israel. That dimension of his thought does not appear in the letter because it was not relevant to the matters at hand.

This is not to deny that specific issues, terminology, and topoi are due to the specific controversy at hand. Perhaps, indeed, Abraham is a focal point in Galatians because he was part of the argument of his opponents. But are we to suppose that Paul had not thought about Abraham before Galatians?

It seems to me that the burden of proof lies on those who would maintain that the *larger* topoi are created *de novo* by Paul because of a church situation. To adjudicate between large issues which must have been in Paul's thought and the specific terminology and arguments used in the letters which were perhaps evoked by the situation is obviously a delicate and ultimately uncertain process.

At any rate, the theological horizon in Galatians extends back to *Abraham,* whose value for Paul lies in the promise and covenant created ultimately for all who have faith, including Gentiles. Even here Paul's interest in the past is for the sake of the present. This is, of course, a typical approach to the past for a Jew and is to be expected of the apostle. It does not mean that the past is devalued. "Scripture . . . preached the gospel beforehand to Abraham"— doubtlessly for the benefit of Paul and his times.

With the inclusion of Abraham in the horizon, the bestowal of the law as an event in salvation history becomes a thorn in Paul's theology, and he struggles with it—although the cards are stacked against him in this case. Distinction between νόμος and γραφή emerges (γραφή was not mentioned in the letters discussed earlier) as a way of handling the tension. Νόμος consistently carries a negative connotation (but cf. Gal 5:14 and 6:2); γραφή points to God's message of truth contained in the writings. Moses is not mentioned by name, though he is perhaps referred to obliquely in 3:19. Any overarching scheme of salvation history will contain discontinuity as well as continuity; the bestowal of the law remains a tension-filled ambiguity in Paul's thinking.

The Christ-event. God sent the Son, born of a woman (4:4). The emphasis, however, lies in the salvatory death. Christ "gave himself for our sins" (1:4, the first time in our letters; see also 2:20). The purpose of the death is to "deliver us from the present evil age" (1:4). This includes redemption from the curse of the law (3:13; 4:5) and thus an act of liberation (5:1). There is no statement that explicitly says the death of Christ is an act of justification. Surely this is implied, however, in 3:24: "So that the law was our custodian until Christ came, that we might be justified by faith."

Language about the cross is scattered throughout the letter, but rarely in statements about the past. Even 3:1 refers to the proclamation about Jesus, not to the crucifixion itself, and the reference to Jesus hanging on a tree (3:13) emerges because of a scriptural argument. References to the cross are primarily embedded in descriptions about the quality of faithful existence. In contrast, only one reference to the resurrection of Christ appears in this letter (1:1).

The church. As in the letters discussed above, the founding of the church is a crucial dimension of God's intervention into history. The nuances in Galatians, however, are noticeably different. The role of the Spirit, for example, becomes prominent in a way not present in our other literature (but see 1 Thess 1:5–6). In 3:1–5 Paul refers to the founding experience of the Galatians in terms of their reception of the Spirit. The church is birthed κατὰ πνεῦμα (4:29). God sent the "Spirit of his Son" upon the church, an act that seems parallel and in sequence to the sending of the Son himself (4:6). The Spirit is surely related by implication to baptism in 3:2–5; the latter is pointed to in 3:26–29 as the "historical" founding event which creates sonship and equality among members.

Of course, behind Christ and Spirit is God's activity, and this is expressed in Galatians in familiar terms: God has called the church in grace (1:6), and the chosenness of believers is described in terms of being "known by God" (4:9).

Key to the founding reality of the church is the relation to God in faith rather than in "works of the law." That δικαιοσύνη language is focused on founding must not blind us to its relevance for present and future: it describes the relation between person and God which is the permanent salvatory relationship. Nor should the focus on Gentiles in this letter be taken to mean that this relationship is any the less relevant for Jews. Paul makes it clear that the life of faith based on justification by grace is that quality which distinguishes *all* those who believe in Christ (2:15–16).

Related to all this is other language which can be mentioned but not explored. The founding experience can be described in terms of Christ living in the believer (2:20) or being formed in the believer (4:19). Crucifixion language is used to describe this relationship and thus to define the quality of being formed in Christ. Paul (and thus the believer) has been crucified with Christ (2:20). In what I think is a truly revealing statement, Paul speaks of being crucified to the world (6:14). The cross marks the separation between this world and the new world of the church. In Galatians, at least, this is the basic function of cross language. It shows the radical distinction between church and world, and the principle upon which that distinction is created and sustained.[11]

The Present

The church. As in the letters discussed above, statements about founding are in almost all instances also statements about the present. Certainly this

---

[11] Scroggs, *Christology*, 24–28.

is true about two key realities described above—the work of the Spirit and the relationship with God founded on justification by faith. Since the Galatians are poised at the moment of leaving a faithful relationship with God, Paul focuses on the choice they face. This emphasis leads to statements that reveal dimensions of the reality of the church as well as some judgments about what it means to be "outside" that reality.

Although expected words such as "grace," "peace," and "love" appear occasionally in Galatians, and although faith is prominent because of the argument of the letter, the word that seems to dominate this letter is "freedom": "For freedom Christ has set us free" (5:1). This word did not appear in 1 Thessalonians or Philippians. Of course, the emphasis on it in Galatians is again due to the argument. The basic idea of freedom as denoting the reality of the believer in faith is, however, consistent with other descriptions of the new humanity found in this letter.

Filial language is fairly prominent; there are about nine references to the church as offspring of God (υἱός seven times; τέκνα twice, and once Paul calls the Galatians *his* τέκνα). This language is, of course, especially crucial in 3:29–4:7, where it is an important part of the argument.

The qualities of living in relationship by faith are laid out in the catalogue in 5:22–23 and are said to be grounded in the work of the Spirit. Indeed, this life constitutes "walking by the Spirit" (5:16, 25). The emphasis on the work of the Spirit in the lives of the believers may explain why there are few references to present guidance by God, although Paul has received revelations in the past (2:2). A guide not seen before, however, appears in this letter—namely, "the scripture" (3:8, 22; 4:30). The sacred writings do reveal truth (at least if read as Paul reads them).

Does Paul see the church as Jewish or Gentile? Terms referring to the two classes of people are prominent, and it is clear from the letter that its recipients are Gentile. That the church belongs to one or the other *category* is, however, not certain from what Paul actually says. This is but part of the larger ambiguity that pervades the letter. Since the God who justifies Jew and Gentile by faith is the God of Abraham, it would seem that Paul *assumes* a continuity between Israel and the church.

Crucial to Paul's understanding at this point is the enigmatic phrase "Israel of God" (6:15). I take this to be a reference to the church—perhaps a phrase stolen from a slogan of his opponents. Assuming that this is correct, it then implies that all those who "walk by this rule"—that is, live before God in justification by faith—are true Israelites. Thus, the church—if it is really the church—is the Israel called into existence by God in the promises to Abraham.

Existence outside the church. There is a sharp and irreconcilable separation between the reality of the "Israel of God" and that of the rest of the world. The world's reality is one of slavery, not freedom, to powers that are not authored by God (4:3, 8–9). There is no need here to enter the debate about what these powers are, except to say that they are opposed to God's intentions. It is to be observed, however, that when Paul speaks of his human opponents in the letter, he assigns them human motivations and does not *say* that he sees Satan lurking behind every opposition (unless the "angel from heaven" in Gal 1:8 is an oblique reference).

This existence in slavery pertains to nonbelieving Jews as well as to Gentiles (4:9), since life under law is as much a false life before God as the idolatry of the pagans. This is true also of Jews before the advent of Christ (4:3–4). Ambiguity in Paul's statements, however, is obvious here. The Jew before Christ is "no better than a slave"; yet he is an heir (4:1). The law is a παιδαγωγός, but such a servant is not only a negative force. For several reasons, no doubt, Paul cannot make his judgments upon pre-Christ Israel quite as condemnatory as those upon the pagan world.

A life of flesh is the result of this slavery. (Interestingly, Paul uses κατὰ σαρκά in Galatians only in the allegory of the two sons.) The works of the flesh are denoted in contrast to fruit of the Spirit (5:19–21). The implication— and one I think correct—is that *all* life outside of faithful existence before God is a life of flesh. This means that life under law is a life of flesh and subject to the same condemnatory description found in 5:19–21. Interestingly, Paul does not threaten the Galatians with the ultimate result of bondage except in 5:21: those who live by the flesh "shall not inherit the kingdom of God."

The apostle. Paul's self-description and his grasp of his place in salvation history are so apparent in this letter that little needs to be said. "Apostle" appears for the first time as a self-designation. Paul has a prophetic calling, which means he is part of God's preordained plan; he is guided by revelation; his gospel is thus God's truth. Moreover, he knows that his role is part of God's larger plan (2:7–10).

The Future

As is well known, Paul says little about the future in Galatians. His few comments suggest only vaguely the contours of the eschatological horizon. The Spirit not only guides the present but is said to be the source of eternal life (6:8). Δικαιοσύνη language is also given a future cast. Through the Spirit the believer waits for the hope of justification (5:5; the reference in 2:16 is ambiguous).

V. CONCLUSIONS

The horizons of salvation history shift as we move from 1 Thessalonians and Philippians to Galatians. In the former it begins with the Christ-event and ends with life in heaven for the believers. In the latter it begins with the promise to Abraham and (effectively) extends to the present situation of the Galatians. "Extends" may not, however, be an appropriate term. Perhaps it should be replaced by "jumps over"; that is, the time between Abraham and Christ may be one of disjunction.

This does not mean that Paul began to think about God's intervention in the world before Christ only with the Galatian situation any more than that he stopped thinking about the future consummation. The different situations call forth different horizons of salvation history. We can fairly conclude from our evidence that Paul's theological structure extends at least from Abraham to the consummation. On the other hand, we cannot conclude from the absence of pre-Abrahamic allusions that Paul's structure did not include such reflections.

On the basis of these letters alone, what can we judge about the character of Paul's structure of salvation history? On the one hand, it certainly includes the vistas of God's relationship with Israel, interpreted in terms of God's foreordained intention to include Gentiles as well as Jews within the ultimate aim of salvation. On the other hand, even with the addition of Galatians, it could still be given a Marcionite interpretation. The Christ-event brings something radically new to human possibility, because only with that event do humans—Jews as well as Gentiles—have the possibility of living in a faithful relationship with God.

The past of Israel is shrouded in ambiguity. It lived in slavery and yet contained the promise for the future, a future now realized in the church for both Jew and Gentile. There are *two* covenants; the relation between the two is not clarified, but they seem opposing rather than complementary.

The time-honored debate concerning salvation history and justification by grace through faith peaks at this point. Paul's theological structure is salvation history, but the criterion that determines whether one has been grafted into that history is whether one lives in faithful existence before God. I would argue that E. Käsemann's conclusion about Romans is already accurate here: "Just as the church must not take precedence over Christ, but must be Christ-determined without itself determining Christ, so salvation history must not take precedence over justification. It is its sphere. But justification remains the centre, the beginning and the end of salvation history."[12]

This would seem to return us to an argument about the core or center of Paul's theology. To this I say only two things: (1) justification language has its place *within* the larger structure of salvation history; and (2) justification language is not the *only* language that Paul uses to describe the faithful relationship with God. It is, indeed, crucial language, and our understanding of Paul would be impoverished without it. But the apostle has other terms and other metaphors to point to what could be said to be a true covenantal relationship between God and God's people — now seen to include the entire world.

I do think one thing is clear from our letters, especially Galatians. Paul does *not* think just "signing up" is all that is required to belong to the "Israel of God." God calls Jew and Gentile into a faithful relationship with him, and the believer's steadfastness in remaining in that relationship is at least in part due to the believer's "work of faith" (1 Thess 1:3). Paul's theological task is to describe what constitutes that faithful relationship, using whatever terminology is helpful.

---

[12] E. Käsemann, *Perspectives on Paul* (Philadelphia: Fortress, 1971) 76.

15 CRUCIFIED WITH CHRIST

A Synthesis of the Theology of
1 and 2 Thessalonians, Philemon,
Philippians, and Galatians

Richard B. Hays
Yale Divinity School

LET US PRETEND that Paul's writings had vanished from history, that his letters, never canonized as Christian scripture, had been forgotten by posterity. Now let us pretend that some chance discovery should unearth in a cave a collection of perfectly preserved manuscripts consisting only of 1 and 2 Thessalonians, Philippians, Philemon, and Galatians. Our assignment: write a synthetic account of the theology of these five letters.

I. AIMS AND METHODS
OF THEOLOGICAL SYNTHESIS

Before attempting the exotic stunt promised by the subtitle of this paper, I offer a rough account of my working assumptions, along with an *apologia* to readers who may, with fair cause, doubt the value or intelligibility of the project proposed here. To render an account of Pauline theology, we must perform two fundamental tasks: *descriptive,* to sketch the "theology" of each Pauline letter considered individually; and *synthetic,* to construct a composite account of Pauline theology by "synthesizing" the results of the individual sketches. Difficult problems of method beset both phases of the project.

The Descriptive Task

What are we looking for when we seek to describe the "theology" of a Pauline letter? Is there a difference between Paul's "symbolic universe" and his "theology"? And how are both of these to be distinguished from the particular statements that Paul actually happens to make in his surviving correspondence?[1]

My working assumptions are these: Paul shares a "symbolic world"—a communally shared imaginative environment—with other early Christians, including the readers of his letters. The dominant images of this symbolic world are located in early Christian tradition (kerygmatic and liturgical) and in Israel's scripture.[2] Paul's particular statements, which are contingent pastoral responses to specific historical situations, are to be read as performances of a competence supplied by this larger communal symbol system; the symbol system is a language, and Paul's letters are utterances within the language. (This way of formulating the matter draws analogically upon a linguistic model first formulated by Noam Chomsky: every individual sentence generated by a speaker is a "performance," a particular speech-act that actualizes a "competence," which is a set of general possibilities that are both given and circumscribed by the lexical and syntactical resources of the speaker's language.[3]) When we seek the "theology" of the letters, however, we are concerned neither with the performance as such nor with the competence as such, but with the ideational *mediating structures* that characterize Paul's critical selection, organization, and interpretation of the elements of the communal symbolic universe. We are focusing neither on *langue* nor on *parole,* but on the syntax of Paul's thought: the characteristic patterns of critical reflection that appear when he appropriates the symbolic universe in responding to specific pastoral situations.

To employ an optical metaphor rather than a linguistic one, we are seeking to trace the contours of the hermeneutical lens through which Paul projects the images of the community's symbolic world onto the screen of the community's life. The contingent arguments of the letters should be read as Paul's

---

[1] These different objects of inquiry correspond to J. Paul Sampley's distinctions between Paul's "thought world," his "thought," and his "communication of them." These terms are employed by Sampley in "From Text to Thought World: The Route to Paul's Ways," pp. 3–14 above.

[2] The centrality of scripture in Paul's symbolic world has not always been appropriately acknowleged in critical treatments of Pauline theology. I have investigated this aspect of Paul's thought in my book *Echoes of Scripture in the Letters of Paul* (New Haven and London: Yale University Press, 1989).

[3] See Noam Chomsky, *Aspects of the Theory of Syntax* (Cambridge, MA: MIT Press, 1965). The use of this linguistic model was suggested by Norman Petersen ("On the Method of Recasting Pauline Theology: A Response to J. Paul Sampley," unpublished paper presented in the Pauline Theology Consultation at the 1986 SBL Annual Meeting). My application of this distinction between competence and performance corresponds closely to Daniel Patte's distinction between the "convictional logic" of Paul's faith and the "argumentative logic" of his letters (*Paul's Faith and the Power of the Gospel: A Structural Introduction to the Pauline Letters* [Philadelphia: Fortress, 1983]).

attempts to persuade his readers to interpret the practical consequences of foundational assumptions (axioms) that they putatively share with him in the light of his convictions — that is, in the light of his own particular theological construal of those assumptions.

We know Paul's symbolic world primarily through its contingent expression in the letters; thus, the distinction between that symbolic world and Paul's own theological thought can be discerned only inferentially. Though such a distinction may be methodologically difficult to make, it is nonetheless indispensable, for it does justice to J. C. Beker's insight that Paul is a "hermeneutic theologian," rather than a systematic one; proposals about the theology of a Pauline letter must reckon with the fact that Paul's statements and exhortations are always in fact *interpretations* of a body of traditions or beliefs, spoken as "a word on target" for a particular situation.[4]

For that reason, we hope to gain clarity initially by isolating the "theology" of individual letters, considered apart from the rest of the Pauline corpus. Looking at a single letter, the critic charged with the descriptive task seeks to give an account of the theological and hermeneutical patterns that emerge in Paul's discourse as he confronts a specific situation with the resources of the communal symbolic world. Why isolate individual letters in this first phase of analysis? The procedure is purely heuristic: it may allow us to recognize important data that would elude us if we began with the whole collection of letters.

The Synthetic Task

Even if we grant the possibility of describing the theology of individual letters, the difficulties of synthesis remain daunting. The more clearly historical scholarship has limned the historical contingency of the letters as pastoral communications, the more difficult it has seemed to give a satisfying account of the unity of Paul's thought. Older synthetic accounts of "Pauline theology," such as those of Rudolf Bultmann or D. E. H. Whiteley, failed to do justice to the particularity and diversity of the letters.[5] On the other hand, more recent efforts at synthesis that take the contingency of the letters seriously into account have been hard pressed to find grounds for asserting their theological coherence. (I have in mind here not only aggressively deconstructive analyses such as Heikki Räisänen's but also, for example, Beker's frank puzzlement over how to fit Galatians into his constructive

---

[4] J. Christiaan Beker, "The Faithfulness of God and the Priority of Israel in Paul's Letter to the Romans," *HTR* 79 (1986) 10.

[5] R. Bultmann, *Theology of the New Testament* (2 vols.; New York: Scribner's, 1951, 1955) 1. 185–352; D. E. H. Whiteley, *The Theology of St. Paul* (Philadelphia: Fortress, 1966).

proposal that apocalyptic is the ground of coherence in Pauline theology.[6])
Under such circumstances, it is tempting to dismiss the synthetic task as
misguided and doomed, an exercise in artificial harmonization.[7]

Still, with few exceptions, readers of the Pauline corpus continue to
register tantalizing impressions of ideational coherence. Are such impressions the projections of our own irrepressible lust for order, which so
captivates us that, as Frank Kermode remarks, it requires "a more strenuous
effort to believe that a [text] lacks coherence than to believe that somehow,
if we could only find out, it doesn't"?[8] Or is there in fact a coherent theological vision out of which Paul's pastoral responses issue? The synthetic
phase of our inquiry seeks to test the impression of coherence by proposing
synthetic construals of Pauline theology based on artificially limited — but
incrementally increasing — bodies of textual data.

Such synthetic proposals are necessarily constructive in character: they
entail an act of imagination on the part of the interpreter. This observation
has several important consequences: (1) Our synthetic proposals are not
neutral accounts of Paul's thought; they must be honestly acknowledged as
our own attempts to make sense of Paul's writings by rearticulating their
message in a form different from the form that Paul himself employed.[9]
Michael Foucault has wryly noted that the role of "commentary" is "to create
new discourses ad infinitum" in which we "say, for the first time, what has
already been said, and repeat tirelessly what was, nevertheless, never said."[10]
So it is, necessarily, with our synthetic attempts. (2) The value of such
proposals can be tested only through the execution of concrete attempts to
perform the synthetic task. There is no fixed method that can be consistently
applied; rather, we hope to generate imaginative accounts of Pauline theology that have the power to elicit consent from the community of putatively
competent readers. In other words, we are working by trial and error. (3) The
primary criterion that must be employed in assessing these synthetic
proposals is the test of satisfaction: does the proposed synthesis illumine the
texts in such a way that informed readers can say, "Yes, that is a good reading

---

[6] See H. Räisänen, *Paul and the Law* (Philadelphia: Fortress, 1986); J. Christiaan Beker, *Paul
the Apostle: The Triumph of God in Life and Thought* (Philadelphia: Fortress, 1980) 58.

[7] See, however, the response to Räisänen by N. T. Wright, "Putting Paul Together Again:
Toward a Synthesis of Pauline Theology," pp. 186–95 above.

[8] Frank Kermode, *The Genesis of Secrecy: On the Interpretation of Narrative* (Cambridge, MA:
Harvard University Press, 1979) 53.

[9] As rightly noted by Robert Jewett, "A Methodological Suggestion Emerging out of the
Beker-Sampley Session," an unpublished paper presented in response to the 1986 SBL Consultation on Pauline Theology.

[10] Michael Foucault, "The Discourse on Language," in *The Archaeology of Knowledge* (New
York: Harper & Row, 1972) 221.

of the texts"? A "good reading" is presumably one that accounts for the content of the letters in such a way that it enables us to recognize and understand elements of these texts that might previously have remained opaque.

My synthetic proposal, then, seeks to let the five selected texts dictate the lines of emphasis and the shape of our construal of Paul's thought, just as though these were the only letters in the Pauline corpus.[11] In other words, I am seeking to sketch what "Pauline theology" would look like if Romans and the Corinthian correspondence did not exist — or if the guild of critical scholars suddenly decreed these longer letters to be deutero-Pauline! (I once had a student who actually wrote a paper contending that Romans was a deutero-Pauline letter because it so flagrantly contradicts the "true" Pauline theology of Galatians.)

The results of such a procedure will, of course, be skewed because of the limitations of the sample. However, as Leander Keck reminds us, the seven-letter corpus may be an equally skewed partial sample.[12] Even if my procedure is successful, it will by no means reveal a comprehensive ground plan of Paul's theology. Instead, it will describe only that portion of the foundation uncovered by our excavations in the five letters under consideration. Major themes may remain buried. My goal will be to give a sketch that captures the contours, concerns, and movement of Paul's thought *as it appears in these five letters*. The heuristic value of such a sketch will, I hope, become evident as we proceed.

II. PAULINE THEOLOGY: SHAPE AND EMPHASES

Symbolic World: The Narrative Framework

Scattered throughout Paul's letters are allusions to a foundational *story* about what God has done to bring salvation to his elect people. Though *not* part of Paul's "theology" in the sense defined above, this narrative provides the symbolic matrix within which Paul's theological reflection lives and moves; the ground of coherence in Paul's thought is to be found not in a system of theological propositions (e.g., "justification by faith" or a "theology

---

[11] I have not made any attempt here to grapple with the problem of the authorship of 2 Thessalonians. My assignment for the Pauline theology project was to treat it, for the purposes of our experiment, as a Pauline letter, and I have done so here. Interestingly, while my own predisposition was to assume its pseudonymity, I found it fitting into my proposed synthesis rather effortlessly. I have no settled conviction on the issue, however, and I would ask readers of this essay not to read it as if it were a defense of the authenticity of the letter.

[12] Leander E. Keck, *Paul and His Letters* (2d ed.; Philadelphia: Fortress, 1988) 16–20.

of the law") but in the kerygmatic story of God's action through Jesus Christ, "who gave himself for our sins in order to deliver us from the present evil age, according to the will of our God and Father" (Gal 1:4).[13] Thus, an account of Paul's theology in our five-letter corpus must begin with a summary reconstruction of the narrative framework of the symbolic world presupposed by that theology, insofar as such a framework can be discerned within these letters.

Nowhere within the letters does Paul narrate this foundational story in detail, but he constantly cites it allusively as a warrant for the claims and arguments he makes. (For especially clear examples, see 1 Thess 1:9–10; 4:13–18; 5:9–10; Phil 2:1–13; Gal 3:13–14; 4:3–7; 5:1.) It is possible, therefore, to piece together an outline of the story's key elements.

(1) God long ago revealed, in his promise to Abraham, his intention to bless "all nations" (Gal 3:6–9). This intention was a result of God's love (1 Thess 1:4; 2 Thess 2:13, 16), which expresses itself in God's election and calling of a people for salvation (1 Thess 2:12; 5:9, 23–24; 2 Thess 2:13–14).

(2) God sent forth his Son, Jesus Christ, in order to liberate people who were in bondage and to make them "sons" of God (Gal 4:1–7; 5:1; how they came to be in bondage is nowhere explained in these letters). This sending of Jesus was God's way of fulfilling the promise made to Abraham (Gal 3:14; see also 4:28). (Within our present corpus, the "sending" motif appears explicitly only in Galatians, but in all the letters, it is pervasively presupposed that Jesus is the instrument of God's will, the one through whom God's redemptive purpose is executed.)

(3) Jesus achieved God's purpose through his death on a cross (Gal 3:1, 13). This death was simultaneously an act of obedience to God (Phil 2:8; Gal 1:4) and of love for those whom he died to save (Gal 2:20). That is why Paul interprets Jesus' death as an act of "faithfulness" (πίστις, Gal 2:20; 3:22): Jesus' obedience to God brings about the fulfillment of God's promise to Abraham and extends the promised blessing to all nations (Gal 3:14).[14] For reasons that Paul does not entirely explain, Jesus' death has multifaceted consequences: to

---

[13] See my earlier work on "narrative substructure" in Pauline theology (*The Faith of Jesus Christ: An Investigation of the Narrative Substructure of Galatians 3:1–4:11* [SBLDS 56; Chico, CA: Scholars Press, 1983]). Readers of that book will recognize that I have tried to come at the issues in a fresh way in the present essay, without recourse to the methods used in the book to identify narrative structure.

[14] I am pleased to note that B. R. Gaventa joins the ranks of those who are persuaded by this interpretation of πίστις Ἰησοῦ Χριστοῦ ("The Singularity of the Gospel: A Reading of Galatians," p. 157 above). James D. G. Dunn remains unconverted ("The Theology of Galatians," p. 141 n. 54). For a more complete discussion of the issue, see Hays, *Faith of Jesus Christ,* 158–76, esp. nn. 105 and 106.

it can be ascribed deliverance from the wrath of God (1 Thess 1:10) and from "the present evil age" (Gal 1:4) and redemption from "the curse of the law" (Gal 3:10). Positively speaking, Jesus' death seems to be the means through which the community has received the gift of the Spirit (Gal 3:14) and "life" with Jesus (1 Thess 5:10; Gal 2:20), with its blessings of freedom (Gal 5:1) and righteousness (Phil 1:11; 3:9[?]; Gal 2:21). Paul's frequent formulaic references to "the χάρις of our Lord Jesus Christ" (e.g., 2 Thess 3:18; Phil 4:23; Phlm 25; Gal 6:18) appear to be based in this interpretation of Jesus' death as an act of love that has vicarious salvific benefits for others.

(4) Jesus was also raised from the dead (1 Thess 1:10; 4:14; Gal 1:1; Phil 3:10, 21; 2:9[?]). By contrast to Paul's great emphasis on Jesus' death, these letters make relatively little explicit theological use of this element of the story. In the one clear instance where Jesus' resurrection is employed as a theological warrant (1 Thess 4:14), it functions as a proleptic sign that points to the general resurrection of the dead (see #6 below).

(5) Those who belong to Christ Jesus find themselves at the turn of the ages, living the chapter between the story's climax and its resolution. Jesus' death/resurrection has put an end to the world as it was and has adumbrated the "new creation" (Gal 6:14–15; see also 2:20), but the present time is a temporal anomaly, an in-between time in which the community "awaits the hope of righteousness" (Gal 5:5). During this interval, the believing community suffers (1 Thess 2:2, 14–16; 3:3–4; 2 Thess 1:4–5; Phil 1:27–30; Gal 4:29; 5:11; 6:12). At the same time, however, the present is a time in which the Holy Spirit is given to the community as a sign of their adoption into God's family (Gal 3:14; 4:6), and the word of God goes forth in power through the preaching of the gospel (1 Thess 1:5; 2 Thess 3:1).

(6) The community's hope is fixed on an event that still lies in the future of the story: the parousia of the Lord Jesus, when the dead will be raised and the Lord Jesus will come from heaven to claim his people and transform them into his likeness, pronouncing judgment on the world (1 Thess 1:10; 2:19; 3:13; 4:13–18; 5:23–24; 2 Thess 1:6–10; Phil 3:11, 20–21; 4:5). Galatians makes few explicit references to this last act of the story, but—if it be read through the lens of the Macedonian correspondence—apparent allusions to the events of parousia and judgment may be found in 1:4, 8–9[?]; 5:5, 10, 21; 6:4–5, 7–10, 15.

Within this narrative structure, Paul understands the vocation and temporal location of his communities. As he confronts pastoral problems in his churches, he responds to them by thinking through the situation in the light of the story, plotting the community's place within the unfolding narrative. For example, he finds the Galatians' desire to be under law upsetting because it seems (to him) to represent a retrogression to an earlier phase of the story, and therefore a de facto denial of the efficacy of Jesus' death (Gal 2:21; 4:8–11).[15] Or, to cite another clear instance, he answers the Thessalonians' concerns about believers who have died by assuring them that when Jesus returns "the dead in Christ will rise first" and be together with those who are left alive (1 Thess 4:13–18). Rather than consoling them with philosophical arguments about death or explaining that the souls of the departed have gone to be with God, he unfolds a narrative of future events in which he believes he and his readers will participate.

Patterns of Critical Reflection

Several preliminary "grammatical" remarks may be made about Paul's use of this foundational story. First, it is striking that the narrative — as I have outlined it here — is primarily about *God's* action through Jesus Christ. The story has subplots that detail the responses of Paul himself (e.g., Phil 3:4–14; Gal 1:13–24) or of the people to whom he preached (e.g., 1 Thess 1:3–10; Gal 4:12–20), but these subplots derive their sense and significance from their participation in the larger narrative in which Jesus Christ is the protagonist.[16]

Second, Paul's references to the story focus to a remarkable extent on two key moments: the death of Jesus and "the Day of the Lord." The particular pathos of Paul's theology results from the suspension of the community's present experience between these poles. Jesus' death has somehow transmuted the human condition in such a way that Paul can say that the world has been crucified through his cross (Gal 6:14). From a whole series of passages, particularly in Galatians, it is evident that Paul thinks of the cross as the pivotal point of what Amos Wilder called "the world plot."[17] On the other hand, however, the final resolution of that plot is still to come in the parousia.

The Thessalonian correspondence places great emphasis on the future element of Paul's apocalyptic narrative framework ("not yet"), whereas Galatians concentrates heavily on the transformation of present experience as a result of Christ's death ("already"). Happily for our purposes, Philippians combines these emphases and shows that they are logically related in Paul's thought world through a *narrative* sequence: "The one who began a good work in you will bring it to completion at the day of Christ Jesus" (Phil 1:6). This same narrative logic is manifest in Philippians 3: Paul has "suffered the

---

[15] See Hays, *Faith of Jesus Christ,* 223–35.

[16] See pp. 240–43 below, for further discussion of the response of the community.

[17] Amos Wilder, *Early Christian Rhetoric: The Language of the Gospel* (Cambridge, MA: Harvard University Press, 1971) 58.

loss of all things" (3:8), but because Christ Jesus has claimed him (3:12) he presses on to what lies ahead, while awaiting the day when the Lord Jesus Christ "will change our lowly body to be like his glorious body" (3:21). Thus, the apparent theological discrepancy between Galatians and 1–2 Thessalonians in relation to eschatology may be understood as an effect of the interplay between contingent factors and coherent structure: Paul addresses different problems by appealing to different parts of one and the same foundational narrative.[18]

As Paul interprets this narrative framework in our five-letter corpus, he highlights three themes: the relation of Israel and Gentiles in God's election; Jesus as representative figure who enacts the destiny of God's people; and the community's vocation to participate in the way of the cross. Paul's distinctive handling of each of these characteristic emphases merits careful attention.

Israel, Gentiles, election. In Galatians a major issue surfaces concerning the interpretation of *election* (element #1 in the above plot summary): can uncircumcised Gentiles participate fully in the community of those who experience the blessing of the God of Israel? Circumstances in Thessalonica had not required Paul to address this problem, but the challenge of the Jewish Christian "teachers" at Galatia compelled him to articulate a theological rationale for his non-law-observant mission to Gentiles.[19]

In 1 Thessalonians, Paul appears to assume without argument that his Gentile Christian converts at Thessalonica have become participants in the covenant community of Israel. Because the matter is not yet a point of controversy for Paul, he does not formulate the claim thetically, but his language assumes this position at several points. Not only does he remark that his readers have "turned to God from idols, to serve a living and true God" (1 Thess 1:9; surely the God of Abraham?), but—even more tellingly—he exhorts them to take wives "in holiness and honor, not in the passion of lust like the Gentiles (τὰ ἔθνη) who do not know God" (1 Thess 4:4–5; the warrant for this exhortation is given in v. 7: "For God has not called us for uncleanness, but in holiness"). It is often noted that in these passages Paul has appropriated the language of Hellenistic Jewish apologetics and missionary preaching, but the extraordinary implications of these texts for his ecclesiology are rarely noted. Paul writes as if this Gentile Christian community

---

[18] This suggestion could be worked out in much more detail if the scope of this essay permitted.

[19] As this way of formulating the matter suggests, I accept the general outlines of J. Louis Martyn's reconstruction of the historical situation ("A Law-Observant Mission to Gentiles: The Background of Galatians," *SJT* 38 [1985] 307–24). Whether Paul had previously worked out his own position on this problem is not particularly important for our purposes.

is "Gentile" no longer; though they remain uncircumcised, he has transferred to them the communal ascriptions appropriate to Israel. Whether his comment in 1 Thess 4:5 is completely artless or whether it is a conscious and clever metaphorical deformation of Jewish linguistic convention, Paul is addressing his readers as non-Gentiles.

We may connect these passages directly to Phil 3:3: "*We* are the circumcision, who worship God in Spirit and boast in Jesus Christ and do not trust in the flesh." Although the claim occurs in the midst of a rhetorically heated passage, there is ample reason to think that Paul means what he says: it is believers in Jesus Christ who have legitimate claim to Israel's destiny and prerogatives.[20] Περιτομή functions here as a nonliteral honorific term meaning "covenant people," and it has been appropriated to describe Christian believers, whether they are physically circumcised or not. To make an issue out of physical circumcision is to put confidence in the flesh rather than in Christ. Thus, the shorter letters of the Macedonian correspondence presuppose the theological position that Paul is forced to argue explicitly in Galatians: Gentiles participate in the promised blessing ἐκ πίστεως 'Ιησοῦ Χριστοῦ, not through circumcision or Torah obedience.

When we turn to Galatians with these issues in view, we perceive that the letter is not concerned primarily to establish a doctrine of justification by faith as opposed to justification through human achievement; rather, it is concerned primarily to argue that God's promise to Abraham always had the Gentiles in view and that God's covenant was never intended only for the Jewish people (Gal 3:6–9).[21] The existence of Gentile Christian communities where the Spirit is palpably and powerfully present (3:2–5) is evidence that these Gentile believers are "children of promise" like Isaac, children of the free woman rather than children born κατὰ σάρκα to the slave woman, who represents "the present Jerusalem . . . in slavery with her children" (4:21–31). That is why Paul can refer provocatively to the church as "the Israel of God" (6:16). In this eschatological Israel, embracing both Jews and Gentiles, neither circumcision nor uncircumcision matters (5:6; 6:15), because where the promise is fulfilled, the old distinctions have been abolished in the "new creation," the new life in which those who are "in Christ" already participate (2:20; 3:26–29).

---

[20] Correctly, N. T. Wright: "[T]he church is regarded in these letters as the covenant community, which in several quite different but complementary ways is regarded by Paul as heir to the titles, prerogatives, and role in God's plan that had been taken by Israel (or the righteous within Israel) in standard Jewish thought" ("Putting Paul Together," p. 204).

[21] Here I follow Dunn's analysis; however, see pp. 238–40 below, for further response to Dunn.

In other words, Paul does not interpret the foundational story as a simple linear *Heilsgeschichte* from Abraham to the present moment. Rather, for Paul, Christ's death has introduced a surprising discontinuity in Israel's story, simultaneously necessitating and enabling a new reading of scripture that discloses its witness to the gospel. Christians have become Isaac; Jews have become Ishmael! Paul's revisionary rereading of scripture — worked out in some hermeneutically jarring ways in Gal 3:6–29 and 4:21–31 — fractures traditional Jewish models for discerning the coherence of scripture's message.[22] At the same time, however, he insists that God's act in Jesus Christ illuminates a previously uncomprehended narrative unity in scripture.[23] It turns out, according to Paul, that scripture from the first was always "about" God's intention to bless the Gentiles through Christ.

If we read Galatians as a response to this range of concerns, it becomes evident that the letter's references to "sonship" and "adoption," to "righteousness," and to God's "calling" all should be understood as aspects of Paul's response to the issue of participation in the covenant promises. The Gentile Galatians, who once were "enslaved under the στοιχεῖα τοῦ κόσμου" (4:3) have been set free and brought into the family of God's own people. At the same time, Paul also argues in this letter that the law is among the στοιχεῖα and that Jews as much as Gentiles must be adopted through Christ into God's family. That, of course, is an explosive claim, but it is a necessary inference from the narrative framework in which Paul reasons, for "if righteousness were through law, then Christ died gratuitously" (2:21; see also 3:21).

This last quotation suggests that δικαιοσύνη connotes "covenant membership" or "covenant status."[24] Δικαιοσύνη is the status conferred on Abraham as a result of God's gracious promise. This status is likewise conferred on others whom God calls through Christ, not through the law, which has no power to give life (3:21) and no authority to supersede or limit the covenant promise to Abraham and Christ his "seed" (3:15–18). It is not just coincidental that righteousness/justification language is absent from 1–2 Thessalonians and Philemon; this terminology appears only in the letters where the question of covenant membership for Gentile Christians is a disputed matter. (These five letters offer virtually no support for Käsemann's interpretation of δικαιοσύνη θεοῦ as God's salvation-creating power — unless Gal 5:5 should be so construed; virtually all the references to God's own righteousness appear in Romans.)

---

[22] Of course, there is ample precedent in Israel's prophetic tradition for the sort of reversal that Paul works here on the conventions of confident piety.

[23] This claim is developed more fully in Hays, *Echoes of Scripture.*

[24] Here I am in agreement with Wright, "Putting Paul Together," p. 201.

One of the motifs that does surface with surprising frequency in this five-letter corpus is the theme of God's *calling* (see, e.g., 1 Thess 2:12; 4:7; 5:24; 2 Thess 1:11; 2:13–14; Phil 3:14; Gal 1:6, 15; 5:8, 13). The references speak variously of being called into God's kingdom or to holiness or for freedom; ὁ καλῶν ὑμᾶς becomes in several of the passages an epithet for God. In every case the image presupposes that God summons a people that were previously ignorant of or estranged from him into relationship with himself. The background of this imagery, I suggest, is to be found in Deutero-Isaiah, where there are repeated references to God's calling of the Servant/Israel (e.g., Isa 41:9; 42:6; 43:1; 49:1; 51:2 [re: Abraham!]; 54:6). If one hears such echoes in Paul's use of καλεῖν, the close association of the "calling" imagery with the idea of Israel as a covenant people becomes the more evident. Just as God called the Servant/Israel by gathering them from the corners of the earth so that they might be "a covenant to the people, a light to the nations," so God now calls the "Israel of God" (= the church) for a similar reason, so that the gospel might be proclaimed.[25]

The Messiah and the people of God. The above reflections lead on to the formulation of an obvious and crucial question: How is the calling of *Israel* (which Paul dramatically reinterprets in these letters to include Gentile Christians) related to the narrative framework that we have described above, which focuses on the action of *Jesus,* especially his death on the cross? Precisely at this point Christian theology usually falls mute, despite the obvious importance of the issue. As Gerhard Ebeling noted (speaking of the Reformers' theology), it is very difficult to discern any "strict inner connexion" between christology and the doctrine of justification by faith.[26] This traditional difficulty is illustrated by James D. G. Dunn's essay in this volume, which virtually ignores christology. If, as Dunn rightly summarizes Paul's position, the "initial expression of God's covenant purpose was in terms of promise and faith and always had the Gentiles in view from the first,"[27] then why was the death of Jesus necessary? Abraham's faith was certainly not directed toward the crucified Christ. If Abraham was justified by believing God, why can't the Gentiles do the same, without necessity for the Son of God to die on a cross?[28]

---

[25] It is important to note that Paul never speaks of the church as the "new Israel," as though the old one had been supplanted. Rather, believers in Jesus simply *are* Israel. They are the true remnant that stands in continuity with the past Israel, rather than in contradiction to that Israel. Nonetheless, Paul certainly leaves himself open in Galatians to a supersessionist interpretation.

[26] Gerhard Ebeling, *Word and Faith* (Philadelphia: Fortress, 1963) 203.

[27] Dunn, "Theology of Galatians," p. 125.

[28] Gal 1:4 affirms that Jesus Christ "gave himself for our sins," but Paul — in the letters of our restricted "canon"— does not develop a sacrificial atonement theory.

The connection between Paul's narrative framework (= his christology) and his reinterpretation of "Israel" (= his doctrine of justification) becomes intelligible only in the light of two crucial elements in Paul's interpretation of the kerygmatic story: the apocalyptic significance of the cross and the inclusion of the faithful in the Messiah's destiny.[29] Let us consider each of these elements in turn.

In Paul's theology, God's action in Jesus Christ has cosmic consequences — not merely local significance for the Jewish people — because Jesus' death is construed within *apocalyptic* horizons. Beverly Roberts Gaventa, following a line of interpretation pioneered by J. Louis Martyn, contends that the central theological claim of Galatians is "that the gospel proclaims Jesus Christ crucified to be the inauguration of a new creation."[30] Jesus' death terminates the old age and ushers in a new one, in such a way that the very structure of reality is transformed. (By way of distant analogy, one might think of the remarkable precipitous collapse of communist governments in Eastern Europe late in 1989; the old regime is crumbling before our eyes, the new is already coming into being, promising freedom.) The old age, to which the law belongs, perishes in the ἀποκάλυψις of the cross. Thus, believers living in the eschatological twilight zone at the turn of the ages are called upon to recognize and embody the new creation in which the old barriers between Jew and Gentile are dissolved (note especially Gal 3:26–29; 6:14–16).

Believers participate in the blessings and power of the new age, however, not only because a cosmic revolution is under way but also because they are personally united with Jesus and thus mysteriously transformed. As N. T. Wright explains, the Messiah represents his people, God's Israel, in such a way that his destiny contains and determines theirs: "they are 'in' him such that what is true of him is true of them."[31] That is why Paul can write Χριστῷ συνεσταύρωμαι (Gal 2:19). That is why the promise originally made only to Abraham and his singular σπέρμα (= Christ, Gal 3:16) is now made available to others: "If you are Christ's then you are Abraham's σπέρμα, heirs according to promise" (3:29). That is why the blessing of Abraham comes upon the Gentiles *in* Christ Jesus (3:14). That is why the faith and obedience of Jesus are both life-giving and life-shaping for God's people (Gal 2:20–21; 3:21–22). That is why the self-emptying, death, and exaltation of Christ Jesus in the Philippians hymn (Phil 2:6–11) is a saving event rather than a

[29] These two elements are highlighted in the essays by Gaventa ("Singularity of the Gospel") and Wright ("Putting Paul Together"), respectively.
[30] Gaventa, "Singularity of the Gospel," p. 159; see J. Louis Martyn, "Apocalyptic Antinomies in Paul's Letter to the Galatians," *NTS* 31 (1985) 410–24.
[31] Wright, "Putting Paul Together," p. 205.

bizarre cosmic spectacle. That is why Paul expects Christians ultimately to be raised up along with Jesus and to share his glory (1 Thess 4:14; 2 Thess 2:14; Phil 3:20–21).

Paul thinks of the fate of God's people as bound up in the fate of Jesus. The logic of salvation is a logic of *participation* in the destiny of Jesus, the divinely sent protagonist of the gospel story.[32] For that reason, there is a vital organic connection between christology and ecclesiology (Israelology?) in Paul's thought. The life of God's elect is prefigured and carried by the life, death, and resurrection of Jesus.

That this life entails neither a sectarian escape from reality nor a private inner spiritual experience is guaranteed when the participation of Israel in the fate of the Messiah is coupled with the apocalyptic interpretation of the cross. The gospel of Jesus Christ offers a proclamation about the transformation of creation through Jesus' death and a call to all who hear to participate in the freedom of the children of God.[33]

It will occur to some readers that this account of Pauline theology is relentlessly "mythological." Such ideas as the destruction of the old age through the death of Jesus or the "mystical" participation of the people of God in the fate of God's Son are not readily intelligible outside the universe of discourse in which they appear in Paul's letters. Can such images be demythologized in such a way that their content is successfully carried over into a universe of discourse more hospitable to modern scientific/historical sensibilities? I tend to think not; Paul's theology will retain its coherence and integrity only for readers who continue to find its symbolic world habitable. The present essay, however, is concerned with theological synthesis, not hermeneutical transfer. The one task that does remain for us is to show how Paul employs these ideas and images in describing and prescribing the *response* of the community of faith to the action of God narrated in the gospel.

The community's cruciform role in the drama. Much of Paul's explicit argumentation is concerned with the Christian community's *response* to God's action in Christ. Because the story of God's saving purpose is not yet finished, the community has a role to play in its outworking in the present time. One of Paul's most characteristic theological emphases is his steadfast insistence on the *cruciform* character of that role. The community called to live "in Christ" will necessarily live in a way that corresponds to the pattern of faith/obedience defined by Christ's death on the cross.

---

[32] See Hays, *Faith of Jesus Christ*, 248–54.

[33] Of course, this call to freedom sets up difficult issues for a community in a social world where slavery was a normal institution; see my remarks on Philemon, p. 245 below.

For the most part, Paul regards this cruciform existence in the present time not as an ideal to be pursued but as a fact of experience. "I have been crucified with Christ" (Gal 2:20): among the many things that Paul means by this extraordinary claim is that he is a participant in Christ's suffering. He tells the Thessalonians that they have become "imitators of us and of the Lord, for you received the word in much affliction with joy of the Holy Spirit" (1 Thess 1:6). These sufferings are also said to correspond to the experience of the "churches of God in Christ Jesus which are in Judea," whose sufferings in turn mirror the death inflicted on "the Lord Jesus and the prophets" by their own countrymen (1 Thess 2:14–15; see also the allusions to persecution in Gal 4:29; 5:11; 6:12). Similarly, he encourages the Philippians by saying, "It has been granted to you that for the sake of Christ you should not only believe in him but also suffer for his sake, engaged in the same conflict which you saw and now hear to be mine" (Phil 1:29–30). As this citation suggests, suffering in the likeness of Jesus and for his sake is seen not as a misfortune but as a privilege; Paul can regard this conformity to Jesus' death as a consummation to be wished by the faithful (e.g., 2 Thess 1:4–5). He describes his own hope in terms of conformity to the emptying-death-resurrection paradigm of Christ's career[34] (Phil 2:5–11): "that I may know him and the power of his resurrection, and may share his sufferings, becoming like him in his death, that if possible I may attain the resurrection from the dead" (Phil 3:10–11).

Just as clearly, Paul regards this hope not as a private goal for himself only but as a normative paradigm for all Christian believers. He explicitly urges them to *imitate* him in contrast to others who are "enemies of the cross of Christ" (Phil 3:17–18). He agonizes over the Galatians, whom he entreats to "become as I am," because he hopes to see "Christ formed in [them]" (Gal 4:12, 19). I have argued elsewhere—and therefore will not repeat the arguments here—that, when he exhorts the Galatians to "bear one another's burdens, and so fulfill the law of Christ" (Gal 6:2), he is urging them to assume the same posture of self-sacrificial giving for the sake of others that he urges upon the Philippians by appealing to the story-warrant of Christ, who took the form of a slave and humbled himself by becoming obedient unto death on a cross (Phil 2:1–13; see also Gal 5:13b: "Through love become slaves of one another"). Νόμος Χριστοῦ is a way of describing this pattern of renouncing one's own privileges and interests for the sake of others.[35]

[34] Noted by Wright, summing up a widely held interpretation ("Putting Paul Together," p. 205).
[35] Richard B. Hays, "Christology and Ethics in Galatians: The Law of Christ," *CBQ* 49 (1987) 268–90.

One unexpected consequence of our heuristic experiment of working with a Pauline corpus consisting of 1–2 Thessalonians, Philemon, Philippians, and Galatians is that we are led to read Galatians in a way that highlights these themes of imitation, union with Christ, and participation in his sufferings. I take this to be a significant finding that future attempts to describe Pauline theology should reckon with seriously. Issues concerning the law and justification are present in Galatians, to be sure, but they appear to belong to the contingent level of argumentation rather than to the theological hermeneutic out of which Paul responds to the questions at hand. Gal 2:20–21, with its emphasis on union with Christ's grace-giving death, looks more and more like the hermeneutical center of the letter.

How does this union occur? Unfortunately for us, the matter is not as clear as we might wish. The warrant for the claim of union with Christ's death and participation in his life is apparently given in Gal 3:27: "For as many of you as were baptized into Christ have put on Christ." Playing out our letters-found-in-a-cave fantasy, we might ask, what does it mean to be "baptized into Christ"? Is this a reference to some cultic ceremony? A metaphorical way of talking about the believer's imaginative identification ("through faith," 3:26) with the fate of the hero of the community's foundational story? Since our corpus contains no other references to baptism, the matter remains mysterious. (But perhaps we can hope for the discovery of additional evidence. . . .)

It is clear, in any case, that union with Christ has definite ethical implications for Paul. The metaphor of being crucified with Christ is given an explicit ethical turn in Gal 5:24: "Those who belong to Christ Jesus have crucified the flesh with its passions and desires" (see also Gal 6:14). Furthermore, to "put on Christ" is to assume something of the character and vocation of the "Son of God who loved me and gave himself for me" (Gal 2:20). That is what Paul means by insisting that "it is no longer I who live, but Christ who lives in me." And that is why the exemplary character qualities of the triadic πίστις-ἀγάπη-ὑπομονή formula (1 Thess 1:3; see also 2 Thess 1:3–4, Phlm 5) mirror attributes that are ascribed elsewhere in these letters to Christ or to God (e.g., πίστις in 1 Thess 5:24; 2 Thess 3:3; Phil 3:9; Gal 2:20; 3:22;[36] ἀγάπη in 1 Thess 1:4; 2 Thess 2:13, 16; 3:5; Gal 2:20; ὑπομονή in 2 Thess 3:5). The character of the community of faith is to be a reflection of the character of God, as revealed in the cross of Christ.

For that reason, the community itself has a witness-bearing function in the world (1 Thess 1:8). The community's unity in faith and suffering love stands

---

[36] I am well aware that the exegesis of these last three citations as references to Jesus' faithfulness is open to debate; nonetheless, I stand by the interpretation given here.

as a witness to the hostile world of God's judgment and salvation (Phil 1:27–30), of hope for the new creation (Gal 5:5–6; 3:28). As "children of promise" the eschatological community reflects the free Jerusalem above (Gal 4:26–28). Therefore they must live as "children of God without blemish in the midst of a crooked and perverse generation, among whom [they] shine as lights in the world" (Phil 2:14–15). They can be designated simply "the saints" because they are a (covenant) community called to be devoted to the service of God. That is one of the reasons why they must practice community discipline (2 Thess 3:6–15; Gal 6:1–5) and cultivate practices that build the community up in love (1 Thess 4:9–12; 5:12–22; Phlm 4–7; Phil 2:1–4; Gal 5:13–15).

In fact, one way of summarizing the role given to the eschatological community is to say that the community, by living a life "worthy of the gospel of Christ" (Phil 1:27)—that is, a life that faithfully corresponds to his obedience and self-sacrificial love—becomes the embodiment of the new creation at the turn of the ages. Because the parousia of the Lord Jesus is still a future event, the community in the present time knows "the fellowship (κοινωνία) of his sufferings" (Phil 3:10). But that κοινωνία is already a sign of grace in the world, because of its correspondence to the cross.[37]

Paul's passionate rejection of the law-gospel of the Galatian teachers must be understood in this frame of reference. The problem with the law-gospel is not (just?) that it promotes works-righteousness; the problem is that, by redividing the world between Jew and Gentile, it reinstantiates the distinction that Christ's death had broken down (Gal 3:28) and brings division in the eschatological community (5:15–21). The law-gospel turns back the cosmic clock and effectually denies the presence of the new age in the community that should receive its identity solely from the story of the cross.

III. CONCLUSION: "STRAINING FORWARD TO WHAT LIES AHEAD"

At the conclusion of this attempt at synthesis, there are, to be sure, several loose ends. I will, for the sake of discussion, identify six of them. Of these, three are Paul's own loose ends—important unresolved theological problems that threaten the internal coherence of his thought and therefore render the

---

[37] The role of the community here is not only as vehicle of the message: the community's life actually has a hermeneutical function. For various reflections on this issue, see J. Christiaan Beker, "Recasting Pauline Theology: The Coherence-Contingency Scheme as Interpretive Model," pp. 21–24 above, and the important programmatic essay by Wayne Meeks, "A Hermeneutics of Social Embodiment," *HTR* 79 (1986) 176–86.

task of synthesis problematic. The other three loose ends are problems that we must cope with somehow in our hermeneutical efforts to appropriate Paul's witness constructively.

Synthetic Challenges: Paul's Unfinished Agenda

The positions staked out by Paul in our five letters, taken together, pose a series of theological dilemmas that are not adequately addressed, let alone resolved, in the texts before us. Space forbids discussion of these issues, but I list some of them here as matters that demand further consideration.

Why then the Law of Moses? No reader with a sympathetic understanding of Judaism can come away from Galatians without feeling that Paul has dodged the essential theological issues concerning the law as divine revelation. In answer to his own question, "Why then the law?" Paul makes a number of interesting proposals: the law was given to restrain sin[38] until the promised σπέρμα should come (3:19); the law was never intended to give life (3:21); the law was our παιδαγωγὸς εἰς Χριστόν (3:24). These statements hang together reasonably well with the contention that the law is not contrary to the promises of God (3:21). But how can Paul also say that being under the law is a state of slavery, equivalent to being in bondage to the στοιχεῖα (4:1-11)? How can he brush aside circumcision—which was given to Abraham as a sign of the covenant promise—as being of no importance while simultaneously appealing to the Abraham story as a key support for his law-free gospel? Does he really mean to suggest in Gal 3:19 that the law was not given by God? (I do not think that is what he means, but he comes dangerously close to saying it; this is the Paul that Marcion knew and loved.) Paul owes his Jewish Christian critics a better solution than he has produced here in Galatians.

Judgment and mercy. How can the gracious God who sent Jesus Christ to die for us—including Gentile sinners—also inflict "vengeance on those who do not know God and upon those who do not obey the gospel of our Lord Jesus" (2 Thess 1:8)? The problem is emphasized by the inclusion of 2 Thessalonians within the data base, but the theological issue also arises from the other letters, which are not reticent about pronouncing God's wrath and destruction on unbelievers (e.g., 1 Thess 1:10; 2:16; 4:6; Phil 1:28; 3:18–19; Gal 1:6-10; 4:30; 5:4, 10–12, 21; 6:7-8). The problem is hardly unique to Paul, but it is sharpened by the intensity of his proclamation of the grace of Jesus Christ.

---

[38] Here I stand in agreement with Dunn's exegesis ("Theology of Galatians," p. 136 n. 41).

Slavery and freedom. The letter to Philemon, by urging this man to receive Onesimus back "no longer as a slave but more than a slave, as a beloved brother . . . both in the flesh and in the Lord" (Phlm 16), suggests that Paul's language in Galatians about liberation from bondage through Christ has a literal application.[39] The symbolic world of the gospel impinges on and reshapes social relations: this is a necessary corollary of Paul's view that the Christian community is the place where the new creation breaks through into human experience. When slavery is given an unremittingly negative valence, as it is in Galatians (especially 4:1–11; 4:21–5:1), it is hard to avoid the inference that the institution of slavery has no place among Christians: it would appear to be a social embodiment of the "yoke of slavery" from which Christ has set us free, a vestige of the old order.[40] On the other hand, the very same letter can also urge Christians to "become slaves of one another" (5:13). In Philippians Paul describes himself and Timothy as "slaves of Christ Jesus" (1:1), while at the same time holding up Jesus who "emptied himself, taking the form of a slave" (2:7) as paradigmatic for the community of faith. Obviously Paul uses the slavery metaphor in different ways, but the uses would seem to work against one another, particularly at the level of discerning the practical social implications of the gospel story.[41] This is a theological problem because it raises questions about the coherence of Paul's eschatology.

Hermeneutical Challenges: Making Paul's Theology Make Sense to Us

Finally, though this essay does not presume to address questions about how we, as belated readers rifling through someone else's mail, can appropriate Paul's message, I cannot help noting three issues that confront us at every turn when we try to synthesize an account of Paul's thought that makes sense to us.

---

[39] My interpretation of Philemon at this point is indebted to Norman R. Petersen, *Rediscovering Paul: Philemon and the Sociology of Paul's Narrative World* (Philadelphia: Fortress, 1985).

[40] It is striking that Paul never explains in these letters how human beings became subject to bondage. This is not, however, necessarily a "loose end" in Paul's systematic thinking; it is, rather, a lacuna in the story, a part of the tale that Paul does not happen to recount within this body of writings. The references to Adam in 1 Corinthians and Romans, of course, fill in part of this gap.

[41] For a nuanced discussion of the way in which social realities condition the ranges of meaning that Paul's original readers might have assigned to this metaphor, see Dale B. Martin, "Slave of Christ, Slave of All: Paul's Metaphor of Slavery in 1 Corinthians 9" (Ph.D. diss., Yale University, 1988).

Apocalyptic eschatology. If the coherence of Paul's gospel is integrally bound up with the imminent parousia expectation, does that render his whole thought world problematical for readers who have seen history go on as before? Is it possible to give a persuasive account of the redemptive significance of Christ's death if we see no clear evidence that his death and resurrection have signaled the turn of the ages and the new creation? Or is it possible to discern the signs of the new creation, as Paul did, in the activity of the Spirit in the church?

Vicarious inclusion in corporate salvation. My whole discussion of the participation of the people of God in the destiny of Christ raises this issue. Can such conceptualities be grasped as intelligible by those of us who live on this side of Luther, Jefferson, and Bultmann? Or, alternatively, does Paul's theology implicitly pronounce anathema on all forms of Christian piety that make our relation to God contingent on individual subjective response?

Interpretation of Israel's scripture. How are we to comprehend Paul's strange interpretations of scripture (e.g., Gal 3:16; 4:21–31)? To what extent does an understanding of Paul's letters depend on our ability to discern the nuances of his manifold allusions to scripture and to early Christian traditions? The more I have worked with Paul, the more convinced I have become of the accuracy of Beker's characterization of Paul as a "hermeneutic theologian." But if he is a hermeneutic theologian, we must seek to comprehend his writings as intertextual performances that presuppose and depend on their relation to a body of precursor "texts," many of which are irretrievably lost to us. The effect of this loss is not only a muffling of the rhetorical force of the performance but also a semantic leakage. In order to begin recovering some of what has been lost, I propose that the best place to focus our efforts is on Paul's use of scripture, for there we at least have access to the texts to which he alludes. Galatians, with its long exegetical arguments, raises the issue far more directly than the other letters examined previously in our project, but even the Macedonian correspondence is full of scriptural allusions (a few illustrations: Phil 1:19/Job 13:16; Phil 2:10–11/Isa 45:23; 1 Thess 3:9/Ps 115:3 LXX; 1 Thess 3:13/Zech 14:5[?]; 1 Thess 5:8/Isa 59:17). If the specific task of "Pauline theology" is to study the hermeneutical transformations that Paul performs in appropriating elements of his symbolic universe for the situation of his readers, what better place to start than with careful analysis of Pauline uses of scripture? That is, of course, a major project for another time, but we would do well to pay careful attention to Paul's interpretations of scripture as a key to understanding his theology.

16 SALVATION HISTORY

Theology in 1 Thessalonians, Philemon,
Philippians, and Galatians: A Response to
N. T. Wright, R. B. Hays, and R. Scroggs

David J. Lull
Executive Director, Society of Biblical Literature

I. FORMAL DEFINITIONS
OF "PAUL'S THEOLOGY"

THE ATTEMPT TO SKETCH a "synthesis" of the "theology" in Paul's letters must take into account the *ad hoc* character of Paul's letters.[1] These letters do not present Paul's thought in a systematic form. Instead, they present his thought as practical reflection on concrete issues of faith and life in the Christian communities founded by Paul. That fact poses two problems for our task: How are "Paul's theology" and particular arguments in his letters related? And how should a "synthesis" deal with differences among the letters? These problems are compounded by the absence of a consensus about what "theology" is. Moreover, a "synthesis" inevitably employs categories that are more or less foreign to Paul's own thought.

N. T. Wright formally defines "Pauline theology" as "that integrated set of beliefs which may be supposed to inform and undergird Paul's life, mission, and writing, coming to expression in varied ways throughout all three."[2] Whereas Wright's construal of theology as an "integrated set of beliefs" presupposes or implies that Paul's theology, in form and content, is primarily *propositional*, R. B. Hays and R. Scroggs draw attention to the *narrative* structure of Paul's theology. These two formal ways of construing Paul's theology, however, are not as incompatible as they are often made out to be if Paul's "theology" is identified with his critical reflection on the meaning and truth

---

[1] Since in my judgment 2 Thessalonians is deutero-Pauline, references to it will be confined to the notes.

[2] N. T. Wright, "Putting Paul Together Again: Toward a Synthesis of Pauline Theology," p. 184 above.

of the "gospel" for particular occasions in his churches. This "critical reflection" is to be found in the letters themselves, not "beyond" them.[3]

Wright, more than either Hays or Scroggs, is aware of the social function
of "Paul's theology" when he describes "beliefs" as community "boundary
markers."[4] But this definition is too narrow. As Wayne A. Meeks has shown,
the beliefs that Paul shared with his readers, as well as those he sought to
persuade them to accept, served not only to mark the boundaries of the
Christian community as the people of God but also to establish appropriate
patterns of behavior and social structures within this community.[5] The belief
in the one, true, living God (1 Thess 1:9), for example, establishes the demand
for "holiness" (1 Thess 4:1–8), forms the basis for consolation to those who
grieve (1 Thess 4:13–14) and for the assurance of vindication against one's
enemies (Phil 1:27–30), and provides backing for the elimination of conventional social divisions (Gal 3:20, 28) and for disregarding the religious
rituals that marked those divisions (Gal 5:6; 6:15; Phil 3:2–7). "Beliefs" as
well as "foundational stories," therefore, are essential to the formation and
maintenance of Christian character and Christian community.

In this respect, "Paul's theology" can be understood as "political theology"
and "moral theology." In regard to the term "political," I mean it in the precise
sense in which it is used today as a qualification of a certain type of reflection
on the meaning and truth of the gospel for the concrete political dimensions
of the lives and social structures of particular people. When Paul transfers the
characteristics and attributes of Israel as the people of God to the mixed
Christian community of Gentiles and Jews, when he declares an end to social
divisions between women and men, and when he makes an appeal on behalf
of the freedom of a slave, he does so on the basis of critical reflection on the
political meaning and truth of the crucified Messiah for his readers.

Wright's principal, constructive thesis — that Paul's theology seeks to refor-
mulate in Christian terms traditional Jewish beliefs in the "one God" and in
the divinely appointed destiny of Israel as God's "chosen people"—points in
the right direction. He is also correct in pointing out that early Christian
beliefs about God's action in Jesus as the Christ — beliefs shared by Paul — led
Paul to transfer the "covenantal hope for Israel's vindication," as well as
Israel's "attributes and characteristics," to the community of Christian
believers.[6] That his thesis seems to have had its genesis in Romans and

---

[3] Cf. Victor P. Furnish's formal construal of Paul's theology in "Theology in 1 Corinthians:
Initial Soundings," in *Society of Biblical Literature 1989 Seminar Papers* (ed. D. J. Lull; Atlanta:
Scholars Press, 1989) 246–49.

[4] Wright, "Putting Paul Together," pp. 185, 195.

[5] See Wayne A. Meeks, *The First Urban Christians: The Social World of the Apostle Paul* (New
Haven: Yale University Press, 1983).

[6] See Wright, "Putting Paul Together," pp. 197–201.

1 Corinthians is only a technical objection, given the self-imposed limitations of this project, since the letters under consideration support his thesis. Hays, whose own constructive proposal develops themes only outlined by Wright, begins his study with a description of the grammar of Paul's "hermeneutical" theology as his critical reflection on the "story" that was "foundational" for Paul and his churches.[7] Whereas Wright's "integrated set of beliefs" lies, as it were, in the texts themselves, Hays's "patterns of critical reflection" lie behind the texts, between the "symbolic world," whose "narrative framework" is a "foundational story" shared by Paul and his readers, and the particular "arguments" in the letters. These "patterns" informed Paul's appropriation of the "narrative framework" of his "symbolic world" as he responded to particular pastoral situations.

For Hays, Israel's scripture and early Christian tradition constitute Paul's "symbolic world."[8] One should also include traditions from postbiblical Judaism and from the nonbiblical Greco-Roman world. Even if one can hear echoes of the biblical Holiness Code in 1 Thess 4:3-7, one can also hear echoes of the Hellenistic moral philosophers.[9] Gal 5:19-23 also reflects the mixture of nonbiblical Jewish and Greco-Roman symbolic worlds.[10] In 1 Thess 2:1-11 and 4:9-12 Paul draws on traditions of Hellenistic moral philosophers.[11] In Gal 3:23-25 Paul appropriates a symbol from the social world of Greco-Roman antiquity—namely, the "pedagogue"—a symbol Paul shares with both Hellenistic Jewish and Greco-Roman philosophers.[12] These are but samples from the letters under consideration that demonstrate the need to expand Hays's construal of Paul's "imaginative environment," which surely also drew its symbols from nonliterary sources.

Thus, we might agree that Paul was a "hermeneutic [sic] theologian," as Hays claims.[13] But Paul applied his "hermeneutic" to more than early

---

[7] Richard B. Hays, "Crucified with Christ: A Synthesis of the Theology of 1 and 2 Thessalonians, Philemon, Philippians, and Galatians," pp. 227-46 above.

[8] Ibid., p. 228.

[9] See O. Larry Yarbrough, *Not Like the Gentiles: Marriage Rules in the Letters of Paul* (SBLDS 80; Atlanta: Scholars Press, 1985).

[10] See Anton Vögtle, *Die Tugend- und Lasterkataloge im NT* (NTAbh 16/4-5; Münster: Aschendorff, 1936); Siegfried Wibbing, *Die Tugend- und Lasterkataloge im Neuen Testament und ihre Traditionsgeschichte unter besonderer Berücksichtigung der Qumran-Texte* (BZNW 25; Berlin: Töpelmann, 1959); and Ehrhard Kamlah, *Die Form der katalogischen Paränese im NT* (WUNT 7; Tübingen: Mohr [Siebeck], 1964).

[11] See Abraham J. Malherbe, "'Gentle as a Nurse': The Cynic Background to I Thess ii," *NovT* 12 (1970) 204-17; idem, "Exhortation in First Thessalonians," *NovT* 25 (1983) 238-56.

[12] See Richard N. Longenecker, "The Pedagogical Nature of the Law in Galatians 3:19-4:7," *JETS* 25 (1982) 53-61; David J. Lull, "'The Law Was Our Pedagogue': A Study in Gal 3:19-25," *JBL* 105 (1986) 481-98; and Norman H. Young, "*Paidagogos*: The Social Setting of a Pauline Metaphor," *NovT* 29 (1987) 150-76.

[13] Hays attributes this phrase to J. Christiaan Beker, "The Faithfulness of God and the

Christian tradition and Israel's scripture. Moreover, Paul's letters focus as much on the interpretation of "experience" in the light of scripture and tradition (more broadly defined) as on the reverse. By "experience" I mean, on the one hand, the encounter with the crucified and exalted Christ and the presence of God's Spirit in early Christian communities and, on the other, the transformations and crises in the social structure of emerging Christian communities that occasioned the letters. In Paul's letters, such experiences are interpreted in relation to scripture and tradition, just as the meaning and truth of the "imaginative environment" Paul inherited are worked out in relation to those experiences.

All three authors have identified Paul's theology as strongly *theocentric*. Wright describes Paul's theology as a reformulation of "monotheism," and Hays observes that God is the primary agent in Paul's "foundational story." Scroggs begins his essay with a material definition of Paul's theology as "what he thinks about the transcendent and its intervention into immanent reality."[14] Although he intends to limit himself to *direct* statements in the letters about "transcendent intervention," Scroggs, like Hays, sees a narrative pattern in the "thought" of these letters, which he calls "salvation history." Whereas Hays finds a single "narrative framework" behind the letters, Scroggs distinguishes between the narrative pattern in 1 Thessalonians and Philippians (from Christ to the gathering of the saints in heaven) and the one in Galatians (from the promise to Abraham to the hope of justification and eternal life). With his category of "transcendent *intervention*," Scroggs introduces into his definition of Pauline theology a clearly modern notion. The term "intervention," which implies or presupposes the belief that the universe is a closed system of causes and effects in which God from time to time "intervenes," is a relatively modern belief based on Newtonian physics. For Paul and his contemporaries, however, it would be less anachronistic to speak simply of the story of the unfolding in history of God's redemption of the world—a story whose central narrative is about Jesus as the crucified Messiah whom God had promised to send to Israel for the salvation of the whole world. I understand this formulation to be in basic agreement with Scroggs's definition of "salvation history" as a "grand story," in which the term "intervention" neither appears nor seems necessary.[15]

This "grand story" has "a spatial and temporal dimension," to borrow Ernst Käsemann's comment on "salvation history."[16] For Paul, God's promise to

---

Priority of Israel in Paul's Letter to the Romans," *HTR* 79 (1986) 10 (see p. 229 above).

[14] Robin Scroggs, "Salvation History: The Theological Structure of Paul's Thought," p. 212 above.

[15] Ibid., pp. 215–16.

[16] Ernst Käsemann, *Perspectives on Paul* (Philadelphia: Fortress, 1971) 68.

Abraham, Moses' introduction of the Jewish law, the coming and crucifixion of Jesus as the Messiah, and early Christian encounters with the risen Jesus were events in history. So also was the "new creation" (Gal 6:15), whose coming was visible in the Gentiles' adherence to ways of holiness (1 Thess 4:1–8), in demonstrations of the power of the Spirit of God in the community (1 Thess 1:5–6; Phil 3:3; Gal 3:1–5, 14; 4:6), and in the abolition of conventional social divisions between Jew and Gentile, slave and free, male and female (Gal 3:28; cf. 1 Thess 4:1–8; Phil 3:3; and Philemon).

Scroggs's category of "salvation history" raises again a set of issues that Rudolf Bultmann raised in response to Oscar Cullmann.[17] To what extent does the past in "salvation history" already determine what each individual must decide in faith—namely, whether to constitute one's own existence on the basis of God's eschatological act in Jesus Christ? To what extent has that decision been made "once and for all"? To what extent is human existence no longer understood as being constituted by "constantly new decisions"?[18]

Is there a way of construing "salvation history" as genuine *history* that would not be in tension with the genuine *temporality* of human existence? I think there is, as long as history is understood as the sphere in which new *possibilities* emerge among which human beings must choose as they constitute their own existence.[19] That is how Paul viewed history: he saw in the introduction of the Mosaic law and in the death and resurrection of Jesus the emergence of new possibilities for human existence. Scroggs's denial of "triumphalism" in the "salvation history" in Paul's letters is congenial with this view of history.[20]

The category of "salvation history" may also be associated with the notion that salvation is an *evolutionary development* in history. "Salvation history," however, can be disassociated from this notion; and if Paul's theology is to be described in terms of "salvation history," we will have to make it clear that Paul's view is not of an "evolutionary development" in history. In the letters under consideration (and in the other letters as well), the movement of

---

[17] See Oscar Cullmann, *Christ and Time: The Primitive Christian Conception of Time and History* (rev. ed.; Philadelphia: Westminster, 1964); idem, *Salvation in History* (New York: Harper, 1967).

[18] Rudolf Bultmann, "History of Salvation and History," in *Existence & Faith: Shorter Writings of Rudolf Bultmann* (ed. S. M. Ogden; New York: World, 1960) 239. For the continued debate over the category of "salvation history," see Günther Klein, "Individualgeschichte und Weltgeschichte bei Paulus: Eine Interpretation ihres Verhältnisses im Galaterbrief," *EvT* 24 (1964) 126–65; and Rainer Schmitt, *Gottesgerechtigkeit—Heilsgeschichte—Israel in der Theologie des Paulus* (Europäische Hochschulschriften 23/240; Frankfurt am Main: Lang, 1984).

[19] See David J. Lull, *The Spirit in Galatia: Paul's Interpretation of Pneuma as Divine Power* (SBLDS 49; Chico, CA: Scholars Press, 1980) 131–33 and 170–71.

[20] See Scroggs, "Salvation History," p. 215.

history is guided by the "will" of God (Gal 1:4) or of the divine Christ figure (Phil 2:6–11). Although the analogy of the heir "coming of age" (Gal 4:1–7) might be construed in terms of a natural "evolutionary development" in history, Paul emphasizes that the time of inheritance was "appointed" by God (Gal 4:2, 4), not by historical developments.

Yet the focal events in the "salvation history" in these letters do respond to "historical developments." For instance, however the debate about the preexistence of the Christ figure in Phil 2:6–11 comes out, the narrative of self-divestiture and self-humiliation, of obedience "even to the point of death, and that on a cross," includes temporal and contingent acts of the historical Jesus. The exaltation of Jesus Christ as "Lord" (2:11) and the salvation that Christ's sovereignty makes possible (1:28; 2:12–13) are understood as God's response to historical events in the life of Jesus (as the διὸ καί ["therefore"] in 2:9, which refers to Jesus' act of "obedience unto death" in 2:8, implies). In a similar fashion, Paul presupposes or implies that God declared Abraham "righteous" in response to his "faith in God" (Gal 3:6). And he held the view that the law was introduced in response to "transgressions" (Gal 3:19).[21] Nevertheless, Paul believed that it was God alone who, before all these "historical developments," determined that "God would justify the Gentiles by faith" (Gal 3:8). In these letters, therefore, "salvation history" is the story of the interplay of God's foreordained plan for the salvation of the world and historical events.

Käsemann warns us, however, that theologies of history contributed to the "faith in progress" that was shattered by World War I (at least in Europe) and to the "Nazi eschatology" that replaced it, and that Paul's "salvation history" was used "erroneously and improperly" as a "shield for Nazi eschatology."[22] It is important to emphasize, however, that if there is a "triumphalism" in Paul's "salvation history," it is a *Jewish* "triumphalism"—to be sure, a Jewish *Christian* "triumphalism," but a *Jewish* one nevertheless.[23] That is to say that it is a "triumphalism" in which a claim is made not against Jews but rather on behalf of Gentiles who, so far from surpassing Jews as the chosen people of God, are *adopted* as members of that elect people (Gal 3:26–4:7) and who are joined to the "*Israel* of God" (Gal 6:16). It is the triumph of Israel's own ancient hope—namely, that God will bless all the nations by Abraham (Gen 12:18 and 22:18)—that Paul proclaims and defends (Gal 3:6–14; cf. 1 Thess 4:5; Phil 3:3).

---

[21] For the exegetical difficulties of the prepositional phrase τῶν παραβάσεων χάριν ("because of transgressions") in Gal 3:19, see Lull, "'The Law Was Our Pedagogue,'" 483–85.

[22] Käsemann, *Perspectives on Paul*, 64.

[23] Cf. Krister Stendahl, *Paul among Jews and Gentiles and Other Essays* (Philadelphia: Fortress, 1976) 131–32.

We must ask, therefore, whether for Paul "salvation history" came to an end with the death and resurrection of Jesus. At Cullmann's suggestion that Christ occupies the *midpoint* of "salvation history," Bultmann objected that the New Testament understands Christ to be the *end* of "salvation history."[24] Bultmann, however, underestimated the *future* in Paul's eschatology.

Included in the "symbolic universe" that Paul and his readers shared with Jewish apocalypticism is God's judgment of the wicked and the vindication of the righteous on the "Day of the Lord." In 1 Thessalonians, that "day" is the coming of the risen and exalted Jesus, when the "dead in Christ" will be united with living Christians (1 Thess 4:13–18); but no new "salvation event" is envisioned, since Christians already "belong to the day," and salvation is "through our Lord Jesus Christ" (1 Thess 5:1–11). The warning of future destruction for the enemies of God's people and the promise of vindication for the people of God is found in 1 Thess 5:3; Phil 1:27–30; 3:2–21.[25] With the latter passage, the theme of God's victory over the power of death, which we found already in 1 Thess 4:14–17 and which we find in Gal 6:8–9, is expressed in terms that imply that the sovereignty accorded Jesus Christ in Phil 2:9–11 is not yet complete (3:21). Striking a similar note, Phil 1:6 speaks of the "good work" that had begun as being completed "at the day of Jesus Christ," which refers to being kept "pure and blameless for the day of Christ" (1:11). Although this future element of "salvation history" is not absent from Galatians, it is muted: the "present age," from which Christ's death brings deliverance, remains "evil" (1:4); "righteousness" is obtained by faith but it is also awaited in faith (2:16; 5:5); a "new creation," in which the Spirit triumphs over the power of "the flesh with its passions and desires" (5:16–25), has begun (6:15), but death has not yet been defeated (6:7–8). In our letters, therefore, "salvation history" still has a future, but it is clear that the same Jesus Christ who was crucified and raised will be the agent of future salvation, just as Christ is the source of salvation in the present.

We have not yet grasped Paul's theology, however, until we have understood the basic question or questions to which his theology provides answers. Throughout these letters, Paul reveals a concern about how one can become "blameless in holiness" or "righteous" before God (1 Thess 3:13; 5:23–24; Phil 1:10; 3:6, 9; Gal 2:16–17, 21; 3:6, 8, 11, 21, 24; 5:4–5). This question can be asked in terms of the seeming impossibility of being "holy" or "righteous" in an "evil" age (Gal 1:4), in which the "flesh" demands gratification of its

---

[24] See Bultmann, "History of Salvation," 235–39.

[25] In 2 Thess 2:1–11 the parousia is envisioned as the coming of the risen Christ as an apocalyptic warrior, the breath of whose mouth vanquishes God's enemies (cf. 1:5–12). For literature on the apocalyptic "combat myth," see Adela Yarbro Collins, *The Combat Myth in the Book of Revelation* (HDR 9; Chico, CA: Scholars Press, 1976).

"passions and desires" (Gal 5:16–24). Paul answers this question by assuring his readers that God was at work in them for their salvation (Phil 2:13–14), that Jesus, by his death, had delivered them from the coming wrath of God (1 Thess 1:10; 5:9), and that through sharing in Jesus' death they had been rescued from "the present evil age" (Gal 1:4). He also assures them that Christ dwells within them (Gal 2:19–20), that the "flesh with its passions and desires" and the "world" have been rendered impotent, and that a "new creation" has begun (Gal 5:24; 6:14–15), and he admonishes them to obey the instructions of the Spirit of God (1 Thess 4:1–12; Gal 5:16–25). One question that Paul's theology answers, therefore, is, How can persons gain freedom from slavery to fleshly passions and desires, so that they can live in holiness and righteousness among others in the world and before God? In these letters, the answer is that only Christ and the Spirit of God received from the crucified and risen Christ bring this freedom and make holiness and righteousness possible.

This question of holiness and righteousness is also asked in concretely social terms. In the letters to Philemon and to the churches in Galatia, Paul seeks to present the meaning and truth of the lordship of Jesus Christ in terms of the structure of social relations within Christian communities. As he does so, he captures an ancient hope for a truly cosmopolitan world. Among those who adhere to the lordship of Jesus Christ, Jew and Greek, slave and free, male and female are all to be one, just as God is one and Christ is one. In 1 Thessalonians, holiness pertains not only to the heart but also to relations between men and women and to mutual love among members of the community (a theme also expressed in Gal 5:13). For Paul and his readers, therefore, the meaning and truth of the gospel of Jesus Christ provided answers to the question of how to live in social as well as inward holiness and righteousness among others in the world and before God.[26]

Krister Stendahl argues that "justification by faith" in Paul's letters answers the question about the right of Gentiles to participate in God's promises, not the question about how human beings can find a gracious God; that is, it "functions within his reflection on God's plan for the world," which is the

---

[26] In the letters under consideration, one can find statements that challenge the political conventions of Paul's day (see, e.g., 1 Thess 4:11; Phil 3:20; Gal 3:28; 4:26; cf. Phil 3:3 and Philemon), but when Wright claims that Paul's affirmation of the lordship of Jesus as the Christ intends to pose a challenge to the political sovereignty of Caesar and that Paul's apocalyptic eschatology refers to the imminent destruction of Jerusalem and the vindication of Christians, he finds support not in Paul's letters (with the exception of 1 Thess 2:14–16) but in the book of Acts, the Synoptic Gospels, and Ephesians (see above, pp. 207–11). When we turn to the Corinthian correspondence and Romans, we find that Paul did not fear the imminent destruction of Jerusalem before he had opportunity to reach the Gentiles with the gospel; rather, he feared Jerusalem's rejection of his "gift" of the Gentiles.

"key" to Paul's theology.[27] As correct as Stendahl is here, we need to guard against two distortions of Paul's theology. The first is that of underestimating the importance in Paul's theology of the question about how to find a gracious God. Stendahl's criticism is directed against the interpretation of Paul's letters in terms of the relatively modern "introspective conscience of the West," which is preoccupied with individual, subjective guilt and forgiveness. But Stendahl's critique does not rule out interpreting Paul's reflection on the question about the place of Gentiles in God's plan for the redemption of the world as an answer to the *Gentiles'* question precisely about how *they* are to find a gracious God, a God who cares about their lives, who knows and loves them.

The fact that Gentiles "turned to God from idols, to serve a living and true God" (1 Thess 1:9), that they came "to know God, or rather to be known by God" (Gal 4:8–9), shows that they found in Paul's gospel an answer to their quest for a gracious God. The assurance that the risen Jesus will deliver Christian Gentiles from "the coming wrath" (1 Thess 1:10), that God has not destined them "for wrath, but to obtain salvation" through the Lord Jesus Christ (1 Thess 5:9), and that the Lord Jesus Christ "gave himself" for their "sins" to "rescue" them from "the present evil age," according to God's "will" (Gal 1:4), answers a question that is less about guilt and forgiveness than about God's blessing and curse. That God would bless Israel and curse the Gentiles was well known among Gentiles, who ridiculed the Jews and their God as misanthropic, for they knew that this God's gracious blessing would be reserved only for Abraham's heirs, from whom Gentiles were excluded. These Gentiles would encounter a gracious God in Paul's salutations (1 Thess 1:1; Gal 1:3; and Phil 1:2), in the assurance of their participation in God's promises (Gal 3:6–14; 6:16), in the promise of their inclusion among Abraham's heirs (Gal 3:26–4:7), and in the affirmation that God was "at work" in them "both to will and to work for God's good pleasure" (Phil 2:13). They would also hear from Paul that their "commonwealth" was in "heaven" from which they "await a savior, the Lord Jesus Christ," who will transform their "lowly bodies" to be "like his glorious body" (Phil 3:20–21) and that God will supply their every need according to God's "riches in glory in Christ Jesus" (Phil 4:19). The "blessing" to which they had been graciously joined by Christ, therefore, is not forgiveness but freedom.

---

[27] Stendahl, *Paul among Jews and Gentiles,* 131. In his critique of Stendahl, Käsemann argues that the "doctrine" of justification by faith "is the key to salvation history, just as, conversely, salvation history forms the historical depth and cosmic breadth of the event of justification." These scholars disagree about the interpretation of "justification by faith," but they agree about "salvation history" being the "horizon" of Paul's theology (see Käsemann, *Perspectives on Paul,* 60–78; Stendahl, *Paul among Jews and Gentiles,* 129–32).

The second distortion of Paul's theology that we must avoid is that of continuing to interpret his "salvation history" in individualistic and subjective terms—even after rejecting the individualistic and subjective interpretation of "justification by faith"—as if God's redemptive activity is directed primarily to the freedom of individuals from subjective guilt. In the phrase "salvation history," the term "history" focuses attention on the *objective* dimension of salvation, the *extra nos* and *pro nobis* aspects of God's promise to Abraham and his "seed," the giving of the law, Jesus' obedience unto death, and the coming "Day of the Lord." These redemptive acts of God are presented by Paul as events in history that objectively affect the conditions of human existence in the world. The pattern of this "salvation history" is clearest in Galatians:[28]

—God's promise to Abraham created a world of hope for Gentiles based on God's own faithfulness (Gal 3:6–15).
—The giving of the law introduced a protective guardian and disciplinarian into a world in the grips of the power of sin until the coming of the promised Messiah (Gal 3:19–25).
—Through the death and resurrection of Jesus, God broke the grip of the power of sin (Gal 1:4) and sent God's Spirit into the hearts of Jews and Gentiles alike who believed that Jesus was the promised Messiah, identifying them as children of God, thereby inaugurating the fulfillment of God's promise to bless the Gentiles through Abraham's "seed" (Gal 4:1–7).
—And in the life to come, those who have based their lives on the flesh will be destroyed, but those who have based their lives on the Spirit will be given "eternal life" (Gal 6:8).

II. SALVATION HISTORY

I turn now to the pattern of "salvation history" in our letters. In what follows I attempt to test how far the pattern of "salvation history" in Galatians fits 1 Thessalonians, Philippians, and Philemon.

Scroggs presents "salvation history" in these letters according to a pattern of past, present, and future. According to Scroggs, the *present* of this history is the present of the church, and the ultimate *future* is eternal life for believers. Although he places the Christ-event in the *present,* he also puts it in the *past,* which begins with Christ in 1 Thessalonians and Philippians, but with

---

[28] Cf. the "narrative pattern" of Paul's "symbolic world" in Hays's essay in this volume (pp. 232–33 above).

Abraham in Galatians.[29] This confusion is due to the ambiguity of Scroggs's temporal categories, which seem to refer to time relative to the reader. Although it is not entirely clear what their point of reference is, it would appear that the *present* is the period between the coming of Christ and the life to come. This scheme is reminiscent of Hans Conzelmann's formulation of "salvation history" in Luke-Acts, according to which the church occupies *die Mitte der Zeit.*[30]

Scroggs's scheme also obscures the pattern of "salvation history" in Galatians, where the pattern of Paul's "salvation history" is the clearest in the letters under consideration. In Galatians, the introduction of the law of Moses 430 years after God's covenant with Abraham begins a period between Abraham and the coming of Christ (Gal 3:15–25), so that the age of Abraham is separated from the age of Christ by the period of the law. Moreover, the age of Christ cannot be said to belong to the past in the same sense that the law belongs to the past, since the period of the law came to an end with the coming of the age of Christ (Gal 3:23–25). Scroggs's description of the past in the pattern of "salvation history" in Galatians, therefore, obscures Paul's understanding of the era before the coming of Christ.

In what follows I take the clear pattern of "salvation history" in Galatians as the clue to Paul's "salvation history," which can also be seen in 1 Thessalonians and Philippians. Galatians makes it clear that the death and resurrection of Jesus inaugurated the age of God's indivisible redemption of Jews and Gentiles alike. In Galatians, the appearance of Jesus Christ as the object of faith is the key to the pattern of "salvation history," which is clearly marked out by phrases that distinguish its main periods: "before . . . , but since . . . no longer . . ." (Gal 3:23–25); and "when . . . , but when the fullness of time had come . . ." (Gal 4:3). That pattern is:

—*Before Christ,* the covenant with Abraham awaits fulfillment and the law is introduced as a disciplinarian.
—*The Christ-event* and the Spirit fulfill the covenant with Abraham.
—*The life to come* will complete the work of Christ and the Spirit.

Before Christ

At the center of the age before the coming of Christ is God's covenant with Abraham, in which God promised to bless the Gentiles through Abraham

[29] See Scroggs, "Salvation History," pp. 216, 217–21.
[30] Hans Conzelmann, *The Theology of St. Luke* (New York: Harper & Row, 1961); originally published under the title *Die Mitte der Zeit.*

(Gal 3:6–9).[31] The inclusion of the Gentiles in the fulfillment of God's promise to redeem the world must have been constitutive of Paul's self-understanding as a preacher of the gospel of Christ to the Gentiles (Gal 2:7–9; cf. 1:15–16; 2:3).[32] Against the objection that this theme is polemical and occasion-dependent, in both 1 Thessalonians and Philippians — which, like Galatians, are addressed to Gentile Christians — signs that the age had come when God would fulfill the promise to include Gentiles in the redemption of the world play an important role. The eschatological gift of the Spirit at the Thessalonians' reception of Paul's gospel provides evidence of their faith (1 Thess 1:2–10), a faith that was to be lived out in a "holiness" that would set them apart from their former Gentile life and that God's holy Spirit had taught them (1 Thess 4:1–8).[33] The Philippians are also marked by their worship in the eschatological Spirit of God, which is the sign of "the true circumcision" (Phil 3:3). These Gentiles are members of the heavenly "commonwealth," from which Jesus will come as their savior and Lord to transform them into a "glorious" existence like his (Phil 3:20–21). God's promise concerning the salvation of Gentiles also lies behind such passages as 1 Thess 1:9–10 and 5:9–10, which imply that Paul's gospel offered to Gentiles a share in God's blessing promised to the righteous — namely, deliverance from God's wrath. It also lies behind the dispute to which Phil 3:2–16 is addressed.

The period before the coming of Christ is also an age in which everything was in the grip of the power of sin (Gal 3:22). Although the term "sin" does not appear in 1 Thessalonians, it lies behind such passages as 1:10 and 5:9 (God's wrath is against sin), 2:11–12 (a life "worthy" of God is in contrast to a life of sin), 3:13 and 5:23 (a heart "unblamable in holiness" is one free from the grip of sin), 4:5 (a Jewish stereotype of Gentile sinners), and 4:7 ("uncleanness" denotes immorality in general and belongs to the Jewish stereotype of Gentiles as sinners; cf. Gal 2:15). More significant than the absence of the term "sin" in 1 Thessalonians — the term also appears infrequently in Galatians — is the absence of an explicit description of the period before Christ. Since that description can be inferred from the passages from 1 Thessalonians cited above, and since it belongs to Paul's Jewish heritage, it is almost certain that it is not a mere inference drawn from Paul's revelatory

---

[31] For the importance of the division between *before* and *after* Christ, see Rudolf Bultmann, *Theology of the New Testament* (2 vols.; New York: Scribner's, 1951, 1955) vol. 1, part 2.

[32] See T. David Gordon, "The Problem at Galatia," *Int* 41 (1987) 32–43; Lull, *Spirit in Galatia*, 32–33; E. P. Sanders, *Paul, the Law, and the Jewish People* (Philadelphia: Fortress, 1983) 19; and Stendahl, *Paul among Jews and Gentiles*.

[33] Since the Spirit is a form of "divine guidance," I am puzzled by Scroggs's statement that "the emphasis on the work of the Spirit in the lives of the believers may explain why there are few references to present guidance by God" (see above, p. 223).

experience of Christ nor a situation-dependent "fighting doctrine" against the so-called judaizers in Galatia.

Paul's understanding of the period before Christ as an age in the grip of the power of sin is also missing from Philippians. Not only is the term "sin" missing from the letter, but nowhere is there any description of the period before Christ. Although 2:8 refers to Jesus' death on a cross, the "hymn" to which it belongs does not contain any explicit interpretation of the soteriological significance of the cross. That significance has to be inferred from the strophe concerning Jesus' exaltation (2:9–11), according to which God makes Jesus the cosmocrator. Can we infer from that that the exalted Jesus, as cosmocrator, reigns over "sin"— one of the powers on, above, and beneath the earth—and that before Christ "sin" vied for power? The only other reference to the death of Jesus, however, speaks of "imitating" the *suffering* of Jesus (3:10), not of Jesus' sacrificial death "for us" or "for our sins."

In Galatians, Paul reflects on the law, which also belongs to this era. Because of the transgressions that were committed in the age before Christ came, the law was introduced as a disciplinarian (Gal 3:19–25) and the στοιχεῖα τοῦ κόσμου acted as overseers (Gal 4:3).[34] The idea that the law was temporary rather than eternal and was meant only for the era before Christ— a view found in Galatians—is not found in 1 Thessalonians, where the term νόμος does not appear at all because the Law of Moses was not at issue there. The Jewish stereotype of Gentiles that lies behind 1 Thess 4:5, 7 presupposes that Paul still held them up to the standard of the Jewish law. The term νόμος does not appear in Philippians either, even though chap. 3 indicates that a dispute had arisen concerning circumcision. Paul responded to that dispute by arguing that the ritual of circumcision—and by implication the observance of the whole law, to which circumcision was the initiatory rite—no longer had the value it had had before the coming of Christ. The era of law-observant worship had been replaced by an age in which God is worshiped "in the Spirit," a form of worship that makes Christians the "true circumcision" (Phil 3:3). The idea that the coming of Christ brought an end to the era of the law, therefore, was not a mere reflex to the crisis in Galatia over the law; rather, it was part of Paul's "salvation history."

Before Christ, righteousness was impossible. One could be blameless according to the righteousness of the law (Phil 3:6), but that righteousness

---

[34] Scroggs might be right that it is unnecessary "to enter the debate" about what the powers mentioned in Gal 4:3 and 8–9 are (p. 224 above), but in 4:1–2 Paul compares the στοιχεῖα by analogy to household slaves who supervise the affairs of minors until they come into their age of inheritance, just like the law, which Paul compares to the "pedagogue" (3:23–25). At the appointed time, God sent an agent who liberates Jew and Gentile alike (cf. 4:8–9 and the first person plurals in 4:3) from these στοιχεῖα.

is not the same as God's righteousness, which depends not on the law but on faith (Phil 3:9; Gal 3:11–12, 21; cf. Gal 2:21; 3:25). The law was not able to make anyone righteous (Gal 2:16), because before Christ everything was enslaved to sin (Gal 3:22). Only through Christ and the Spirit could one become righteous (Gal 2:16; 3:25; 5:5; Phil 3:9).[35]

The Christ-event

In Galatians the Christ-event is identified with the crucifixion of Jesus (Gal 1:4; 2:19–21; 3:1, 13; 5:24; 6:14).[36] Even if the "preexistence" of God's messianic emissary is implied in the sending formula of Gal 4:4,[37] as it is in Phil 2:6–11,[38] the central event in the coming of Christ is the cross. For Paul, the cross overshadows all events in the historical life of Jesus, of which Paul hands on only that Jesus had been born into the normal conditions of human existence and as a Jew (Gal 4:4) and that he died on a cross. In Phil 2:7–8, the Jewishness of Jesus is eclipsed by the descent of the preexistent Christ into the universal human condition of mortal existence in order to dramatize his unconditional obedience — his obedience unto death, even death on a cross.

The sending of Christ (Gal 4:3–4) is closely related to the sending of the Spirit (Gal 4:6), which marks the Christ-event as an eschatological event. Whether the emphasis is on Christ or the Spirit, the benefits of this eschatological event are the same: baptism into Christ (Gal 3:26–29) and the presence of the Spirit among Gentiles (1 Thess 1:4–7; Phil 3:3; Gal 4:3–7) mark them as members of the eschatological people of God. The coming of Christ and the coming of the Spirit bring an end to the era of the law (Gal 3:1–5, 23–25; 5:18; Phil 3:2–16), because Christ and the Spirit defeat the power of evil in the flesh (Gal 5:16–24; 1 Thess 4:1–8). Through the power of Christ and of the Spirit, believers become righteous (1 Thess 1:10; 5:9; Phil 3:9; Gal 2:16; 3:11, 25; 5:5).

The new age of God's redemptive act in Jesus Christ signals the breaking of the grip of the power of sin on all things (Gal 1:3–4; 3:22) and as such

---

[35] In 1 Thess 1:10 and 5:9 the idea of deliverance from God's wrath presupposes or implies that those who are delivered are the righteous.

[36] Cf. the reference to the scars of Paul's persecution, an allusion to his "imitation" of the suffering of Christ (Gal 6:17).

[37] See Hans Dieter Betz, *Galatians: A Commentary on Paul's Letter to the Churches in Galatia* (Hermeneia; Philadelphia: Fortress, 1979) 206.

[38] For the debate about christology in the Philippians hymn, see James D. G. Dunn, *Christology in the Making: A New Testament Inquiry into the Origins of the Doctrine of the Incarnation* (Philadelphia: Westminster, 1980); Carl R. Holladay, "New Testament Christology: A Consideration of Dunn's *Christology in the Making*," *Semeia* 30 (1984) 65–82.

it follows and brings to an end the age for which the law functioned as a disciplinarian (Gal 3:19–25). Since the faith of which Abraham's faith was the prototype has been revealed in those Jews and Gentiles alike who believe in Jesus as the Christ,[39] the age of the law, together with the age for which it was introduced, came to an end.[40] The new life is to be based on the eschatological gift of the Spirit with which the new life began, instead of on the law, which the Spirit makes obsolete (5:16–25).[41] The promise to bless the Gentiles through Abraham has been fulfilled (Gal 3:6–14).[42] Whether it is through the Spirit (Gal 5:16–25) or through the enthronement of Jesus Christ as Lord of the universe (Phil 2:6–11; 3:20–21), the Christ-event inaugurates God's victory over the powers of evil.

1 Thess 1:10 and 5:9–10, which associate Jesus' death with deliverance from God's coming wrath, are evidence that Paul preached to Gentiles the "kerygma of the cross," a message of redemption from sin through the death

---

[39] Paul does indeed talk about Christ bringing "something radically new to human possibility" (so Scroggs, p. 225 above). But Paul also talks about Abraham's "faith" (Gal 3:6–9) and about Isaac's being a child of the "promise" and of his having been "born according to the Spirit" (Gal 4:28–29), which imply that the faith and Spirit that characterize the "new" possibility of human existence brought by Christ existed in the time of Abraham, Sarah, and Isaac. It is not easy to reconcile these seemingly contradictory claims, which are reminiscent of the "structural inconsistency" in Bultmann's existentialist interpretation of the New Testament to which Schubert M. Ogden points (*Christ Without Myth: A Study Based on the Theology of Rudolf Bultmann* [New York, Evanston, London: Harper & Row, 1961]; cf. the interpretation of "the significance of Abraham for the Christian faith" by Hendrikus Boers in *Theology out of the Ghetto: A New Testament Exegetical Study concerning Religious Exclusiveness* [Leiden: Brill, 1971] 74–104). I am less convinced today that Abraham and Isaac are nonhistorical "types" for faith in Christ, but I cannot think of any other way to resolve this tension (see Lull, *Spirit in Galatia,* 157–60). Perhaps it is better to leave it unresolved. In any case, Scroggs's resolution of the tension by affirming one half—the other half is not even acknowledged—is a weakness in his interpretation of "salvation history" in Galatians.

[40] Paul's periodization of history in Galatians is more complex than Scroggs indicates with his statements that in Galatians, with the exception of 5:14 and 6:2, "νόμος consistently carries a negative connotation," that "life under law is . . . a false life before God," and that the law, in its role as a παιδαγωγός, "is not only a negative force" (pp. 221 and 224 above). As I have argued at length elsewhere, a distinction must be made between the function of the law *before the coming of Christ* and its status *after the coming of Christ* (see Lull, "'The Law Was Our Pedagogue'").

[41] This view is more fully developed in Lull, *Spirit in Galatia;* idem, "'The Law Was Our Pedagogue.'"

[42] Scroggs affirms precisely what Paul denies in Gal 3:21—namely, that the two covenants are *opposed* (see p. 225 above). In Galatians 3, where the term "covenant" is reserved for God's promise to bless the Gentiles through Abraham (3:16–18), Paul is careful not to call the law a "covenant," although in Galatians 4 he mentions "two covenants" (4:24a). The εἰς clauses in 3:23 and 24a, as well as the ἵνα clause in 3:24b, seem to suggest that the Abrahamic covenant and the law *are* "complementary" (against Scroggs). The law finds its fulfillment in the fulfillment of the Abrahamic covenant and comes to an end with the coming of Christ (3:25).

of Jesus. It is important to note, however, that in both passages the emphasis lies on Jesus' *resurrection* rather than on his death, and that in 5:9–10, as in 4:13–18, the emphasis is on the promise of the life to come, in which both the living and the dead will be united in life with Christ, rather than on their redemption from sin. This emphasis on resurrection is due to the setting of 5:9–10 in the context of "consolation" for those who grieve.

It is through faith that Jews and Gentiles participate in the Christ-event and its benefits. Paul can even speak of "the coming" or the "revelation" of faith (Gal 3:23, 25). The content of what Paul preached can simply be called "the faith" (Gal 1:23; 3:2, 5) or "the faith of the gospel" (Phil 1:27), and members of the churches of Christ are simply called "believers" (1 Thess 1:7; 2:10, 13) and "the household of faith" (Gal 6:10). The unqualified use of the πιστ- word group in such passages as 1 Thess 1:3 and Gal 3:7–12 are to be understood as faith *in God,* as 1 Thess 1:8 and Gal 3:6 suggest. According to Phil 1:29, on the other hand, the phrase in 1:25 is shorthand for faith *in Christ,* just as it can be inferred from the context that Christ is the content of faith in Gal 3:14, 23–25, and 5:5–6. The content, or object, of faith is Jesus' death and resurrection (1 Thess 4:14) or simply Jesus Christ (Phil 1:29; 3:9; Gal 2:16, 20; 3:22, 26).[43]

Through faith, Gentiles received the eschatological gift of the Spirit (Gal 3:2, 5), by which they are marked as recipients of God's "promise" (Gal 3:14). Through baptism, believers put on Christ—that is, they become united with Abraham's seed (Gal 3:26–29). Paul can also say that God and Christ dwell in them (Phil 1:6; 2:13; Gal 2:20; 4:19), which expresses a change in the dominant force in their lives, just as the image of putting on Christ expresses the same change by denoting the sphere of power or field of force within which believers live. It is in this locative, as well as normative and instrumental, sense that "walking in the Spirit" (Gal 5:16, 25) is to be understood.

Existence in faith is still life "in the flesh" (Gal 2:20), where the "Tempter" remains a threat (1 Thess 3:5).[44] To cope with life in the flesh, Paul exhorts the Thessalonians to put on the "breastplate of faith" (1 Thess 5:8). He instructs the Galatians to live by and in the Spirit, which opposes the power of evil in the flesh, and whose "fruit" includes faith (Gal 5:16–24). He writes that it is in the Spirit, received from faith, that Jews and Gentiles eagerly await the righteousness for which they hope (Gal 5:5). So faith is oriented to the future as well as to the Christ-event.

[43] I have not joined those who understand διὰ/ἐκ πίστεως 'Ιησοῦ Χριστοῦ as a subjective genitive (see Hays, "Crucified with Christ," p. 232 n. 14 above).
[44] Cf. 2 Thess 2:1–12.

The Life to Come

The pattern of "salvation history" in Paul's letters concludes with the hope that God will complete the work of Christ and the Spirit. This hope is expressed in Jewish apocalyptic images.[45] In 1 Thessalonians and Philippians, the end of "salvation history" is called "the day/coming of [the Lord Jesus] Christ" (1 Thess 2:19; 3:13; 4:15; 5:2, 4, 5, 8, 23; Phil 1:6, 10; 2:16).[46] On that "day," which will come without warning (1 Thess 5:2, 4), Christ will appear as an apocalyptic warrior, who will rescue those who "belong to the day" and will destroy those who are "of the night" (1 Thess 4:13–5:11).[47]

The implication of these phrases is that judgment as well as salvation is to be expected in the future (1 Thess 1:9–10; 5:10). Paul assures the Philippians and Thessalonians of their deliverance from God's wrath as long as they remain "blameless" (1 Thess 3:13; 5:23; Phil 1:10; 2:16). He reminds the Thessalonians that they "belong to the day," so that they will not be caught by surprise when "the day" comes, provided they remain vigilant (1 Thess 5:1–11).[48] He is confident that at that "day" God will bring to completion the "work" begun in the Philippians (1:6). Paul also reminds the Thessalonians that the living and the dead in Christ will be united in life with Christ at his parousia (1 Thess 4:15).

The phrase "day/coming of Christ" does not appear in Galatians, except perhaps by allusion in the reference to the passing of the present age (1:4; 6:10). In Galatians, Paul speaks explicitly only of the "righteousness" that is the object of hope (5:5) and of the eternal life that the Spirit will give to those who live by the Spirit (6:7; see also 1 Thess 4:13–18; Phil 3:20–21). Elsewhere in Galatians allusions are made to the coming consummation of the age of promise already inaugurated with the coming of Christ and the Spirit, when those who live by the Spirit and do not gratify the desires of the flesh will live in the eschatological realm of God (5:16–25; cf. 1 Thess 2:12)[49] and the blessings of God's peace and mercy will come upon those who live by

---

[45] Throughout his essay, Wright, in contrast to an emerging consensus, uses the adjective "apocalyptic" as a noun. For the consensus, see John J. Collins (ed.), *Apocalypse: The Morphology of a Genre* (*Semeia* 36; Chico, CA: Scholars Press, 1979); and David Hellholm (ed.), *Apocalypticism in the Mediterranean World and the Near East* (Tübingen: Mohr [Siebeck], 1983).

[46] See also 2 Thess 1:10; 2:1, 2, 8.

[47] In 2 Thess 2:1–12, the parousia is more explicitly portrayed in terms of a myth of the coming of "our Lord Jesus Christ" as the triumphant apocalyptic warrior.

[48] Because 2 Thess 2:1–12 is addressed to those who have been falsely informed that "the Day of the Lord has come," it appears to correct a misreading of 1 Thess 5:1–11.

[49] In 2 Thess 1:5–12, those who endure suffering with steadfastness and faith are deemed worthy of membership in the realm of God, the eschatological community of God's people.

this rule of a new creation (Gal 6:15–16; cf. 1:3, which also speaks of grace and peace).

The Jewish Christian tradition that Paul quotes in Gal 1:4 speaks of "*rescue* from the present evil age," which implies that the *present* age, even after the coming of Christ, is *still* "evil."[50] Although the end of "the present evil age" has not yet come, a "new creation" has already begun (Gal 6:15).[51] Christ subdues the powers of evil, not, however, from a throne on high (as in Phil 2:9–11), nor from a glorious resurrection existence in heaven (as in 1 Thess 1:9–10; 4:13–18; Phil 3:20–21), but from the cross (Gal 2:19–21; 3:1, 13; 5:24; 6:14). In the "end," the union of Jews and Gentiles who abide by and in this "new creation" will be completed by their union in God's peace and mercy (Gal 6:16),[52] even as they are already thus united through faith in Jesus Christ (Gal 1:3; 3:28).[53]

In other words, the life to come is presented in all three letters as the consummation of God's work of salvation in Jesus Christ for all, Jews and Gentiles alike.

Summary

The pattern of "salvation history" in 1 Thessalonians, Philippians, and Galatians can be summarized as follows: *before Christ,* the law was a

---

[50] Cf. Betz, *Galatians,* 42.

[51] Scroggs is correct in saying that our letters do not *explicitly* say anything about God as "creator" (see above, p. 220), but God's original creative activity can be inferred from the concept of "a *new* creation." Furthermore, the idea of God as the creator is implied in the phrase "our Father," which Paul frequently uses as a name of God. Nevertheless, Paul evidently did not consider God-the-creator significant for any of the issues to which these letters are addressed. That, of course, does not mean that Paul did not think of God as the creator.

[52] In Scroggs's reading of Gal 6:16, "true Israelites" are to "live before God" by the "rule" of "justification by faith" (see above, p. 223). But neither justification nor faith language appears in Gal 6:11–18. The "rule" by which those who belong to the "Israel of God" live (6:16) is given in 6:15 — namely, "a new creation." What that is was just described as the "crucifixion of the world" and being "crucified to the world"; in 5:13–24 it is "walking by the Spirit" and the "crucifixion" of "the flesh with its passions and desires"; and it was described already in the opening salutation as deliverance from "the present evil age" (1:4), in 2:19b–20 as being "crucified with Christ" and as the indwelling of Christ, and in Paul's reference to the Galatians' experience of beginning with "the Spirit" (3:3). It seems to me that these "participatory" images constitute the primary language of Galatians and, therefore, provide the horizon within which the meaning of the phrase "justification by faith" is to be located.

[53] Wright's discussion of Paul's apocalyptic eschatology is imprecise and misleading (see above, pp. 197–201). In his claim that Paul's letters (including 2 Thessalonians) do not envision "the end of the world," what does Wright mean by "the end of the world"? Whatever Paul means by 1 Thess 4:14–17; Phil 3:20–21; Gal 1:4; and 6:15, he does envision a change in the actual world; that is, these texts do refer to events in "space and time" (cf. Käsemann, *Perspectives on Paul,* 68).

disciplinarian while everything was in the grip of sin and while God's promise to Abraham awaited fulfillment; *in the Christ-event,* Christ and the Spirit bring freedom and the fulfillment of the Abrahamic covenant; and *in the life to come,* the work of Christ and the Spirit will be completed. This pattern of "salvation history" was constitutive of Paul's self-understanding as an apostle to the Gentiles. In this pattern, Jews and Gentiles are united in God's indivisible redemption of the world through faith in Jesus Christ.

III. POSTSCRIPT

In Jesus Christ, Paul found fulfillment of the twin pillars of his thought: God's promise to set the world free from the grip of the power of sin, and God's promise to unite Jews and Gentiles in the redemption of the world. Both pillars were part of Paul's thought—the traditions of his ancestors for which he was zealous in his "former life in Judaism" (Gal 1:14)—before he became a preacher of the gospel of Christ to the Gentiles. From his new faith that the crucified Jesus, whom God raised from the dead, was the promised Messiah, Paul concluded that this Messiah, and not the Law of Moses, would set both Jew and Gentile free from the grip of the power of sin, and therefore that this Messiah, and not the Law of Moses, would unite Jews and Gentiles in God's redemption of the world.

The problem for which the coming of faith in Jesus Christ is the solution is thus twofold. In the first instance, the problem is that of the bondage of all things to sin (Gal 3:22) and only secondarily that of bondage to the law (Gal 3:23–25). The law was introduced to deal with transgressions during the era when everything was in the grip of sin (Gal 3:19–25), when everyone was still a "minor" (Gal 4:1–7). The law, however, separated Jews and Gentiles into two distinct peoples (cf. Gal 2:1–21; 3:28). The coming of Christ, therefore, is also a solution to the problem of the law, in the sense that Christ breaks the grip of the power of sin and replaces the law with the eschatological gift of the Spirit, which is available to all who believe, Jew and Gentile alike, and alone is able to set people free, to give them life, and to make them "righteous" (1 Thess 1:10; 5:9; Phil 3:9; Gal 2:16; 3:11, 21, 25; 5:5; 5:16–25). Christ and the Spirit also unite Jews and Gentiles into one people, because Christ is one (Gal 3:28–29) and life in the Spirit is one (Gal 5:22–23). It is in this sense that Christ liberates both Jew and Gentile from the law and effects the adoption of both as children of God who inherit God's promises (Gal 4:1–7; cf. 4:21–31).

Bibliographies

Pauline Theology:
General Bibliography

Compiled by Calvin J. Roetzel

Allo, E. B. *Paul: Apôtre de Jésus-Christ.* Paris: Cerf, 1942.

Amiot, F. *Les Idées Maîtresses de Saint Paul.* Paris: Cerf, 1959.

Baeck, Leo. "The Faith of Paul." In *Judaism and Christianity,* 139–68. New York: Atheneum, 1958.

Baird, W. "Pauline Eschatology in Hermeneutical Perspective." *NTS* 17 (1970–71) 314–27.

Baumgarten, Jorg. *Paulus und die Apokalyptik: Die Auslegung apokalyptischer Überlieferungen in den echten Paulusbriefen.* WMANT 44. Neukirchen-Vluyn: Neukirchener Verlag, 1975.

Beker, J. Christiaan. *Paul the Apostle: The Triumph of God in Life and Thought.* Philadelphia: Fortress, 1980.

Ben-Chorin, Schalom. *Paulus: Der Völkerapostel in jüdischer Sicht.* Munich: Paul List, 1970.

Benoit, Pierre. "Genèse et évolution de la pensée paulinienne." In *Paul de Tarse, Apôtre de notre temps,* 75–100. Série monographique de "Benedictina" Section Paulinienne 1. Rome: Abbaye de S. Paul, 1979.

Betz, H. D. "Paul's Concept of Freedom in the Context of Hellenistic Discussions about Possibilities of Human Existence." In *Protocol Series of the Colloquies of the Center for Hermeneutical Studies in Hellenistic and Modern Culture* 26, edited by W. Wuellner, 1–13. Berkeley: Graduate Theological Union and University of California, 1977.

———. "The Problem of Rhetoric and Theology according to the Apostle Paul." In *L'Apôtre Paul: Personnalité, style et conception du ministère,* edited by A. Vanhoye, 16–48. BETL 73. Leuven: Leuven University Press, 1986.

Blank, J. "Erwägungen zum Schriftverständnis des Paulus." In *Rechtfertigung: Festschrift für E. Käsemann zum 70. Geburtstag,* edited by J. Friedrich et al., 37–56. Tübingen: Mohr (Siebeck), 1976.

Boers, Hendrikus. "The Foundations of Paul's Thought: A Methodological Investigation—The Problem of the Coherent Center of Paul's Thought." *ST* 42 (1988) 55–68.

———. "The Meaning of Christ in Paul's Writings: A Structuralist-Semiotic Study." *BTB* 14 (1984) 131–44.

Bornkamm, Günther. *Paul.* New York: Harper & Row, 1969.

Brisebois, Mireille. *Saint Paul: Introduction à Saint Paul et ses lettres.* Lectures Bibliques 19. Montreal: Editions Paulines, 1984.

Bultmann, Rudolf. *Theology of the New Testament.* 2 vols. New York: Scribner's, 1951, 1955.

Cerfaux, L. *Christ in the Theology of St. Paul.* New York: Herder & Herder, 1959.

Conzelmann, Hans. *An Outline of the Theology of the New Testament.* New York: Harper & Row, 1968.

Cosgrove, Charles H. "Justification in Paul: A Linguistic and Theological Reflection." *JBL* 106 (1987) 653–70.

Court, J. M. "Paul and the Apocalyptic Pattern." In *Paul and Paulinism: Essays in Honour of C.K. Barrett,* edited by M. D. Hooker and S. G. Wilson, 57–66. London: SPCK, 1982.

Dahl, N. A. "The Messiahship of Jesus in Paul." In *The Crucified Messiah and Other Essays,* 37–47. Minneapolis: Augsburg, 1974.

———. *Studies in Paul: Theology for the Early Christian Mission.* Minneapolis: Augsburg, 1977.

Davies, W. D. *Jewish and Pauline Studies.* Philadelphia: Fortress, 1984.

———. *Paul and Rabbinic Judaism: Some Elements in Pauline Theology.* London: SPCK, 1948.

———. "Paul and the Law: Reflections on Pitfalls in Interpretation." In *Paul and Paulinism: Essays in Honour of C.K. Barrett,* edited by M. D. Hooker and S. G. Wilson, 4–16. London: SPCK, 1982.

de Boer, W. P. *The Imitation of Paul: An Exegetical Study.* Kampen: Kok, 1962.

Dietzfelbinger, Christian. *Die Berufung des Paulus als Ursprung seiner Theologie.* WMANT 58. Neukirchen-Vluyn: Neukirchener Verlag, 1985.

Donfried, Karl Paul. "Justification and Last Judgment in Paul." *ZNW* 67 (1976) 90–110.

Eichholz, G. *Die Theologie des Paulus im Umriss.* Neukirchen-Vluyn: Neukirchener Verlag, 1972.

Feuillet, A. "Loi de Dieu, loi du Christ et loi de l'Esprit d'après les Epîtres pauliniennes: Les rapports de ces trois lois avec la Loi Mosaïque." *NovT* 22 (1980) 29–65.

Fitzmyer, Joseph A. "The Gospel in the Theology of Paul." *Int* 33 (1979) 339–50.

———. *Paul and His Theology: A Brief Sketch.* 2d ed. Englewood Cliffs, NJ: Prentice Hall, 1989.

———. "Reconciliation in Pauline Theology." In *No Famine in the Land: Studies in Honor of John L. McKenzie,* edited by J. W. Flanagan and A. W. Robinson, 155–77. Claremont, CA: Scholars Press for the Institute of Antiquity and Christianity, 1975.

Furnish, Victor Paul. *The Moral Teaching of Paul: Selected Issues.* 2d ed. Nashville: Abingdon, 1985.

———. *Theology and Ethics in Paul.* Nashville: Abingdon, 1968.

Gaston, L. *Paul and the Torah.* Vancouver: University of British Columbia Press, 1987.

Goppelt, L. *Theology of the New Testament:* Volume 2, *The Variety and Unity of the Apostolic Witness to Christ,* edited by J. Roloff. Grand Rapids: Eerdmans, 1982.

Güttgemanns, Erhard. *Der leidende Apostel und sein Herr: Studien zur paulinischen Christologie.* FRLANT 90. Göttingen: Vandenhoeck & Ruprecht, 1966.

Hahn, F. "Taufe und Rechtfertigung: Ein Beitrag zur paulinischen Theologie in ihrer Vor- und Nachgeschichte." In *Rechtfertigung: Festschrift für E. Käsemann zum 70. Geburtstag,* edited by J. Friedrich et al., 95–124. Tübingen: Mohr (Siebeck), 1976.

Hooker, M. D. "Paul and Covenantal Nomism." In *Paul and Paulinism: Essays in Honour of C.K. Barrett,* edited by M. D. Hooker and S. G. Wilson, 47–56. London: SPCK, 1982.

Hübner, Hans. *Das Gesetz bei Paulus: Ein Beitrag zum Werden der paulinischen Theologie.* FRLANT 119. Göttingen: Vandenhoeck & Ruprecht, 1978. English translation, *Law in Paul's Thought.* Edinburgh: T. & T. Clark, 1984.

———. "Pauli Theologiae Proprium." *NTS* 26 (1979–80) 445–73.

Hunter, A. J. M. *Paul and his Predecessors.* London: SCM, 1940.

Hurd, John C. "Pauline Chronology and Pauline Theology." In *Christian History and Interpretation: Studies Presented to John Knox,* edited by W. R. Farmer et al., 225–48. Cambridge: Cambridge University Press, 1968.

Jewett, Robert. *Paul's Anthropological Terms: A Study of Their Use in Conflict Settings.* AGJU 10. Leiden: Brill, 1971.

Jones, F. S. *"Freiheit" in den Briefen des Apostels Paulus: Eine historische, exegetische und religionsgeschichtliche Studie.* GTA 34. Göttingen: Vandenhoeck & Ruprecht, 1987.

Käsemann, Ernst. "Die Anfänge christlicher Theologie." *ZTK* 57 (1960) 162–85. English translation, "The Beginnings of Christian Theology." In *New Testament Questions of Today,* 82–107. Philadelphia: Fortress, 1969.

———. "Gottesgerechtigkeit bei Paulus." *ZTK* 58 (1961) 367–78. English translation, "'The Righteousness of God' in Paul." In *New Testament Questions of Today,* 168–82. Philadelphia: Fortress, 1969.

———. *Perspectives on Paul.* Philadelphia: Fortress, 1971.

———. "Zum Thema der urchristlichen Apokalyptik." *ZTK* 59 (1962) 267–84. English translation, "On the Subject of Primitive Christian Apocalyptic." In *New Testament Questions of Today,* 108–37. Philadelphia: Fortress, 1969.

Keck, Leander E. "Justification of the Ungodly and Ethics." In *Rechtfertigung: Festschrift für E. Käsemann zum 70. Geburtstag,* edited by J. Friedrich et al., 197–209. Tübingen: Mohr (Siebeck), 1976.

———. "Paul and Apocalyptic Theology." *Int* 38 (1984) 229–41.

Kertelge, Karl. "Der Ort des Amtes in der Ekklesiologie des Paulus." In *L'Apôtre Paul: Personnalité, style et conception du ministére,* edited by A. Vanhoye, 184–202. BETL 73. Leuven: Leuven University Press, 1986.

———. *"Rechtfertigung" bei Paulus: Studien zur Struktur und zum Bedeutungsgehalt des paulinischen Rechtfertigungsbegriffs.* Münster: Aschendorff, 1967.

———. "Das Verständnis des Todes Jesu bei Paulus." In *Der Tod Jesu: Deutungen im Neuen Testament,* 114–36. Freiburg: Herder, 1976.

Klaiber, Walter. *Rechtfertigung und Gemeinde: Eine Untersuchung zum Paulinischen Kirchenverständnis.* FRLANT 127. Göttingen: Vandenhoeck & Ruprecht, 1982.

Klein, G. "Apokalyptische Naherwartung bei Paulus." In *Neues Testament und christliche Existenz: Festschrift für Herbert Braun,* edited by H. D. Betz and L. Schottroff, 241–62. Tübingen: Mohr (Siebeck), 1973.

———. "Präliminarien zum Thema 'Paulus und die Juden.'" In *Rechtfertigung: Festschrift für E. Käsemann zum 70. Geburtstag,* edited by J. Friedrich et al., 229–43. Tübingen: Mohr (Siebeck), 1976.

———. "Ein Sturmzentrum der Paulusforschung." *VF* 33 (1988) 40–56.

———. "Sündenverständnis und theologia crucis bei Paulus." In *Theologia Crucis-Signum Crucis: Festschrift für Erich Dinkler zum 70. Geburtstag,* edited by C. Andresen and G. Klein, 249–82. Tübingen: Mohr (Siebeck), 1979.

Kleinknecht, K. T. *Der leidende Gerechtfertigte: Die alttestamentlich-jüdische Tradition vom 'leidenden Gerechten' und ihre Rezeption bei Paulus.* WUNT 2/13. Tübingen: Mohr (Siebeck), 1984.

Knox, John. *Chapters in a Life of Paul.* Nashville: Abingdon, 1950.

Knox, W. L. *St. Paul and the Church of the Gentiles.* Cambridge: Cambridge University Press, 1939.

Kreitzer, L. J. *Jesus and God in Paul's Eschatology.* JSNTSup 19. Sheffield: JSOT Press, 1987.

Krentz, Edgar. "The Spirit in Pauline and Johannine Theology." In *The Holy Spirit in the Life of the Church,* edited by P. Opsahl, 47–65. Minneapolis: Augsburg, 1978.

Kümmel, Werner Georg. *The Theology of the New Testament according to Its Major Witnesses Jesus-Paul-John.* Nashville: Abingdon, 1973.

Kuss, O. *Paulus: Die Rolle des Apostels in der theologischen Entwicklung der Urkirche.* Auslegung und Verkündigung 3. Regensburg: Pustet, 1971.

Lang, F. "Gesetz und Bund bei Paulus." In *Rechtfertigung: Festschrift für E. Käsemann zum 70. Geburtstag,* edited by J. Friedrich et al., 305–20. Tübingen: Mohr (Siebeck), 1976.

Lindars, Barnabas. "The Sound of the Trumpet: Paul and Eschatology." *BJRL* 67 (1984–85) 766–82.

Lohmeyer, E. *Probleme paulinischer Theologie.* Darmstadt: Wissenschaftliche Buchgemeinschaft, 1954.

Longenecker, Richard N. "The Nature of Paul's Early Eschatology." *NTS* 31 (1985) 85–95.

Lüdemann, G. *Paulus und das Judentum.* Theologische Existenz heute 215. Munich: Kaiser, 1983.

Lüdemann, Hermann. *Die Anthropologie des Apostels Paulus und ihre Stellung innerhalb seiner Heilslehre.* Kiel: Universitäts Buchhandlung, 1872.

Lührmann, D. "Christologie und Rechtfertigung." In *Rechtfertigung: Festschrift für E. Käsemann zum 70. Geburtstag,* edited by J. Friedrich et al., 351–63. Tübingen: Mohr (Siebeck), 1976.

Luz, Ulrich. *Das Geschichtsverständnis des Paulus.* BEvT 49. Munich: Kaiser, 1968.

Martin, Ralph P. *Reconciliation: A Study of Paul's Theology.* Atlanta: John Knox, 1981. Revised 1989.

Meeks, Wayne A. *The Moral World of the First Christians.* Library of Early Christianity 6. Philadelphia: Westminster, 1986.

———. "The Social Context of Pauline Theology." *Int* 36 (1982) 266–77.

Merklein, Helmut. *Studien zu Jesus und Paulus.* WUNT 48. Tübingen: Mohr (Siebeck), 1987.

Meyer, Paul W. "The Holy Spirit in the Pauline Letters: A Contextual Exploration." *Int* 33 (1979) 3–18.

Morgan, R. "The Significance of Paulinism." In *Paul and Paulinism: Essays in Honour of C.K. Barrett,* edited by M. D. Hooker and S. G. Wilson, 320–38. London: SPCK, 1982.

Munck, Johannes. *Paul and the Salvation of Mankind.* Richmond: John Knox, 1956.

Neugebauer, Fritz. *In Christus — EN XPIΣTΩI: Eine Untersuchung zum paulinischen Glaubensverständnis.* Göttingen: Vandenhoeck & Ruprecht, 1961.

Nock, Arthur Darby. *St. Paul.* New York: Harper, 1938.

O'Brien, P. T. "Thanksgiving within the Structure of Pauline Theology." In *Pauline Studies: Essays Presented to F.F. Bruce on his 70th Birthday,* edited by D. A. Hagner and M. J. Harris, 50–66. Exeter: Paternoster, 1980.

Patte, Daniel. *Paul's Faith and the Power of the Gospel: A Structural Introduction to the Pauline Letters.* Philadelphia: Fortress, 1983.

Pedersen, S., ed. *The Pauline Literature and Theology: Anlässlich der 50. Gründungsfeier der Universität vom Aarhus.* Göttingen: Vandenhoeck & Ruprecht, 1980.

Perkins, Pheme. *Ministering in the Pauline Churches.* New York: Paulist, 1982.

Plevnik, Joseph. *What Are They Saying About Paul?* New York: Paulist, 1986.

Pobee, John S. *Persecution and Martyrdom in the Theology of Paul.* JSNTSup 6. Sheffield: JSOT Press, 1985.

Räisänen, H. *Paul and the Law.* WUNT 29. Tübingen: Mohr (Siebeck), 1983. Fortress Press edition, 1986.

———. "Paul's Theological Difficulties with the Law." In *Studia Biblica 1978: III, Papers on Paul and Other New Testament Authors,* edited by E. A. Livingstone, 301–20. JSNTSup 3. Sheffield: JSOT Press, 1980.

Reicke, Bo. "Paulus über das Gesetz." *TZ* 41 (1985) 237–57.

Rese, Martin. "Die Rolle Israels im apokalyptischen Denken des Paulus." In *L'Apôtre Paul: Personnalité, style et conception de ministère,* edited by A. Vanhoye, 311–18. BETL 52. Leuven: Leuven University Press, 1980.

Reumann, John. *"Righteousness" in the New Testament: "Justification" in the United States Lutheran–Roman Catholic Dialogue.* Philadelphia: Fortress; New York: Paulist, 1982.

Ridderbos, Herman. *Paul: An Outline of His Theology.* Grand Rapids: Eerdmans, 1975.

Robinson, John A. T. *The Body: A Study in Pauline Theology.* SBT 5. London: SCM, 1952.

Roetzel, Calvin J. *Judgement in the Community: A Study of the Relationship between Eschatology and Ecclesiology in Paul.* Leiden: Brill, 1972.

Röhser, G. *Metaphorik und Personifikation der Sünde: Antike Sündenvorstellungen und paulinische Hamartia.* WUNT 2/25. Tübingen: Mohr (Siebeck), 1987.

Sanders, E. P. *Paul and Palestinian Judaism: A Comparison of Patterns of Religion.* Philadelphia: Fortress, 1977.

———. *Paul, the Law, and the Jewish People.* Philadelphia: Fortress, 1983.

Schade, Hans-Heinrich. *Apokalyptische Christologie bei Paulus: Studien zum Zusammenhang von Christologie und Eschatologie in den Paulusbriefen.* GTA 18. Göttingen: Vandenhoeck & Ruprecht, 1981.

Schlier, H. *Grundzüge einer paulinischen Theologie.* 2d ed. Freiburg: Herder, 1979.

Schnackenburg, R. "Christologie des Neuen Testaments." In *Mysterium Salutis: Grundriss heilsgeschichtlicher Dogmatik,* edited by J. Feiner and M. Löhrer, 3. 227–38. Einsiedeln: Benziger, 1970.

———. *Neutestamentliche Theologie: Stand der Forschung.* Munich: Kösel, 1965.

Schoeps, Hans Joachim. *Paul: The Theology of the Apostle in the Light of Jewish Religious History.* Philadelphia: Westminster, 1961.

Schrage, Wolfgang. *Die konkreten Einzelgebote in der paulinischen Paränese.* Gütersloh: Mohn, 1961.

Schulz, S. "Die Charismenlehre des Paulus: Bilanz der Probleme und Ergebnisse." In *Rechtfertigung: Festschrift für E. Käsemann zum 70. Geburtstag,* edited by J. Friedrich et al., 443–60. Tübingen: Mohr (Siebeck), 1976.

———. "Der frühe und der späte Paulus: Überlegungen zur Entwicklung seiner Theologie und Ethik." *TZ* 41 (1985) 228–36.

Schweitzer, Albert. *The Mysticism of Paul the Apostle.* London: Adam & Charles Black, 1931. Reprint with a prefatory note by F. C. Burkitt. Northampton: John Dickens, 1967.

Scroggs, Robin. *The Last Adam: A Study of Pauline Anthropology.* Philadelphia: Fortress, 1966.

Stendahl, Krister. *Paul among Jews and Gentiles and Other Essays.* Philadelphia: Fortress, 1976.

Stuhlmacher, Peter. "Das paulinische Evangelium." In *Das Evangelium und die Evangelien,* 157–82. Tübingen: Mohr (Siebeck), 1983.

———. *Das paulinische Evangelium.* FRLANT 95. Göttingen: Vandenhoeck & Ruprecht, 1968.

———. *Reconciliation, Law, and Righteousness: Essays in Biblical Theology.* Philadelphia: Fortress, 1986.

Theissen, Gerd. *Psychological Aspects of Pauline Theology.* Philadelphia: Fortress, 1987.

von der Osten-Sacken, P. *Evangelium und Tora: Aufsätze zu Paulus.* TBü 77. Munich: Kaiser, 1987.

Wedderburn, A. J. M. *Baptism and Resurrection: Studies in Pauline Theology against Its Graeco-Roman Background.* WUNT 44. Tübingen: Mohr (Siebeck), 1988.

———. "Some Observations on Paul's Use of the Phrases 'In Christ' and 'With Christ.'" *JSNT* 25 (1985) 83–97.

Weder, Hans. *Das Kreuz Jesu bei Paulus: Ein Versuch über den Geschichtsbezug des christlichen Glaubens nachzudenken.* FRLANT 125. Göttingen: Vandenhoeck & Ruprecht, 1981.

Westerholm, Stephen. *Israel's Law and the Church's Faith: Paul and His Recent Interpreters.* Grand Rapids: Eerdmans, 1988.

Whiteley, D. E. H. *The Theology of St. Paul.* Philadelphia: Fortress, 1966.

Wikenhauser, A. *Pauline Mysticism.* New York: Herder & Herder, 1960.

Wilckens, Ulrich. "Christologie und Anthropologie im Zusammenhang der paulinischen Rechtfertigungslehre." *ZNW* 67 (1978) 64–82.

———. *Rechtfertigung als Freiheit: Paulusstudien.* Neukirchen-Vluyn: Neukirchener Verlag, 1974.

———. "Statements on the Development of Paul's View of Law." In *Paul and Paulinism: Essays in Honour of C.K. Barrett,* edited by M. D. Hooker and S. G. Wilson, 17–26. London: SPCK, 1982.

1 Thessalonians
Compiled by Raymond F. Collins

Adinolfi, Marco. "Etica 'commerciale' e motivi parenetici in 1 Thess. 4, 1–8." *BeO* 19 (1977) 9–20.

———. "La sanctità del matrimonio in 1 Tess. 4, 1–8." *RivB* 24 (1976) 165–84.

Arróniz, Jose Manuel. "La parusía y su hermeneútica (1 Tes. 4, 13–18)." *Lumen* 32 (1983) 193–213.

Baarda, Tjitze. "'Maar de toorn is over hen gekomen' (1 Thess 2:16c)." In *Paulus en de andere joden,* edited by H. Jansen et al., 15–74. Delft: Meinema, 1984.

Baltensweiler, Heinrich. "Erwägungen zu 1. Thess. 4, 3–8." *TZ* 19 (1963) 1–13.

Bammel, Ernst. "Judenverfolgung und Naherwartung: Zur Eschatologie des ersten Thessalonicherbriefs." *ZTK* 56 (1959) 294–315.

Baumert, Norbert. "*Omeirmenoi* in 1 Thess 2,8." *Bib* 68 (1987) 552–63.

Becker, Jürgen. *Auferstehung der Toten im Urchristentum.* SBS 82. Stuttgart: Katholisches Bibelwerk, 1976.

———. "Die Erwahlung der Völker durch das Evangelium-Theologiegeschichtliche Erwägungen zum 1. Thessalonicherbrief." In *Studien zum Text und zur Ethik des Neuen Testaments: Festschrift zum 80. Geburtstag von Heinrich Greeven,* edited by W. Schrage, 82–101. BZNW 47. Berlin: Walter de Gruyter, 1986.

Broer, Ingo. "'Antisemitismus' und Judenpolemik im Neuen Testament: Ein Beitrag zum besseren Verständnis von 1 Thess 2, 14–16." *Biblische Notizen* 20 (1983) 59–91.

Cavallin, Hans C. "Parusi och uppståndelse. 1 Th. 4:13–18 som kombination av två slags eskatologi." *STK* 59 (1983) 54–63.

Collins, Raymond F. *Studies on the First Letter to the Thessalonians.* BETL 66. Leuven: Leuven University Press, 1984.

———, ed. *The Thessalonian Correspondence.* BETL 87. Leuven: Leuven University Press, forthcoming.

Cranfield, C. E. B. "A Study of 1 Thessalonians 2." *IBS* 1 (1979) 215–26.

Donfried, Karl P. "The Cults of Thessalonica and the Thessalonian Correspondence." *NTS* 31 (1985) 336–56.

———. "Paul and Judaism: 1 Thessalonians 2:13–16 as a Test Case." *Int* 38 (1984) 242–53.

Egelkraut, Helmuth. "Die Bedeutung von 1 Thess 4, 13ff für eine Umschreibung christlicher Zukunftserwartung." In *Zukunftserwartung in biblischer Sicht,* edited by G. Maier, 87–97. Wuppertal: Brockhaus, 1984.

Feuillet, André. "Le 'ravissement' final des justes et la double perspective eschatologique (résurrection glorieuse et vie avec le Christ après la mort) dans la Première Epître aux Thessaloniciens." *RevThom* 72 (1972) 533–59.

García del Moral, Antonio. "'Nosotros los vivos': Convicción personal de Pablo o reinterpretación de un slamo? (I Tes 4,13–5,11)." *Communio* 20 (1987) 3–56.

García-Moreno, Antonio. "La realeza y el señorio de Cristo en Tessalonicenses." *EstBib* 39 (1981) 63–82.

Geiger, G. "1 Thess 2,13–16: Der Initiationstext des christlichen Antisemitismus?" *BLit* 59 (1986) 154–60.

Gillman, John. "Signals of Transformation in 1 Thessalonians 4:13–18." *CBQ* 47 (1985) 263–81.

Gundry, Robert H. "The Hellenization of Dominical Tradition and Christianization of Jewish Tradition in the Eschatology ot 1–2 Thessalonians." *NTS* 33 (1987) 161–87.

Harnisch, Wolfgang. *Eschatologische Existenz: Ein exegetischer Beitrag zum Sachanliegen von 1 Thessalonicher 4,13–5,11.* FRLANT 110. Göttingen: Vandenhoeck & Ruprecht, 1973.

Havener, Ivan. "The Pre-Pauline Christological Credal Formulae of 1 Thessalonians." In *Society of Biblical Literature 1981 Seminar Papers,* edited by K. H. Richards, 105–28. Chico, CA: Scholars Press, 1981.

Henneken, Bartholomaus. *Verkündigung und Prophetie im 1. Thessalonicherbrief: Ein Beitrag zur Theologie des Wortes Gottes.* SBS 29. Stuttgart: Katholisches Bibelwerk, 1969.

Herman, Zvonimir Izidor. "Il significato della morte e della risurrezione di Gesù nel contesto escatologico di 1 Ts 4,13–5,11." *Anton* 55 (1980) 327–51.

Hodgson, Robert, Jr. "1 Thess 4,1–12 and the Holiness Tradition (HT)." In *Society of Biblical Literature 1982 Seminar Papers,* edited by K. H. Richards, 199–216. Chico, CA: Scholars Press, 1982.

Hoffmann, Paul. *Die Toten in Christus: Eine religionsgeschichtliche und exegetische Untersuchung zur paulinischen Eschatologie.* NTAbh n.F. 2. Münster: Aschendorff, 1966.

Holtz, Traugott. "Der Apostel des Christus: Die paulinische 'Apologie' 1 Thess. 2,1–12." In *Als Boten des gekreuzigten Herrn: Festgabe für Bischof Dr. Dr. Werner Krusche,* edited by H. Falcke et al., 101–16. Berlin: Evangelische Verlagsanstalt, 1982.

———. *Der erste Brief an die Thessalonicher.* EKKNT 13. Zurich: Benziger, 1986.

———. "'Euer Glaube an Gott': Zu Form und Inhalt von 1 Thess 1, 9f." In *Die Kirche des Anfangs: Festschrift für Heinz Schürmann zum 65. Geburtstag,* edited by R. Schnackenburg et al., 459–88. Leipzig: St. Benno, 1977.

Hurd, John C. "Paul Ahead of His Time: 1 Thess. 2:13–16." In *Anti-Judaism in Early Christianity:* Volume 1, *Paul and the Gospels,* edited by P. Richardson, 1. 21–36. Studies in Christianity and Judaism 2. Waterloo, Ont.: Wilfred Laurier University Press, 1986.

Hyldahl, Niels. "Auferstehung Christi, Auferstehung der Toten (1 Thess 4,13–18)." In *Die paulinische Literatur und Theologie,* edited by S. Pedersen, 119–35. Aarhus: Aros, 1980.

Jewett, Robert. *The Thessalonian Correspondence: Pauline Rhetoric and Millenarian Piety.* FFNT. Philadelphia: Fortress, 1986.

Kaye, B. N. "Eschatology and Ethics in 1 and 2 Thessalonians." *NovT* 17 (1975) 47–57.

Klijn, A. F. J. "1 Thessalonians 4,13–18 and its Background in Apocalyptic Literature." In *Paul and Paulinism: Essays in Honour of C.K. Barrett,* edited by M. D. Hooker and S. G. Wilson, 67–73. London: SPCK, 1982.

Krentz, Edgar. "Roman Hellenism and Paul's Gospel." *TBT* 26 (1988) 328–37.

Langevin, Paul-Emile. *Jésus Seigneur et l'eschatologie: Exégèse de textes prépauliniens.* Studia 21. Bruges and Paris: Desclée de Brouwer, 1967.

Laub, Franz. *Eschatologische Verkündigung und Lebensgestaltung nach Paulus: Eine Untersuchung zum Wirken des Apostels beim Aufbau der Gemeinde in Thessalonike.* Biblische Untersuchungen 10. Regensburg: Pustet, 1973.

Longenecker, Richard N. "The Nature of Paul's Early Eschatology." *NTS* 31 (1985) 85–95.

Lyons, George. *Pauline Autobiography: Toward a New Understanding.* SBLDS 73. Atlanta: Scholars Press, 1985.

Malherbe, Abraham J. *Paul and the Thessalonians: The Philosophic Tradition of Pastoral Care.* Philadelphia: Fortress, 1987.

Marshall, I. Howard. "Pauline Theology in the Thessalonian Correspondence." In *Paul and Paulinism: Essays in Honour of C.K. Barrett,* edited by M. D. Hooker and S. G. Wilson, 173–83. London: SPCK, 1982.

Mattern, Lieselotte. *Das Verständnis des Gerichtes bei Paulus.* ATANT 47. Zurich: Zwingli, 1966.

Mayer, Bernhard. *Unter Gottes Heilsratschluss: Prädestinationsaussagen bei Paulus.* FB 15. Würzburg: Echter, 1964.

Müller, Peter. *Anfänge der Paulusschule: Dargestellt am zweiten Thessalonicherbrief und am Kolosserbrief.* ATANT 74. Zurich: Theologischer Verlag, 1988.

Neyrey, Jerome H. "Eschatology in 1 Thessalonians: The Theological Factor in 1,9–10; 2,4–5; 3,11–13; 4,6 and 4,13–18." In *Society of Biblical Literature 1980 Seminar Papers,* edited by P. J. Achtemeier, 219–31. Chico, CA: Scholars Press, 1980.

Plevnik, Joseph. "The Parousia as Implication of Christ's Resurrection." In *Word and Spirit: Essays in Honor of David Michael Stanley on his 60th Birthday,* edited by J. Plevnik, 199–277. Willowdale: Regis College, 1975.

———. "The Taking Up of the Faithful and the Resurrection of the Dead in 1 Thessalonians 4:13–18." *CBQ* 46 (1984) 274–83.

Robinson, John A. T. *Jesus and His Coming: The Emergence of a Doctrine.* Nashville: Abingdon, 1957.

Schade, Hans-Heinrich. *Apokalyptische Christologie bei Paulus: Studien zum Zusammenhang von Christologie und Eschatologie in den Paulusbriefen.* GTA 18. Göttingen: Vandenhoeck & Ruprecht, 1981.

Schnelle, Udo. "Der erste Thessalonicherbrief und die Entstehung der paulinischen Anthropologie." *NTS* 32 (1986) 207–24.

Schulz, Siegfried. *Neutestamentliche Ethik.* Zürcher Grundrisse zur Bibel. Zurich: Theologischer Verlag, 1987.

Siber, Peter. *Mit Christus Leben: Eine Studie zur paulinischen Auferstehungshoffnung.* ATANT 61. Zurich: Theologischer Verlag, 1971.

Snyder, Graydon F. "A Summary of Faith in an Epistolary Context." In *Society of Biblical Literature 1972 Seminar Papers,* edited by L. C. McGaughy, 19–35. N.p.: Society of Biblical Literature, 1972.

Steele, E. Springs. "The Use of Jewish Scriptures in 1 Thessalonians." *BTB* 14 (1984) 12–17.

Stegemann, Wolfgang. "Anlass und Hintergrund der Abfassung von 1 Th 2,1–12." In *Theologische Brosamen für Lothar Steiger,* edited by G. Freund and E. Stegemann, 397–416. Heidelberg: [Wiss.-Theol. Seminar], 1985.

Ulonska, Herbert. "Christen und Heiden: Die Paulinische Paränese in I Thess 4,3–8." *TZ* 43 (1987) 210–18.

Viard, André. "L'Evangile de Jésus Christ dans la première Epître aux Thessaloniciens." *Angelicum* 56 (1979) 413–27.

Vidal Garcia, Senen. "La fórmula de resurrección 'christológica simple.'" *Salmanticensis* 27 (1979) 385–417.

Wanamaker, C. A. "Apocalypticism at Thessalonica." *Neot* 21 (1987) 1–10.

Wiederkehr, Dietrich. *Die Theologie der Berufung in den Paulusbriefen.* Studia Friburgensia n.F. 36. Freiburg: Universitätsverlag, 1963.

Wilcke, Hans-Alwin. *Das Problem eines messianischen Zwischenreiches bei Paulus.* ATANT 51. Zurich: Zwingli, 1967.

Yarbrough, O. Larry. *Not Like the Gentiles: Marriage Rules in the Letters of Paul.* SBLDS 80. Atlanta: Scholars Press, 1985.

2 Thessalonians
Compiled by Edgar Krentz

Aus, Roger D. "The Liturgical Background of the Necessity and Propriety of Giving Thanks According to 2 Thes 1:3." *JBL* 92 (1973) 432–38.

———. "The Relevance of Isaiah 66:7 to Revelation 12 and 2 Thessalonians 1." *ZNW* 67 (1976) 252–68.

Bassler, Jouette M. "The Enigmatic Sign: 2 Thessalonians 1:5." *CBQ* 46 (1984) 496–510.

Baur, Ferdinand Christian. "Die beiden Briefe an die Thessalonicher, ihre Unechtheit und Bedeutung für die Lehre der Parusia Christi." *Theologischer Jahrbücher* 14 (1855) 141–68. English translation in *Paul, the Apostle of Jesus Christ: His Life and Work, His Epistles and His Doctrine*, 2. 314–40. London: Williams & Norgate, 1875–76.

Best, Ernest. *A Commentary on the First and Second Epistles to the Thessalonians*. HNTC. New York: Harper & Row, 1972.

Bornemann, W. *Die Thessalonicherbriefe, völlig neu bearbeitet*. MeyerK 10. Göttingen: Vandenhoeck & Ruprecht, 1894.

Bousset, Wilhelm. *The Antichrist Legend: A Chapter in Christian and Jewish Folklore*. London: Hutchinson, 1896.

Braun, Herbert. "Zur nachpaulinischen Herkunft des zweiten Thessalonicherbriefes." *ZNW* 44 (1952) 152–56.

Bruce, F. F. *1 and 2 Thessalonians*. WBC. Waco: Word, 1982.

Collins, Raymond F. "The Second Epistle to the Thessalonians." In *Letters That Paul Did Not Write*, 209–41. GNS 28. Wilmington: Glazier, 1988.

Cullmann, Oscar. "Der eschatologische Charakter des Missions-auftrages und des apostolischen Selbstbewusstseins bei Paulus: Untersuchung zum Begriff des κατέχον (κατέχων) in 2 Thess. 2, 6–7." In *Vorträge und Aufsätze, 1925–1962*, edited by K. Fröhlich, 305–36. Tübingen: Mohr (Siebeck), 1966.

Denis, Albert-Marie. *L'Apôtre Paul prophète messianique des Gentils: Étude thématique de 1 Thess. II,1–6*. ALBO 3/6. Louvain: Publications Universitaires de Louvain, 1957.

Dibelius, Martin. *An die Thessalonicher I, II; An die Philipper*. HNT 11. 3d ed. Tübingen: Mohr (Siebeck), 1937.

Giblin, Charles H. *The Threat to Faith: An Exegetical and Theological Re-Examination of 2 Thessalonians 2*. AnBib 31. Rome: Pontifical Biblical Institute, 1967.

Holland, Glenn Stanfield. "Let No One Deceive You in Any Way: 2 Thessalonians as a Reformulation of the Apocalyptic Tradition." In *Society of Biblical Literature 1985 Seminar Papers*, edited by K. H. Richards, 329–41. Atlanta: Scholars Press, 1985.

———. *The Tradition That You Received from Us: 2 Thessalonians in the Pauline Tradition*. HUT 24. Tübingen: Mohr (Siebeck), 1988.

Holtzmann, H. J. "Zum zweiten Thessalonicherbrief." *ZNW* 2 (1901) 97–108.

Hughes, Frank Witt. *Early Christian Rhetoric and 2 Thessalonians*. JSNTSup 30. Sheffield: JSOT Press, 1989.

Hurd, John C., Jr. "Thessalonians, Second Letter to the." *IDBSup*, 900–901.

Jewett, Robert. *The Thessalonian Correspondence: Pauline Rhetoric and Millenarian Piety*. FFNT. Philadelphia: Fortress, 1986.

Kaye, B. N. "Eschatology and Ethics in 1 and 2 Thessalonians." *NovT* 17 (1975) 47–57.

Koester, Helmut. "Apostel und Gemeinde in den Briefen an die Thessalonicher." In *Kirche: Festschrift für Günther Bornkamm zum 75. Geburtstag*, edited by D. Lührmann and G. Strecker, 287–98. Tübingen: Mohr (Siebeck), 1980.

Krodel, Gerhard. "The 2nd Letter to the Thessalonians." *Ephesians, Colossians, 2 Thessalonians, the Pastoral Epistles,* edited by G. Krodel, 73–96. Proclamation Commentaries. Philadelphia: Fortress, 1978.

Laub, Franz. *Eschatologische Verkündigung und Lebensgestaltung nach Paulus: Eine Untersuchung zum Wirken des Apostels beim Aufbau der Gemeinde in Thessalonike.* Biblische Untersuchungen 10. Regensburg: Pustet, 1973.

———. "Paulinische Autorität in nachpaulinischer Zeit (2 Thess)." In *The Thessalonian Correspondence,* edited by R. F. Collins. BETL 87. Leuven: Leuven University Press, forthcoming.

Lindemann, Andreas. "Zum Abfassungszweck des zweiten Thessalonicherbriefes." *ZNW* 68 (1977) 35–47.

Marshall, I. Howard. *1 and 2 Thessalonians* NCB. Grand Rapids: Eerdmans, 1983.

Marxsen, Willi. *Der zweite Thessalonicherbrief.* Zürcher Bibelkommentare 11.2. Zurich: Theologischer Verlag, 1982.

Mearns, Christopher L. "Early Eschatological Development in Paul: The Evidence of I and II Thessalonians." *NTS* 27 (1981) 137–57.

Milligan, George. *St. Paul's Epistles to the Thessalonians: The Greek Text with Introduction and Notes.* London: Macmillan, 1908.

Morris, Leon. *The First and Second Epistles to the Thessalonians.* NICNT. Grand Rapids: Eerdmans, 1959.

Müller, Peter. *Anfänge der Paulusschule: Dargestellt am zweiten Thessalonicherbrief und am Kolosserbrief.* ATANT 74. Zurich: Theologischer Verlag, 1988.

Oepke, Albrecht. *Die Briefe an die Thessalonicher.* NTD 8. Göttingen: Vandenhoeck & Ruprecht, 1933.

Reese, James M. *1 and 2 Thessalonians.* New Testament Message 16. Wilmington: Glazier, 1979.

Reicke, Bo. "Thessalonicherbriefe." *RGG³,* 6. 851–53.

Rigaux, B. *Saint Paul: Les épîtres aux Thessaloniciens.* Ebib. Paris: Gabalda, 1956.

Schmithals, Walther. "Die Thessalonicherbriefe als Briefkompositionen." In *Zeit und Geschichte: Dankesgabe an R. Bultmann zum 80. Geburtstag,* edited by E. Dinkler, 295–315. Tübingen: Mohr (Siebeck), 1964.

Trilling, Wolfgang. "Literarische Paulusimitation im 2. Thessalonicherbrief." In *Paulus in den neutestamentlichen Spätschriften,* edited by K. Kertelge, 146–51. Freiburg: Herder, 1981.

———. *Untersuchungen zum zweiten Thessalonicherbrief.* ETS 27. Leipzig: St. Benno, 1972.

———. *Der zweite Brief an die Thessalonicher.* EKKNT 14. Neukirchen-Vluyn: Neukirchener Verlag, 1980.

von Dobschütz, Ernst. *Die Thessalonicher-briefe.* MeyerK 10. 7th ed. 1909. Reprint, Göttingen: Vandenhoeck & Ruprecht, 1974.

Wanamaker, C. A. "Apocalypticism at Thessalonica." *Neot* 21 (1987) 1–10.

Whiteley, D. E. H. *Thessalonians in the Revised Standard Version.* New Clarendon Bible. London: Oxford University Press, 1969.

Wrede, William. *Die Echtheit des Zweiten Thessalonicherbriefs.* TU 24/2. Leipzig: Hinrichs, 1903.

Philippians
Compiled by John Reumann

Ahern, Barnabas M. "The Fellowship of His Sufferings (Phil. 3, 10)." *CBQ* 22 (1960) 1–32.

Beare, F. W. *A Commentary on the Epistle to the Philippians.* HNTC. New York: Harper, 1959.

Betz, Hans Dieter. *Nachfolge und Nachahmung Jesu Christi im Neuen Testament.* BHT 37. Tübingen: Mohr (Siebeck), 1967.

Black, David Alan. "Paul and Christian Unity: A Formal Analysis of Philippians 2:1–4." *JETS* 28 (1985) 299–308.

Bonnard, Pierre. "Mourir et vivre avec Jésus-Christ selon saint Paul." *RHPR* 36 (1956) 101–12.

Böttger, P. C. "Die eschatologische Existenz der Christen: Erwägungen zu Philipper 3:20." *ZNW* 60 (1969) 244–63.

Collange, Jean-François. *The Epistle of Saint Paul to the Philippians.* London: Epworth, 1979.

Culpepper, Robert A. "Co-workers in Suffering: Philippians 2:19–20." *RevExp* 77 (1980) 349–58.

Denis, A. M. "La fonction apostolique et la liturgie nouvelle en Esprit: Etude thématique des métaphores pauliniennes de culte nouveau." *RSPT* 42 (1958) 617–56.

Duncan, G. S. "Philippians, Letter to the." *IDB* 3. 790–91.

Eichholz, Georg. "Bewahren und Bewähren des Evangeliums: Der Leitfaden von Phil. 1–2." In *Hören und Handeln: Festschrift für E. Wolf,* edited by H. Gollwitzer and H. Traub, 85–105. Munich: Kaiser, 1962.

Ernst, J. "From Local Community to the Great Church, Illustrated from Church Patterns of Philippians and Ephesians." *BTB* 6 (1976) 237–57.

Ezell, D. "The Sufficiency of Christ: Philippians 4." *RevExp* 77 (1980) 373–87.

Fitzmyer, Joseph A. "To Know Him and the Power of His Resurrection; Phil. 3:10." In *Mélanges bibliques en hommage au R. P. Béda Rigaux,* edited by A. Descamps and A. de Halleux, 411–25. Gembloux: Duculot, 1970.

Fleury, Jean. "Une Société de Fait dans l'Église Apostolique (Phil. 4: 10 à 22)." In *Mélanges Philippe Meylan:* Volume 2, *Histoire de Droit,* 41–59. Lausanne: Lausanne Université, 1963.

Forestell, J. T. "Christian Perfection and Gnosis in Phil. 3, 7–16." *CBQ* 18 (1956) 123–36.

Gaide, G. "L'amour de Dieu en nous (Ph 1. 4–6. 8–11)." *Assemblées du Seigneur* 55 (1969) 62–69.

Garland, D. E. "Philippians 1:1–26: The Defense and Confirmation of the Gospel." *RevExp* 77 (1980) 327–36.

Gärtner, Bertil. "The Pauline and Johannine Idea 'To Know God' Against the Hellenistic Background." *NTS* 14 (1967–68) 209–31.

Glombitza, O. "Der Dank des Apostels: Zum Verständnis von Phil. 4: 10–20." *NovT* 7 (1964–65) 135–41.

Gnilka, Joachim. *Der Philipperbrief.* HTKNT 10/3. Freiburg: Herder, 1968.

——. "La carriere du Christ, appel à l'union et à la charité (Ph. 2)." *Assemblées du Seigneur* 57 (1971) 12–19.

Gremmels, C. "Selbstreflexive Interpretation konfligierender Identifikationen am Beispiel des Apostels Paulus (Phil. 3, 7–9)." In *Religion, Selbstbewusstsein, Identität,* edited by J. Scharfenberg, 44–57. Theologische Existenz heute 182. Munich: Kaiser, 1974.

Hawthorne, Gerald F. *Philippians.* WBC 43. Waco: Word, 1983.

——. *Word Biblical Themes: Philippians.* Waco: Word, 1987.

Hoffmann, Paul. *Die Toten in Christus: Eine religionsgeschichtliche und exegetische Untersuchung zur paulinischen Eschatologie.* NTAbh n.F. 2. Münster: Aschendorff, 1966.

Jones, Maurice. *The Epistle to the Philippians.* Westminster Commentaries. London: Methuen, 1918.

Koester, Helmut. "The Purpose of the Polemic of a Pauline Fragment (Philippians III)." *NTS* 8 (1961–62) 317–32.

Kurz, William S. "Kenotic Imitation of Paul and of Christ in Philippians 2 and 3." In *Discipleship in the New Testament,* edited by F. F. Segovia, 103–26. Philadelphia: Fortress, 1985.

Lightfoot, J. B. *St. Paul's Epistle to the Philippians.* 4th ed. London: Macmillan, 1868.

Mackenzie, D. "Philippians, Epistle to the." In *Dictionary of the Apostolic Church,* edited by J. Hastings, 2. 224–27. New York: Scribner's, 1916.

Mayer, Bernhard. "Paulus als Vermittler zwischen Epaphroditus und der Gemeinde von Philippi: Bemerkung zu Phil 2, 25–30." *BZ* 31 (1987) 176–88.

Merk, Otto. "Nachahmung Christi: Zu ethischen Perspektiven in den paulinischen Theologie." In *Neues Testament und Ethik: Festschrift für Rudolf Schnackenburg,* edited by H. Merklein, 172–206. Freiburg: Herder, 1989.

O'Brien, Peter T. "The Fellowship Theme in Philippians." *Reformed Theological Review* 37 (1978) 9–18.

——. "The Importance of the Gospel in Philippians." In *God Who Is Rich in Mercy: Essays Presented to Dr. D. B. Knox,* edited by P. T. O'Brien and D. G. Peterson, 213–33. Homebush West, New South Wales: Lancer, 1986.

——. *Introductory Thanksgivings in the Letters of Paul.* NovTSup 49. Leiden: Brill, 1977.

Palmer, D. W. "'To die is gain' (Philippians I 21)." *NovT* 17 (1975) 203–18.

Plummer, Alfred. *A Commentary on St. Paul's Epistle to the Philippians.* London: Robert Scott, 1919.

Polhill, J. B. "Twin Obstacles in the Christian Path: Philippians 3." *RevExp* 77 (1980) 359–72.

Portefaix, Lilian. *Sisters Rejoice: Paul's Letter tc the Philippians and Luke-Acts as Seen by First-century Philippian Women.* ConBNT 20. Stockholm: Almqvist & Wiksell, 1988.

Reicke, Bo. "Unité chrétienne et diaconie: Phil. 2:1–11." In *Neotestamentica et Patristica: Eine Freundesgabe O. Cullmann*, 203–12. NovTSup 6. Leiden: Brill, 1962.

Reumann, John. "Justification and the *Imitatio* Motif in Philippians." In *Promoting Unity: Themes in Lutheran Catholic Dialogue: Festschrift for Johannes Cardinal Willebrands,* edited by H. G. Anderson and J. R. Crumley, Jr., 17–29 and 92–99. Minneapolis: Augsburg, 1989.

Sampley, J. Paul. *Pauline Partnership in Christ: Christian Community and Commitment in Light of Roman Law.* Philadelphia: Fortress, 1980.

Schenk, Wolfgang. *Die Philipperbriefe des Paulus: Kommentar.* Stuttgart: Kohlhammer, 1984.

Schulz, Anselm. *Nachfolge und Nachahmung: Studien über das Verhältnis der neutestamentlichen Jüngerschaft zur christlichen Vorbildethik.* Munich: Kösel, 1962.

Schütz, John. *Paul and the Anatomy of Apostolic Authority.* SNTSMS 26. Cambridge: Cambridge University Press, 1975.

Scott, E. F. "The Epistle to the Philippians." *IB* 11. 12–13.

Silva, Moisés. *Philippians.* Wycliffe Exegetical Commentary. Chicago: Moody, 1988.

Stagg, Frank. "The Mind in Christ Jesus: Philippians 1:27–2:18." *RevExp* 77 (1980) 337–47.

Stanley, David M. "'Become Imitators of me.' The Pauline Concept of Apostolic Tradition." *Bib* 40 (1959) 857–77.

———. *Christ's Resurrection in Pauline Soteriology.* AnBib 13. Rome: Pontifical Biblical Institute, 1961.

———. "Imitation in Paul's Letters: Its Significance for His Relationship to Jesus and to His Own Christian Foundations." In *From Jesus to Paul: Studies in Honour of Francis Wright Beare,* edited by P. Richardson and J. Hurd, 127–41. Waterloo, Ont.: Wilfrid Laurier University Press, 1984.

Stuhlmacher, Peter. *Gerechtigkeit Gottes bei Paulus.* FRLANT 87. Göttingen: Vandenhoeck & Ruprecht, 1965.

Tannehill, Robert C. *Dying and Rising with Christ: A Study in Pauline Theology.* BZNW 32. Berlin: Töpelmann, 1967.

Zerwick, Max. "Gaudium et pax custodia cordium (Phil. 3,1; 4,7)." *VD* 31 (1953) 101–4.

Ziesler, J. A. *The Meaning of Righteousness in Paul: A Linguistic and Theological Enquiry.* SNTSMS 20. New York: Cambridge University Press, 1972.

On Phil 2:(5)6–11:

See the research reports in R. P. Martin, *Carmen Christi: Philippians ii. 5–11 in Recent Interpretation and in the Setting of Early Christian Worship.* SNTSMS 4. Cambridge: Cambridge University Press, 1967; and idem, *Philippians.* NCB. London: Oliphants, 1976.

Bakken, Norman K. "The New Humanity: Christ and the Modern Age. A Study Centering in the Christ-Hymn: Philippians 2: 6–11." *Int* 22 (1968) 71–82.

Bartsch, Hans Werner. *Die konkrete Wahrheit und die Lüge der Spekulation: Untersuchung über den vorpaulinischen Christushymnus und seine gnostische Mythisierung.* Frankfurt and Bern: Lang, 1974.

Benoit, Pierre. "Préexistence et incarnation." *RB* 77 (1970) 5–29.

Blanc, R. "La rencontre de Dieu dans l'incognito de Jésus Christ, Phil. 2,5–11." *Positions Luthériennes* 21 (1973) 49–55.

Böld, W. "Gott — Sklave — Weltenherr: Ein Beitrag zur Christusmorphologie von Philipper 2,5–11." In *Beiträge zur hermeneutischen Diskussion,* edited by W. Böld, 30–61. Wuppertal: Brockhaus, 1968.

Bornhäuser, Karl. *Jesus Imperator Mundi.* Gütersloh: Bertelsmann, 1938.

Bornkamm, Günther. "On Understanding the Christ-Hymn (Philippians 2. 6–11)." In *Early Christian Experience,* 112–22. New York: Harper & Row, 1970.

Brown, Schuyler. "The Christ-Event according to Philippians 2: 6–11." *Homiletic and Pastoral Review* 73 (1973) 31–32, 55–59.

Cerfaux, L. "L'Hymne au Christ — Serviteur de Dieu (Phil 2,6–11 = Is 52,13–53,12)." In *Recueil L. Cerfaux: Etudes d'Exégèse et d'Historie Religieuse,* 2. 425–37. BETL 6–7. Gembloux: Duculot, 1954.

Dawe, Donald G. *The Form of a Servant: A Historical Analysis of the Kenotic Motif.* Philadelphia: Westminster, 1963.

Deichgräber, Reinhard. *Gotteshymnus und Christushymnus in der frühen Christenheit: Untersuchung zu Form, Sprache und Stil der frühchristlichen Hymnen.* SUNT 5. Göttingen: Vandenhoeck & Ruprecht, 1967.

De Lacey, D. R. "Image and Incarnation in Pauline Christology — A Search for Origins." *TynBul* 30 (1979) 1–28.

Dunn, James D. G. *Christology in the Making: A New Testament Inquiry into the Origins of the Doctrine of the Incarnation.* Philadelphia: Westminster, 1980.

Dupont, J. "Jésus-Christ dans son abaissement et son exaltation d'après Phil. 2,6–11." *RSR* 37 (1950) 500–514.

Feinberg, Paul D. "The Kenosis and Christology: An Exegetical-Theological Analysis of Philippians 2:6–11." *Trinity Journal* n.s. 1 (1980) 21–46.

Feuillet, A. "L'Hymne christologique de l'épître aux Philippiens (II, 6–11)." *RB* 72 (1965) 352–80, 481–507.

Georgi, Dieter. "Der vorpaulinische Hymnus Phil. 2.6–11." In *Zeit und Geschichte: Dankesgabe an R. Bultmann zum 80. Geburtstag,* edited by E. Dinkler, 263–94. Tübingen: Mohr (Siebeck), 1964.

Gibbs, John G. *Creation and Redemption: A Study in Pauline Theology.* NovTSup 6. Leiden: Brill, 1971.

——. "The Relation between Creation and Redemption according to Philippians II. 5–11." *NovT* 12 (1970) 270–83.

Hanssler, B. "Der Knecht Gottes: Die Dimensionen in einer Auslegung von Phil 2,6–11." *Wort und Wahrheit* 12 (1957) 85–89.

Hengel, Martin. "Hymn and Christology." In *Studia Biblica 1978: III, Papers on Paul and Other New Testament Authors,* edited by E. A. Livingstone, 173–97. JSNTSup 3. Sheffield: JSOT Press, 1968.

Hofius, Otto. *Der Christushymnus Philipper 2, 6–11: Untersuchungen zu Gestalt und Aussage eines urchristlichen Psalms.* WUNT 17. Tübingen: Mohr (Siebeck), 1976.

Hooker, Morna D. "Philippians 2: 6–11." In *Jesus und Paulus: Festschrift für Werner Georg Kümmel,* edited by E. E. Ellis and E. Grässer, 151–64. Göttingen: Vandenhoeck & Ruprecht, 1975.

Howard, George. "Philippians 2: 6–11 and the Human Christ." *CBQ* 40 (1978) 368–87.

Hurst, L. D. "Re-Enter the Pre-Existence of Christ in Philippians 2.5–11?" *NTS* 32 (1986) 449–57.

Hurtado, Larry W. "Jesus as Lordly Example in Phil. 2:5–11." In *From Jesus to Paul: Studies in Honour of Francis Wright Beare,* edited by P. Richardson and J. Hurd, 113–26. Waterloo, Ont.: Wilfrid Laurier University Press, 1984.

Käsemann, Ernst. "A Critical Analysis of Philippians 2: 5–11." In *God and Christ: Existence and Province,* edited by R. W. Funk, 45–88. New York: Harper & Row, 1968. German original, *ZTK* 47 (1950) 313–60.

Knox, W. L. "The 'Divine Hero' Christology in the New Testament." *HTR* 41 (1948) 229–49.

Ligier, L. "L'Hymne christologique de Philippiens 2,6–11, la Liturgie eucharistique et la Bénédiction synagogal 'Nishmat kol hay.'" In *Studiorum Paulinorum Congressus Internationalis Catholicus 1961,* 2. 65–74. AnBib 18. Rome: Pontificio Instituto Biblico, 1963.

Lohmeyer, Ernst. *Kyrios Christos: Eine Untersuchung zu Phil. 2.5–11.* Darmstadt: Wissenschaftliche Buchgesellschaft, 1961. Originally published, Heidelberg: C. Winter, 1928.

Meinertz, M. "Zum Verständnis des Christushymnus Phil 2, 5–11." *TTZ* 61 (1952) 186–92.

Moule, C. F. D. "Further Reflexions on Philippians 2: 5–11." In *Apostolic History and the Gospel: Biblical and Historical Essays Presented to F. F. Bruce,* edited by W. W. Gasque and R. P. Martin, 264–76. Grand Rapids: Eerdmans, 1970.

———. "The Manhood of Jesus in the New Testament." In *Christ, Faith and History,* edited by S. W. Sykes and J. P. Clayton, 95–110. Cambridge: Cambridge University Press, 1972.

Müller, Ulrich B. "Der Christushymnus Phil 2 6–11." *ZNW* 79 (1988) 17–44.

Murphy-O'Connor, Jerome. "Christological Anthropology in Phil. II., 6–11." *RB* 83 (1976) 25–50.

Pintard, J. "Christologie paulinienne: Observations sur l'hymne christologique de l'épître aux Philippiens et sur l'ensemble de la christologie paulinienne." *Esprit et Vie* 83 (1973) 328–33.

Robinson, W. C., Jr. "Christology and Christian Life: Paul's Use of the Incarnation Motif." *ANQ* 12 (1971) 108–17.

Sanders, Jack T. *The New Testament Christological Hymns: Their Historical and Religious Background.* SNTSMS 15. New York: Cambridge University Press, 1971.

Sanders, James A. "Dissenting Deities and Philippians 2: 1–11." *JBL* 88 (1968) 279–90.

Schumacher, Heinrich. *Christus in seiner Präexistenz und Kenose nach Phil 2,5–8.* Scripta Pontificii Instituti Biblici. 2 vols. Rome: Päpstl. Bibel-Institut, 1914, 1921.

Strecker, Georg. "Freiheit und Agape: Exegese und Predigt über Phil 2,5–11." In *Neues Testament und christliche Existenz: Festschrift für Herbert Braun,* edited by H. D. Betz and L. Schottroff, 523–38. Tübingen: Mohr (Siebeck), 1973.

Strimple, R. B. "Philippians 2: 5–11 in Recent Studies: Some Exegetical Conclusions." *WTJ* 41 (1979) 246–68.

Talbert, Charles H. "The Problem of Pre-existence in Philippians 2:6–11." *JBL* 86 (1967) 141–53.

Wagner, G. "La scandale de la croix expliqué par le chant du Serviteur d'Isaie 53: Reflexion sur Philippiens 2/6–11." *ETR* 61 (1968) 177–87.

Wanamaker, C. A. "Philippians 2.6–11: Son of God or Adamic Christology?" *NTS* 33 (1987) 179–93.

Wong, T. Yai-Chow. "The Problem of Pre-Existence in Philippians 2,6–11." *ETL* 62 (1986) 267–82.

Wright, N. T. "ἁρπαγμός and the Meaning of Philippians 2:5–11." *JTS* n.s. 37 (1986) 321–52.

Galatians
Compiled by David J. Lull

Baird, William. "What is the Kerygma? A Study of 1 Cor 15:3–8 and Gal 1:11–17." *JBL* 76 (1957) 181–91.

Barclay, John M. G. *Obeying the Truth: A Study of Paul's Ethics in Galatians.* Studies of the New Testament and Its World. Edinburgh: T. & T. Clark, 1988.

Barrett, C. K. "The Allegory of Abraham, Sarah, and Hagar in the Argument of Galatians." In *Rechtfertigung: Festschrift für E. Käsemann zum 70. Geburtstag,* edited by J. Friedrich et al., 1–16. Tübingen: Mohr (Siebeck), 1976.

———. *Freedom and Obligation: A Study of the Epistle to the Galatians.* Philadelphia: Westminster, 1985.

Barth, Marcus. "The Kerygma of Galatians." *Int* 21 (1967) 131–46.

Betz, Hans Dieter. *Galatians: A Commentary on Paul's Letter to the Churches in Galatia.* Hermeneia. Philadelphia: Fortress, 1979.

———. "In Defense of the Spirit: Paul's Letter to the Galatians as a Document of Early Christian Apologetics." In *Aspects of Religious Propaganda in Judaism and Early Christianity,* edited by E. Schüssler Fiorenza, 99–114. Studies in Judaism and Christianity in Antiquity 2. Notre Dame: University of Notre Dame Press, 1976.

———. "Spirit, Freedom, and Law: Paul's Message to the Galatian Churches." *SEÅ* 39 (1974) 145–60.

Boers, Hendrikus. "The Significance of Abraham for the Christian Faith." In *Theology out of the Ghetto: A New Testament Exegetical Study concerning Religious Exclusiveness,* 74–106. Leiden: Brill, 1971.

Borgen, Peder. "Observations on the Theme 'Paul and Philo': Paul's Preaching of Circumcision in Galatia (Gal. 5:11) and Debates on Circumcision in Philo." In *Die paulinische Literatur und Theologie,* edited by S. Pedersen, 85–102. Teologiske Studier 7. Aarhus: Aros, 1980.

Borse, Udo. *Der Brief an die Galater.* RNT. Regensburg: Pustet, 1984.

Bring, Ragnar. *Commentary on Galatians.* Philadelphia: Muhlenberg, 1961.

Brinsmead, B. H. *Galatians—Dialogical Response to Opponents.* SBLDS 65. Chico, CA: Scholars Press, 1982.

Bruce, F. F. "'Called to Freedom': A Study in Galatians." In *The New Testament Age: Essays in Honor of Bo Reicke:* Volume 1, edited by W. C. Weinrich, 61–72. Macon, GA: Mercer University Press, 1984.

———. "The Curse of the Law." In *Paul and Paulinism: Essays in Honour of C.K. Barrett,* edited by M. D. Hooker and S. G. Wilson, 27–36. London: SPCK, 1982.

———. "Galatian Problems, 3: The 'Other' Gospel." *BJRL* 53 (1970–71) 253–71.

Bultmann, Rudolf. "Zur Auslegung von Galater 2.15–18." In *Exegetica: Aufsätze zur Erforschung des Neuen Testaments,* edited by E. Dinkler, 394–99. Tübingen: Mohr (Siebeck), 1967.

Burton, Ernest de Witt. *A Critical and Exegetical Commentary on the Epistle to the Galatians.* ICC. Edinburgh: T. & T. Clark, 1921.

Callan, Terrance. "Pauline Midrash: The Exegetical Background of Gal 3:19b." *JBL* 99 (1980) 549–67.

Calvin, John. *Galatians, Ephesians, Philippians and Colossians.* Calvin's NT Commentaries 11. Grand Rapids: Eerdmans, 1965.

Cavallin, H. C. C. "'The Righteous Shall Live by Faith': A Decisive Argument for the Traditional Interpretation." *ST* 32 (1978) 33–43.

Cosgrove, Charles H. *The Cross and the Spirit: A Study in the Argument and Theology of Galatians.* Macon, GA: Mercer University Press, 1989.

———. "The Law Has Given Sarah No Children (Gal. 4:21–30)," *NovT* 29 (1987) 219–35.

———. "The Mosaic Law Preaches Faith: A Study in Galatians 3." *WTJ* 41 (1978) 146–64.

Cousar, Charles. *Galatians.* IBC. Atlanta: John Knox, 1982.

Cranfield, C. E. B. "St. Paul and the Law." *SJT* 17 (1964) 43–68.

Crownfield, Frederic R. "The Singular Problem of the Dual Galatians." *JBL* 64 (1945) 491–500.

Dahl, Nils A. "The Atonement—An Adequate Reward for the Akedah?" In *Jesus the Christ: The Historical Origins of Christological Doctrine,* edited by Donald H. Juel, 149–66. Minneapolis: Fortress Press, 1991.

———. "Der Name Israel: Zur Auslegung von Gal. 6,16." *Judaica* 6 (1950) 161–70.

Davies, W. D., P. Meyer, and D. Aune. "Reviews of H. D. Betz, *Galatians: A Commentary on Paul's Letter to the Churches of Galatia.*" *RelSRev* 7 (1981) 310–28.

Donaldson, T. L. "The 'Curse of the Law' and the Inclusion of the Gentiles: Galatians 3.13–14." *NTS* 32 (1986) 94–112.

Dunn, James D. G. "The Early Paulines." In *Baptism in the Holy Spirit: A Reexamination of the New Testament Teaching on the Gift of the Spirit in Relation to Pentecostalism Today,* 103–15. SBT 2/15. London: SCM, 1970.

———. "The Incident at Antioch (Gal 2.11–18)." *JSNT* 18 (1983) 3–57.

———. "'A Light to the Gentiles': The Significance of the Damascus Road Christophany for Paul." In *The Glory of Christ in the New Testament: Studies in Christology in Memory of G. B. Caird,* edited by L. D. Hurst and N. T. Wright, 251–66. Oxford: Clarendon, 1987.

———. "The Relationship between Paul and Jerusalem according to Galatians 1 and 2." *NTS* 28 (1982) 461–78.

———. "Works of the Law and the Curse of the Law (Galatians 3:10–14)." *NTS* 31 (1985) 523–42.

Ebeling, Gerhard. *The Truth of the Gospel: An Exposition of Galatians.* Philadelphia: Fortress, 1984.

Eckert, Jost. *Die urchristliche Verkündigung im Streit zwischen Paulus und seinen Gegnern nach dem Galaterbrief.* Biblische Untersuchungen 6. Regensburg: Pustet, 1971.

Epp, Eldon J. "Paul's Diverse Images of the Human Situation and His Unifying Theme of Freedom." In *Unity and Diversity in New Testament Theology: Essays in Honor of George E. Ladd,* edited by R. Guelich, 100–116. Grand Rapids: Eerdmans, 1978.

Fiorenza, Elisabeth Schüssler. "Neither Male nor Female: Galatians 3:28 — Alternative Vision and Pauline Modification." In *In Memory of Her: A Feminist Theological Reconstruction of Christian Origins,* 205–41. New York: Crossroad, 1983.

Fitzmyer, J. A. "Saint Paul and the Law." *The Jurist* 27 (1967) 18–36. Reprinted, "Paul and the Law." In *To Advance the Gospel: New Testament Studies,* 186–201. New York: Crossroad, 1981.

Fuller, D. P. "Paul and 'the Works of the Law.'" *WTJ* 38 (1975–76) 28–42.

Fung, Ronald Y. K. *The Epistle to the Galatians.* NICNT. Grand Rapids: Eerdmans, 1988.

Gaventa, Beverly Roberts. "Conversion in the Letters of Paul." In *From Darkness to Light: Aspects of Conversion in the New Testament,* 17–51. OBT 20. Philadelphia: Fortress, 1986.

———. "Galatians 1 and 2: Autobiography as Paradigm." *NovT* 28 (1986) 302–26.

Gordon, T. David. "The Problem at Galatia." *Int* 41 (1987) 32–43.

Haacker, K. "Paulus und das Judentum im Galaterbrief." In *Gottes Augapfel: Beiträge zur Erneuerung des Verhältnisses von Christen und Juden,* edited by E. Brocke and J. Sein, 95–111. Neukirchen-Vluyn: Neukirchener Verlag, 1986.

Hahn, F. "Das Gesetzesverständnis im Römer- und Galaterbrief." *ZNW* 67 (1976–77) 29–63.

Hamerton-Kelly, Robert G. "Sacred Violence and 'Works of the Law.'" *CBQ* 52 (1990) 55–75.

Hays, Richard B. "Christology and Ethics in Galatians: The Law of Christ." *CBQ* 49 (1987) 268–90.

———. *The Faith of Jesus Christ: An Investigation of the Narrative Substructure of Galatians 3:1–4:11.* SBLDS 56. Chico, CA: Scholars Press, 1983.

Hester, James. "The 'Heir' and Heilsgeschichte: A Study of Galatians 4:1ff." In *Oikonomia: Heilsgeschichte als Thema der Theologie,* edited by F. Christ, 118–25. Hamburg: Reich, 1967.

Hofius, O. "Das Gesetz des Mose und das Gesetz Christi." *ZTK* 80 (1983) 262–86.

Holtz, Traugott. "Der antiochenische Zwischenfall (Gal 2:11–14)." *NTS* 32 (1986) 344–61.

Howard, George. *Paul: Crisis in Galatia.* SNTSMS 35. Cambridge: Cambridge University Press, 1979.

Hübner, Hans. "Gal 3,10 und die Herkunft des Paulus." *KD* 19 (1973) 21–31.

——. "Galaterbrief." *TRE* 12 (1984) 5–15.

——. "Identitätsverlust und paulinische Theologie: Anmerkungen zum Galaterbrief." *KD* 24 (1978) 181–93.

——. "Nomos in Galatians" and "Boasting in Galatians." In *Law in Paul's Thought,* edited by J. Riches, 15–50 and 101–11. Studies of the New Testament and Its World. Edinburgh: T. & T. Clark, 1984.

——. "Was heisst bei Paulus 'Werke des Gesetzes'?" In *Glaube und Eschatologie: Festschrift für W. G. Kümmel,* edited by E. Grässer and O. Merk, 123–33. Tübingen: Mohr (Siebeck), 1985.

Jewett, Robert. "The Agitators and the Galatian Congregation." *NTS* 17 (1971) 198–212.

Jones, F. Stanley. "ἐλευθερία im Galaterbrief." In *"Freiheit" in den Briefen des Apostels Paulus: Eine historische, exegetische und religionsgeschichtliche Studie,* 70–109. GTA 34. Göttingen: Vandenhoeck & Ruprecht, 1987.

Kertelge, K. "Zur Deutung des Rechtfertigungsbegriffs im Galaterbrief." *BZ* 12 (1968) 211–22.

——. "Gesetz und Freiheit im Galaterbrief." *NTS* 28 (1982) 382–94.

Kieffer, René. *Foi et justification à Antioch: Interprétation d'un conflit (Gal 2,14–21).* LD 111. Paris: Cerf, 1982.

Klein, Günther. "Individualgeschichte und Weltgeschichte bei Paulus: Eine Interpretation ihres Verhältnisses im Galaterbrief." *EvT* 24 (1964) 126–65.

——. "Werkruhm und Christusruhm im Galaterbrief und die Frage nach einer Entwicklung des Paulus: Ein hermeneutischer und exegetischer Zwischenruf." In *Studien zum Text und zur Ethik des Neuen Testaments: Festschrift zum 80. Geburtstag von Heinrich Greeven,* edited by W. Schrage, 196–211. BZNW 47. Berlin: Walter de Gruyter, 1986.

Kümmel, Werner G. "'Individualgeschichte' und 'Weltgeschichte' in Gal. 2:15–21." In *Christ and Spirit in the New Testament: In Honour of C. F. D. Moule,* edited by B. Lindars and S. S. Smalley, 157–73. Cambridge: Cambridge University Press, 1973.

Lambrecht, Jan. "The Line of Thought in Gal. 2.14–21." *NTS* 24 (1977–78) 484–95.

Longenecker, Richard N. "The Pedagogical Nature of the Law in Galatians 3:19–4:7." *JETS* 25 (1982) 53–61.

Lührmann, Dieter. *Der Brief an die Galater.* Zürcher Bibelkommentare Neues Testament 7. Zurich: Theologischer Verlag, 1978.

Lull, David J. "'The Law Was Our Pedagogue': A Study in Gal 3:19–25." *JBL* 105 (1986) 481–98.

——. "The Spirit and the Creative Transformation of Human Existence." *JAAR* 47 (1979) 39–55.

——. *The Spirit in Galatia: Paul's Interpretation of Pneuma as Divine Power.* SBLDS 49. Chico, CA: Scholars Press, 1980.

Lütgert, Wilhelm. *Gesetz und Geist: Eine Untersuchung zur Vorgeschichte des Galater-briefes.* BFCT 22/6. Gütersloh: Bertelsmann, 1919.

Luther, Martin. "Lectures on Galatians" (1535 and 1519). *Luther's Works,* vols. 26 and 27, edited by J. Pelikan. St. Louis: Concordia, 1963, 1964.

Martyn, J. Louis. "Apocalyptic Antinomies in Paul's Letter to the Galatians." *NTS* 31 (1985) 410–24.

——. "A Law-Observant Mission to Gentiles: The Background of Galatians." *Michigan Quarterly Review* 22 (1983) 221–36. Reprinted, *SJT* 38 (1985) 307–24.

——. "Paul and His Jewish-Christian Interpreters." *USQR* 42 (1988) 1–15.

Meeks, Wayne A. "The Image of the Androgyne: Some Uses of a Symbol in Earliest Christianity." *HR* 13 (1973) 165–208.

Minear, Paul S. "The Crucified World: The Enigma of Galatians 6,14." In *Theologia Crucis-Signum Crucis: Festschrift für Erich Dinkler zum 70. Geburtstag,* edited by C. Andresen and G. Klein, 395–407. Tübingen: Mohr (Siebeck), 1979.

Mussner, Franz. *Der Galaterbrief.* HTKNT 9. Freiburg: Herder, 1974.

Oepke, A. *Der Brief des Paulus an die Galater.* 3d ed. Revised by J. Rohde. THKNT 9. Berlin: Evangelische, 1973.

Paulsen, Henning. "Einheit und Freiheit der Söhne Gottes—Gal 3:26–29." *ZNW* 71 (1980) 74–95.

Räisänen, Heikki. "Galatians 2.16 and Paul's Break with Judaism." *NTS* 31 (1985) 543–53.

——. "Paul's Conversion and the Development of His View of the Law." *NTS* 33 (1987) 404–19.

Reike, Bo. "The Law and This World According to Paul: Some Thoughts Concerning Gal. 4:1–11." *JBL* 70 (1951) 259–76.

Ropes, J. H. *The Singular Problem of the Epistle to the Galatians.* HTS 14. Cambridge, MA: Harvard University Press, 1929.

Sanders, James A. "Habakkuk in Qumran, Paul, and the Old Testament." *JR* 39 (1959) 232–44.

Schlier, Heinrich. *Der Brief an die Galater.* 5th ed. MeyerK 7. Göttingen: Vanden-hoeck & Ruprecht, 1971.

Schmithals, Walter. "The Heretics in Galatia." In *Paul and the Gnostics,* 13–64. Nashville: Abingdon, 1972.

——. "Judaisten in Galatien?" *ZNW* 74 (1983) 27–58.

Schürmann, Heinz. "'Das Gesetz des Christus' [Gal 6,2]. Jesu Verhalten und Wort als letztgültige sittliche Norm nach Paulus." In *Neues Testament und Kirche: Festschrift für R. Schnackenburg,* edited by J. Gnilka, 282–300. Freiburg: Herder, 1974.

Schütz, John H. "Tradition, Gospel and the Apostolic Ego: Gal. 1 and 2." In *Paul and the Anatomy of Apostolic Authority,* 114–58. SNTSMS 26. Cambridge: Cambridge University Press, 1975.

Schweizer, Eduard. "Die Elemente der Welt." In *Beiträge zur Theologie des Neuen Testaments,* 147–63. Zurich: Zwingli, 1970.

——. "Slaves of the Elements and Worshipers of Angels: Gal 4:3, 9 and Col 2:8, 18, 20." *JBL* 107 (1988) 455–68.

Strelan, John G. "Burden-Bearing and the Law of Christ: A Re-examination of Galatians 6:2." *JBL* 94 (1975) 266–76.

Tuckett, C. M. "Deuteronomy 21,23 and Paul's Conversion." In *L'Apôtre Paul: Personnalité, style et conception de ministère,* edited by A. Vanhoye, 344–50. Leuven: Leuven University Press, 1986.

Tyson, J. B. "Paul's Opponents in Galatia." *NovT* 4 (1968) 241–54.

——. "'Works of Law' in Galatians." *JBL* 92 (1973) 423–31.

Vielhauer, Philipp. "Gesetzesdienst und Stoicheiadienst im Galaterbrief." In *Rechtfertigung: Festschrift für E. Käsemann zum 70. Geburtstag,* edited by J. Friedrich et al., 543–55. Tübingen: Mohr (Siebeck), 1976.

Williams, Sam K. "Justification and the Spirit in Galatians." *JSNT* 29 (1987) 91–100.

——. "*Promise* in Galatians: A Reading of Paul's Reading of Scripture." *JBL* 107 (1988) 709–20.

Wink, Walter. "The 'Elements of the Universe' in Biblical and Scientific Perspective." *Zygon* 13 (1978) 225–53.

Young, E. M. "'Fulfill the Law of Christ.' An Examination of Galatians 6:2." *Studia Biblica et Theologica* 7 (1977) 31–42.

Young, Norman H. "*Paidagogos:* The Social Setting of a Pauline Metaphor." *NovT* 29 (1987) 150–76.